CW00922966

Archaeology in Law

AUSTRALIA
LBC Information Services—Sydney

CANADA and USA
Carswell—Toronto

NEW ZEALAND
Brooker's—Auckland

SINGAPORE and MALAYSIA
Thomson Information (S.E. Asia)—Singapore

Archaeology in Law

by

John Pugh-Smith and John Samuels

of Gray's Inn,
Barrister
M.A.(Oxon)

Archaeological
Consultant
B.A., Ph.D., F.S.A.,
M.I.F.A.

with contributions from

Richard Harwood and James Rouse

of Middle Temple,
Barrister
M.A., LL.M.(Cantab)

Tax Manager
Grant Thornton
M.A. (Oxon), A.T.I.I.

LONDON
SWEET & MAXWELL
1996

Published in 1996 by Sweet & Maxwell Limited of
100 Avenue Road, Swiss Cottage
London NW3 3PF
Computerset by Tradespools Ltd, Frome, Somerset
Printed and bound in Great Britain by
Hartnolls Ltd, Bodmin

No natural forests were destroyed to make this product; only farmed
timber was used and replanted

A CIP catalogue record for this book is available from the British Library

ISBN 0 421 503 408

©
Sweet & Maxwell
1996

To our wives and children who have tolerantly allowed us to work on this project late into the evenings and at weekends. From our endless discussions they have probably ended up knowing more about archaeology in law than they ever thought they wanted to know!

Acknowledgments

Goodwill and practical advice from many quarters have speeded this project along. In particular we have benefited from substantial contributions by Richard Harwood (Chapter 4 and parts of Chapter 5) and James Rouse (Chapter 7) but they have also taken a great interest in the whole project.

The idea for the book came out of our everyday working lives. We first met in Spring 1991 when the ink of PPG 16 had just dried and John Pugh-Smith urgently needed the services of an independent archaeological witness for a planning inquiry at Daventry. The issues raised by that project focused our attention on the need for a specialist work, the content of which has been formulated and refined by our collective input into a number of seminars and articles as well as individual involvement with the development process. Therefore, we would like to thank the various colleagues, developers, County Archaeologists, English Heritage Inspectors and Planning Inspectors who have made us think about the application of archaeology to planning.

Numerous individuals and organisations have provided us with information, in particular: Dr Geoffrey Wainwright (English Heritage, Chief Archaeologist); Dr Chris Brook (Leicestershire County Council, Conservation Officer); Malcolm Atkins (Hereford and Worcester County Archaeologist); Hugh Corner, Chris Dawes and Dr Roger Bland (Department of National Heritage); Vivien Bodnor (Highways Agency); Gill Lewis (National Rivers Authority); Naomi Field (Lindsey Archaeological Services); Philip Hodgkinson (Simons Estates Ltd); Inspector Peter Jones (Trent Division, Nottinghamshire Constabulary); Ursilla Spence (Nottinghamshire County Council, Archaeological Officer); Jane Gardiner (National House Builders Federation); Ben Ferrari (Royal Commission on the Historical Monuments of England) and Carl Dyer (Berwin Leighton, Solicitors). As the book progressed a draft version was sent out to certain people for their comments. We are grateful for the constructive criticism received from: Iain Newton (Department of National Heritage); Dr David Breeze (Chief Inspector for Ancient Monuments for Historic Scotland); Francis Golding (Secretary to the Royal Fine Art Commission); Liz Poynter (Highways Agency); Howard Carter (Legal Adviser to English Heritage); Dr Richard Morris (Director of the Council for British Archaeology); Mike Bishop (Nottinghamshire County Council, County Archaeologist); and David Morgan Evans (General Secretary to the Society of Antiquaries of London). Separate thanks also go to Charles Mynors (Barrister) for his diligent attention to detail drawn from his wide experience of heritage matters. All comments received have been analysed and, where we thought appropriate, the text adapted or revised. Although their views have been taken into account, the individuals are not responsible for the opinions we express.

We are particularly pleased that Sir Frank Layfield Q.C. has contributed his comments to this publication. It is gratifying that he recognises the need for such a publication and is willing to offer his endorsement.

Research for the book included examination of not only statutory and policy guidance from government departments but also advice from various advisory and professional bodies. Recognising that not all of this will be easily available to our readers who may wish to consult the original sources, we have provided as appendices the most significant material, either in its entirety or as extracts. For permission to reproduce these we would like to thank HMSO, English Heritage, the Highways Agency, the Association of County Archaeological Officers, the Institute of Field Archaeologists and the Joint Nautical Archaeological Policy Committee.

Our publishers, Sweet and Maxwell, have provided consistent support and assistance as well as the occasional goad to ensure that we completed the project on time. However, even they did not anticipate having to search for the typescript amongst the debris of their former office after the IRA bombing of the Isle of Dogs.

Finally, we must acknowledge our secretarial support. Our primary debt is to Sue Garwood, former secretary to John Samuels who managed to endure our frenetic pace of work and produce a typescript out of numerous computer disks and semi-legible handwriting. We also thank her successor, Sarah Rushby who has dealt with our continuing demands at galley and page proof stages. Collectively they have enabled the publisher to produce this book.

Foreword

By Sir Frank Layfield Q.C.

An interest in archaeology, its support, protection and pursuit, has been held for several centuries in Britain. Nevertheless, there have always been threats to its maintenance and continuance. Only when the country had the capacity to destroy existing buildings, work and structures speedily and on a large scale did it become clear that archaeological sites required protection from destruction, alteration and neglect.

The need for protection first took legislative form in the 1880s when the first Ancient Monuments Act was passed. In the ensuing decades the threat to archaeological remains steadily increased. It was not until the 1980s that the scale, character and pace grew so spectacularly that elaborate and extensive archaeological legislative provisions came into being, together with a range of administrative structures which were built to carry out the official requirements. Those arrangements would, even if they stood alone have been difficult to appreciate fully and to apply successfully.

However, those provisions with regard to archaeological law and administration cannot be applied as a single system. Since 1909 a long and complicated set of statutory provisions for town and country planning came into being, of which the most recent enactment is the Environment Act 1995. The latter sequence of Acts has been universally regarded as difficult to understand in detail. As one year follows another there is little sign of either branch of law becoming easier for practitioners to understand and apply.

If both branches of law have to be read, understood and applied together when practising and when dealing with archaeological sites and similar problems, the difficulties are much greater. It follows that assistance on how to apply the two branches of law is of particular value.

Concurrently with the increases in the legislative difficulties, the scientific and technical aspects have been growing in importance in the archaeological world. The techniques of geophysical survey, the means to identify buried remains and the scientific examination of environmental indicators, together with advances in the understanding of conditions in the past, are examples of the third stream of thought that needs to be applied in practice, effectively, accurately and reasonably quickly.

It is the outstanding merit and value of this book that it enables practitioners to equip themselves in a way which will be usable both in the office and in the field. I recommend this book not merely for the extent of supporting material, although it is extensive, but also because the text is so laid out that it is easy to use. The contents are copiously and clearly signposted. The book is very well documented. One of the main features is Chapter 6 on Development Control, which describes the planning system with clarity and brevity. It also identifies the necessary practical consider- ations that affect the administration of the system, such as planning policies, environmental assessments, conditions, section 106 agreements and other control processes in their archaeological contexts.

Archaeological law and practice commences with a clear summary of the growth of the subject up to 1990. That is followed by a useful description of the present organisation and its relationship with the Government, local government, UNESCO, English Heritage, Royal Commission and interested groups. The way in which the procedures are followed when seeking scheduling, and the status of Ancient Monuments and archaeological areas are described. The book then tackles the mechanics of Ancient Monument legislation, including changes in ownership, guardianship and numerous related matters linked to the Town and Country Planning Act 1980 and regualtions where relevant.

The text provides helpful comments on subjects that do not form part of the central subjects. The most valuable of those subjects is one on "Fiscal Considerations". The chapter is relatively short and gives a clear guide to the U.K. tax system and is intended to alert readers to such arrangements and transactions which could cause financial penalties to be incurred but not obviously so. This is a chapter which will be much appreciated.

Brief but useful occurrences are dealt with in a separate chapter which handles such matters as Human Remains, Treasure Trove, Historic Build- ings, Historic Parks, Ecclesiastical Buildings and many subjects. The final chapter provides some useful indications of future problems and potential developments affecting archaeology through legislation and other controls.

This book provides an excellent practitioners' guide.

Contents

Table of Cases

Table of Statutes

All references are to paragraph numbers

Table of Statutory Instruments

Table of Department of the Environment Circulars

Table of Planning Policy Guidance Notes

Table of Abbreviations

AAI	Area of Archaeological Importance
ACAO	Association of County Archaeological Officers
AEA	Association of Environmental Archaeologists
AIA	Association for Industrial Archaeology
AMAA	Ancient Monuments and Archaeological Areas Act 1979
AMAC	Ancient Monuments Advisory Committee
AONB	Area of Outstanding Natural Beauty
BM	British Museum
BSAC	British Sub Aqua Club
CA	County Archaeologist or Community Archaeologist
CAO	County Archaeological Officer
CBA	Council for British Archaeology
CCC	Council for the Care of Churches
CIA	Coal Industry Act 1994
CSA	Council for Scottish Archaeology
CUCAP	Cambridge University Committee for Aerial Photography
DMRB	Design Manual for Roads and Bridges, Vol. 11. DOT 1993 with revisions 1994
DMV	Deserted Medieval Village
DNH	Department of National Heritage
DOE	Department of the Environment
DOE (NI)	Department of the Environment for Northern Ireland
DOT	Department of Transport
EA	Environmental Assessment
EAD	EC Directive 85/337 on the Assessment of the Effects of Certain Private and Public Projects on the Environment
EAR	Town and Country Planning (Assessment of Environmental Effects) Regulations 1988

EH	English Heritage
ES	Environmental Statement
ESA	Environmentally Sensitive Area
FC	Forestry Commission
GDO	General Development Order
GIS	Geographical Information System
GPDO	Genereal Permitted Development Order 1995
GPES	Guide on Preparing Environmental Statements for Planning Projects. DOE 1995
HA	Highways Agency
HBMC	Historic Buildings and Monuments Commission
HMSO	Her Majesty's Stationary Office
HS	Historic Scotland
IFA	Institute of Field Archaeologists
LDA	Land Drainage Act 1991
LPA	Local Planning Authority
MA	Museums Association
MAFF	Ministry of Agriculture and Fisheries
MAP 2	*Management of Archaeological Projects*, English Heritage 1991
MARS	Monuments at Risk Programme. A three-year project launched in 1994 by English Heritage in association with the Royal Commission on the Historical Monuments of England to assess the condition and survival of archaeological sites througout England.
MOLAS	Museum of London Archaeological Service
MPG	Mineral Policy Guidance Note
MPP	The Monuments Protection Programme
NAS	Nautical Archaeological Society
NMM	National Maritime Museum
NMR	National Monuments Record
NMS	National Museum of Scotland
NMW	National Museum of Wales
NPPG	National Planning Policy Guideline
NRA	National Rivers Authority
NT	National Trust

xl

NTS	Non-Technical Summary
OFWAT	Director-General of Water Services
OIEL	Open Individual Export Licence
PAN	Planning Advice Note
PAYE	Pay As You Earn
PPG	Planning Policy Guidance
PPG15	*Planning Policy Guidance: Planning and the Historic Environment*, Department of the Environment and Department of National Heritage 1994
PPG16	*Planning Policy Guidance: Archaeology and Planning,* Department of the Environment 1990
PPS	*Proceedings of the Prehistoric Society*
QB	Queen's Bench (Division of the High Court of Justice)
RCAHMS	Royal Commission on Ancient and Historical Monuments of Scotland
RCAHMW	Royal Commission on Ancient and Historical Monuments in Wales
RCHME	Royal Commission on the Historical Monuments of England
RFAC	Royal Fine Arts Commission
RPG	Regional Policy Guidance (Note)
SAM	Scheduled Ancient Monument
SDD	Scottish Development Department
SMC	Scheduled Monument Consent
SMR	Sites and Monuments Record
SOSE	Scretary of State for the Enviroment
SOSW	Secretary of State for Wales
SSSI	Sites of Special Scientific Interest
TAN	Technical Advice Note (Wales)
TCPA	Town and Country Planning Act 1990
UCO	Use Classes Order 1987
UDP	Unitary Development Plan
VAT	Value Added Tax
WHS	World Heritage Site
WIA	Water Industry Act 1991
WO	Welsh Office
WRA	Water Resources Act 1991

1. Introduction

To many people archaeology conjures up images of fabulous buried treasure **1.1** or ivy-covered romantic ruins. In reality it includes all evidence of man's activities from the earliest times to the recent past. European legislation includes archaeology within the phrase "cultural heritage", and in many ways this is a useful definition for such an all-embracing subject. For the modern archaeologist everything from discarded rubbish and abandoned settlements to whole landscapes is grist to the mill in an attempt to understand earlier societies. Sometimes archaeological evidence supports historical documentary sources but often it is the only evidence of life in the past. Monuments can be impressive and artefacts intrinsically beautiful, but more often the remains are buried beneath the ground and the individual finds fragmentary and unphotogenic. The skill of the archaeologist is using all of this evidence to create a view of the past.

Britain has been settled on an increasingly dense scale for the past 5,000 **1.2** years and the evidence of the past is all around us. The remains of earlier societies have been long recognised, sometimes treated with veneration and often with curiosity. Since the sixteenth century efforts have been made to record and investigate archaeological remains, and from the early eighteenth century concern has been expressed about the survival of some monuments. In 1882 the first Ancient Monuments Act was passed to protect monuments considered to be of national importance. Various pieces of legislation followed culminating in the Ancient Monuments and Archaeological Areas Act 1979 and the National Heritage Act 1983, supported by government policy statements such as PPG 16 (Archaeology and Planning) in 1990 and PPG 15 (Planning and the Historic Environment) in 1994 to safeguard a wider range of archaeological remains. In some ways this is a response to the growth of archaeology as a subject of serious study; but it also reflects a growing awareness by the public of its collective past. It is also a reaction to the pace of modern development which not only creates new amenities, replacing existing features at the same site, but also destroys earlier buried remains.

Archaeology and development may seem strange bedfellows but both are **1.3** aspects of social change. Most people find archaeology interesting. Developers are normally sympathetic to the interests of archaeologists while probably wishing that the archaeological implications of their development were elsewhere; and archaeologists are fundamentally interested in archaeology not planning. Too often the problems which arise are due to ignorance or a misunderstanding of the legal requirements, compounded by the increasing amount of archaeological jargon.

The purpose of this book is to set out clearly the scheme of current **1.4**

1

archaeological legislation and government guidance and to discuss its implications within the planning system. Because some of the legislation and much of the guidance will not be easily available, the principal publications have been reproduced as appendices.

1.5   Behind the complexity of legislation and guidance is a desire to protect and enjoy our archaeological heritage. The effectiveness of this depends upon a proper understanding of the framework within which the archaeologist and the developer work.

1.6   Commencing with a short and rapid introduction to the historical development of archaeology as a subject, the book then provides a general overview of the organisation of archaeological activity in Britain today. A description and analysis of the principal legislation is followed by identification of other legal protection and guidance on particular aspects of archaeology.

1.7   As development is now one of the primary stimuli for archaeological activity, the scope and nature of the planning system is described in broad outline and the archaeological implications upon it. A substantial section of this chapter analyses recent planning inquiry decisions and comments upon apparent trends.

1.8   Many aspects of archaeology have financial effects and consequent taxation concerns. These have been described, although it is a complex subject where specialist advice may be necessary for individual cases.

1.9   The final chapter concludes that the legislation and guidance concerning archaeology is extensive and complex. It is also a growing consideration within the planning system.

1.10   This book is biased towards England, although comments are made about some of the more significant differences in Wales and, to a lesser extent, other parts of the United Kingdom. To have covered all of the variations in Scotland and Northern Ireland would have required much more general background in terms of legislation and practice beyond the scope and scale to achieve a readily accessible publication.

2. Historical Background

An appreciation of any subject's past development assists with an under- **2.1**
standing of its present situation and can, to some extent, enable its future
directions to be anticipated. For archaeology, its historical background is
particularly important. This is partly because it is a relatively recent subject
and only just developing a more fully formed and rounded approach. It is also
because much of the evidence used today will rely upon earlier research
based upon different approaches; and, as a professional body, archaeologists
claim to be considering the needs of future generations.

A primary aim of the modern archaeologist is to enable the present **2.2**
generation to understand past cultures and societies; although it is the
spectacular finds of buried treasure which are more likely to be deemed
newsworthy by the media. The history of archaeological study is much the
same. It is a counterpoint between the academic examination of man-made
artefacts or structures and the excitement of finding precious objects set
against improving techniques of discovery and recording.

Our earliest historians, Caesar, Tacitus and Bede, provide fascinating and **2.3**
often accurate accounts of events and their background. Each is concerned to
explain what has happened from his particular point of view and archaeological evidence is usually incidental. For most of the medieval period, history
was a rag-bag mixture of fact and fantasy from which items were selected
without regard to proof or evidence. Licences granted by King John and Henry
III for treasure hunting, from which the Crown might benefit, was the full
extent of archaeological research.

Renaissance scholarship in England in the late fifteenth and sixteenth **2.4**
centuries began to describe and query the meaning of archaeological
remains.[1] Inspired by an intense sense of patriotism and support for the
Tudor Monarchy, John Leland was commissioned by Henry VIII to search the
libraries of the country for lost or forgotten works. Extending far beyond this
to a topographical, historical and archaeological survey, Leland presented his
New Year's gift to the king in 1546:

> "... after that I had perpended the honest and profitable studies of these
> historiographes, I was totally inflamed with a love to see thoroughly all
> those parts of this your opulent and ample realm that I had redde of in the
> aforesaid writers. In so much that all my other occupations intermitted, I
> have so travelled in your dominions both by the sea coasts and the
> middle parts, sparing neither labour nor costs by the space of these six

---

[1] Kendrick, *British Antiquity* (1950).

years past, that there is almost neither cape nor bay, haven, creak or pier, river or confluence of rivers, breeches, washes, lakes, meres, fenny waters, mountains, valleys, moors, heaths, forests, woods, cities, burroughs, castles, principal manor places, monasteries, and colleges, but I have seen them, and noted in so doing a whole world of things very memorable."[2]

2.5 Although Leland was not available in published form until 1710, followed by a second edition in 1745, a more popular account of the country's antiquities was Camden's *Britannia*. First published in 1586, it provided detailed descriptions of antiquities and the second edition in 1600 was illustrated. Other studies and publications followed throughout the seventeenth century including several county histories, usually with a strong bias towards genealogy. It was one of these antiquaries, William Dugdale, who put forward one of the most trenchant arguments for the study of the past: "Every man naturally is desirous of knowledge, and therefore man without learninge, and the remembrance of things past, falls into a beastlye sottishness and his life is noe better to be accounted of than to be buryed alive".[3]

2.6 Contemporary with the study of the past came a desire to collect objects, usually indiscriminately. Animals, birds, fossils, weapons, coins or anything that was unusual might be considered suitable. The collections of the two John Tradescants, father and son gardeners to Charles I, were to form the basis of the Ashmolean Museum in Oxford[4] while the later, more extensive and classical collections of Sir Hans Sloane became the British Museum.[5] Many other modern museums owe the basis of their collections to the often indefatigable obsession of Victorian collectors, more commonly for classical Greek and Roman objects but also for local artefacts, whether Roman pottery and coins or prehistoric flints and pottery.

2.7 Recording of archaeological remains reached a peak by the mid-eighteenth century with William Stukeley (1687–1765) who not only described what he saw and discussed its significance but provided fine illustrations published in several volumes, *Itinerarium Curiosum*.[6] He was also involved in the refounding of the Society of Antiquaries of London in 1707 which through its meeting and fellowship, fostered and continues to encourage the debate and dissemination of archaeological studies.[7]

2.8 Occasional digging into archaeological remains had probably been carried out from time immemorial but Stukeley may have been the first to undertake what might be described as the earliest recorded scientific excavation.[8] Many others, during the eighteenth and nineteenth centuries, carried out excavations but with a few exceptions most were no more than treasure hunting expeditions with little or no attempt to record accurately what was found. The exceptions were Bryan Faussett (1720–76) and James

[2] Leland, *The Itinerary of John Leland the Antiquary* (1745), Vol. 1, p.xxii.
[3] Quoted in Ashbee, *The Bronze Age Round Barrow in Britain* (1960), p.14.
[4] Piggott, *Ruins in a Landscape: Essays in Antiquarianism* (1976), p.106.
[5] Crook, *The British Museum: a case study in architectural policies* (1972), pp.42–49.
[6] Stukeley, *Itinerarium Curiosum* (1724) 2 vols.
[7] Evans, *A History of the Society of Antiquaries* (1956); Piggott, *William Stukeley* (1985).
[8] Marsden, *The Early Barrow Diggers* (1974), p.4.

Douglas (1753–1819), both working in North Kent[9]; Sir Richard Colt Hoare (1758–1838) and William Cunnington (1754–1810) both working in Wiltshire[10]; and Thomas Bateman (1821–61) in Derbyshire.[11] Each is notable for the quality of their excavations, attention to recording, and publication. Many were more cavalier in attitude and there was considerable disquiet about their plundering activities,[12] typified perhaps by the Reverend Stephen Isaacson's doggerel:

> "Uprouse ye then, my barrow-digging men, It is our opening day!
> And all exclaimed, their grog whilst swigging,
> There's naught on earth like barrow digging!"[13]

Meanwhile, considerable progress had been made with establishing the **2.9** chronology of man's past in Europe through a combination of geology, archaeology and rationalisation. The result was that towards the end of the nineteenth century, with a few dissenting voices, the concept of man's antiquity before the Romans had been established within a broad framework of three periods known as Stone, Bronze and Iron Ages. Cross-fertilisation of ideas and approaches between the studies of natural history, geology and archaeology was beginning to produce a more scientific approach to excavation. An outstanding example, which set standards not surpassed for at least 20 years and forms the basis of today's excavation techniques, was the work of General Pitt Rivers (1827–1900). His excavations in Cranborne Chase between 1880 and 1890 (subsequently published in four privately printed volumes[14]) were remarkable, not only for their approach and quality of recording, but also publication, making the primary record of his discoveries available to all in a form which allowed independent interpretation. As Professor Glyn Daniel was later to comment, "unlimited by considerations of finance, time or labour, Pitt Rivers was able to make these excavations a model of scientific excavation".[15]

General Pitt Rivers was remarkable and energetic in his pursuit of his **2.10** archaeological interests and the broader issues of archaeology.[16] Appointed in 1883 as the first Inspector of Ancient Monuments, under "The Act for the Better Protection of Ancient Monuments 1882", he proved to be energetic and effective in encouraging the preservation and understanding of archaeological remains. The Act itself was almost entirely due to the campaigning zeal and political adroitness of Sir John Lubbock but was the outcome of over 50 years of concern.[17] Attached to the Act was a schedule of 68 monuments in

---

[9] Marsden, *ibid.*, pp.5–11; Jessup, *Man of Many Talents: an informal biography of James Douglas 1753–1819* (1975).

[10] Colt Hoare, *The History of Ancient Wiltshire* (1810); Cunnington, *From Antiquary to Archaeologist* (1975).

[11] Bateman, *Ten Years' Diggings in Celtic and Saxon Grave-hills* (1861) (2nd ed. 1978).

[12] Marsden *op.cit* (n. 8 above), p.48.

[13] From *Barrow Digging by a Barrow-Knight* by Rev. Stephen Isaacson published in 1845 and quoted by Marsden *op.cit* (n. 8 above), frontispiece.

[14] Pitt-Rivers, *Excavations in Cranborne Chase* (1887–98), 4 vols.

[15] Daniel, *The Origins and Growth of Archaeology* (1967), p.236.

[16] Thompson, *General Pitt-Rivers* (1977); Bowden, *Pitt Rivers: The Life and Archaeological Work of Lieutenant-General Augustus Lane Fox Pitt-Rivers, DCL, FRS, FSA* (1991).

[17] Saunders, "A Century of Ancient Monuments Legislation 1882–1992" in *The Antiquaries Journal* (1983), Vol. LXIII, part 1, pp.11–33.

England, Wales, Scotland and Ireland which owners could put into the State's Guardianship but retain the freehold to themselves.

2.11   Organised through the Office of Works and later the Ministry of Works, the Ministry of Public Buildings and Works, the Department of the Environment, and now the Department of National Heritage, the number of protected monuments gradually increased and broadened in range. Additional powers of protection were granted under later legislation including the Ancient Monuments Protection Act 1900 with successive Acts in 1913 and 1931. The first successful prosecution for damage to a monument was in 1906 when the 17-year-old son of a superintendent to the Prudential Life Insurance and a local preacher was fined £3 and costs for scratching his name on one of the stones forming the Castlerigg Stone circle. It was unfortunate for the young man that in addition to his name he had added his address.[18]

2.12   The excavation techniques of Pitt Rivers were to form the basis of future excavations, culminating in the great set-piece projects of Mortimer Wheeler at Maiden Castle (Dorset), Verulamium (St Albans) in the 1930s and later in the 1950s at Stanwick (North Yorkshire). They were carried out with considerable showmanship that brought archaeology to popular attention. Involvement in archaeology and new fieldwork and analytical techniques were to bring about major changes in the organisation of archaeology and range of information available.

2.13   From the mid-nineteenth century there had been a steady growth in county, local and later specialist societies dedicated either entirely to the study of archaeology or combinations of archaeology, local history, and natural history.[19] The result was an increasing popular interest in the study of the past with survey and fieldwork reported in an impressive range of county journals, and the publications of specialist societies.

2.14   By the 1930s archaeology had begun to develop into an academic discipline sometimes taught at universities. The number of professional archaeologists, often based in local and regional museums, increased and the basis of modern archaeology was created. In addition to the popularisation by Mortimer Wheeler, academic archaeologists such as Gordon Childe and later Christopher Hawkes provided the theoretical framework. Dramatic discoveries such as the Sutton Hoo Saxon Ship in Suffolk in 1939 fired the academic and public imagination, bringing the Saxons to life.

2.15   The most dramatic new fieldwork technique to be developed was aerial photography. Since the eighteenth century the influence of buried remains on corn crops had been recognised. The opportunity to view these from aircraft allowed better recognition and plotting. This work was pioneered after the First World War by O.G.S. Crawford, the first archaeological officer at the Ordnance Survey and founder of the archaeological publication, *Antiquity*. Second World War intelligence requirements educated a number of academics in the uses of aerial photography, several of whom later became leading archaeologists. Construction of military bases also financed the excavation of several important sites.[20]

2.16   It was in the late 1940s and 1950s, with increased central government expenditure on research and sites threatened by development, that new

---

[18] Saunders, *idem*, p.16.

[19] Hudson, *A Social History of Archaeology* (1981), pp.15–41; Piggott, *Ruins in a Landscape: Essays in Antiquarianism* (1976), pp.171–95.

[20] Grimes, *Excavations on Defence Sites, 1939–1945* (1960).

techniques of geophysical survey began to be developed and, from the USA, came the radical discovery of radio-carbon dating ("C14"). At first cumbersome and producing dubious results, resistivity and magnetometry techniques for identifying buried remains were slow in their advent. Likewise radio-carbon dating while offering the potential key to independent dating was expensive and fraught with problems. It was to be the more prosaic method of dendrochronology, or tree-ring dating, which provided the necessary correlation for the vagaries of radio-carbon.

By the mid 1960s the current techniques of fieldwork and analysis were becoming more widely used. Scientific examination of pollen, snails, beetles and other environmental indicators allowed the creation of more complete pictures of conditions in the past. Archaeology was becoming a popular subject and there was a growing number of professional archaeologists. However, it was the boom development years of the late 1960s, with large scale remodelling of towns and cities and the impact of the new motorway and road network, that was to create the framework of modern archaeological organisation.[21] Yet, after several decades of reaction to archaeological crises and escalating expenditure by central government on rescue archaeology, it was not the Ancient Monuments and Archaeological Areas Act 1979 which solved the problems. Rather it has been the creation of English Heritage by the National Heritage Act 1983 and the publication of Planning Policy Guidance Notes "PPG 16" in 1990 and "PPG 15" in 1994 which have done more to safeguard the long-term future of archaeological remains in Britain.

2.17

---

[21] Rhatz, *Rescue Archaeology* (1974); Jones, *Past Imperfect. The Story of Rescue Archaeology* (1984).

3. The Organisation of British Archaeology

1. INTRODUCTION

Given the diffuse background to the development of the study of archae- **3.1**
ology, its present organisation in Britain, not surprisingly, consists of a
myriad of bodies and individuals.[1] The interests of archaeologists are
represented through a range of national, county and local societies, specialist
interest groups and a professional body, the Institute of Field Archaeologists.
The total number of professional archaeologists is probably around 2,500, of
which 1,121 are members of the Institute of Field Archaeologists,[2] but there
has always been a strong tradition of the amateur archaeologist, many of
them leading specialists in their field.

Professional archaeologists can be employed by universities, museums, **3.2**
English Heritage, The National Trust, local authorities and commercial
organisations. It is common practice that many archaeologists will be
members of several societies as well as serving on the management
committees of professional organisations. To the outsider this might appear a
bizarre situation, where the same person can be employed as professional
archaeologist by a monitoring body such as English Heritage or a local
authority and yet, through his professional organisation or special interest
society, also exert an opinion as part of a pressure group. In mitigation, it can
only be said that professional integrity is rarely challenged.

Within the planning system, the various roles of the archaeologist can be **3.3**
broken down into three groups: monitors (or, as they often prefer to be called,
curators); contractors and consultants; survey and interest groups. However,
the distinctions are often blurred because of the way in which each group
operates. For example, English Heritage, as adviser to all government
departments on archaeological matters, has its own archaeological unit,
Central Archaeological Services, which not only undertakes analysis, survey
and excavation work for English Heritage but can be employed on a
commercial basis. Likewise, many local authorities support archaeological
units which advise them on archaeological issues and also accept commercial projects. Many archaeological contractors and consultants receive

---

[1] Hunter and Ralston, "The Structure of British Archaeology" in Hunter and Ralston,
   Archaeological Resource Management in the UK: An Introduction (1993), pp.30–43.
[2] IFA, *Annual Report No. 11* (1994), p.22.

substantial funding through English Heritage and local authorities. It is a complex web and close attention should be paid to individual interests.

2. CENTRAL AND LOCAL GOVERNMENT IN ENGLAND AND WALES

3.4   The central government office concerned with archaeological issues is the Department of National Heritage ("the DNH"). The DNH was created in 1992 as a new entity collecting together activities, some of them quite small in terms of bureaucracy, from six previous departments including the former Heritage Division of the Department of the Environment ("the DOE"). Circular 20/92 ("Responsibilities for Conservation Policy and Casework") details the division of responsibilities between the DNH and the DOE. In essence, the DNH now has policy responsibility for all aspects of archaeology, including the protection of wrecks, as well as conservation of the built environment. It has also taken over sponsorship responsibilities for English Heritage, the National Heritage Memorial Fund, the Royal Commission on the Historical Monuments of England, the Royal Fine Art Commission, the Millennium Fund and other heritage public bodies. However, close co-operation is still maintained with the DOE, particularly where cases raise wider policy questions or where the DOE is not disposed to accept advice from English Heritage on applications and appeals.

3.5   English Heritage (formally the Historic Buildings and Monuments Commission for England) is a non-departmental public body. Established in 1984 by the National Heritage Act 1983 it is the government's official adviser on all matters concerning the conservation of the historic environment. It is also the major source of public funding for rescue archaeology, conservation areas and repairs to historic buildings and ancient monuments including the management and presentation of some 400 historic properties in the nation's care. Until the implementation of PPG 16 in 1990, which placed the financial onus of any archaeological work associated with development on the developer, English Heritage was the largest funder of rescue archaeology. Since then it has been able to concentrate its energies to a greater degree on the formulation of archaeological policy although continuing to fund projects such as surveys of sites and buildings, excavations and publications. Its annual publication, *Archaeology Review*, graphically illustrates the wide range of activities undertaken and sponsored.

3.6   The Commissioners who oversee the work of English Heritage are normally appointed for a three-year term by the Secretary of State for National Heritage. (Following the recommendations of the Nolan Committee, expressions of interest in these posts are now sought publicly through newspaper advertisements.) They are required to have knowledge of, or experience in, a relevant field. Commission meetings are held in private due to matters of commercial confidentiality as well as confidential advice to government departments. A list of the names of current Commissioners can be found in the Annual Report.

3.7   In addition to advising the Secretary of State on any matters concerning scheduled monuments, English Heritage has undertaken an ambitious project, the Monument Protection Programme (MPP) to assess the validity of existing scheduled monuments and recommend additional scheduling of

24,500–28,000 monuments by 2003.[3] A national census of all archaeological sites, the Monuments at Risk Programme (MARP), is also being sponsored with the intention of assessing the physical impact on monuments since 1945, their present condition and long-term future.[4] Planning advice by English Heritage on archaeological issues has been provided in two publications, *Development Plan Policies for Archaeology*, English Heritage (1992) and *Conservation Issues in Strategic Plans*, Countryside Commission, English Heritage, English Nature (1993).

As well as being accountable to the Secretary of State for National   **3.8** Heritage, English Heritage also advises the DOE directly on related planning issues (including listed buildings). In addition, its activities may be scrutinised by the National Audit Office and Parliamentary Select Committees, including the Public Accounts Committee. The Parliamentary Ombudsman is also entitled to investigate complaints made about English Heritage.

Most day-to-day planning decisions will be made by the relevant unitary,   **3.9** borough or district council acting as the local planning authority ("the LPA"). Usually, the LPA will act on its own archaeological advice. This might be provided by the County Archaeologist, employed by the county council. Less commonly, an archaeologist may be employed by the LPA, usually called either a City, District or Community Archaeologist. Here, the situation can become more complex; and for the sake of clarity in this book the archaeological adviser will be referred to simply as the County Archaeologist.

Often based within a planning department but sometimes in museum   **3.10** services, the County Archaeologist will usually be responsible for the maintenance of the Sites and Monuments Record (SMR) which provides a county-based register of known archaeological sites.[5] His other tasks will normally include advising on regional and structural plans, and planning applications with archaeological issues. In metropolitan areas and where unitary status has been granted to particular authorities, SMRs are jointly maintained by the relevant councils. However, English Heritage maintains and administers the SMR for Greater London. An Association of County Archaeological Officers (ACAO) and Association of District Archaeological Officers (ADAO) have been formed, and recently combined into the Association of Local Government Archaeological Officers (ALGAO).

In Wales, central government responsibility for both planning and heritage   **3.11** issues is undertaken by the Welsh Office. It is advised by Cadw, the Welsh Historic Monuments Executive Agency, created in 1984. However, unlike its English counterpart, Cadw is not a fully independent body as it remains under the jurisdiction of the Secretary of State for Wales, who is responsible for administration of the Welsh Office. Recent administration changes also now mean that the formulation of planning policy no longer mirrors the English equivalents.

All local government planning functions are now administered solely   **3.12** through unitary authorities (since April 1996). In respect of archaeology four trusts are responsible: Clwyd-Powys Archaeological Trust, the Dyfed Archaeological Trust Limited, the Glamorgan-Gwent Archaeological Trust

---

[3] Report from the Committee of Public Accounts, *Protecting and Managing England's Heritage Property* (1993 H.C. 252), p.25.
[4] UNESCO, *The World Heritage Convention: An Idea in Action* (1991), p.4.
[5] Oliver, *Archaeology Review 1993–4* (1994), p.2.

Limited, the Gwynedd Archaeological Trust. They fulfil the County Archaeologist's role for the whole of the Principality including collecting information for the SMR, though it is maintained by the planning department of Clwyd County Council. However, the role of the Trusts is both curatorial and contractual through their provision not only of advice and guidance to planning authorities and other statutory bodies, but also assessment, evaluation and investigation for landowners and developers.

3. GOVERNMENT FOR OTHER PARTS OF THE UNITED KINGDOM

3.13   Whilst the scope of this work is primarily intended to cover the law affecting England and Wales it should be noted that the Scottish Office Development Department is responsible for planning and archaeological issues through its executive agency, Historic Scotland. The Royal Commission on the Ancient and Historical Monuments of Scotland is sponsored by Historic Scotland.

3.14   Although the Scottish legal system is fundamentally different, the planning system is broadly similar. Currently, the relevant statutory framework is found in the Town and Country Planning (Scotland) Act 1972. The provisions of the Ancient Monuments and Archaeological Areas Act 1979 are directly applied to Scotland. National Planning Policy Guideline 5 ("Archaeology and Planning"), known colloquially as "NPPG 5" and Planning Advice Note "PAN 42" ("Archaeology – the Planning Process and Scheduled Monument Procedures"), collectively, are the Scottish equivalent of PPG 16 although the wording is not a mirror of its English counterpart.

3.15   Local government administration is divided on a tiered basis between regional, island and local councils. The SMR is covered by the regional and island councils although, at the time of writing, the Lothian, Tayside and Western Isles do not have a local government archaeological service. Determination of planning applications is the same as the English system. Since April 1, 1996, local government administration has been based upon 32 unitary authorities. They have taken over the SMR previously operated by the regional and island councils where they existed.

3.16   The organisation of both planning and archaeology are radically different again in Northern Ireland. There, the Department of the Environment (Northern Ireland) oversees both areas advised by the Environment Service, a grouping responsible for the countryside, wildlife, historic monuments and buildings, as well as environmental protection. The Town and Country Planning Service prepares area plans which, following adoption, form the statutory framework. Governing legislation is by way of Parliamentary Orders in Council. The most recent and relevant to archaeology is the Historical Monuments and Archaeological Objects (Northern Ireland) Order 1995.

3.17   Local government has one tier made up of district and borough councils. Whilst some run local museums and employ archaeologists there are no formal appointments. There is also no SMR equivalent to that found on the mainland part of the United Kingdom. However, a centralised SMR has been built up since the 1970s, known as the Northern Ireland Monuments and Buildings Record.

3.18   On the Isle of Man planning applications are determined by the Department of Local Government and Environment. Advice on archaeological issues is given by Manx National Heritage, a body made up of representatives from the Manx Museum and National Trust, members of the Tynwald (the Manx parliament), local authorities and organisations, a member from Liverpool University and one from The National Trust for England and Wales.

On Guernsey, planning applications are dealt with by the Land Develop- **3.19**
ment Committee and archaeological issues by the Heritage Committee which, whilst not bound by any specific law, operates under a Code of Practice similar to that of the Museums Association. Elected members of the local parliament, the States of Deliberation, serve on both committees. A similar arrangement operates on Jersey, where the Planning and Environment Committee deals with both planning and heritage/archaeological matters.

4. MUSEUMS

A wide range of museums exists throughout Britain which may be either **3.20**
purely archaeological in nature or combine wider areas of interest. They might be considered in terms of national, regional or local significance although their geographical and subject areas will often overlap. National interest will be reflected in the: British Museum, London; National Museum of Scotland, Edinburgh; Ulster Museum, Belfast; the National Museum of Wales, Cardiff. However, a number of the other larger museums such as the Museum of London or the Ashmolean Museum, Oxford would normally be considered significant centres. Other museums can be part of local government services, universities, independent charitable organisations or private collections.

The Museums and Galleries Commission which is funded by the Depart- **3.21**
ment of National Heritage has produced guidance—*Standards in the Museum Care of Archaeological Collections* (MGC 1992). It is becoming more common for regional museums to produce their own guidance on acceptance of materials. This can be critical as it becomes a standard requirement that all archaeological records and finds from excavations stimulated through the planning system are deposited in museums. However, it should be noted that not all museums may be considered suitable by the planning authority as places for deposit. Neither will all museums accept material from excavations.

In addition to 10 regional Area Museum Councils, which offer advice and **3.22**
support to the museums in their regions, there are a number of other museum organisations: Association of Independent Museums, The Museums Association, Society of Museum Archaeologists and Scottish Museum Archaeologists.

The interests and roles of museums have changed considerably in the past **3.23**
decade or so. Collecting policies now tend to be more detailed and the increased cost of conservation and storage a significant problem.

5. UNESCO

3.24 The United Nations Educational, Scientific and Cultural Organisation (UNESCO) is relevant to British archaeology following the United Kingdom's signature at the World Heritage Convention in 1984. The Convention, adopted by UNESCO in 1972, provides for the identification and conservation of World Heritage Sites (WHS) and requires a World Heritage List to be established under the management of an inter-governmental World Heritage Committee (WHC) which, in turn, is advised by the International Council on Monuments and Sites (ICOMOS) and the World Conservation Union.

3.25 Each Member State makes its own nominations and is required to do all it can to ensure that adequate protection is available through its own legislation. Nominations are assessed first by ICOMOS, which is an international non-governmental body of people professionally concerned with conservation. This assessment is considered by the WHC elected by the World Heritage Convention signatories and then by UNESCO. In order to be eligible, a site must be of "outstanding universal value" in one or more of six defined categories.

3.26 It is the stated aim of UNESCO that the intention of inclusion in the list of WHS is "the better protection of World Heritage properties ... So the immediate and obvious benefit of international listing is to strengthen the hand of those who are committed to their protection and enjoyment".[6] Recognising that "international notoriety and moral support are not enough",[7] there is also a World Heritage Fund which provides financial assistance for the identification, technical co-operation and training necessary for the conservation of WHS. Most of the money available is spent in the Third World.[8]

3.27 Over 300 heritage or man-made sites have now been registered as WHS from over 100 signatories to the World Heritage Convention. There is also a further category of natural sites with nearly 100 entries, which illustrates the broad range of the concept, which is designed to protect "the most precious treasures of mankind's cultural and natural heritage".[9] The United Kingdom currently has 14 WHS. Further discussion on WHS can be found in Chapter 5, Section 6.

6. CONSULTANTS AND CONTRACTORS

3.28 Prior to PPG 16 in 1990, the archaeological excavation of sites threatened by development had been funded on an ad hoc basis by central government through the Ministry of Public Buildings and Works, later the Department of the Environment (DOE) and more recently through English Heritage. Some funding had been provided by local authorities and occasionally by developers. From the late 1960s funding was often channelled through committees set up initially to deal with specific projects but often transforming

---

[6] See further para.- 6–64, below for legal status.

[7] UNESCO *op: cit.* (n. 4 above), p.4.

[8] Cleere, "British Archaeology in a Wider Context" in Hunter and Ralston, *Archaeological Resource Management in the UK: An Introduction* (1993), p.123.

[9] UNESCO *op.cit.* (n. 4 above).

themselves into permanent bodies to deal with all archaeological issues in either a city or town or on a regional basis. The effect was that by the late 1970s a network of archaeological units, usually charitable trusts and sometimes limited companies, had been established covering most of England, Wales and Scotland. Their funding was given a particular fillip by the Manpower Services Commission (MSC) which financed large scale excavation projects.

However, the reorganisation by English Heritage of funding on a project only basis and greater pressures on MSC and local authority expenditure in the 1980s, saw a reduction in the number of units and staff employed. The result was a fragmentation of what had been virtually complete national coverage in a non-competitive situation and the rise of independent archaeological contractors and consultants, including specialised services in aerial photographic interpretation and geophysical survey, and a sharpened awareness of financial competitiveness. In addition, some of the local authority based units have been hived off in order to separate their monitoring or curatorial roles from competitive contract tendering. While many archaeologists may regret the changes, it has brought greater professional and financial accountability.   **3.29**

Already in the 1970s and 1980s, in recognition of the increasing costs of rescue archaeology and the need for minimum standards, the DOE had published guidelines on a variety of aspects.[10] English Heritage has continued this approach with publications on research priorities such as Roman and Medieval Pottery Studies[11] as well as the *Management of Archaeological Projects*.[12] The increased professional awareness of archaeologists through the Institute of Field Archaeologists and the Association of County Archaeological Officers, has encouraged a number of guidelines which underpin the work of any professional archaeologist.[13]   **3.30**

7. ROYAL COMMISSIONS ON HISTORICAL MONUMENTS

National survey and data collection is the responsibility of the Royal Commissions for England, Wales and Scotland, funded by central government but not part of the Civil Service. Originally founded by Royal Warrant in 1908, the intention was "to make an inventory of the Ancient and Historical Monuments and Constructions connected with or illustrative of the contemporary culture, civilisation and conditions of life of the people ... from the earliest times to the year 1700, and to specify those which seem   **3.31**

---

[10] DOE, *Principles of Publication in Rescue Archaeology* (1975); Young, *Guidelines for the Processing and Publication of Roman Pottery from Excavations* (1980).

[11] Fulford and Huddleston, *The Current State of Romano-British Pottery Studies: A Review for English Heritage* (1991); Mellor, *Medieval Ceramic Studies in England* (1994).

[12] English Heritage, *The Management of Archaeological Projects* (2nd ed., 1991).

[13] IFA, *Code of Conduct* (1994); IFA, *Standard and Guidance for Archaeological Desk-Based Assessments* (1994); IFA, *Standard and Guidance for Field Evaluations* (1994); IFA, *Standard and Guidance for Archaeological Excavations* (1994); IFA, *Standard and Guidance for Archaeological Watching Briefs* (1994); ACAO, *Model Briefs and Specifications for Archaeological Assessments and Field Evaluations* (1994). See Appendices.

most worthy of preservation".[14] Overseen by Crown-appointed Commissioners, teams of skilled investigators worked on a county basis to produce a series of magisterial volumes. Originally, they were primarily concerned with standing buildings. However, the scope of investigation has been broadened in recent years to include all archaeological remains within surveys. In addition to the county surveys, monographs on specific sites or topics have also been produced; and since the progress on county inventories was undoubtedly slow, these studies have become more common.

3.32   Over the years the role and function of the Royal Commissions gradually changed and radical reviews resulted in new Royal Warrants. For the RCHME this enabled it to meet better the needs of those concerned with archaeology:

> "... to provide for the survey and recording of ancient and historical monuments and constructions connected with, or illustrative of, contemporary culture, civilisation and conditions of the life of the people in England from the earliest times (including ancient and historical monuments and constructions in, on or under the sea bed within the United Kingdom territorial sea adjacent to England) by compiling, maintaining and curating the National Monuments Record of England as the basic national record of the archaeological and historical environment; by identifying, surveying, interpreting and recording all buildings, sites and ancient monuments of archaeological, architectural and historical interest in England or in, on or under the sea bed within the territorial sea adjacent to England, in order both to enhance and update the National Monuments Record of England, and also to respond to statutory needs; by providing advice and information relevant to the preservation and conservation of such buildings, sites and ancient monuments of archaeological, architectural and historical interest; by collecting and exchanging data with other record holders and providing an index to data from other sources; by promoting the public use of information available in the National Monuments Record of England by all appropriate means; by establishing and maintaining national standards in surveying, recording and curating of records relating to archaeology and historical architecture and providing guidance on these matters to other bodies; by exercising responsibility for the oversight of local Sites and Monuments Records; and by continuing and furthering the work of the survey of London."[15]

3.33   Although the county inventories have been abandoned there has been an increased publication of specialist surveys and greater attention to computer compilation of national data. An overview and assistance with County Sites and Monuments Record is maintained, which has been greatly aided by a programme of plotting archaeological features on aerial photographs.

3.34   In addition, the Royal Commissions have absorbed the archaeological function of the Ordnance Survey which from the late eighteenth century had identified and depicted monuments in its cartographic surveys and since 1920 had maintained its own specialist archaeological staff. This historic database forms a significant element of the National Monuments Record.

---

[14] RCHME, *An Inventory of the Historical Monuments in Buckinghamshire* (1912), p.xiv.

[15] DNH, *Royal Warrant* (RCHME) (1994).

8. OTHER SURVEY BODIES

Various organisations such as English Heritage, The National Trust, local **3.35** authorities, universities, museums and grant-giving bodies will sponsor archaeological surveys which can be undertaken either by their own staff, or by independent consultants and contractors. In addition, there are two other surveys which will be commonly mentioned in archaeological reports.

Victoria History

Beginning with its first publication in 1900 and subsequently running almost **3.36** parallel to, sometimes overlapping with, the earlier work of the Royal Commission is the Victoria History: *The Victoria History of the Counties of England* "is a National Historic Survey which, under the direction of a large staff comprising the foremost students in science, history, and archaeology, is designed to record the history of every county in England in detail. This work was, by gracious permission, dedicated to Her Late Majesty Queen Victoria, who gave it her own name".[16] Run by an advisory committee and now based at the University of London Institute of Historical Research, the organisation is dependent upon grant aid and without a role in the monitoring of archaeology but provides an invaluable source of information.

English Place-Name Society

The English Place-Name Society undertakes research and publishes volumes **3.37** on the place names of English counties and, again, is dependent upon grant aid.

9. INTEREST GROUPS

Numerous archaeological societies exist, ranging from national, county and **3.38** locally-based societies to specialist period and subject societies. Most counties will have a society, some also embracing history and natural history and there are many local societies. Most will produce publications, a few have their own museums and some continue to sponsor research and excavation although this is becoming more rare. There are a number of national specialist societies covering the main periods: The Prehistoric Society, The Society for the Promotion of Roman Studies, The Society for Medieval Archaeology and the Society for Post-Medieval Archaeology. There are numerous more specialised interest groups such as the Lithic Study Society, Hillfort Study Group, Roman Pottery Study Group, Medieval Pottery Research Group, Medieval Settlement Research Group, Fortress Study Group, Vernacular Buildings Group and the Nautical Archaeology Society.[17] Each of these groups exist not only to provide a forum for the discussion of their specialist interests but often produces guidelines and

---

[16] Page, *The Victoria County History of the County of Nottingham* (1906), p.vii.
[17] A useful list of special interest groups will be found in Hayworth, *British Archaeological Yearbook* 1995–6 (1995), pp.155–164.

research priorities for their studies. However, several bodies in particular will be encountered during any consideration of archaeology today.

Institute of Field Archaeologists

3.39   The only professional body for archaeologists, the Institute of Field Archaeologists, was founded in 1982. By 1994 it had a total membership of 1,121. These comprised five honorary members, 574 members, 306 associates, 135 practitioners and 101 affiliates.[18] A *Code of Conduct*[19] and *Standards and Guidance*[20] on various aspects of archaeological work have been produced as well as papers and monographs on other technical matters and issues of concern to the membership. It is likely that about one-half of the total number of full-time field archaeologists in Britain belong to the Institute.

Society of Antiquaries of London

3.40   The premier society for archaeologists was founded in 1707. Membership is obtained only through sponsorship by members and a secret ballot. It represents a wide range of antiquarian archaeological interests and has been successful in influencing government opinion.

Society of Antiquaries of Scotland

3.41   Founded in 1780 and similar to the Society of Antiquaries of London, the Society of Antiquaries of Scotland is a major guardian of Scottish Heritage. Its museum became part of the National Museums of Scotland but the society was relieved of the charge of management by the National Museum of Antiquaries of Scotland Act 1954.

Council for British Archaeology (CBA)

3.42   Founded in 1944 as a co-ordinating educational and policy-making body for amateur and professional archaeologists, membership is open to any individual or organisation. In Scotland there is an equivalent, the Council for Scottish Archaeology. With regional sub-groups and specialist national committees, it has been influential at both local and national levels as a campaigning body. The CBA has a quasi-statutory role as a body which the Secretaries of State for National Heritage and for Wales have directed should be notified of listed building applications which involve demolition.[21] It is also a consultative body for nominations to the Cathedrals Fabric Commission. It is usually represented on the committees of other organisations such as The National Trust, various archaeological trusts, Diocesan Advisory Committees, and specialist interest societies. Accordingly, the CBA is in a good position to monitor and influence trends in archaeology. The regional

---

[18] IFA, *Annual Report No. 11* (1994), p.22.
[19] See n. 11 above.
[20] See n. 11 above.
[21] Information from Richard Morris, Director CBA.

CBA groups will often make comments on planning applications and sometimes submit evidence at planning inquiries.

RESCUE (Trust for British Archaeology)

Out of the development boom of the 1960s and, in particular the motorway construction programme, came the creation in 1971 of the Trust for British Archaeology commonly known as RESCUE.[22] An independent campaigning organisation drawing support from many of the leading archaeologists of the day, it has been influential in drawing public and political attention to the large-scale destruction of archaeological remains. Although since the appearance of PPG 16 archaeology is to be treated within the planning system, RESCUE still sees a role for itself as a pressure group.

3.43

10. CONCLUSIONS

The organisation of British archaeology has changed dramatically over the past 30 years and particularly since the publication of PPG 16 in 1990. Archaeology is now planted firmly within the planning system and archaeologists, whether working for charitable trusts or independent contractors and consultants, are following not only government guidance on the requirements of archaeological work but standards set by their own professional body with advice from English Heritage and County Archaeologists. Accompanying this is the requirement for competitive tenders, professional indemnity and public liability insurance.

3.44

Archaeological societies, specialist interest and pressure groups have also recognised the changes and have an opportunity to express their views and exert influence. The foundations have been set for the long-term benefit of archaeology and it is to be hoped that archaeologists will continue their professional development alongside an improving system.

3.45

---

[22] Barker, "The Origins and Development of RESCUE" in Rhatz, *Rescue Archaeology* (1974), pp.280–285.

4. Ancient Monuments and Archaeological Areas Act

1. INTRODUCTION AND DEFINITIONS

The Ancient Monuments and Archaeological Areas Act 1979 (AMAAA) **4.1** contains the principal code relating to ancient monuments. It consolidates and amends legislation dating back to the Schedule to the Ancient Monuments Protection Act 1882 which had introduced the concept of "scheduling" monuments to give them protected status. In addition, the AMAAA introduces a broader perception of archaeological remains through the designation of Areas of Archaeological Importance (AAI).

AMAAA was amended by the National Heritage Act 1983. This estab- **4.2** lished the Historic Buildings and Monuments Commission for England to exercise many of the Secretary of State's functions in England. Referred to in AMAAA as "the Commission", this body is commonly known as English Heritage, and is referred to in this book as such.

The powers granted by AMAAA are exercised by the Secretary of State, **4.3** English Heritage and local authorities.[1] The responsibilities of the Secretary of State, in England, were transferred from the Department of the Environment to the Department of National Heritage in 1992.[2] In Wales it is administered by the Welsh Office, advised by Cadw, and in Scotland by the Scottish Office through Historic Scotland, an executive agency within the Scottish Office Development Department.

"Monument" is defined by section 61(7) as: **4.4**
"(a)   any building, structure or work, whether above or below the surface of the land, and any cave or excavation;

---

[1] Local authorities for the purpose of AMAAA are defined by s.61(1) as:

   (a)   in England and Wales, the council of a county or district, the council of a London borough and the Common Council of the City of London;
   (b)   in Scotland, the planning authority within the meaning of Part IX of the Local Government (Scotland) Act 1973.

For more recent local government changes, refer to paras 3.9, 3.12 and 3.15 for relevant unitary authorities.

[2] Circular 20/92, *Responsibilities for Conservation Policy and Casework*. The powers of the Secretary of State need not be exercised by the minister personally, civil servants can act in his name without express delegation (*Carlton Ltd v. Commissioners of Works* [1943] 2 All E.R. 560).

(b) any site comprising the remains of any such building, structure or work or of any cave or excavation;

(c) any site comprising, or comprising the remains of, any vehicle, vessel, aircraft or other movable structure or part thereof which neither constitutes nor forms part of any work which is a monument within paragraph (a) above;

and any machinery attached to a monument shall be regarded as part of the monument if it could not be detached without being dismantled."

4.5 The definition of "remains" is wide. It includes any trace or sign of the previous existence of the thing in question.[3] Three exceptions are provided in section 61(8). Subsection (7)(a) does not apply to "any ecclesiastical building for the time being used for ecclesiastical purposes". This means religious purposes of a Christian and, possibly non-Christian church.[4] Subsection (7)(c) does not include:

"(a) a site comprising any object or its remains unless the situation of that object or its remains in that particular site is a matter of public interest;

(b) a site comprising, or comprising the remains of, any vessel which is protected by an order under section 1 of the Protection of Wrecks Act 1973 designating an area around the site as a restricted area."

Exception (a) requires that the presence of the object in its site is a matter of public interest. AMAAA is not concerned with the protection of objects alone.

4.6 The site of a monument is a flexible concept. It includes not only the land on or in which the monument is situated but any land "comprising or adjoining it ... essential for the monument's support and preservation".[5] This determination is made by the Secretary of State, the Commission or a local authority exercising in relation to that monument any of their functions under AMAAA.[6]

4.7 Three types of monuments are provided for in AMAAA:

(a) scheduled monuments;

(b) ancient monuments;

(c) protected monuments.

Scheduled monuments

4.8 A scheduled monument is a monument that is included in the Schedule of monuments kept by the Secretary of State pursuant to section 1(1).[7] Scheduling is the principal means of protecting a monument under AMAAA.

---

[3] AMAAA, s.61(13).

[4] *Attorney-General, ex rel Bedfordshire County Council v. Trustees of Howard United Reformed Church, Bedford* [1976] A.C. 363.

[5] AMAAA, s.61(9).

[6] *ibid.* s.61(9).

[7] *ibid.* ss.1(10), 6(1).

Ancient monuments

Ancient monument means: **4.9**

> "(a)   any scheduled monument; and
> (b)   any other monument which in the opinion of the Secretary of State is of public interest by reason of the historic, architectural, traditional, artistic or archaeological interest attaching to it."[8]

The powers to acquire monuments compulsorily and to enter into guardianship agreements extend to ancient monuments.[9]

It should be noted that a different definition of "ancient monument" applies for the purposes of English Heritage's general duties and functions. This is "any structure, work, site, garden or area which in the Commission's opinion is of historic, architectural, traditional, artistic or archaeological interest".[10] **4.10**

Protected monuments

A protected monument is: **4.11**

(a)   any scheduled monument; and
(b)   any other monument under the ownership or guardianship of the Secretary of State, the Commission or a local authority under AMAAA.[11]

Protected monument status is relevant for the offence of damaging certain ancient monuments under section 28.

2. THE SCHEDULING PROCESS

The Schedule is maintained by the Secretary of State.[12] When the AMAAA Schedule was first compiled it included certain monuments already subject to protection.[13] The Secretary of State has the power to include in the Schedule any monument which appears to him to be of national importance.[14] He may also exclude any monument from the Schedule or amend a monument's Schedule entry.[15] **4.12**

The discretion to schedule is broad. In *R. v. Secretary of State for the Environment, ex p. Rose Theatre Trust Co.*,[16] the Secretary of State **4.13**

---

[8] AMAAA, s.61(1), (12).

[9] Under National Heritage Act 1983, s.33(1), (2).

[10] *ibid.* s.33(8).

[11] *ibid.* s.28(3).

[12] *ibid.* s.1(1).

[13] *ibid.* s.1(2). Monuments included in the last list published under s.12 of the Ancient Monuments Consolidation and Amendment Act 1913 and those for which the Secretary of State had served notice under s.6(1) of the Ancient Monuments Act 1931 that he intended to include on a s.12 list.

[14] AMAAA, s.1(3).

[15] *ibid.* s.1(5). Amendment includes excluding anything previously included as part of the monument or adding anything not previously so included.

[16] [1990] 1 Q.B. 504.

considered that the remains of the Rose Theatre in Southwark were of national importance but that they should not be scheduled. Schiemann J. considered that there was a wide area of discretion as to whether the remains were of national importance. There was then a broad discretion whether to schedule.[17]

4.14   The Secretary of State's criteria for scheduling ancient monuments was first published in *Historic Buildings and Ancient Monuments, First Report from the Environment Committee 1986–87*.[18] The present, revised, version is contained in Annex 4 to Planning Policy Guidance Note 16, *Archaeology and Planning* (PPG 16) and in Annex 3 to PPG 16 (Wales):

> "These criteria (which are not in any order of ranking) are used for assessing the national importance of an ancient monument and considering whether scheduling is appropriate. The criteria should not however be regarded as definitive; rather they are indicators which contribute to a wider judgment based on the individual circumstances of a case:
>
> (i)   *Period*: all types of monuments that characterise a category or period should be considered for preservation.
>
> (ii)   *Rarity*: there are some monument categories which in certain periods are so scarce that all surviving examples which still retain some archaeological potential should be preserved. In general, however, a selection must be made which portrays the typical and commonplace as well as the rare. This process should take account of all aspects of the distribution of a particular class of monument, both in a national and a regional context.
>
> (iii)   *Documentation*: the significance of a monument may be enhanced by the existence of records of previous investigation or, in the case of more recent monuments, by the supporting evidence of contemporary written records.
>
> (iv)   *Group Value*: the value of a single monument (such as a field system) may be greatly enhanced by its association with related contemporary monuments (such as a settlement and cemetery) or with monuments of different periods. In some cases, it is preferable to protect the complete group of monuments, including associated and adjacent land, rather than to protect isolated monuments within the group.
>
> (v)   *Survival/Condition*: the survival of a monument's archaeological potential both above and below ground is a particularly important consideration and should be assessed in relation to its present condition and surviving features.
>
> (vi)   *Fragility/Vulnerability*:   highly   important   archaeological evidence from some field monuments can be destroyed by a single ploughing or unsympathetic treatment; vulnerable monuments of this nature would particularly benefit from the statutory protection which scheduling confers. There are also existing standing structures of particular form or complexity whose value can again be severely reduced by neglect or careless treatment and which are similarly well suited by scheduled monument pro-

---

[17] [1990] 1 Q.B. 504 at 513.
[18] Vol.2, p.35.

tection, even if these structures are already listed historic buildings.

(vii) *Diversity*: some monuments may be selected for scheduling because they possess a combination of high quality features, others because of a single important attribute.

(viii) *Potential*: on occasion, the nature of the evidence cannot be specified precisely but it may still be possible to document reasons anticipating its existence and importance and so to demonstrate the justification for scheduling. This is usually confined to sites rather than upstanding monuments."

The criteria are not exclusive. Even if the criteria are met, the Secretary of State is not obliged to schedule. For example, in *Rose Theatre* the Secretary of State was allowed to consider the potential liability to pay compensation because of scheduling. He is entitled to balance the consequences on landowners and others in halting development; to consider the effects on co-operation with the developer; and whether the monument is under threat.[19] **4.15**

In Wales and Scotland the respective Secretaries of State are advised by their executive agencies, Cadw and Historic Scotland.[20] The Secretary of State must consult English Heritage before scheduling a monument situated in England.[21] PPG 16 notes "In practice, most proposals for scheduling originate with English Heritage, some at the request of local authorities or amenity groups, but the decision rests with the Secretary of State".[22] The views of English Heritage, whilst something that the Secretary of State must take into account before scheduling, cannot be decisive. **4.16**

The one statutory limit on the Secretary of State's power is that he may not schedule any monument that is occupied as a dwelling house by any person other than a person employed as its caretaker or his family.[23] **4.17**

The Secretary of State has equivalent powers to exclude monuments from the schedule and to amend entries. The power to amend is wide and may exclude anything previously included as part of the monument and add anything not previously so included.[24] The boundary of a site is a matter for the Secretary of State[25] but is in practice delineated by a red line on the scheduling map. **4.18**

The owners and occupiers of sites, local authorities and other persons are not entitled to be consulted. However, owners are, as a matter of policy, normally consulted although there may not be time in cases where development is impending.[26] English Heritage's Monument Protection Programme is evaluating all archaeological remains in England to identify those suitable for scheduling. This is being carried out in liaison with county authorities.[27] **4.19**

In Wales and Scotland the Secretary of State is obliged to inform the owner **4.20**

---

[19] [1990] 1 Q.B. 504 at 516–518.
[20] PPG 16 (Wales), Annex 1, para. 2.
[21] AMAAA, s.1(3).
[22] PPG 16, Annex 3, para. 1.
[23] AMAAA, s.1(4).
[24] *ibid.* s.1(5).
[25] *Rose Theatre* (n. 16 above) at 518.
[26] PPG 16, Annex 3, para. 2.
[27] *ibid.* para. 3.

and any occupier of the monument and the relevant local authority of the inclusion or exclusion of the monument on the Schedule or the amendment of the entry. A copy of the entry, where there is one, must be sent to the owner and occupier.[28] The procedure in England is different. The Secretary of State notifies English Heritage of his act and the new entry.[29] English Heritage then inform the owner, occupier and local authority.[30]

4.21 The Secretary of State is obliged to publish, from time to time, a list of all scheduled monuments.[31] He may publish amendments to the list. The list, as amended, is evidence that the monuments listed are scheduled and with the details purported to be in the Schedule.[32]

4.22 In England, the list and amendments to it are provided to English Heritage by the Secretary of State.[33] These are then published by English Heritage.[34] This published list is then evidence of the inclusion of any monument listed in the Schedule and of any matters purporting to be reproduced in the list from entries in the Schedule.[35]

3. SCHEDULED MONUMENT CONSENT

4.23 The principal effect of scheduling is that consent is needed to permit most works on a monument. Works are defined as including "operations of any description" and in particular flooding[36] or tipping[37] operations and operations for the purposes of agriculture[38] or forestry.[39]

4.24 The works requiring consent are in three categories (s.2(2)):

"(a) any works resulting in the demolition or destruction of or any damage to the scheduled monument;

(b) any works for the purpose of removing or repairing a scheduled monument or any part of it or making any alterations or additions thereto;

(c) any flooding or tipping operations on land in, on or under which there is a scheduled monument."

Subsection (a) is concerned with the effect of the works. The nature of the works and their purpose are, save for certain defences and consents, irrelevant.

Subsection (b) covers works with the purpose of repairing, removing, altering or adding to scheduled monuments. It will apply even if the works

---

[28] AMAAA, s.1(6).
[29] *ibid.* s.1(6A).
[30] *ibid.* s.1A(1).
[31] *ibid.* s.1(7).
[32] *ibid.* s.1(8).
[33] *ibid.* s.1(7A), (8A).
[34] *ibid.* s.1A(2), (3).
[35] *ibid.* s.1A(3).
[36] Meaning "covering land with water or any other liquid or partially liquid substance" (AMAAA, s.61(7)).
[37] Tipping is defined as "tipping soil or spoil or depositing building or any other materials or matter (including waste materials or refuse) on any land" (AMAAA, s.61(1)).
[38] Within the meaning of the town and country planning legislation.
[39] AMAAA, s.61(1).

are universally considered to be an improvement. Consent is still required. Implicitly the person executing (and so on) the works must know that the works are to a scheduled monument to be guilty of an offence.[40]

Subsection (c) covers certain operations, tipping and flooding. Consent is required even if the operations have no effect on the scheduled monument.

Scheduled monument consent is granted in writing by the Secretary of State.[41] The consent may be granted unconditionally or subject to conditions. Conditions may specify the manner in which works are to be executed and the person carrying out the works.[42] A condition may require that a person authorised by English Heritage or the Secretary of State (outside England) be afforded an opportunity, before the works are begun, to examine the monument and site and carry out archaeological excavations.[43] **4.25**

Like planning permissions, scheduled monument consent is, unless otherwise provided, for the benefit of the monument not its owner.[44] A subsequent owner can therefore normally carry out the consent. However, unlike planning permissions, outline consent cannot be granted.[45] **4.26**

Scheduled monument consent ceases to have effect unless works under it are started within five years, or any longer or shorter period specified in the consent.[46] No definition of start is provided in AMAAA but the equivalent position of planning permissions is that physical works must be executed out for the purpose of implementing the permission. **4.27**

Executing or causing or permitting works to be executed without authorisation is a criminal offence.[47] Criminal offences under section 2 are considered in section 30 below. Works are authorised if they are carried out in accordance with the terms of the consent and the conditions attaching to it.[48] **4.28**

The Secretary of State must notify his decision to the applicant and any person who has made representations.[49] **4.29**

4. APPLICATIONS FOR SCHEDULED MONUMENT CONSENT

Applications are governed by Schedule 1, Part I of AMAAA.[50] Paragraphs 1 and 2 of that Schedule provide for regulations relating to the form and procedural requirements of applications. The current regulations for England **4.30**

---

[40] Unlike subsection (2)(a) or (c), no express defence of not knowing that it was a scheduled monument is provided.

[41] AMAAA, s.2(3)(a).

[42] *ibid.* s.2(4).

[43] *ibid.* s.2(6).

[44] *ibid.* Sched. 1, Pt I.

[45] PPG 16, Annex 3, para. 5.

[46] AMAAA, s.4(1), (2).

[47] *ibid.* s.2(1).

[48] *ibid.* s.2(3).

[49] *ibid.* Sched. 1, para. 3(4).

[50] *ibid.* s.2(11). Where scheduled monument consent is required for an infrastructure project proposed under the Transport and Works Act 1992 the application procedure is amended by the Transport and Works Applications (Listed Buildings, Conservation Areas and Ancient Monument Procedure) Regulations 1992 (S.I. 1992 No. 3138).

and Wales are the Ancient Monuments (Applications for Scheduled Monument Consent) Regulations 1981.[51]

4.31   The form used for the application is set out in the Regulations.[52] The applicant must certify that he is the owner of the monument, or that he has given the requisite notice to some or all of the owners and has been unable to ascertain the names and addresses of any other owners.[53] Guidance on the application process is provided in PPG 16, Annex 3, paragraphs 5 to 9 and in notes for applicants from English Heritage.

4.32   Before consent is given, the Secretary of State must hold a public local inquiry[54] or give the applicant, and other persons in the Secretary of State's discretion, an informal hearing.[55] However, the practice of the Secretary of State is to informally notify applicants of the decision before it is issued, and offer the opportunity to request a hearing before the Secretary of State's decision is issued.[56] Before making his decision, the Secretary of State shall consider any representations made to him and the report of any inquiry or hearing.[57] If the monument is in England, he must consult English Heritage.[58] Otherwise, no formal right of appeal exists although the Secretary of State's action may, occasionally, be capable of challenge in the High Court by way of judicial review. This area is dealt with below in paragraphs 4.134 *et seq.*

5. CLASS CONSENTS

4.33   With the wide definition of works, scheduling has a considerable effect on the ability of landowners to manage their property. Certain acts, perhaps because they have been done before, are unlikely to have any effect on the monument. For them, it is desirable to avoid the expense and complexity of scheduled monument consent. Alternatively, works may be planned under other powers in AMAAA or be carried out by government agencies. Given the degree of government approval already required, the consent process is an unnecessary delay and burden.

4.34   The Secretary of State can give a general consent for certain classes and descriptions of works.[59] The Secretary of State's power is exercised following consultation (if it affects England) with English Heritage.[60] The class consent

---

[51] S.I. 1981 No. 1301.

[52] 1981 Regulations; AMAAA, para. 2(1) and Sched. 1. Although published in English, in Wales the WO has a duty to provide a translation in Welsh if requested.

[53] AMAAA, para. 2(1), Sched. 1. The owner for these purposes is the estate owner of the fee simple or a person with a tenancy with at least seven years to run (AMAAA, para. 2(3), Sched. 1; 1981 Regulations, reg. 4).

[54] Witnesses can be summoned to attend and oaths administered. The Secretary of State may make orders as to payment of his, and parties, costs (AMAAA, Sched. 1, para. 4; Local Government Act 1972, s.250).

[55] AMAAA, Sched. 1, para. 3(2).

[56] PPG 16, Annex 3, para. 9. The policy appears to be to avoid hearings of the application unless the Secretary of State is minded to refuse.

[57] AMAAA, Sched. 1, para. 3(3)(a), (b).

[58] AMAAA, Sched. 1, para. 3(3)(c). The Secretary of State must send a copy of an application for a consent in England to English Heritage as soon as practicable after receiving it (AMAAA, Sched. 1, para. 2A).

[59] Under AMAAA, s.3(1).

[60] AMAAA, s.3(1).

may attach conditions.[61] The present class consent in England and Wales is the Ancient Monuments (Class Consents) Order 1994[62] which authorises 10 classes of works. It is reproduced in Appendix A.

4.35 Several classes cover acts by occupiers that are unlikely to cause damage. They include agricultural, horticultural and forestry works of the same kind that have been carried out in the previous six years (Class 1). This class is subject to detailed restrictions set out in the Order.

4.36 Works for the repair or maintenance of machinery are exempted (Class 4) as are works urgently necessary for safety and health (Class 5). Classes 2 and 3 cover underground coal mining and works by the British Waterways Board respectively.

4.37 Class consents cover various acts by or authorised by archaeological bodies. Works by English Heritage and the Royal Commissions on Historic Monuments are exempted (Classes 6 and 10). The other class consents cover archaeological evaluations connected with scheduled monument consent applications, works under agreements concerning ancient monuments[63] and works grant-aided under AMAAA.[64]

4.38 Some monuments may be vulnerable to works carried out under the class consent. In respect of a specified monument, the Secretary of State may direct that the general consent does not apply.[65] Scheduled monument consent must be applied for if the works are to be carried out once notice of the direction has been served on the occupier, or in the absence of an occupier, the owner.[66]

4.39 A direction may be withdrawn, as with permitted development rights under a Town and Country Planning General Development Order.[67] Before making or withdrawing a direction in relation to a monument in England, the Secretary of State must consult English Heritage.[68]

6. REVOCATION OR MODIFICATION OF SCHEDULED MONUMENT CONSENT

4.40 The Secretary of State has power to revoke or modify a scheduled monument consent by direction.[69] The modification can include changing the period for starting the works.[70] The procedure for modification or revocation is set out in Schedule 1, Part II. In addition, the Secretary of State must consult English Heritage before making such a direction in respect of a monument in England.[71]

4.41 The Secretary of State must serve notice of any proposed revocation or

---

[61] AMAAA, s.3(2).

[62] S.I. 1994 No. 1381. The Ancient Monuments (Class Consents) (Scotland) Order 1996 (S.I. 1996 No. 1501) applies in Scotland.

[63] AMAAA, s.17.

[64] *ibid.* s.24, classes 7, 8 and 9.

[65] *ibid.* s.3(3).

[66] *ibid.* s.3(4). If the application for consent is refused, compensation may be recoverable (see s.9, below).

[67] See further para. 6.18, below.

[68] AMAAA, s.3(3).

[69] *ibid.* s.4(3).

[70] *ibid.* s.4(4).

[71] *ibid.* s.4(3).

modification on the owner, the occupier, any other person the Secretary of State considers would be affected[72] and, if in England, English Heritage.[73] Upon receipt of the notice, works must not be carried out contrary to the proposed modification or revocation.[74] This restriction applies until the Secretary of State gives a direction or states that he will not give one, or until the expiry of 21 months from the date of service on the occupier (or if there is no occupier) the owner.[75] Objections may be made by persons served, within 28 days of service.[76]

4.42   If no such objections are made, or they are withdrawn, the Secretary of State may make the direction.[77] If such an objection is not withdrawn, the Secretary of State must hold a public inquiry or allow that person to have an informal hearing. If an informal hearing takes place, all persons served, and other persons in the Secretary of State's discretion, are entitled to be heard.[78]

4.43   The consultation process is more restricted for revocations and modifications than for the granting of consent. The Secretary of State is not obliged to consider representations made by persons who are not served by notices or who appear at inquiries or informal hearings.[79]

7. ACQUISITION AND GUARDIANSHIP OF ANCIENT MONUMENTS AND OF LAND IN THEIR VICINITY

4.44   Sections 10 to 17 set out provisions for the acquisition and guardianship of ancient monuments and of land in their vicinity. The Secretary of State has the power to acquire compulsorily any ancient monument to secure its preservation.[80] In England, this power is exercised only after consultation with English Heritage.[81]

4.45   Any compulsory purchase is carried out under the Acquisition of Land Act 1981.[82] The Secretary of State publishes a draft compulsory purchase order, giving notice to owners and occupiers in local newspapers. Objections are dealt with by public local inquiry or by informal hearing. The Secretary of State may then make the order, with or without modification.[83]

---

[72] AMAAA, Sched. 1, para. 5.

[73] *ibid.* Sched. 1, para. 5A.

[74] *ibid.* Sched. 1, paras. 5(3), (4), 8.

[75] *ibid.* Sched. 1, para. 8(4).

[76] *ibid.* Sched. 1, para. 5(5).

[77] *ibid.* Sched. 1, para. 6(1).

[78] *ibid.* Sched. 1, para. 6(3). Since the Secretary of State sends a copy of any resulting direction to all those given an opportunity of an informal hearing (Sched. 1, para. 7) it is envisaged that only a few, identified individuals or bodies will be given the chance to appear.

[79] AMAAA, Sched. 1, para. 6(4).

[80] *ibid.* s.10(1). The minister introducing AMAAA in the House of Commons at Second Reading said that this power "will never be used, except when it is the only way of securing the preservation of a monument" (*Hansard*, H.C. Vol. 965, col. 1361, Kenneth Marks, Under-Secretary of State for the Environment (April 4, 1979)).

[81] AMAAA, s.10(1).

[82] *ibid.* s.10(2).

[83] Acquisition of Land Act 1981, s.2, Sched. 1.

An ancient monument may be acquired by agreement or gift[84] by the **4.46** Secretary of State, English Heritage (in England) or a local authority (where the ancient monument is situated in or in the vicinity of their area).[85] The Secretary of State must consult English Heritage before acquiring a monument in England.[86] English Heritage may acquire an ancient monument only with the consent of the Secretary of State.[87]

Equivalent provisions allow the public bodies to acquire easements over **4.47** land adjoining or in the vicinity of monuments in their ownership.[88] Unlike acquisition of land or a monument, a limited owner can grant easements and other rights over the land.[89]

The powers to acquire ancient monuments include land adjoining or in the **4.48** vicinity which the Secretary of State, English Heritage or the local authority consider to be reasonably required for certain purposes, namely[90]:

(a) to maintain the monument or its amenities;
(b) to provide or facilitate access to the monument;
(c) to exercise proper control or management with respect to the monument;
(d) to store equipment or materials for purpose (a);
(e) to provide facilities and services for the public for or in connection with affording public access to the monument.

The scope of the acquisition power is therefore determined by a functional, and judgmental, test.

8. GUARDIANSHIP

The Secretary of State, English Heritage and local authorities may become **4.49** guardians of ancient monuments.[91] This enables the public body to assume responsibility for maintaining an ancient monument, having full control and management of it,[92] without disturbing its ownership.[93] Guardianship requires the consent of the owner, any occupier and the public body taking guardianship. It usually occurs when the owner/occupier is unable or unwilling to maintain the monument.

Land adjoining or in the vicinity of a monument taken into guardianship **4.50**

---

[84] In the form of a deed or will.
[85] AMAAA, s.11(1), (1A), (2), (3)(3A). Various provisions (including powers of entry, mortgages) of Pt I of the Compulsory Purchase Act 1965 apply to acquisition by agreement in England and Wales (AMAAA, s.11(4)).
[86] AMAAA, s.11(1), (3).
[87] *ibid.* s.11(1A), (3A).
[88] *ibid.* s.16(1)–(3).
[89] *ibid.* s.18(2)(a).
[90] *i.e.* the purposes in s.15(1)(a)–(e).
[91] AMAAA, s.12. Like the power to schedule, there cannot be guardianship of a monument occupied as a dwelling-house by any person other than a person employed as its caretaker or his family (s.12(10)).
[92] AMAAA, s.13(1), (2).
[93] *ibid.* s.12(11).

can itself be taken into guardianship either at that time or later.[94] The public body then has full control and management of the land and can use it for the purposes of acquisition above.[95] It is entitled to acquire rights over adjoining land or land in the vicinity as if they were easements.[96]

4.51 Guardianship can only be constituted by a person having certain long-term interests in the property.[97] Guardianship is constituted by a deed executed by such a person and any occupier.[98] Any other person with an interest in the ancient monument may be a party to the guardianship deed.[99]

4.52 Limited owners can constitute guardianship (provided they have the appropriate long-term interests) and can be a party to the deed.[1] Limited owners are defined as bodies corporate or corporate sole with an interest in land or other persons with certain interests.[2]

4.53 The Secretary of State may only consent to becoming guardian of a monument in England after consultation with English Heritage.[3] English Heritage may become guardian of a monument in England, having obtained the consent of the Secretary of State.[4]

4.54 Whilst guardianship does not affect title to the monument, it is binding upon any person deriving title from a person executing a guardianship deed, unless this derives from a disposition made before the deed was executed.[5] A deed executed by a limited owner is binding upon every successive owner of any estate or interest in the land. However, the guardianship deed does not affect a pre-existing incumbrance binding the land which the limited owner was not capable of overreaching.[6] The guardianship deed is a local land charge.[7] A right acquired over adjoining land is treated as a legal easement, being enforceable by the guardian, and is a local land charge.[8]

4.55 The public body's duty is to maintain a monument under its guardianship.[9] It has very wide powers to exercise full control and management and to do everything necessary for its maintenance.[10] This includes fencing, repairing, and covering in a monument or doing anything else required to repair it or

---

[94] AMAAA, s.15(2).

[95] *ibid.* s.15(3).

[96] *ibid.* s.16(4).

[97] *ibid.* s.12(3). They are an estate in fee simple absolute in possession; a leasehold estate or interest with at least 45 years to run (or which can be renewed for at least 45 years); or an interest in possession during that or another person's life.

[98] *ibid.* s.12(4).

[99] *ibid.* s.12(5). The interest need not be amongst those in s.12(3).

[1] *ibid.* s.18(1).

[2] *ibid.* s.18(3). Those persons are tenants for life or statutory owners under the Settled Land Act 1925; trustees for sale; and trustees for charities or commissioners or trustees for ecclesiastical, collegiate or other public purposes (s.18(4)).

[3] AMAAA, s.12(1).

[4] *ibid.* s.12(1A). English Heritage do not need to consult with, or obtain the consent of, the Secretary of State before acquiring an easement over land in the vicinity (s.16(1A)).

[5] *ibid.* s.12(9).

[6] *ibid.* s.18(7). For example, a mortgage.

[7] *ibid.* s.12(7).

[8] *ibid.* s.16(4), (7).

[9] *ibid.* s.13(1).

[10] *ibid.* s.13(2), (3).

protect it from decay or injury.[11] The powers include specific archaeological investigation powers: to examine it, open it up and make excavations.[12] The public body may also remove the whole or any part of the monument to another place to preserve it.[13] These powers are subject to the terms of the guardianship deed.[14] In practice, these deeds often contain detailed, specific provisions. The only other check on the public body is the availability of judicial review, but a court would be reluctant to intervene in this area requiring specialist knowledge.

4.56

There are powers to terminate the guardianship. The relevant public body and the person immediately affected by the operation of the deed (bound by it and in possession or occupation of the land)[15] may agree to the exclusion of part of the monument from the guardianship or the renouncement of the guardianship.[16] The public bodies are under stricter limits in agreeing to terminate guardianship than entering into it. It must be satisfied thatsatisfactory arrangements have been made to ensure the preservation of the monument (or the relevant part) or it is not practicable (on grounds of cost or otherwise) to preserve it.[17] Local authorities must consult with the Secretary of State before entering into such agreement. Whilst the Secretary of State must consult with English Heritage (for monuments in England), English Heritage are not obliged to consult with the Secretary of State before it enters into an agreement.[18] This appears to be a drafting error in the Act.

4.57

Certain occupiers can unilaterally terminate a guardianship. They must have an interest in the monument which would qualify them to establish guardianship but must not be bound by the deed. They may then terminate by notice in writing to the guardian.[19] This shows the importance of getting all persons interested in the monument to be party to the guardianship deed.

Guardianship ends if the monument is acquired by its guardian.[20] The effect of acquisition by another public body is unclear. In practice, the guardian should agree to end the guardianship alongside any such acquisition. The guardianship of land adjoining can be terminated in the same way (other than when the monument is acquired by its guardians or ceases to exist).[21] Additionally it ceases when guardianship of the monument ceases. An easement acquired under AMAAA may be terminated by the grantor (unless the agreement provides to the contrary) or by his successor in title, if the monument ceases to be under guardianship otherwise than by being acquired by its guardians or ceasing to exist.[22]

4.58

---

[11] *ibid.* s.13(7).

[12] *ibid.* s.13(4)(a), (b).

[13] *ibid.* s.13(4)(c).

[14] The public body may enter the land to exercise the powers permitted by this section and the guardianship deed (s.13(5)). Adjoining land under guardianship is not expressed to be subject to the deed. A separate power of entry applies (s.15(4)).

[15] *ibid.* s.61(3).

[16] *ibid.* s.14(1). In England and Wales the agreement must be under seal (s.14(4)).

[17] *ibid.* s.14(3).

[18] *ibid.* s.14(2).

[19] *ibid.* s.14(1).

[20] *ibid.* s.14(1).

[21] *ibid.* s.15(5).

[22] *ibid.* s.16(6).

9. TRANSFER OF OWNERSHIP AND GUARDIANSHIP

4.59   The public bodies can transfer monuments of which they are owners or guardians under AMAAA between each other (including between local authorities).[23] This power is subject to the following restrictions:

(a)   in guardianship monuments, the consent of the persons who are bound by any deed and in possession or occupation of the land is required[24];

(b)   English Heritage may not be party to a transfer outside England[25];

(c)   the Secretary of State must consult with English Heritage before a monument is transferred between him and a local authority[26];

(d)   English Heritage may only transfer a monument to a local authority after consultation with the Secretary of State[27];

(e)   English Heritage may only receive a monument from a local authority with the consent of the Secretary of State.[28]

10. AGREEMENTS CONCERNING ANCIENT MONUMENTS

4.60   Acquisition and guardianship put the monuments under the control, and sometimes ownership, of a public body. There are other mechanisms for protecting monuments without the cost and degree of government intervention involved in exercising those powers.

4.61   The Secretary of State may enter into an agreement with the occupier of an ancient monument or of any land adjoining or in the vicinity of it.[29] Similar powers are vested in English Heritage, in respect of ancient monuments in England, and local authorities.[30] Any person with an interest in the land may also be a party to the agreement in addition to the occupier.[31]

4.62   The agreement may deal with one or more of the following matters[32]:

(a)   the maintenance and preservation of the monument and its amenities;

(b)   the carrying on of work, or doing other things in relation to the monument or land, specified in the agreement;

(c)   public access and the provision of facilities, information and other services for the public in this connection;

(d)   restricting the use of the monument and land;

(e)   prohibiting acts in relation to the monument or land;

---

[23] AMAAA, s.21(1).

[24] *ibid.* s.21(2).

[25] *ibid.* s.21(3).

[26] *ibid.* s.21(4).

[27] *ibid.* s.21(5).

[28] *ibid.* s.21(6).

[29] *ibid.* s.17(1).

[30] *ibid.* s.17(1A), (2).

[31] *ibid.* s.17(3). A limited owner may enter into an agreement provided that he meets the other criteria in s.17.

[32] *ibid.* s.17(4).

(f) the public body making payments in respect of the agreement, whether covering works under it or as consideration for restrictions, prohibitions or obligations on other parties.

It may also contain incidental or consequential provisions which appear necessary or expedient.[33] The power is therefore, very wide. The real restriction is that it must relate to the monument or land adjoining or adjacent. Provided an agreement does so, it can only be challenged on the ground that it is, as a matter of public law, unreasonable.[34]

4.63 The agreement can only be modified by a further agreement between the parties and the public body concerned.[35] PPG 16 provides, as an example, the use of a section 17 agreement to encourage the beneficial management of sites on agricultural land, such as a barrow or deserted settlement. It would run for a number of years with an initial payment for capital costs and payments for a management regime, such as pest and weed control.[36]

4.64 However, an agreement cannot provide scheduled monument consent. English Heritage and local authorities do not have the power to grant it. The Secretary of State cannot provide that consent by means of a section 17 agreement.[37] To do so would bypass the procedures in AMAAA.

4.65 An agreement may provide that successors in title to any of its parties are bound in whole or part. However, a party deriving title by a disposition made before the agreement is not bound.[38] A limited owner can bind the successive owners of any estate subject to earlier incumbrances.[39]

11. PUBLIC ACCESS

4.66 The acquisition, guardianship and agreement-making powers have as a possible purpose the provision of public access. The right of public access to monuments under the ownership or guardianship of the public bodies under AMAAA is enshrined in section 19(1). However, it is subject to contrary provisions in applicable guardianship deeds.[40] Additionally, it only applies to monuments owned by virtue of AMAAA. There is not a right of access for monuments owned for other purposes (for example, part of a Ministry of Defence property). However, public access can be permitted to monuments under the control or management of the Secretary of State for any other purpose.[41] The public body controls access by means of powers and regulations.[42] Contravening the regulations attracts criminal sanctions.[43]

---

[33] AMAAA, s.17(4).

[34] *c.f.* planning obligations under the Town and Country Planning Act 1990, s.106: *Tesco Stores Limited v. Secretary of State for the Environment* (1995) 70 P. & C.R. 184.

[35] The power of the Lands Tribunal to discharge or modify restrictive covenants under s.84 of the Law of Property Act 1925 does not apply to s.17 agreements (AMAAA, s.17(7)).

[36] PPG 16, Annex 3, para. 16.

[37] AMAAA, s.17(8).

[38] *ibid.* s.17(5).

[39] *ibid.* s.18(8).

[40] *ibid.* s.19(9).

[41] *ibid.* s.19(3).

[42] *ibid.* s.19(2), (5), (6) and s.19(3), (4), (4A) respectively.

[43] *ibid.* s.19(7).

4.67   The Secretary of State, English Heritage and local authorities are empowered for monuments under their ownership or guardianship:

(a)   to control times of normal public access[44];

(b)   entirely exclude the public from access to all or part of the monument, in the interests of safety or for the maintenance or preservation of the monument[45];

(c)   determine admission charges[46];

(d)   refuse access to persons likely to injure the monument or disturb the public enjoying it.[47]

4.68   The power to determine admission charges and refuse access to individuals is additionally exercisable in respect of monuments under the Secretary of State's control or management. This control or management is otherwise than under AMAAA. The refusal power is vested in persons authorised by the relevant public body to refuse admission to any person they have reasonable cause to believe is likely to do anything which would tend to injure or disfigure the monument or its amenities or to disturb the public in their enjoyment of it. It allows staff to exclude potentially unruly elements.

4.69   The regulation-making power[48] in respect of public access is broad and overlaps the other powers under section 19. It is vested in the Secretary of State[49] and local authorities, but not in English Heritage. It can apply to any monument, or all monuments, under that body's ownership or guardianship under AMAAA. Further, the Secretary of State can apply regulations to any monuments under his control or management for any other reason.

4.70   In particular, regulations may[50]:

(a)   prescribe the time of public access;

(b)   make any necessary provision for the preservation of the monument and its amenities or of any property of the Secretary of State or local authority;

(c)   prohibit or regulate any act or thing which would tend to injure or disfigure any such monument or its amenities or to disturb the public in their enjoyment of it;

(d)   prescribe admission charges.

Local authority regulations are subject to confirmation by the Secretary of State who is empowered to make modifications before confirmation.[51]

4.71   The Secretary of State may, after consultation, also make regulations for purpose (c) above in respect of monuments under the ownership or guardianship of English Heritage.[52] Other matters regulating public access

---

[44] AMAAA, s.19(2). The local authority power is exercisable only by regulations made under s.19(3).

[45] ibid. s.19(2). Local authorities may only entirely exclude the public for the purpose of conserving the monument with the consent of the Secretary of State.

[46] ibid. s.19(5).

[47] ibid. s.19(6).

[48] ibid. s.19(3).

[49] If the Secretary of State's regulation only applies to monuments in England, he must consult with English Heritage.

[50] AMAAA, s.19(4).

[51] ibid. s.19(8). A local authority cannot, therefore, circumvent the requirement of the Secretary of State's consent in s.19(2)(b) by proceeding by way of regulations.

[52] ibid. s.19(4A), (4B).

are covered by English Heritage's section 19 powers. This keeps the power to create criminal offences under the control of the Secretary of State.

The public bodies are empowered to provide facilities, information and **4.72** other services for the public or in connection with public access to monuments under their ownership or guardianship under AMAAA, or under the Secretary of State's control or management.[53] These facilities may be on the monument or on land associated with it.[54] Charges may be made for these facilities.[55]

12. COMPENSATION

Scheduling, and the need for scheduled monument consent, considerably **4.73** restricts the right of a monument's owner to do works on it. Without such a restriction scheduling would be ineffective. Compensation is payable by the Secretary of State, or if in England, English Heritage, for the refusal of scheduled monument consent in certain circumstances.

Compensation is guided by the principle that compensation is not payable **4.74** for the refusal of planning permission. If planning permission needs to be obtained (and has not been) compensation for refusal of scheduled monument consent should not be forthcoming.

Compensation is recoverable under section 7 by a person with an interest **4.75** in a monument[56] where scheduled monument consent is refused in three circumstances:

(a) planning permission has been granted before the monument was scheduled and was still effective when scheduled monument consent for the works reasonably necessary for carrying it out was applied for;

(b) the works are not development,[57] or they receive planning permission under a general development order[58]; or

(c) the works are reasonably necessary for the continuation of any use occurring immediately before the application for scheduled monument consent.[59]

The desirability of preserving an ancient monument (scheduled or other- **4.76** wise) is a material consideration in a planning decision.[60] Accordingly, a planning permission is unlikely to be granted in situations where the archaeological significance of the site is appreciated. This is illustrated by the facts of *R. v. West Oxfordshire District Council, ex p. Pearce Homes Ltd.*[61] The local planning authority had passed a resolution that planning permission be granted to construct flats and convert a property, subject to the

---

[53] AMAAA, s.20(1).

[54] *ibid.* s.20(2). "Associated land" must be land adjoining or in the vicinity (*c.f.* s.21(2)).

[55] *ibid.* s.20(3).

[56] Including a mortgagee (AMAAA, s.27(3)).

[57] Under the Town and Country Planning Act 1990, ss.55, 336(1).

[58] Currently the Town and Country Planning (General Permitted Development) Order 1995 (S.I. 1995 No. 418).

[59] AMAAA, s.7(2).

[60] PPG 16, para. 18; *Hoveringham Gravels Ltd v. Secretary of State for the Environment* [1975] Q.B. 754.

[61] [1986] J.P.L. 523.

developer entering into a section 52 agreement. The development was to be on the site of the Bishop of Winchester's palace in Witney. The Oxford Archaeological Unit then carried out excavations revealing the true import-ance of the site. The local authority reversed its decision to grant planning permission and the Secretary of State scheduled the site. The developers did not attempt to obtain scheduled monument consent to pursue the development.

4.77   Compensation is not recoverable under (b) if the works would (or might) totally or partially demolish or destroy the monument unless the works are for, or incidental to, agriculture or forestry.[62]

4.78   Compensation is payable under (c) even if the use contravenes legal restrictions, such as the Town and Country Planning Acts or covenants.[63] Where conditional scheduled monument consent is granted, compensation is only recoverable under (c) where the conditions make the use effectively impossible to continue.[64]

4.79   The compensation covers expenditure, loss or damage consequent upon the refusal. This could include extra costs because the work was not done; or a loss of profits or value. The calculation of compensation should take into account any undertaking by the Secretary of State to grant scheduled monument consent for some other works.[65] Notice of the compensation award is normally notified to the relevant local authority and is registrable as a local land charge.[66]

4.80   If compensation is paid under section 7 and scheduled monument consent is subsequently granted for all or any of the works in question or conditions that triggered compensation are modified, then all or part of the compensa-tion may be recovered by the Secretary of State or English Heritage.[67] The recovery is by way of a condition in the new consent that the works are not to be carried out until compensation is paid back.[68] In the event of dispute, the Lands Tribunal will determine the amount recoverable.[69]

4.81   Compensation can also be obtained from the Secretary of State or English Heritage under section 9 in three circumstances[70]:

(a)   if a class consent is varied or is directed not to apply to a scheduled monument and scheduled monument consent is subsequently refused or granted subject to different conditions to the class consent[71];

(b)   if a scheduled monument consent is modified or revoked[72]; or

(c)   if a scheduled monument consent is suspended because of a proposed modification or revocation.[73]

---

[62] AMAAA, s.7(4).

[63] *ibid*. s.7(2).

[64] *ibid*. s.7(5).

[65] *ibid*. s.9(6).

[66] *ibid*. s.8(2), (2A), (5), (6).

[67] *ibid*. s.8. The compensation must exceed £20 and proper notice of the compensation must have been given to the relevant local authority (s.8(2), (2A)).

[68] *ibid*. s.8(3). Compensation cannot be recovered if the new consent is not carried out.

[69] *ibid*. s.8(4).

[70] *ibid*. s.9(1), (2).

[71] *ibid*. s.9(2)(a), (3).

[72] Under AMAAA, s.4.

[73] Under AMAAA, Sched. 1, para. 8.

The compensation is for loss, damage or expenditure incurred. Unlike **4.82** section 7, expenditure is only recoverable if it is rendered abortive by the change in authorisation. The expenditure does, however, include preparatory plans and similar professional matters.[74] Otherwise compensation is not recoverable for acts before consent was granted. Compensation under sections 7 and 9 is calculated under section 5 of the Land Compensation Act 1961.[75]

13. CARRYING OUT URGENT WORKS

The Secretary of State is empowered to execute works on the site of a **4.83** scheduled monument if they appear to be urgently necessary for the preservation of the monument. He must give the owner and any separate occupier not less than seven days' notice in writing.[76] For scheduled monuments in England, the Secretary of State may authorise English Heritage to carry out the works,[77] in which case it must give the notice.[78] These powers are regarded as powers of last resort, but have been used in a number of cases where owners have failed to keep monuments in good repair.

Where the Secretary of State or English Heritage carry out works to repair **4.84** damage, they will receive the benefit of any compensation order made under section 35 of the Powers of Criminal Courts Act 1973 in respect of that damage.[79]

14. FINANCIAL PROVISIONS

Assistance is available from the government to assist in managing and **4.85** preserving monuments. The Secretary of State may:

(a) defray or contribute to the cost of acquisition of an ancient monument[80];

(b) undertake, or assist in, or defray or contribute to the cost of removal of an ancient monument or part of it to another place to preserve it[81];

(c) undertake, or assist in, or defray or contribute to the cost of the preservation, maintenance and management of any ancient monument[82];

(d) contribute to the costs of a local authority in providing section 20 facilities.[83]

In England, these powers are exercised not by the Secretary of State but by **4.86**

---

[74] AMAAA, s.9(4).
[75] *ibid.* s.27(1).
[76] *ibid.* s.5(1).
[77] *ibid.* s.5(3).
[78] *ibid.* s.5(4).
[79] *ibid.* s.5(2), (5).
[80] *ibid.* s.24(2).
[81] *ibid.* s.24(2).
[82] *ibid.* s.24(2).
[83] *ibid.* s.24(3).

English Heritage.[84] Despite the scope of the powers, these grants are principally given for the costs of repair, archaeological recording and consolidation of monuments. More rarely they are given towards the purchase of monuments and the capital costs of schemes for their presentation or display.[85]

4.87   Local authorities may undertake, or assist in, or defray or contribute towards the cost of the preservation, maintenance and management of any ancient monument in or in the vicinity of their area.[86]

4.88   Funding under these powers cannot be given in respect of any monument occupied as a dwelling house other than by its employed caretaker or his family.[87]

4.89   The Secretary of State or a local authority may receive voluntary contributions towards the cost of any expenditure incurred by them under Part I of AMAAA.[88]

15. ARCHAEOLOGICAL INVESTIGATION

4.90   The public bodies are given express statutory powers to carry out or fund archaeological investigations of land which may contain an ancient monument or anything else of archaeological or historic interest.[89] The Secretary of State's power is exercised in England by English Heritage.[90] However, English Heritage also have their own statutory powers to carry out archaeological research.[91] Local authorities have the power in respect of land in their area or in the vicinity.[92]

4.91   The Secretary of State and local authorities may publish the results of work they funded or carried out under this power.[93] English Heritage can publish findings under the general duty to promote the public's knowledge of ancient monuments.[94]

16. ARCHAEOLOGICAL AREAS

4.92   Part I of AMAAA provides protection to identified and scheduled monuments. However, Part II of AMAAA sought to introduce the recognition of areas of archaeological remains such as will be found in historic towns by creating new powers for rescue archaeology whilst seeking to strike a balance between archaeology and development.

4.93   The public bodies are empowered to designate Areas of Archaeological

---

[84] AMAAA, s.24(3A). An ancient monument here is a scheduled monument or one which in English Heritage's opinion meets the public interest criteria (s.24(3B)).

[85] PPG 16, Annex 3, para. 15.

[86] AMAAA, s.24(4).

[87] ibid. s.24(5).

[88] ibid. s.31.

[89] ibid. s.45. This includes investigations on the seabed in territorial waters (s.45(4)).

[90] ibid. s.45(1), (1A).

[91] National Heritage Act 1983, s.33(2), (6).

[92] AMAAA, s.45(2).

[93] ibid. s.45(3).

[94] National Heritage Act 1983, s.33(1).

Importance (AAIs).[95] No criteria are set out in AMAAA but the area must merit designation. That involves considering the archaeological or historical importance of the area and the effect of the powers. Essentially the effect is that notice must be given of works, and archaeological investigations can then be carried out whilst the development is delayed for several months.

Five areas have been designated: the historic town centres of Canterbury, Chester, Exeter, Hereford and York.[96] The Secretary of State takes the view that PPG 16 deals with archaeological interests more comprehensively than areas of archaeological importance so no more should be designated until the effectiveness of the PPG has been assessed.[97]   **4.94**

17. DESIGNATION

The Secretary of State may designate areas within Great Britain. He is required to consult with the relevant local authorities and English Heritage (if the area is within England).[98] Notice of the draft order is required to be published in the London Gazette and at least one local newspaper[99] and copies made available.[1] The order may not be made until at least six weeks after this has been done. The Secretary of State should consider representations made by the public before making the order, which may be modified to reduce its scope.[2] However there is no provision for an informal hearing or public inquiry. On making the order, the Secretary of State must again publish notice and deposit copies with the local authorities and, in England, English Heritage.[3]   **4.95**

Local authorities may designate areas, within their own area.[4] Before publishing notice of the draft order, in the same way as the Secretary of State,[5] they must consult other local authorities for the area and English Heritage, if in England.[6] There is a six-week period before the order can be made.[7] The order only takes effect when confirmed by the Secretary of State. The Secretary of State[8] will exercise his current policy against further designation orders.[9] Upon confirmation, the local authority must publish notice of the making of the order and deposit copies with other local authorities and, in England, English Heritage.[10]   **4.96**

---

[95] National Heritage Act 1983, s.33(1).

[96] PPG 16, Annex C, para. 19.

[97] *ibid*. para. 20.

[98] *ibid*. s.33(1); Sched. 2, para. 2(a), (aa).

[99] *ibid*. Sched. 2, paras 2(b), 3(2). If the area is in Scotland, notice is given in the Edinburgh Gazette rather than the London Gazette (AMAAA, Sched. 2, para. 19).

[1] AMAAA, Sched. 2, paras 4, 5.

[2] *ibid*. Sched. 2, para. 6.

[3] *ibid*. Sched. 2, para. 7.

[4] *ibid*. s.33(2).

[5] *ibid*. Sched. 2, para. 9(b), (10).

[6] *ibid*. Sched. 2, paras 9, 9A.

[7] *ibid*. Sched. 2, para. 13.

[8] *ibid*. Sched. 2, para. 13.

[9] PPG 16, Annex C, para. 20.

[10] AMAAA, Sched. 2, para. 14.

4.97   A consequence of the abolition of the Greater London Council is that English Heritage is empowered to designate areas within Greater London.[11] The procedure followed is essentially the same as for local authorities.[12]

4.98   Designation orders must be accompanied by maps showing the area affected.[13] They cannot come into operation until six months after they have been made by the Secretary of State or confirmed by him.[14]

18. VARIATION OR REVOCATION

4.99   The Secretary of State may revoke or vary, by reducing the area, a designation order at any time.[15] This includes orders made by local authorities or English Heritage. He must follow the same procedure as when he designates an area.[16]

19. INVESTIGATING AUTHORITIES

4.100   An investigating authority is usually appointed by the Secretary of State in respect of each area.[17] This is usually a local archaeological unit. English Heritage are consulted on appointments and cancellations in England.[18] Notice of appointment is given to relevant local authorities and, for Greater London, English Heritage.[19] If no investigating authority is appointed its functions are exercised by English Heritage (in England) and the Secretary of State (elsewhere).[20] The investigating authority may authorise in writing other persons to act on its behalf.[21]

20. NOTICES

4.101   Notice of operations which involve tipping, flooding or otherwise disturb the ground, must be given six weeks before they are carried out[22] unless the operations are undertaken with the consent of the investigating authority[23] or are exempted by the Secretary of State by order.[24] This notice must specify

---

[11] AMAAA, s.33(2A).

[12] *ibid.* Sched. 2, para. 15.

[13] *ibid.* Sched. 2, paras 1, 8.

[14] *ibid.* Sched. 2, para. 16. No time limit is provided for orders made by English Heritage. The better approach is to treat them the same way as local authority orders with a six-month delay.

[15] AMAAA, s.33(4).

[16] *ibid.* Sched. 2, para. 18.

[17] *ibid.* s.34(1).

[18] *ibid.* s.34(1), (2).

[19] *ibid.* s.34(3).

[20] *ibid.* s.34(4).

[21] *ibid.* s.34(5).

[22] *ibid.* s.35(1), (2).

[23] *ibid.* s.37(1).

[24] *ibid.* s.37(2).

the nature of the proposed operations, the site and the commencement date. If the site is being cleared first, the developer's[25] estimate of when clearance will be complete must also be provided.[26] It must be served with a certificate by a person entitled to carry out the operations, whether because of an interest, compulsory purchase or by being a statutory undertaker, stating the entitlement and, if not the developer, confirming his authorisation.[27]

The form of the notice and certificate is prescribed by the Operations in Areas of Archaeological Importance (Forms of Notice, etc.) Regulations 1984.[28] The developer must serve the notice on the relevant local authority.[29] If the developer is a local authority, notice must be served on the Secretary of State.[30] The local authority must copy a notice and certificate served on it to the investigating authority or the body exercising its functions within seven days.[31] **4.102**

If the operations are to be carried out after clearance, the developer must notify the investigating authority immediately on such clearance.[32] Carrying out operations without proper notice is an offence.[33] Injunctive remedies are also available. **4.103**

21. EXEMPTIONS FROM THE NOTICE REQUIREMENTS

As with scheduled monument consent, the Secretary of State may issue a class consent allowing operations, unconditionally or subject to conditions.[34] This is contained in the Areas of Archaeological Importance (Notification of Operations) (Exemption) Order 1984.[35] These provide for 11 exemptions. Most are operations which, because of their nature, are likely to have little effect on buried remains. Infrastructure and utilities operations are generally exempted.[36] Reflecting the effectiveness of some voluntary arrangements, mining operations are exempt if they are carried out in accordance with the Code of Practice for Minerals Operators, dated April 1982.[37] There is an exemption for further operations within five years, but at **4.104**

---

[25] The developer is the person carrying out or proposing to carry out operations (AMAAA, s.35(3)).
[26] AMAAA, s.35(4).
[27] *ibid.* ss.35(4)(b), 36(1), (2), (3).
[28] S.I. 1984 No. 1285.
[29] AMAAA, s.35(5)(a), (aa).
[30] *ibid.* s.35(5)(c).
[31] Forms of Notice Regulations 1984, reg. 4(a).
[32] AMAAA, s.35(7). The local authority he notified should have warned him of this obligation and given the name and address of the investigating authority within 14 days of its receipt of the notice (Form of Notice Regulations 1984, reg. 4(b)). Clearance means the demolition and removal of existing buildings and structures and the removal of other materials to clear the surface of the land. It does not include levelling the surface or removing materials from below the surface (AMAAA, s.41(1)(d)).
[33] AMAAA, s.35(1).
[34] *ibid.* s.37(2).
[35] S.I. 1984 No. 1286.
[36] 1984 Order, Sched., paras 5–9.
[37] *ibid.* para. 4.

least six weeks after an operations notice is issued for that site.[38] Operations given scheduled monument consent, including by the class consent order, are also exempt.[39] This is a particularly important exemption, given the width of the class consent order. It means that any area of archaeological importance designation does not give any greater protection to a site than scheduling.

22. INSPECTION AND EXCAVATION

4.105   Once the operations notice is served, the investigating authority has the right to enter the site at any reasonable time.[40] However, such entry can be for two purposes: inspecting the site to record matters of archaeological or historical interest and to determine whether it is desirable to excavate; observing operations on the land to examine and record objects, other material or matters of archaeological or historical interest discovered during the operations.

4.106   The investigating authority is entitled to excavate the site but only if it gives notice within four weeks of the service of the operations notice. It must serve notice upon the developer, the councils served with the operations notice, the Secretary of State and, in England, English Heritage.[41] The investigating authority then has four months and two weeks to carry out excavations. This period runs either from six weeks after the service of the operations notice, or from the date of receipt of notification of clearance of the site, or any earlier date agreed with the developer.[42]

4.107   If clearance operations have not finished six weeks after service of the operations notice, the investigating authority can then carry out excavations. However, they must not obstruct the clearance operations or other operations not subject to an operations notice.[43] If the investigating authority has properly served notice of intention to excavate, then it is an offence to carry out operations covered by the notice during the period they are entitled to excavate.[44]

4.108   The Secretary of State may, by direction, remove the investigating authority's power to inspect or excavate all or part of a site or make it subject to conditions.[45] Such directions can be varied or revoked.[46] The direction must be served on the investigating authority, the relevant councils, the developer, any person issuing a certificate with the operations notice, and, in England, English Heritage. The same bodies should be notified of any variation or revocation.[47]

---

[38] 1984 Order, Sched., para. 10.

[39] *ibid.* para. 11.

[40] AMAAA, s.38(1).

[41] *ibid.* s.38(3).

[42] *ibid.* s.38(4).

[43] *ibid.* s.38(5).

[44] *ibid.* s.38(7). The offence is under s.35(1). This is subject to the usual exemptions and defences under s.37.

[45] *ibid.* s.38(8). If the site is in England, English Heritage must be consulted.

[46] *ibid.* s.38(9), (10).

[47] *ibid.* s.38(9), (11).

23. BODIES WITH COMPULSORY ACQUISITION POWERS

Additional powers provide for archaeological investigation at the behest of authorities with compulsory purchase powers before they have served an operations notice.[48] Since under the certification requirements, the authority cannot serve an operations notice until it has a right to enter on or take possession of the site, an informal notification procedure operates to allow investigation before the land is acquired. **4.109**

If the investigating authority is notified of operations[49] which such an authority proposes to carry out or authorise another person to carry out in an AAI, the investigating authority has the right to enter, at any reasonable time, the site and any land giving access to the site for the purpose of inspecting the site to record matters of archaeological or historical interest and to determine whether it is desirable to excavate.[50] Before the operations are commissioned, the authority must serve an operations notice, as normal. The right to inspect runs for one month from its first exercise.[51] **4.110**

As with other inspections in AAIs the Secretary of State may revoke or condition the inspection power.[52] In this case, notice must be served by the Secretary of State on the investigating authority, the authority with compulsory purchase powers, the owner and occupier of the land and English Heritage (if in England).[53] **4.111**

24. OTHER INSPECTIONS

Where an operations notice is served, it is not simply the investigating authority who can inspect. A person authorised in writing by the Secretary of State may enter, inspect and record any matters of archaeological or historical interest observed in the course of the inspection. Similar rights in respect of buildings and other structures are granted to persons authorised in writing by the Royal Commission on Historical Monuments.[54] **4.112**

25. CROWN LAND

Crown land[55] is exempted from most laws governing the use of land. This exemption is relaxed, to a limited degree, in respect of ancient monuments. A **4.113**

---

[48] This means any person or body of persons who could be or have been authorised to acquire an interest in land compulsorily (AMAAA, s.39(5)).

[49] As defined by AMAAA, s.35(2). Operations exempted by an order under AMAAA, s.37 are excluded (AMAAA, s.39(1)).

[50] AMAAA, s.39(1) (from s.38(1)(a)).

[51] *ibid.* s.39(2).

[52] *ibid.* s.39(3), adopting the provisions of s.38(8).

[53] *ibid.* s.39(4).

[54] *ibid.* s.40.

[55] *i.e.* land in which there is a Crown or Duchy interest. A Crown interest is an interest belonging to Her Majesty in the right of the Crown, or belonging to a Government department, or held in trust by Her Majesty for the purposes of a Government department, and includes any estate or interest held in right of the Prince and Steward of Scotland. A Duchy interest belongs to Her Majesty in right of the Duchy of Lancaster, or the Duchy of Cornwall (AMAAA, s.50(4)).

monument on Crown land may be scheduled.[56] Additionally, AMAAA applies, subject to consents, to anything done on the land other than by or on behalf of the Crown, provided that it does not affect any interest of the Crown.[57]

4.114 The appropriate authority must have consented before:

    (a) any power to enter or do anything on land under AMAAA is exercised; and

    (b) before any interest in land is acquired compulsorily.[58]

An operations notice is not effective unless the appropriate authority certificates its consent to the exercise of section 38 and 40 powers.[59] The appropriate authority is the government department, Chancellor of the Duchy (for the Duke of Lancaster), Duke of Cornwall or the Crown Estate Commissioners to whom the land belongs.[60]

26. METAL DETECTORS

4.115 Provisions dealing with metal detectors were first introduced in AMAAA. Commenting on the hobby of metal detecting, the minister said in the House of Commons: "That may be an innocent pastime, but in irresponsible hands these devices can lead to irreparable damage and loss of knowledge."[61]

4.116 The use of metal detectors[62] in protected places is banned save with the written consent of English Heritage or, outside England, the relevant Secretary of State. A "metal detector" is defined as "any device designed or adapted for detecting or locating any metal or mineral in the ground".[63] Whilst the provision was intended to deal with amateur treasure hunters, much equipment, such as geophysical survey equipment, used by professional archaeologists is included within the definition.[64] Archaeologists should be careful to obtain consents under these provisions where necessary.

4.117 A protected place is a scheduled monument or a monument under the ownership or guardianship of a public body under AMAAA or situated in an area of archaeological importance.[65] It therefore applies to protected monuments and areas of archaeological importance. The scope is wide, but, unlike "ancient monument", certain.

Contravention is a criminal offence punishable on summary conviction by a fine not exceeding £200.[66] The offence may be committed by the owner of the property or someone authorised by him. The metal detector ban is not principally to protect the landowner's rights to objects found on his property: it is to protect the archaeological heritage from unprofessional excavation.

---

[56] AMAAA, s.50(1)(a).

[57] *ibid.* s.50(1)(b).

[58] *ibid.* s.50(2).

[59] *ibid.* s.50(3).

[60] *ibid.* s.50(4).

[61] *Hansard* (Mr Marks), H.C. Vol. 965, col. 1362 (April 4, 1979).

[62] A "metal detector" is defined as "any device designed or adapted for detecting or locating any metal or mineral in the ground" (AMAAA, s.42(2)).

[63] AMAAA, s.42(2).

[64] *ibid.* s.42(1).

[65] *ibid.* s.42(2).

[66] *ibid.* s.42(1).

The removal of objects of archaeological or historical interest discovered **4.118** by the use of a metal detector in a protected place without written consent is also an offence. It is punishable by the statutory maximum fine, currently £5,000, on summary conviction and an unlimited fine on indictment.[67] Additionally, it may amount to theft if the removal is without the landowner's consent or the object is treasure trove.

A consent to use a metal detector may be granted unconditionally or **4.119** subject to conditions.[68] Failure to comply with a condition amounts to one of two separate offences. These are:

(a) using a metal detector in a protected place in accordance with a consent failing to comply with any condition attached to it;

(b) removing or otherwise dealing with any object which he has discovered by the use of a metal detector in a protected place in accordance with a consent failing to comply with any condition attached to it.[69]

In the latter case the condition need not relate to the removal of objects: it can be any condition. The penalties are the same as for the equivalent offences committed without consent.

Two statutory defences are provided. The accused can be acquitted, where **4.120** charged with using a metal detector without consent, if he can show that it was used for a purpose other than detecting or locating objects of archaeological or historical interest.[70] This is known as the "car keys" defence.

Secondly, believing that the metal detector was not being used in a **4.121** protected place is a defence to charges of either using a metal detector or removing objects without consent. However, the defendant must prove that he had taken all reasonable precautions to find out whether it was a protected place.[71] Since protected places are defined by scheduling, ownership or guardianship, this defence is really only applicable if the defendant has asked the owner or relevant public bodies and been misinformed.

27. POWERS OF ENTRY

Persons authorised in writing by the Secretary of State may enter land at any **4.122** reasonable time to inspect any scheduled monument for the following purposes:

(a) to ascertain its condition;

(b) to ascertain whether any works contrary to section 2(1) are being carried out;

(c) to ascertain whether it has been or is likely to be damaged;

(d) in connection with any application for scheduled monument consent;

(e) in connection with any proposal by the Secretary of State to modify or revoke a scheduled monument consent;

---

[67] AMAAA, s.42(3).
[68] *ibid.* s.42(4).
[69] *ibid.* s.42(5).
[70] *ibid.* s.42(6).
[71] *ibid.* s.42(7).

(f) to observe the execution of works to which a scheduled monument consent relates to ensure compliance with the consent;

(g) to inspect the condition of land and the scheduled monument in question after the completion of works to ensure compliance with scheduled monument consent;

(h) whilst works under scheduled monument consent are being carried out, to inspect the land (including buildings and structures) with a view to recording any matters of archaeological or historical interest;

(i) to observe the execution of works under scheduled monument consent with a view to examining and recording any objects or other material of archaeological or historical interest, and recording any matters of archaeological or historical interest discovered during the course of those works.[72]

4.123 English Heritage has powers under AMAAA to inspect for purposes (b), (f) and (g) to consider proceedings and for (d) and (e) to advise the Secretary of State on those matters.[73] The investigating authority for an area of archaeological importance has the power to enter a site subject to an operations notice for purposes equivalent to (h) and (i) and to determine whether it would be desirable to carry out excavations in the site.[74]

4.124 With the consent of the owner and occupier, a person authorised by the Secretary of State may enter land to erect and maintain notice boards and marker posts on or near the site of a scheduled monument to preserve it from accidental or deliberate damage.[75] In England this power is vested in English Heritage rather than the Secretary of State.[76]

Persons authorised in writing by the Secretary of State may at any reasonable time enter land where the Secretary of State knows or has reason to believe there is an ancient monument to inspect the land with a view to recording any matters of archaeological or historical interest.[77] These persons may, with the consent of the owner, carry out excavations. English Heritage officers have powers of entry to obtain information for the ancient monuments records.[78]

4.125 There is also a power of entry for survey and valuation purposes in connection with acquisition proposals or compensation.[79] Officials from the Inland Revenue Valuation Office and those authorised by the acquiring or compensation-paying public body can exercise this power.[80] Searching and boring can be carried out to determine the nature of the subsoil or the presence of minerals as part of a survey.[81]

---

[72] For (a)–(c) see AMAAA, s.6(1); (d)–(e) see AMAAA, s.6(2); (f)–(g) see AMAAA, s.6(3); (h)–(i) see AMAAA, s.6(4). Here scheduled monument consent includes a class consent under an Order (AMAAA, s.6(6)).

[73] AMAAA, s.6A(1), (2), (3).

[74] *ibid.* s.38(1).

[75] *ibid.* s.6(5).

[76] *ibid.* s.6A(4).

[77] *ibid.* s.26(1).

[78] National Heritage Act 1983, s.36.

[79] AMAAA, s.43(1).

[80] *ibid.* s.43(2).

[81] *ibid.* s.43(3). Two weeks notice of this must be given. If statutory undertakers (essentially infrastructure operators: s.61(2)) object that these works would be

The relevant public bodies have a power of entry in respect of carrying out **4.126** their functions under guardianship.[82] The powers of the Secretary of State and English Heritage to carry out urgent works[83] and compulsory superintendence[84] are powers of entry. The entry powers may only be exercised in respect of buildings occupied as dwelling-houses with the consent of the occupier[85] (except those for valuation).

At least 24 hours' notice must be given of an intention to enter. Fourteen **4.127** days' notice of entry to carry out works must generally be given. The exceptions are urgent works, and excavations on land believed to contain an ancient monument or covered by an operations notice.[86]

A person exercising the entry powers may bring assistance or equipment reasonably required.[87] If required, he must produce evidence of authority before entering.[88] In an archaeological investigation or examination, samples may be removed for archaeological analysis.[89]

A person entering to carry out excavations or operations or to observe **4.128** operations may take temporary custody of any object of archaeological or historical interest discovered by this. He may remove it from the site to examine, test, treat, record or preserve it.[90] The object should be promptly returned to the owner unless he consents to it being retained for a longer period.[91]

A person entering must comply with reasonable requirements to prevent **4.129** interference with or delay to works.[92] This does not apply if the works are contrary to the scheduled monument operations notice controls. Requirements are not reasonable if they would effectively frustrate the exercise or purpose of the entry power.[93]

28. INFORMATION

To serve notices, carry out investigations or bring prosecutions, the public **4.130** authority needs to know who is involved in the land and what their involvement is. The public bodies may require occupiers or persons receiving rent from land to state the nature of their interests and the names and addresses of the other people with interests in the land.[94] No time limit for replying is provided in AMAAA. Any request will have to be complied with in a reasonable time.

---

seriously detrimental to their undertaking, then the works require the authorisation of the Secretary of State (s.44(9)).

[82] AMAAA, s.15(4).
[83] *ibid.* s.5.
[84] *ibid.* s.25.
[85] *ibid.* s.44(1); National Heritage Act 1983, s.36(4)(a).
[86] AMAAA, s.44(2).
[87] *ibid.* s.44(4).
[88] *ibid.* s.44(3).
[89] *ibid.* s.44(5).
[90] *ibid.* s.54(1).
[91] *ibid.* s.54(2).
[92] *ibid.* s.44(6).
[93] *ibid.* s.44(7).
[94] *ibid.* s.57(1).

29. CHALLENGING DECISIONS

4.131 Decisions of public bodies under AMAAA can be challenged in the courts by two alternative methods:

(a) statutory application to the High Court under section 55 of the AMAAA;

(b) judicial review in the High Court.

Statutory application under section 55

4.132 AMAAA provides that certain actions under the Act may only be challenged by application to the High Court on a point of law under a procedure laid out in the Act. This procedure is very similar to that used in section 288 of the Town and Country Planning Act 1990 to challenge decisions of the Secretary of State on applications for planning permission.

This statutory challenge applies to:

(a) Area of Archaeological Importance designation orders and orders under section 33(4) varying or revoking such orders;[95]

(b) any decision of the Secretary of State on an application for scheduled monument consent;[96]

(c) the giving by the Secretary of State of a direction under section 4 modifying or revoking a scheduled monument consent.[97]

The right of challenge extends to any person aggrieved and not just to the major participants, so that any third party who has participated at the public inquiry can, in principle, pursue an application.[98]

4.133 The statutory grounds of challenge are limited to establishing either that the order or the action is not within the powers of AMAAA,[99] or that any of the relevant requirements of AMAAA, regulations made under it or the Tribunals and Inquiries Act 1992 have not been complied with (*i.e.* there has been a breach of natural justice).[1] However, even if the grounds are made out,

---

[95] AMAAA, s.55(2).

[96] *ibid.* s.55(3)(a).

[97] *ibid.* s.55(3)(b).

[98] For decisions on *locus standi* see cases on planning permission appeals: a person is aggrieved in the ordinary meaning of the words (*Times Investments Ltd v. Secretary of State for the Environment and Tower Hamlets L.B.C.* [1990] 3 P.L.R. 111). Persons allowed to bring challenges include objectors heard at the public inquiry (*Turner v. Secretary of State for the Environment* (1973) 23 P. & C.R. 123); pressure groups (*Save Britain's Heritage v. Secretary of State for the Environment* [1991] 2 All E.R. 10); neighbouring landowners (*Bannister v. Secretary of State for the Environment* [1995] J.P.L. B13).

[99] AMAAA, s.55(1). From planning cases, *i.e.* that the Secretary of State has erred in law on the same principles as a judge at first instance (see *Ashbridge Investments Ltd v. Minister of Housing and Local Government* [1965] 1 W.L.R. 1320), but the weighing of evidence and decisions of fact and degree are for the Secretary of State, not the court (*Catton v. Secretary of State for the Environment* [1976] J.P.L. 663). Errors of fact, if material, are errors of law (*Elmbridge B.C. v. Secretary of State for the Environment* [1980] J.P.L. 463).

[1] AMAAA, s.55(1), (6). Substantial prejudice must be established before the order or action will be quashed on this ground (AMAAA, s.55(5)(b)). See, *e.g. Peak Park Joint*

the court is still, in the exercise of its discretion, entitled not to grant any relief.[2]

The application must be brought within six weeks of the publication of the order, or the action being taken, as appropriate.[3] The validity of an order or action to which section 55 applies may not be questioned in any legal proceedings whatsoever other than by challenge under this section.[4]

Judicial review

Other decisions of the Secretary of State, local authorities or English Heritage under AMAAA may be challenged by an application for judicial review in the High Court. But judicial review is not an alternative method of appeal against a decision.[5] The court can only grant one or more of the prerogative remedies of certiorari (to quash a decision), prohibition (to prevent an *ultra vires* act) or mandamus (requiring a decision to be made) and a declaration or injunction.[6]   **4.134**

Moreover, the court will only grant relief to a person with a "sufficient interest" in the matter. In *R. v. Secretary of State for the Environment, ex p. Rose Theatre Trust Co.*,[7] Schieman J. controversially held that members of the public, and a company formed by them for the purpose of the proceedings, did not have sufficient interest to challenge the Secretary of State's decision not to schedule a monument. The owner or potential developer of a site would have standing to challenge its scheduling.   **4.135**

Relief can be granted if there has been some illegality, procedural impropriety or irrationality.[8] The latter is better known as *Wednesbury* unreasonableness: "although the local authority has kept within the four corners of the matters they ought to consider, they have nonetheless come to a conclusion so unreasonable that no reasonable authority could ever have come to it."[9]   **4.136**

Speed is also essential, as applications must be made "promptly and in any

---

Planning Board v. Secretary of State for the Environment (1979) 39 P. & C.R. 361 at 385 and *Greater London Council v. Secretary of State for the Environment* [1983] J.P.L. 793.

[2] It must be clear that there is a real possibility that the matter would have been decided differently. The planning authorities are reviewed in *Bolton M.B.C. v. Secretary of State for the Environment* (1990) 61 P. & C.R. 343, C.A.

[3] AMAAA, s.55(1), (4). For a decision on a scheduled monument consent application, time runs from the date of the decision letter (see for planning decision *Griffiths v. Secretary for the Environment* [1983] 1 All E.R. 439).

[4] AMAAA, s.55(7). A refusal or failure by the Secretary of State to take a decision on an application for scheduled monument consent can be challenged in other proceedings.

[5] The court will not redetermine questions of fact.

[6] R.S.C., Ord. 53, r.1. Damages will only be awarded in addition to one of these remedies if the application includes a private law claim (Supreme Court Act 1981, s.31(4)).

[7] [1990] 1 Q.B. 504.

[8] The headings were considered in *Court of Civil Service Unions v. Minister for the Civil Service* [1985] A.C. 374, H.L.

[9] *Associated Provincial Picture Houses v. Wednesbury Corporation* [1948] 1 K.B. 223 at 233.

event within three months", unless the court considers that there is good reason for extending the time.[10]

30. CRIMINAL OFFENCES

4.137 Prosecutions may be brought by the normal prosecution authorities, namely the Crown Prosecution Service and the police or by the Secretary of State. Local authorities are empowered to prosecute where offences affect the interests of inhabitants of their area.[11]

The Planning and Compensation Act 1991 gave prosecution powers to English Heritage. It may now prosecute for any offence under Part I of AMAAA committed in England.[12]

Control of works affecting scheduled monuments

4.138 Executing or causing or permitting to be executed works (within section 2) without authorisation is an offence.[13] This includes carrying out works which do not have consent, or carrying out works without complying with the terms of the consent[14] or any conditions attached to it.[15]

A number of defences are provided. Where the accused is required to prove any matter, he must do so on the balance of probabilities.

Destruction or damage (section 2(2)(a))

4.139 It is a defence for the accused to prove that he took all reasonable precautions and exercised due diligence to avoid or prevent damage to the monument.[16] This may include finding out the position and form of the monument.

Destruction or damage (section 2(2)(a)) and flooding or tipping (section 2(2)(c))

4.140 It is a defence to a charge involving carrying out these acts without authorisation that the accused did not know and had no reason to believe that the monument was within the area affected by the works or that it was a scheduled monument.[17] Unlike the defence above, the accused is not obliged to check whether there is a scheduled monument. However, a relatively low level of information may give him reason to believe that it is scheduled: for example, the age of the site, or involvement by English Heritage or an archaeological unit.

---

[10] R.S.C., Ord. 53, r.4 and Supreme Court Act 1981, s.31(6).
[11] Local Government Act 1972, s.222.
[12] National Heritage Act 1983, s.33(2A).
[13] AMAAA, s.2(1).
[14] *ibid.* s.2(3)(b).
[15] *ibid.* s.2(6).
[16] *ibid.* s.2(7).
[17] *ibid.* s.2(8).

Breach of condition

It is a defence to failing to comply with a condition that the accused took all **4.141**
reasonable precautions and exercised all due diligence to avoid the contravention.[18] Failing to comply with a condition or a term of the consent means
that the works are unauthorised. They may constitute an offence under
section 2(2).[19]

Health and safety

It is a defence to prove that the works were urgently necessary in the interests **4.142**
of safety or health and that notice in writing of the need for the works was
given to the Secretary of State as soon as reasonably practicable. This
includes works carried out without consent and works in breach of a
condition (for example, removing a dangerous roof before archaeological
inspection).

The Ancient Monuments (Class Consents) Order 1994 now gives consent
to these urgent works provided that they are limited to the minimum
measures immediately necessary and notice in writing is given to the
Secretary of State justifying in detail the need for the works as soon as
reasonably practicable.[20] This consent will usually be relied upon instead of
the statutory defence.

Sentence

The offence is subject to the maximum fine in summary courts of £5,000 or **4.143**
an unlimited fine in the Crown Court.[21]

The courts have imposed substantial fines. However, the fines are lower
where the offence, though negligent, is inadvertent and not an intentional
flouting of the law. In *R. v. Seymour*,[22] the ploughing of two fields seriously
damaged remains of the Roman town of Alcester. There had been ambiguity
in correspondence with English Heritage as to whether ploughing was
permitted but the court stated that if in doubt landowners should seek
adequate and accurate advice. The concern of the defendant for national
heritage and, conversely, any personal gain from the offence are factors in
sentencing. In that case, the Court of Appeal reduced the fine from £10,000 to
£3,000.

The financial means of the defendant are important. In *J.O. Sims Ltd*,[23] a **4.144**
fine of £75,000 against a company with annual profits around £100,000 was
held to be excessive for negligent damage to remains of Winchester Palace in
Southwark. A fine of £15,000 was substituted by the Court of Appeal.

---

[18] AMAAA, s.2(6).
[19] *ibid.* s.2(9).
[20] S.I. 1994 No. 1381, class 5.
[21] AMAAA, s.2(10).
[22] [1988] 1 P.L.R. 19.
[23] (1993) 96 Cr.App.R 125.

False certificate on an application for scheduled monument consent

4.145 Issuing a certificate of ownership on a scheduled monument consent application which contains a statement that the issuer knows to be false or misleading in a material particular, or is reckless as to it, is a summary offence. The maximum fine is level 3 on the standard scale, currently £1,000.[24]

Breach of the regulations on public access

4.146 Contravening or failing to comply with regulations controlling public access is a summary offence.[25] It is punishable by a fine to a maximum of level 3 on the standard scale, currently £1,000. Failing to comply with restrictions on access or pay charges which are not the subject of regulations is not an offence under section 19(7). However, it may be an offence under other parts of AMAAA, other legislation or at common law.

Damaging a protected monument

4.147 A protected monument is a scheduled monument or a monument under the ownership or guardianship of the Secretary of State, English Heritage or a local authority under AMAAA.[26] A person commits an offence if he, without lawful excuse, destroys or damages a protected monument:

  (a) knowing that it is a protected monument; and
  (b) intending to destroy or damage the monument or being reckless as to whether the monument would be destroyed or damaged.[27]

Acts done by the owner or under his authority are included unless they are for the execution of works the subject of scheduled monument consent or a class consent.[28] On summary conviction the sentence can be a fine at the statutory maximum and six months' imprisonment. On indictment, the maximum fine is unlimited and a sentence of two years' imprisonment can be imposed.[29]

4.148 There is an overlap between this offence and carrying out works on a scheduled monument without consent (section 2). However, this section 2 offence covers works which did not cause destruction or damage. It is of strict liability, whereas this section 28 offence requires intentionality or recklessness. The section 2 offence is regulatory in purpose. It seeks to protect by ensuring that works are done with the Secretary of State's consent. Section 28 is really concerned with vandalism or a blatant disregard of the importance of scheduled monuments by their owner. That is reflected in the availability to the court of imprisonment.

---

[24] AMAAA, Sched. 1, para. 2(4).
[25] *ibid.* s.19(7).
[26] *ibid.* s.28(3).
[27] *ibid.* s.28(1).
[28] *ibid.* s.28(2).
[29] *ibid.* s.28(4).

Compensation orders can be made against persons convicted of damaging **4.149** monuments.[30] The orders are normally in favour of the owner. However, if the monument was under the guardianship of a public body when the offence occurred, any compensation is payable to that public body rather than the owner.[31]

Failure to give notice of operations in an area of archaeological importance

Carrying out operations without giving proper notice of operations in areas of **4.150** archaeological importance is a criminal offence.[32] It is also a criminal offence to carry out operations without notifying the investigating authority upon completion of clearance operations.[33] The operations notice must be as prescribed by section 35[34] and regulations.[35] The offence is punishable by a fine, the statutory maximum on summary conviction and an unlimited fine on indictment.[36] Local authorities covering part of an area may prosecute even if the operations are in a part of the area covered by another local authority.[37]

Three defences are provided. It is a defence for the defendant to show that **4.151** he did not know and had no reason to believe that the site was within an area of archaeological importance.[38] There is no obligation upon the defendant to have tried to check whether it was within such an area. The second defence is that the operations were urgently necessary in the interests of safety or health and that notice in writing of this need was given to the Secretary of State as soon as reasonably practicable.[39]

If the allegation is disturbing the ground, it is a defence to show that all reasonable precautions were taken and all due diligence exercised to avoid or prevent disturbance of the ground.[40]

Other offences

If a person in issuing a certificate under section 36 makes a statement in it **4.152** which he knows to be false or misleading in a material particular, or is reckless as to this and it is false or misleading in a material particular, he commits an offence. This is punishable summarily, with a maximum fine at level 3, currently £1,000.[41]

---

[30] Powers of Criminal Courts Act 1973, s.35.
[31] AMAAA, s.29. If the Secretary of State or English Heritage carry out urgent works to repair the damage, they are entitled to any compensation order (AMAAA, s.5(2), (5)).
[32] AMAAA, s.35(1), (8).
[33] *ibid.* s.35(1), (8).
[34] *ibid.* s.35(8).
[35] Operations in Areas of Archaeological Importance (Forms of Notice) Regulations 1984 (S.I. 1984 No. 1285).
[36] AMAAA, s.35(9).
[37] *ibid.* s.35(10).
[38] *ibid.* s.37(6)(a).
[39] *ibid.* s.37(6)(b).
[40] *ibid.* s.37(5).
[41] *ibid.* s.36(4).

4.153   Intentionally obstructing a person acting in the exercise of a power of entry is a criminal offence. It is punishable on summary conviction by a maximum fine of £200.[42]

4.154   A person who fails, without reasonable excuse, to provide information required under section 57 is guilty of a summary offence. The maximum fine is £200.[43]

If a person knowingly misstates information which has been required under section 57, he is guilty of an offence. On summary conviction the potential penalty is the statutory maximum fine, currently £5,000. On conviction on indictment, the fine is unlimited.[44]

4.155   Where an offence has been committed by a corporate body (such as a company), directors, managers, company secretaries and person holding similar office are also criminally liable if the offence was committed with their consent or connivance or is attributable to their neglect.[45]

31. INJUNCTIONS

4.156   Unlawful acts on scheduled monuments or in areas of archaeological importance can cause irreparable damage and destroy historic information. Bringing criminal proceedings may punish the offender, but is unlikely to restore the monument. Where unlawful acts need to be stopped immediately, or remedial action taken, injunctions can be obtained from the civil courts. Failure to comply with an injunction is a contempt of court, punishable by fines or imprisonment.

The Secretary of State

4.157   The Secretary of State may seek injunctions to enforce AMAAA by asking the Attorney-General to bring proceedings. The Attorney-General is the guardian of the public interest on behalf of the Crown. He is entitled to bring actions to protect that interest, even if no private interest of the Crown is involved. This can include seeking injunctions to prevent breaches of the law, but the power must be exercised with caution.[46]

English Heritage

4.158   English Heritage can bring proceedings for an injunction to restrain any contravention of Part I of AMAAA (relating to ancient monuments).[47] The contravention need not be criminal and "restrain" allows the granting of a mandatory injunction to remedy a breach.[48]

---

[42] AMAAA, s.44(8).

[43] *ibid*. s.57(2).

[44] *ibid*. s.57(3).

[45] *ibid*. s.58(1).

[46] *Gouriet v. Union of Post Office Workers* [1978] A.C. 435.

[47] National Heritage Act 1983, s.33(2A), as inserted by the Planning and Compensation Act 1991.

[48] *c.f. Croydon London Borough Council v. Gladden* (1994) 68 P.&C.R. 300 concerning injunctions under Town and Country Planning Act 1990, s.187B.

Local authorities

Local authorities have a general power to bring proceedings "for the **4.159** promotion or protection of the interests of the inhabitants of their area" under section 222 of the Local Government Act 1972. This includes obtaining injunctions to restrain breaches of the criminal law. However, this power is to be exercised exceptionally.[49] The court must infer that the defendant's unlawful operations will continue unless and until effectively restrained by the law and nothing short of an injunction will be effective to restrain them.

If the notice provisions for areas of archaeological importance are breached **4.160** the local authority has an express statutory power to apply for an injunction. A local authority may seek a High Court injunction to restrain operations, if:

(a) they are in being or are about to be carried out in, or partly in, its area;

(b) those operations are or will contravene section 35; and

(c) the site contains or is likely to contain anything of archaeological or historical interest which will be disturbed, damaged, destroyed or removed without proper archaeological investigation if operations are carried out on the site without regard for the provisions on areas of archaeological importance.[50]

If breaches of AMAAA are also breaches of the planning legislation then injunctions may be obtained under those Acts.[51]

Third parties

Other persons such as landowners, pressure groups or neighbours are only **4.161** entitled to seek injunctions to protect their private interests. But they may bring proceedings to enforce AMAAA with the consent of the Attorney-General in a relator action. The third party (the relator) must seek the acceptance of the Attorney-General that the proceedings are in the public interest. If he concludes that they are, the action proceeds as a normal civil action but in the Attorney-General's name. The relator is responsible for pursuing the action and is liable for any costs.

---

[49] *City of London Corporation v. Bovis Construction Limited* [1992] 3 All E.R. 697, C.A.

[50] AMAAA, s.35(10).

[51] *i.e.* Town and Country Planning Act 1990, s.187B (breach of planning control); Planning (Listed Buildings and Conservation Areas) Act 1990, s.44A (listed buildings and demolition of buildings in conservation areas).

5. Other Forms of Legal Protection and Guidance

1. HUMAN REMAINS

Archaeologists are likely to disturb human remains in two circumstances: **5.1** when digging for known or suspected bodies or when hitherto unsuspected bodies are found in an excavation.

If the excavation is intended to remove human remains, appropriate **5.2** authority should first be obtained. This is normally a licence for the removal of human bones from the Home Office under the Burial Act 1857.[1] The licence, for which the fee is £10, permits the removal of bodies subject to any specified conditions. These conditions commonly include:

(a) "the removal shall be effected with due care and attention to decency";
(b) "the ground from which the remains are interred shall be screened from the public gaze while the work of removal is in progress";
(c) arrangements for scientific examination;
(d) the disposal of the remains, whether by archival storage in a museum or reinterment in a place where burials may lawfully take place.

If the remains are less than 100 years old, the Home Office requires licence **5.3** applicants to notify surviving next of kin or, if this is unreasonably difficult, to advertise in the local press and by site notice that a licence is being sought.

However, there are a number of circumstances where human remains can **5.4** be removed or dealt with under other powers.

A faculty is required, under ecclesiastical law, to permit the removal of remains from ground consecrated according to the rites of the Church of England.[2] The power to grant a faculty is vested in the diocesan bishop, but is usually exercised by the chancellor of the diocese as judge of the consistory court. If the purpose is to remove the remains from one consecrated place of burial to another, and a faculty is obtained, then a Burials Act licence is not required.[3] Because of the desire for scientific investigation and the possible retention of remains in a museum, a licence is usually required for archaeological investigation.

---

[1] Burial Act 1857, s.25.
[2] *Adlam v. Colthurst* (1867) L.R. 2 A. & E. 30.
[3] Burial Act 1857, s.25.

5.5   When land containing human remains is to be used for development the following provisions may be applicable:

(i)   Under the Town and Country Planning Act 1990, remains may be removed from burial grounds acquired or appropriated under the Planning Acts or by compulsory purchase powers.[4] The removal is subject to the directions of the Secretary of State and, if from consecrated land, any conditions imposed by the bishop of the diocese.[5] Relatives and personal representatives are entitled to remove remains, and other remains must be reinterred in a burial ground.[6]

(ii)   The New Towns Act 1981 permits development corporations, highways authorities and the Secretary of State to remove human remains from consecrated land and burial grounds acquired under the Act.[7]

(iii)   By virtue of section 3 of the Disused Burial Grounds Act 1884 it is unlawful "to erect any buildings upon any disused burial ground except for the purpose of enlarging a church, chapel, meeting house, or other places of worship". However, section 5 provides a statutory exception where the burial ground has been sold or disposed of under the authority of any public Act of Parliament.[8]

(iv)   The Disused Burial Grounds (Amendment) Act 1981 permits the removal and reinterment or cremation of human remains from a disused burial ground[9] where development is proposed to take place.

(v)   The Pastoral Measure 1983 permits the removal and reinterment or cremation of remains in redundant churches or land subject to a redundancy scheme.[10]

5.6   Burial ground "includes any churchyard, cemetery or other ground, whether consecrated or not, which has at any time been set apart for the purposes of interment".[11] Although normally applied to recognised Christian interments, the scope of the Act would seem to apply to all burials undertaken on a formalised basis. However, the requirements of the

---

[4] Town and Country Planning Act 1990, ss.239, 240. Town and Country Planning (Churches, Places of Religious Worship and Burial Grounds) Regulations 1950 (S.I. 1950 No. 792).

[5] Town and Country Planning Act 1990, s.240(1)(c).

[6] 1950 Regulations, regs 9, 10.

[7] New Towns Act 1981, s.20(2), (5).

[8] *Re St Saviour's Rectory Trustees and Oyler* (1886) 31 Ch. 412 is authority for the proposition that a private Act does not come within the exception. The burial ground must have been sold under authority of the (public) Act of Parliament (see *Attorney General v. London Parochial Charities Trustees* [1896] 1 Ch. 541) and the Act must relate to the land and not to the person selling it (see *London County Council v. Greenwich Corporation* [1929] 1 Ch. 305) *e.g.* railway land under the Transport Acts 1947–1962.

[9] Disused Burial Grounds (Amendment) Act 1981, ss.1(1), 2(1). The burial ground must have been owned by or on behalf of a church or other religious body provided that it is not consecrated land *(ibid.* s.5). The procedure is set out in the Schedule to the Act.

[10] Pastoral Measure 1983, s.65, Sched. 6.

[11] Open Spaces Act 1906, s.20 (for the Disused Burial Grounds (Amendment) Act 1981); Town and Country Planning Act 1990, s.240(3); New Towns Act 1981, s.20(11).

legislation contradict the guidance in PPG 16 in favour of preservation *in situ* of important archaeological remains.

No faculty or Burial Act licence is required under these powers.[12] These measures are all concerned with the removal of human remains to permit other uses of the site. Archaeologists are likely to deal with them when working for developers. The powers are not designed to facilitate archaeological investigation. If remains are to be analysed, or kept in a museum, a burial licence should be obtained.   **5.7**

Records must be kept by the burial authority (usually the local authority) of disinterments in its cemeteries.[13]

Remains in non-Church of England burial grounds are not subject to the faculty jurisdiction or the Pastoral Measure 1983. The other powers, in particular the Burials Act 1857, do apply. There may additionally be requirements under the law of the religion concerned.   **5.8**

If remains are disturbed accidentally, a burial licence should promptly be sought from the Home Office. The discovery of previously unknown remains should be reported to the police. Every person is under a duty to give information which may lead to the coroner having notice of circumstances requiring the holding of an inquest.[14] The police will contact the coroner if an inquest may be necessary, that is, if the body is less than 100 years old. If there is reasonable cause to suspect that the death was violent, unnatural or occurred suddenly from an unknown cause, then an inquest must be held.[15] Otherwise, it is for the coroner's discretion.   **5.9**

2. TREASURE TROVE

Treasure trove has been defined as follows: **5.10**

> "... where any gold or silver in coin, plate or bullion is found concealed in a house, or in the earth, or other private place, the owner thereof being unknown, in which case the treasure belongs to the King or his grantee, having the franchise of treasure trove ..."[16]

Whenever treasure is hidden in the earth, or other secret place, with the intention of recovering it there is a prima facie presumption that it belongs to the Crown or franchisee unless somebody else can show better title. (Numerous grants of franchise were made in the medieval period but only four are dealt with regularly. Duchy of Cornwall, Duchy of Lancaster, City of London and City of Bristol and all operate in the same manner as the Crown.) For example, in the case of *Attorney-General v. British Museum Trustees*[17] the disputed treasure comprised a number of objects of great antiquity and   **5.11**

---

[12] Town and Country Planning Act 1990, s.240(2); New Towns Act 1981, s.20(7); Disused Burial Grounds (Amendment) Act 1981, s.2(7); Pastoral Measure 1983, s.65(8).

[13] Local Authorities Cemeteries Order 1977 (S.I. 1977 No. 204), art. 11(9) as substituted by the Local Authorities (Amendment) Order 1986 (S.I. 1986 No. 1782).

[14] *R. v. Clerk* (1702) 1 Salk 377.

[15] Coroners Act 1988, s.8(1).

[16] *Chitty's Prerogatives of the Crown* (1830, p.152), cited with approval by the courts including in *Attorney General of the Duchy of Lancaster v. G.E. Overton (Farms) Limited* [1981] Ch. 333.

[17] [1903] 2 Ch. 598 at 608, *per* Farwell J.

beauty of Celtic origin dating between 300 B.C. to A.D. 600–700. The value of the items rendered it unlikely that the treasure had been abandoned except under stress of imminent danger. Indeed, the care with which three plaited chains (with fastenings) and a further chain had been put inside a hollow collar with repousse ornaments and collected together with the other items comprising a model boat (with thwarts, a number of oars, spars, etc.), two gold torques and a bowl with four small rings at the edges, collectively pointed against the likelihood of imminent danger. Despite suggesting a number of ways in which the treasure might have been abandoned, the claimants did not succeed in defeating the Crown's interest.

5.12   The precise meaning of "gold and silver" was considered in the more recent case of *Attorney-General of the Duchy of Lancaster v. G.E. Overton (Farms) Limited.*[18] There, some 7,811 Roman coins, made of a silver alloy, had been discovered below ploughshare level in a field at Coleby, Lincolnshire. A sample of 923 coins had been cleaned and examined by the British Museum. The silver content of 15 coins, on the basis of a limited analysis, ranged between 0.2 per cent and 5.85 per cent. Indeed, only three of the coins showed any trace of silvering, of which two showed a silver content of 5 per cent and 18 per cent respectively. The judge's view was that the silver content was insufficient to deem the coins treasure trove. Accordingly, they were held to belong to the owners of the field.

5.13   Any person finding treasure trove must make it known to the district coroner. In practice, this requirement is most easily achieved by notifying the police. Whilst the common law crime of concealment was abolished by the Theft Act 1968[19] the failure to inform the authorities and the removal of the find may be theft. At any criminal trial, the court will determine if the find is treasure trove.[20]

Once notified, the coroner is under a duty, as with an inquest, to summon a jury and to hold an inquiry to ascertain the status of the find.[21]

5.14   The finder of treasure trove, once it has been established as being the property of the Crown, is entitled to a reward if he has reported the find promptly and handed it over to the proper authorities. The reward is equal to the full market value if it is retained by either the Crown, a franchisee or by a museum. If the treasure is not retained then it will be returned to the finder, who may do with it as he wishes. Should the finder desire, the British Museum will sell the treasure for the best price obtainable. Where the coroner has found that more than one person was concerned in the finding, then the reward may be divided between the finders.[22] In practice objects are only now acquired by museums, not by the Crown. Since 1977, an independent Treasure Trove Reviewing Committee has advised the government and specifically, since 1993, the Secretary of State for National Heritage on valuations. The committee can seek independent advice. It can also invite finders to submit evidence who are only eligible for rewards.

5.15   The decision of the coroner can be challenged in one of two ways. The first is in the High Court by way of a statutory right under section 13 of the Coroner Act 1988. However, the application can only be made by or under the

---

[18] [1981] Ch. 333.
[19] Theft Act 1968, s.32(1)(a).
[20] *R. v. Hancock* [1990] 2 Q.B. 242.
[21] Coroners Act 1988, s.30.
[22] Home Office Circular 10/89.

authority of the Attorney-General. In this context, a fresh inquest for the consideration of new evidence can take place if it can be shown that the jury might have come to a different conclusion even though it cannot be shown that the holding of the new inquest may not necessarily produce a different verdict.[23] Secondly, there is judicial review. As this is a public law remedy concerned with the decision-making process of an inferior court, the grounds of challenge are somewhat limited to errors of law.[24]

Where objects are not found to be treasure trove, the dispute then falls to be **5.16** resolved between the finder and the landowner. The current legal position, following the decision of the Court of Appeal in *Parker v. British Airways Board*[25] is that the claims of the occupier of land will normally prevail over those of the finder where the article is attached to or buried in the land. On the other hand, where the article is merely lying on the surface, then the finder will have a stronger claim unless he is a trespasser or the occupier has manifested an intention to exercise total control over the land. In *Parker* the Court held, on the specific facts, that a passenger, who had found a bracelet on the floor of an executive lounge at Heathrow, was entitled to keep it. The Court of Appeal followed this approach in *Waverley Borough Council v. Fletcher*[26] and, on the facts, rejected the defendant's claim despite his assertion that he was not a trespasser. His case was that he was pursuing a legitimate recreational activity when, at the time he was using his metal detector in a public park, he found a medieval gold brooch which he had retrieved by digging down some nine inches through hard ground.

During the 1994–95 Parliamentary Session, the Government introduced **5.17** the Treasure Bill measures through the House of Lords to reform this area of the law but, due to lack of time, it failed in the Commons. However, a subsequent government-supported Private Member's Bill has led to this piece of legislation completing its various Parliamentary stages and it is expected to receive Royal Assent shortly. The Act cannot come into force until a Code of Practice dealing with rewards and operation of the Bill has been drawn up.

The main points covered by the Bill include the following: **5.18**

(a) All objects other than coins will become treasure trove provided that they contain at least 10 per cent, by weight, of gold or silver and are at least 300 years old.

(b) All coins found in hoards will become treasure trove whatever they are made of, provided that at least two of the coins are at least 300 years old but not single finds.

(c) It will not matter whether objects had been buried in the ground with the intention of recovery, or buried in a grave or simply lost provided they satisfy the above requirements.

(d) All objects found together with such items will be deemed to be treasure trove, whatever they are made of.

(e) Treasure will not include objects which are either unwanted natural objects or minerals, as extracted from a natural deposit.

---

[23] *E. v. Rapier (deceased)* [1988] Q.B. 26.
[24] *R. v. Manchester Coroner, ex p. Tal* [1985] Q.B. 67.
[25] [1982] Q.B. 1004.
[26] [1995] 4 All E.R. 756.

(f)   The Secretary of State for National Heritage, with the approval of Parliament, will be able to designate additional classes of object as treasure trove and also remove classes of object from the definition.

(g)   All finds that are likely to be treasure trove will have to be reported to a coroner within 14 days of the discovery. Failure to declare finds to coroner establishes a new offence of non-declaration of treasure with a maximum fine at level 5 (£5,000) or up to three months' imprisonment or both.

(h)   Coroners will be required to make reasonable efforts to ensure that occupiers and landowners are informed of any reported finds of treasure trove on their land.

(i)   Coroners will no longer need to summon inquest juries.

(j)   Rewards will be dealt with by a separate Code of Practice which will be drawn up after consultation with interested parties, *i.e.* metal detectorists, landowners and the archaeological community.

(k)   The Bill will extend to England, Wales and Northern Ireland but not Scotland which already has a much broader definition of treasure.

(l)   The Bill will exempt the Church of England in respect of objects found associated with human burials on consecrated ground and objects covered by the Church of England's own legal system, except those which might be considered treasure trove under the existing system.

In addition, it was proposed that a voluntary Code of Practice would be introduced to cover the reporting of archaeological objects not covered by the Treasure Bill.

3. SHIPWRECKS AND MILITARY REMAINS

5.19   Maritime archaeology has achieved greater importance in recent years. The raising of the *Mary Rose* and the inspections of the *Titanic* and the *Bismark* have shown the power of technology. There has also been a growing recognition of the numbers of ancient craft, historic wrecks, drowned harbours and settlements. Against that, increased mineral operations and recreational activity, through diving, on the seabed has increased the risk of irreparable damage.

5.20   "Wreck" was first described in *Termes de la Ley*, a legal dictionary published in law French in 1527 and translated into English in 1620:

> " 'Wrecke' or 'varech' (as the Normans, from whom it came, call it) is where a ship is perished on the sea, and no man escapeth alive out of the same, and the ship or part of the ship so perished, or the goods of the ship come to the land of any lord, the lord shall have that as a wrecke of the sea. But if a man, or a dog or a cat, escape alive, so that the party to whom the goods belong, come within a yeare and a day, and prove the goods to be his, he shall have them again ..."

5.21   "Wreck" is now defined by statute as including "jetsam, flotsam, lagan and derelict found on the shores of the sea or any tidal water".[27] The meaning of

---

[27] Merchant Shipping Act 1995, s.255(1).

"derelict" was considered in *The Lusitania*.[28] This passenger liner was sunk by a German submarine in 1915 in international waters. In 1982, 95 items were recovered by divers and a remote-controlled submarine. When they were brought to England, litigation commenced as to their ownership. The court held that a "derelict" is a ship, whether afloat or sunk, that has been abandoned by her master and crew without any intention of returning to her. It is a separate question as to whether the owner has abandoned title to the wreck.

Merchant Shipping Act 1995

If a wreck, or parts of it, are recovered in United Kingdom territorial waters, **5.22** or recovered in other waters and then brought into United Kingdom territorial waters, then the receiver of wrecks must be notified, and if the wreck was not recovered by its owner, the property should be delivered to the receiver.[29] The owner then has a year to claim the wreck, paying salvage fees and expenses due.[30] If the wreck was found in United Kingdom territorial waters and remains unclaimed, then it belongs to the Crown under a "droit of Admiralty".[31] If the wreck was found in other waters, as with the *Lusitania*, then no "droit of Admiralty exists".[32] The salvors, who recovered the wreck, usually receive 50 per cent of the value recovered for their efforts.

It is an offence to board a wreck without permission from the receiver (or, **5.23** for recent casualties, the master).[33] It is also an offence to wrongfully remove any part of a wreck.[34]

Ancient Monuments and Archaeological Areas Act 1979

Shipwrecks and any other monuments in United Kingdom territorial waters **5.24** (12 miles) around Great Britain may be scheduled and be subject to the other protection, of AMAAA.[35] The width of the meaning of "monument",[36] including buildings, aircraft, vessels or vehicles and their remains, covers most submerged items of archaeological interest.

Protection of Wrecks Act 1973

The Secretary of State can designate restricted areas around the sites of **5.25** historic wrecks for their protection. He must find that the site, in United Kingdom territorial waters would, or may, be the site of a wrecked vessel and

---

[28] *Pierce v. Bemis (The Lusitania)* [1986] 1 Q.B. 384.

[29] Merchant Shipping Act 1995, s.236. The receiver is appointed by the Secretary of State for Trade and Industry.

[30] *ibid.* s.243.

[31] *ibid.* s.241.

[32] *The Lusitania*, n. 28 above.

[33] Merchant Shipping Act 1995, s.246(1). It is a summary offence, with a level 3 (£1,000) fine.

[34] *ibid.* s.246(2)(c). The offence is summary with a maximum fine of level 4 (£2,500).

[35] AMAAA, s.53(1).

[36] *ibid.* s.61(7).

because of the historical, archaeological or artistic importance of the vessel or its contents the site ought to be protected from unauthorised interference.[37] Within the restricted area it is an offence to tamper with, damage or remove any part of the vessel or object from it; carry out diving or salvage Trove.

operations; or deposit anything that might damage the wreck or obstruct access to it without a licence from the Secretary of State.[38]

5.26   Only persons competent and properly equipped to carry out salvage operations in a manner appropriate to the historical, archaeological or artistic importance of the wreck or persons with a legitimate reason for doing something in the restricted area may be granted a licence. The licence may be subject to conditions.[39]

Protection of Military Remains Act 1986

5.27   The sanctity of military wrecks, especially those which contain human remains, is of considerable public importance. In 1955 the Admiralty decided that wrecks known to contain human remains should be left undisturbed unless there were special circumstances. The special circumstances were a danger to navigation; the presence of explosives; a strong risk of unauthorised access which might be reduced by a controlled salvage operation to remove attractive items; or valuable historical research by reputable groups.[40]

5.28   In 1973, the desecration of the wreck of the *Royal Oak* in Scapa Flow by amateur divers led to local by-laws. In the 1980s, public concern increased after the salvage of gold from *HMS Edinburgh* and an unauthorised entry into *HMS Hampshire*. The Protection of Military Remains Act 1986 was introduced as a result.[41] It is an offence to interfere with the wreckage of crashed, sunken or wrecked military vessels or aircraft without a licence, whether in the United Kingdom, United Kingdom territorial waters or (in the case of United Kingdom vessels or aircraft) in international waters.[42]

5.29   The Act applies to military vessels sunk or stranded after the start of the First World War which have been designated by the Secretary of State, and any military aircraft lost. The place where their remains rest is a protected place.[43] It is an offence to tamper with, damage, remove or unearth these remains or enter any opening in such vessels or aircraft.[44] Diving, salvage or

---

[37] Protection of Wrecks Act 1973, s.1(1).

[38] *ibid.* s.1(3). The offence is triable either way with a maximum fine of £5,000 in the magistrates' court and an unlimited fine in the Crown court (*ibid.* s.3(4)). There are defences of emergency action, necessity due to stress of weather or navigational hazards, or exercising statutory functions (*ibid.* s.3(3)).

[39] *ibid.* s.1(5).

[40] *Hansard*, H.L., Vol. 473, col. 821 (April 17, 1986).

[41] For background, see the Second Reading debate (*Hansard*, H.L., Vol. 473, cols 811–824 (April 17, 1986)).

[42] The 1986 Act only extends to military remains in international waters if they are British remains. Criminal liability for acts in international waters is only imposed on persons on British ships or who have various forms of British citizenship (Protection of Wrecks Act 1973, s.3).

[43] Protection of Wrecks Act 1973, s.1(1), (2), (6).

[44] *ibid.* s.2(1), (2). The offence is triable either way: in the magistrates court the maximum fine is £5,000; in the Crown court it is unlimited (*ibid.* s.2(7)).

excavations are prohibited if they are for a purpose that is likely to be tampering, etc.[45]

Merely looking at remains in a protected place is not an offence. However, sites can be designated as controlled sites, where diving to investigate or record details of remains without authority is an offence.[46]   **5.30**

Licences to do acts prohibited by the Act are issued by the Secretary of State for Defence. These can apply to individuals or give blanket exemptions in respect of certain groups of people or individual sites. Conditions can be attached to any licence.[47]   **5.31**

International law

The international law of salvage is governed by the London Salvage   **5.32**
Convention 1989. Shipwrecks would normally be covered by the Convention. However, states need not apply the Convention to "maritime cultural property of prehistoric, archaeological or historic interest" situated on the sea-bed.[48] This opt-out was not taken up by the United Kingdom when it implemented the Convention in the Merchant Shipping (Salvage and Pollution) Act 1994.

The United Nations Law of the Sea Convention 1982, which has not been   **5.33**
ratified by the United Kingdom, imposes a duty on states to "protect objects of an archaeological and historic nature found at sea" and to co-operate for this purpose.[49]

Code of Practice for seabed developers

A code of practice for co-operation between seabed developers and archaeol-   **5.34**
ogists has been published.[50] It encourages archaeological evaluation of proposals for development (*e.g.* mining, drilling). The physical preservation of remains is encouraged. If development is unavoidable because of economic or social needs and physical preservation is not possible, archaeological investigation may be an acceptable alternative.

4. IMPORT AND EXPORT OF ARCHAEOLOGICAL ARTEFACTS

Archaeological finds are an important element in a nation's knowledge of its   **5.35**
history. Some finds contribute to the nation's identity and sense of itself. Consequently many countries have been concerned to protect their national archaeological treasures from being exported.

A further reason for controls has developed in recent years. Unrestrained import, export and sale of archaeological artefacts encourages the acquisition of those artefacts for their monetary value.

---

[45] Protection of Wrecks Act 1973, s.2(3)(b).
[46] *ibid.* ss.1(2)(b), 2(3)(a).
[47] *ibid.* s.4.
[48] London Salvage Convention, art. 30.1(d).
[49] *ibid.* art. 303.1.
[50] Joint Nautical Archaeology Policy Committee, January 1995. See Appendix P.

5.36   However, the pillaging of archaeological sites for valuable items is of increasing concern. The primary historical and archaeological value of an object comes from its context and association with other items and features.

The ancient monuments, shipwrecks and military remains legislation and the law of treasure trove provide some protection to sites in the United Kingdom.

5.37   The first step in international efforts to control the trade in illegally obtained artefacts was the UNESCO Convention of 1970 on the means of prohibiting and preventing the illicit import, export and transfer of ownership of cultural property. However this has not been ratified by the United Kingdom.

5.38   There is United Kingdom legislation on exportation, protecting antiques. Recent European Union (E.U.) legislation restricts exportation outside the member states of the Union and provides a mechanism for the return of artefacts.

There may therefore be a requirement for a United Kingdom or European Union licence. Both licences are administered by the Department of National Heritage for the United Kingdom and the Isle of Man.

5.39   The President of the Board of Trade is responsible for licences for arms and military equipment produced less than 100 years before the date of exportation and, regardless of age, all atomic energy-related items, nuclear equipment, certain other categories of industrial and electronic equipment and goods capable of being used for chemical, biological or nuclear weapon purposes. Interestingly, the Department of National Heritage suggests that some of these items could otherwise be regarded as antiques.

United Kingdom export controls

5.40   A licence is required for the export of antiques, defined as goods manufactured or produced more than 50 years ago. The licence regime is contained in the Export of Goods (Control) Order 1992.[51] This is made under section 1 of the Import, Export and Customs Powers (Defence) Act 1939, a piece of emergency wartime legislation which survived the Second World War.

5.41   The 1992 Order defines antiques as:

> "Any goods manufactured or produced more than 50 years before the date of exportation except:
> (1)   postage stamps and other articles of philatelic interest;
> (2)   birth, marriage or death certificates or other documents relating to the personal affairs of the exporter or the spouse of the exporter;
> (3)   letters or other writings written by the exporter or the spouse of the exporter; and
> (4)   any goods exported by, and being the personal property of, the manufacturer or producer thereof, or the spouse, widow or widower of that person".[52]

5.42   Export is permitted if a licence is granted by the Secretary of State and all

---

[51] (S.I. 1992 No. 3092). This has been replaced for all matters except antiques by the Export of Goods (Control) Order 1994 (S.I. 1994 No. 1191).
[52] 1992 Order, Sched. 1, Group 2.

the conditions attaching to the licence are complied with.[53] A licence is required for the export of antiques to other member states of the European Union and to the Channel Islands.

An Open General Export Licence has been granted by the Secretary of State.[54] This removes the need to apply for a United Kingdom licence in respect of certain objects below specified values. This includes archaeological material from outside the United Kingdom which is valued at less than £39,600. Archaeological material found in United Kingdom soil or United Kingdom territorial waters is not exempted by this Licence.

5.43

Regular, reputable exporters can obtain an Open Individual Export Licence (OIEL). This allows the export of objects of a type covered by the licence without the need to apply for individual United Kingdom licences. Various record-keeping requirements are imposed on such persons under the OIEL and the 1992 Order.[55]

5.44

A United Kingdom licence is not required if a European Union licence has been granted.[56]

Any goods exported or brought to a quay or other place for export without the necessary licence become prohibited goods.[57] The goods are forfeit.[58] The exporter and his agents are liable to a penalty on summary conviction of three times the value of the goods or level 3 (£1,000), whichever is the greater.[59] In addition, the exporter, his agent or the shipper are liable to a customs penalty of up to level 5 (£5,000).

5.45

Any person knowingly concerned in export or attempted export with intent to evade the prohibition on export commits an offence. They are liable on summary conviction to a penalty of three times the value of the goods or the prescribed sum (£5,000) and six months' imprisonment. On indictment the penalty is unlimited and a sentence of up to seven years' imprisonment can be imposed.[60]

5.46

It is an offence to knowingly or recklessly make a false statement to obtain a licence or permission. Any licence or permission obtained thereby will be void.[61] Failure to comply with a condition attached to a licence or the recording requirements of the 1992 Order is an offence.[62] The maximum sentence for either offence is a two-year jail term and fine on indictment or a fine of the statutory maximum (£5,000) on summary conviction.[63]

5.47

A person may be required by a Customs officer, under article 6 of the 1992 Order, to declare on leaving the United Kingdom whether he has goods subject to the Order and to produce them. Customs and Excise are empowered to search persons for such goods.[64] It is an offence, punishable by

5.48

---

[53] 1992 Order, art. 3.

[54] Open General Export Licence (Antiques) dated September 3, 1993.

[55] 1992 Order, art. 8.

[56] Open General Export Licence (Antiques), para. 1(j).

[57] Import, Export and Customs Powers (Defence) Act 1939, s.3(1).

[58] *ibid.* s.3(1); Customs and Excise Management Act 1979, s.68. Forfeiture only takes effect when the goods are seized (*Lockyer v. Offley* (1786) 1 T.R. 252).

[59] Customs and Excise Management Act 1979, s.68(1).

[60] *ibid.* s.68.

[61] 1992 Order (n. 51 above), art. 5(1).

[62] 1992 Order, art. 5(3). The article provides a defence if the condition was changed without the licence holder's consent and the goods had already been exported.

[63] *ibid.* art. 5(2), (3).

[64] *ibid.* art. 6(1).

a customs penalty of £1,000 to fail, without reasonable excuse, to make any declaration, produce any goods, or submit to any search, required under the Order.[65] Knowingly or recklessly making a false declaration under article 6 is an offence. It is punishable by a £2,000 Customs penalty on summary conviction, and an unlimited Customs penalty and two years' imprisonment on indictment.[66]

Restricting trade within the European Union

5.49 The Treaty of Rome eliminates restrictions on imports and exports between member states.[67] A specific exception is provided in that member states can prohibit or restrict imports, exports or goods in transit to protect national treasures possessing artistic, historic or archaeological value.[68] This allows the United Kingdom licensing system to apply to export to other member states.

Restricting exports from the European Union

5.50 An export licence is required for the export of archaeological objects outside the European Union by E.C. Regulation 3911/92 on the export of cultural goods.

Cultural goods include:

(a) "archaeological objects more than 100 years old which are the products of excavations and finds on land or under water, archaeological sites, archaeological collections"[69];

(b) "elements forming an integral part of artistic, historical or religious monuments which have been dismembered, of an age exceeding 100 years"[70];

(c) archives more than 50 years old[71];

(d) various other items, depending upon their value, including old maps and books and antique items more than 50 years old.

5.51 Export licences can be issued by the member state where the item is located.[72] An export licence cannot be issued if the cultural goods have been unlawfully exported from another member state, either directly or via a non-European Union country. Temporary licences can be granted, providing for the return of the objects to the United Kingdom by a certain date. Failure to meet the return date, or making a transfer of ownership, will also contravene the United Kingdom licence requirements and so constitute an offence under domestic legislation.[73]

5.52 In the United Kingdom, applicants for European Union licences have to

---

[65] 1992 Order, art. 6(2).

[66] *ibid.* art. 6(3).

[67] Treaty of Rome, Arts 30, 34.

[68] *ibid.* art. 36.

[69] E.C. Regulation 3911/92, Annex A1.

[70] *ibid.* Annex A2.

[71] *ibid.* Annex A11.

[72] *ibid.* Art. 2.

[73] Open General Export Licence (Antiques), para. 5.

declare, if the object was exported from another member state on or after January 1, 1993, that it was lawfully exported. If supporting documentation is available, it should be provided.

Regulation 3911/92 allows member states not to require an export licence **5.53** for archaeological objects which are the product of excavations and finds on land or under water or archaeological sites provided that:

(a) they are of limited archaeological or scientific interest;
(b) they are not the direct product of excavations, finds and archaeological sites within a member state; and
(c) their presence on the market is lawful.[74]

The United Kingdom has exercised this discretion by excluding from the **5.54** European Union licensing requirements:

(a) numismatic items of a standard type which are published in a reference work on numismatics;
(b) objects, other than numismatic items, which possess no special or rare features of form, size, material, decoration, inscription or iconography and which are not in an especially fine condition for the type of object.

This exemption is applicable provided that the objects: **5.55**

(a) do not form part of a recognised archaeological collection of special historical significance;
(b) are not the direct product of excavations, finds and archaeological sites within a member state, *i.e.* they have not come straight onto the market after being recently discovered;
(c) are lawfully on the market—objects which are stolen will not qualify; or
(d) do not fall with any other category of the Annex to Regulation 3911/92.

The member state concerned may refuse a licence where the cultural goods **5.56** are covered by legislation protecting national treasures of artistic, historical or archaeological value.[75] So, whilst the licensing system is imposed on a community-wide basis, whether licences are granted is a matter for the member state. The decision would generally be the same as one made under domestic law.

The main effect of Regulation 3911/92 is to prevent the export from the **5.57** European Union of cultural objects that have been unlawfully removed from a member state.

Return of cultural objects that have been unlawfully removed

In conjunction with Regulation 3911/92, the European Union adopted **5.58** Directive 93/7 on the Return of Cultural Objects Unlawfully Removed from

---

[74] E.C. Regulation 3911/92, Art. 2, para. 4.
[75] Art. 2, para. 3.

the Territory of a Member State. This has been implemented in law in the Return of Cultural Objects Regulations 1994.[76]

The 1994 Regulations allow the Secretary of State to protect unlawfully removed cultural objects. The member state from where the objects have been removed can apply to the court for their return.

5.59   The 1994 Regulations apply to the same cultural objects as Regulation 3911/92 and objects in the public collections of state-funded museums, archives, libraries, or in ecclesiastical institutions. The member state from where the object has been removed ("the requesting state") must classify it as amongst national treasures possessing artistic, historic or archaeological value under its national legislation or administrative procedures.[77] The classification can be made after the object has been removed.

5.60   For the 1994 Regulations to apply, the object must have been unlawfully removed on or after January 1, 1993.[78] Unlawful removal means:

(a)   removal in breach of the member state's rules for the protection of national treasures or of Regulation 3911/92; or

(b)   that the object is not returned at the end of a period of lawful temporary removal or there is a breach of another condition governing the temporary removal.[79]

5.61   The requesting state applies to the member state ("the requested state") where it believes the object is located. It must provide the information needed to facilitate the search.[80] The requested state's relevant authority (here the Secretary of State for National Heritage) is then obliged to seek the object and identify its possessor or holder.[81]

5.62   Where a cultural object is found in the United Kingdom and there are reasonable grounds for believing that it has been unlawfully removed from the territory of a member state, that state will be notified, whether or not the find is the result of a requested search.[82]

The Secretary of State will enable the member state concerned to check that the object is a cultural object. If the check is positive (within two months) the Secretary of State will take any necessary measures to preserve the object. He can take interim measures to prevent the procedure being evaded.[83]

5.63   The Secretary of State can apply to the court[84] for orders to enable the checks to take place, to preserve the object and obtain any necessary interim protection.[85] These include injunctions against those holding the object and orders allowing the Secretary of State to take possession of the object.[86] Additionally, the Secretary of State can obtain a court order to enter and search premises for unlawfully removed cultural objects.[87] This is if

---

[76] (S.I. 1994 No. 501)

[77] E.C. Directive 93/7, Art. 1.

[78] 1994 Regulations, reg. 1(3).

[79] E.C. Directive 93/7, Art. 1(2).

[80] 1994 Regulations, reg. 3(2).

[81] *ibid.* reg. 3(1).

[82] *ibid.* reg. 3(3).

[83] *ibid.* reg. 3(4).

[84] The High Court (in England and Wales) or the Court of Session (in Scotland).

[85] 1994 Regulations, reg. 4(1).

[86] *ibid.* reg. 4(3).

[87] *ibid.* reg. 5(1).

admission has been refused, the case is urgent, or asking for admission would defeat the object of entry *i.e.* the object would be destroyed or removed.[88]

The Secretary of State's powers are purely to protect the object. For it to be returned the requesting state is given a right of action against the possessor or holder of the object.   5.64

The requesting state must prove to the court that the object is the cultural object sought and has been unlawfully removed from the territory of the member state.[89] The object's return will not be ordered if "the proceedings were brought more than one year after the member state became aware of the location of the cultural object and of the identity of its possessor or holder".[90] It is not clear if this limitation applies where the member state knows that the object is in a third country (where it cannot secure its return) and it is then brought into a member state, for example, for auction in London.

Additionally, the action must be brought within the "special limitation period": a certain time from the date of the unlawful removal of the object. For public collections and ecclesiastical goods subject to special protection by the requesting state's law this is 75 years.[91] For other cultural goods the special limitation period is 30 years.[92]   5.65

The requesting state will pay fair compensation to the possessor of the item if the court is satisfied that he exercised due care and attention in acquiring the object.[93]

The export licensing system in practice

The export licensing system is complex. The stages to consider are the following: 5.66

    (a)   Whether an European Union licence is required:
        (i)   is it being exported outside the European Union?
        (ii)   is it covered by Regulation 3911/92 by type and value? and
        (iii) is it outside the limited archaeological value exemption?
    (b)   If not, is a United Kingdom licence required:
        (i)   is the type and value covered by the 1992 Order? and
        (ii)   is the type and value outside the Open General Export Licence?
    (c)   If a United Kingdom licence is required, does the exporter have an Open Individual Export Licence which covers the goods?
    (d)   If he does not have an OIEL, a licence must be sought or an export certificate obtained.

An application for an individual EU or United Kingdom export licence will usually be referred to an "expert adviser". This is a senior keeper or curator in a British national museum or gallery. Objects imported in the last 50 years are usually not referred.   5.67

The expert adviser will then consider the object under the "Waverley Criteria" which are:

---

[88] 1994 Regulations, reg. 5(2).
[89] *ibid.* reg. 6.
[90] *ibid.* reg. 6(6).
[91] *ibid.* reg. 6(7).
[92] *ibid.* reg. 6(8).
[93] *ibid.* reg. 7.

(i)   Is the object so closely connected with our history and national life that its departure would be a misfortune?

(ii)   Is it of outstanding aesthetic importance?

(iii)   Is it of outstanding significance for the study of some particular branch of art, learning or history?

5.68   If the expert adviser objects under these criteria, the application is referred to the Reviewing Committee on the Export of Works of Art, a non-statutory body appointed by the Secretary of State for National Heritage. It consists of seven permanent members who are joined by three independent experts on the object which is the subject of the application. They consider written submissions by the expert adviser and the applicant. The Committee then makes a recommendation to the Secretary of State.

5.69   The Secretary of State will normally either grant the licence or defer the decision for a specified period to allow a buyer to come forward to keep the object in the United Kingdom. The period is usually between two and six months.

If the owner rejects an offer to purchase the object at or above a fair market value recommended by the Committee, the export licence will normally be refused. If an offer is accepted by the owner, the export licence application lapses.

5.70   The Secretary of State may refuse an application on other grounds, for example that the property is stolen. He may be obliged not to grant a licence by European law, for example because the object has been unlawfully exported from a member state.

The Commonwealth Scheme

5.71   Following the difficulties faced by the New Zealand government in legal action to recover a Maori carving that had been unlawfully exported,[94] the Commonwealth Law Ministers declared in February 1983 that the "protection of significant items of cultural heritage was a legitimate concern of the state". After 10 years of discussions, the Law Ministers agreed the "Scheme for the Protection of the Material Culture Heritage" in November 1993. It is a recommendation to Commonwealth governments and does not have the status in international law of a treaty.

The United Kingdom decided that it would not, at the present time, join the Scheme, but would give informal support through diplomatic and other channels.

5.72   The Scheme is similar to the European Directive. It is based on export prohibition. Only nationally important objects should have their export restricted. If such an artefact is exported without a permit and is brought into another Commonwealth country, that country is expected to take the necessary steps to secure its return. As with the European Union legislation, each country must set up a central authority to deal with these matters.

5.73   The Scheme provides a variety of options to secure return.[95] The returning state can order the artefact's return unless the holder challenges the decision in the courts. Alternatively either the returning state or the requesting state

---

[94] *Attorney-General of New Zealand v. Ortiz* [1984] A.C.1. The action ultimately failed.

[95] Scheme, para. 9.

can bring proceedings in the country where the object is held to secure an order for its return.

Compensation is payable to innocent purchasers. The requesting state must make a claim within five years of knowing the whereabouts of the property. States may make it a criminal offence to import an artefact that has been unlawfully exported. A number of Commonwealth states, including Australia, already do this.[96]

Other actions

A state could bring an action at common law if it could establish a proprietary claim to the object. For example, a proprietary claim would arise in favour of the British government if an object was treasure trove.   **5.74**

Export control laws often provide that goods unlawfully exported are forfeit to that government. However, forfeiture may only take place when the goods are seized.[97] Additionally, forfeiture provisions may be construed as a penal statute of a foreign country and not enforced in English courts.[98]

5. OTHER STATUTORY CONTROLS

In addition to the specific legislative and policy controls identified above, some bodies are legally required to pay attention to archaeological sites and remains within their ownership or control. The relevant legislation is grouped under the following subject headings.   **5.75**

Agriculture, forestry and the countryside

Section 18 of the Agriculture Act 1986 provides for the designation and management of environmentally sensitive areas (ESAs), respectively by the Minister for Agriculture, Fisheries and Food (MAFF) and the Secretary of State for Wales. The intention is to conserve and enhance the natural beauty of an area, its flora, fauna, geological, physiographical features or to protect buildings or other objects of archaeological, architectural or historic interest through the maintenance and adoption of particular agricultural methods which are likely to facilitate such conservation, enhancement or protection. ESA status is given, for example, within England, to a number of areas including the Pennine Dales, the South Downs and the Somerset Levels and Moors and, within Wales, to the Cambrian Mountains, the Llyn Peninsula and the Shropshire Borders, within which both scheduled and unscheduled archaeological sites can be found. Designation as an ESA does not, however, affect the status of that area in terms of national planning policies or development control regulations[99] although English Heritage is now a   **5.76**

---

[96] See the Australian Protection of Movable Cultural Heritage Act 1986.

[97] *Attorney-General of New Zealand v. Ortiz* (n. 94 above), considering the New Zealand Historic Articles Act 1962 and the Customs Acts 1913 and 1966.

[98] *Attorney-General of New Zealand v. Ortiz* (n. 94 above): the Court of Appeal held that the statute was unenforceable, reversing Staughton J. The House of Lords expressed no opinion on this issue.

[99] PPG 7, para. 3.18.

statutory consultee as well as the Countryside Commission and English Nature.[1] Management agreements are often utilised to achieve these aims.

5.77   The Environment Act 1995 also contains two statutory provisions affecting archaeology in an agricultural context. The first is to be found in section 97, which concerns the protection of important hedgerows in England and Wales. Under the consultation provisions in respect of the subordinate regulations to enforce protection is a reference to bodies concerned with "environmental conservation". This term is defined by section 97(8) as including features of archaeological or historic interest. Secondly, section 99(2) requires MAFF to consult with English Heritage in respect of ESAs and the making of any other statutory instrument which is concerned with the management of land and whose primary purpose is the conservation and enhancement of any features of archaeological interest.

5.78   The Forestry Act 1967 concerns afforestation, management, protection and practices within Great Britain. Its relevance to archaeology arises generally in connection with the requirement by section 1(3A) for the Forestry Commissioners, in the discharge of their functions under the Forestry Acts 1967 to 1979, to achieve a reasonable balance between the development of afforestation, the management of forests and the production and supply of timber with the conservation and enhancement of natural beauty, flora, fauna and geological or physiographical features of special interest. Specifically, section 40(2)(a) excludes land from compulsory purchase by the Minister which is the site of an ancient monument or other object of archaeological interest. Subsection (2)(b) also excludes land which forms part of a park, garden or pleasure ground or which forms part of a home farm attached to, and usually occupied with, a mansion house or is otherwise required for the amenity and convenience of a dwelling house.

5.79   The Countryside Act 1968 is part of the body of legislation dealing with the protection, enjoyment and access to the general countryside including the provision of country parks, leisure and refreshment facilities. Specifically, section 12(1) enables local planning authorities, whose area includes the whole or part of a National Park in conjunction with the Countryside Commission or the Countryside Council for Wales, to provide study centres and other facilities for learning about the history, natural features, flora and fauna of the National Park and the objects of architectural, archaeological or historical interest therein. National Park authorities, when established, will take over these functions of local planning authorities.[2]

5.80   Part II of the Wildlife and Countryside Act 1981 conferred additional controls through amendment of the National Parks and Access to the Countryside Act 1949 and the Countryside Act 1968. Under section 39 management agreements can be made between local planning authorities and owners and occupiers of land for the purpose of conserving or enhancing the natural beauty or amenity of any land or promoting its enjoyment by the public. The terms of the agreement, which often apply to Sites of Special Scientific Interest, restrict methods of cultivation and other agricultural operations, including forestry, or the exercise of other rights over the relevant land as well as the making of payments by the relevant planning authority.

---

[1] Environment Act 1995, ss.99(2), (3).
[2] *ibid.* s.68.

The coal industry, mines and quarries

With the nationalisation and then de-regulation of the coal industry a number of statutory provisions need to be borne in mind. Under the Coal Industry Act 1994 (CIA), the British Coal Corporation is now replaced by the Coal Authority. This body holds, manages and disposes of the Corporation's assets including all unmined coal-reserves. It licenses coal-mining operations. It also remains responsible for subsidence arising from opencast and mining operations. Section 3(7) of the CIA specifically requires the Authority, when formulating any proposals for workings on or in relation to any of its land or other property, which has been used for the carrying on of any coal-mining operations but is no longer to be put to such use, to have regard to the desirability of preserving natural beauty, of conserving flora, fauna and geological or physiographical features of special interest and of protecting sites, buildings, structures and objects of architectural, historic or archaeological interest and to take into account the effect of the proposals on the foregoing. Licensing provisions are dealt with under Part II of the CIA. Section 28 deals with the attachment of conditions, which can also cover the foregoing considerations. In the case of all future coal-mining proposals requiring planning permission, section 53(2) highlights the environmental duties which must now be expressly considered by planning authorities, including archaeology. Subsection 53(3) further places a requirement on applicants to have regard to these issues in the formulation of coal-mining proposals, including mitigation measures.

5.81

The Coal Mining Subsidence Act 1991 continues to apply where ancient monuments and listed buildings are damaged. Section 19 places a duty, where it is reasonably practicable and in the public interest, to restore any affected monument or listed building to a condition comparable with its former state before the subsidence damage occurred. Section 20 provides like provisions in respect of ecclesiastical property in conjunction with the Church Commissioners.

5.82

The Mines (Working Facilities and Support) Act 1966 deals with all minerals other than coal. Section 7(1) enables a person having an interest in any land who does not have sufficient private rights to protect his property to apply to the Secretary of State for Trade and Industry for restrictions to be imposed on the working of the minerals under his land and land adjacent to it to secure sufficient support for his buildings or land. Subsection 7(8) confers the same rights, respectively, to the Secretary of State for National Heritage, the Secretary of State for Wales or the relevant local authority where any building or work is an ancient monument and is in guardianship or under other protection provisions exercised by one of these public bodies.

5.83

Public utilities and statutory undertakers

Permitted development rights are given under planning legislation to those organisations providing the services generically known, historically, as public utilities and statutory undertakers. Particular archaeological considerations relevant to planning and environmental assessment are considered later in this book in Chapter 6. The following specific statutory provisions also need to be borne in mind.

5.84

The Electricity Act 1989 deals with the privatisation and re-organisation of

5.85

this industry. Section 3(3) requires the Secretary of State for Trade and Industry (and the Director General of Electricity Supply), respectively, in the discharge of their functions and when considering a licence application for a licence to generate, transmit or supply electricity, to take account of the effect on the physical environment of those activities. Section 38 and Schedule 9, paragraph 1 specifically require licence holders to have regard to the desirability of preserving natural beauty, of conserving geological or physiographical features of special interest and of protecting buildings.[3] and other objects of architectural, historic or archaeological interest. They must also do what they reasonably can to mitigate any effects which their proposals would have on these features. Paragraph 2 also requires a licence holder, within 12 months of the grant of his licence, to prepare and from time to time modify, a statement setting out the manner in which he proposes to perform his duties under paragraph 1 in consultation with, amongst others, English Heritage and Cadw.

Surprisingly, no comparable statutory requirements are to be found either in the Telecommunications Act 1984 or the Gas Act 1986.

5.86 The Water industry was privatised under the Water Act 1989. It created three new agencies: the National Rivers Authority (NRA), to which were transferred the regulatory functions of the former water authorities; the new private sector companies responsible for water alone or water and sewerage undertakings; and the Director-General of Water Services (OFWAT), who has the principal function of regulating the performance of the water and sewerage undertakers. However, a further statutory consolidation led to the repeal of the 1989 Act by the Water Consolidation (Consequential Provisions) Act 1991 and its replacement by five consolidating Acts: the Consequential Provisions Act, the Water Industry Act 1991 (WIA), the Water Resources Act 1991 (WRA) and the Land Drainage Act 1991 (LDA). A further complication, in terms of understanding, arises from the statutory re-creation and re-statement of the duties and powers of the NRA by the WRA and then its separate integration into a new Environmental Agency ("the Agency"), combining the functions of Her Majesty's Inspectorate of Pollution, the NRA and certain waste regulation authorities, under the Environment Act 1995. For the purposes of clarity, reference is still made to the NRA in this chapter although it should be borne in mind that its statutory functions under the WIA and the LDA are transferred to the Agency under section 2 of this Act.

5.87 The conservation duties imposed on the privatised water companies and the NRA are very similar in terms of their statutory framework. In respect of the former, section 3 of the WIA, whilst mirroring the approach taken by the Electricity Act 1989, specifically requires the Secretary of State for the Environment (SOSE), the Minister for Agriculture Fisheries and Food (MAFF), the Director of OFWAT and every water company to have regard, amongst other matters, to the desirability of protecting and conserving buildings,[4] sites and objects of archaeological, architectural or historic interest[5] and to the desirability of maintaining the availability to the public of any facility for visiting or inspecting the foregoing.[6] Section 16 of the

---

[3] "Building" includes any structure (Electricity Act 1989, Sched. 9, para. 1(3)).
[4] "Building" includes any structure (Water Industry Act 1991, s.3(10)).
[5] WIA s.3(2).
[6] *ibid.* s.3(3).

WRA imposes the same duties on the NRA. A *Code of Practice on Conservation, Access and Recreation* was published jointly by the SOSE, MAFF and the Welsh Office in 1989, pursuant to the power given by section 5(1) of the WIA and section 18(1) of the WRA.

The LDA 1991 deals with internal drainage boards, their supervision by the NRA and certain financial provisions. Section 61A contains the same provisions in respect of general environmental and recreational duties as are found in the WIA and the WRA. A separate Code of Practice has been published for internal drainage boards.   **5.88**

Other public bodies

Under the Coast Protection Act 1949, passed after the great floods of 1947, local authorities for each maritime district are required to maintain and improve coastal defences; and for this purpose they are given compulsory purchase powers. However, section 47(d) expressly excludes these powers from implicitly authorising or requiring any person to carry out any work or do anything in contravention of the AMAAA 1979.   **5.89**

Section 6(1) of the Land Powers (Defence) Act 1958 enables land to be used for limited training purposes by the armed forces. However, subsection 6(4) expressly excludes deemed authorisation under these powers to injure or deface any scheduled ancient monument. Given the large number of such monuments on Salisbury Plain, a major military training ground, the intent of this piece of legislation is less esoteric than may first appear to be the case.   **5.90**

6. WORLD HERITAGE SITES

A World Heritage Site (WHS) is a cultural or natural site of outstanding universal value.[7] As already explained in Chapter 3, the World Heritage Convention, adopted by UNESCO in 1972, provides for the identification and conservation of such sites and requires a World Heritage List to be established.   **5.91**

The United Kingdom became a signatory to the World Heritage Convention in 1984. Currently, there are 15 WHS in the United Kingdom, of which 12 can be considered wholly or partly archaeological: Durham Cathedral and Castle; Ironbridge Gorge; Fountains Abbey, St Mary's Church and Studley Royal Park; Stonehenge, Avebury and associated sites; Blenheim Palace and Park; the City of Bath; Hadrian's Wall Military Zone; Palace of Westminster, the Abbey of Westminster and St Margaret's Church; the Tower of London; Canterbury Cathedral with St Augustine's Abbey and St Martin's Church; the Castles and Town Walls of King Edward in Gwynedd; and Edinburgh Old and New Towns. The English WHS were nominated by the United Kingdom Government on the recommendation of the Department of the Environment   **5.92**

---

[7] PPG 15, para. 6.35. See further article by David Morgan Evans, John Pugh-Smith and John Samuels, "World Heritage Sites: Beauty Contest or Planning Constraint?" [1994] J.P.L. 503 on practical consideration of WHS. The article was written when PPG 15 was still in draft form though the final wording of paras. 2.22 and 6.35, dealing with the planning status of WHS, does not alter the conclusions of the article.

(Department of National Heritage in future advised by English Heritage). The one Welsh recommendation, Caernarfon, Gwynedd, came to the Government from the Welsh Office advised by Cadw.

5.93   Not all sites put forward by the United Kingdom have been accepted by the World Heritage Committee (WHC). For example, at their eleventh session in December 1987, which accepted Blenheim, Bath, Hadrian's Wall and the Westminster complex, it was decided to "defer" examination of the nominations for the ecclesiastical sites of Lough Erne and that for New Lanark. The examination of the Lake District was deferred until the position of cultural landscapes has been clarified. The WHC also noted that the United Kingdom had withdrawn its nomination of Diana's Peak and High Peak, St Helena and of St David's Bishop's Palace and Close.[8]

5.94   The definition of WHS within the United Kingdom shows no consistency of approach. Designated areas have often been chosen to coincide with existing boundaries of conservation areas, scheduled ancient monuments or, as at Studley Royal, with ownership by the National Trust. Equally, drawing lines on maps to define the extent of the archaeological remains or their setting, or that of historic buildings, is not always satisfactory. For example, the Neolithic causewayed enclosure called Windmill Hill is included within the Avebury WHS; but another causewayed enclosure, called Robin Hood's Ball, is excluded from the Stonehenge part of the WHS, the boundary of which does not precisely follow an Article 4 Direction Area.[9] Furthermore, recent discoveries at Avebury have uncovered important remains either side of the WHS boundaries, suggesting that they should now be extended.[10]

5.95   The significance of WHS designation in the exercise of planning controls was not formally recognised until the publication of PPG 15 in September 1994. Paragraphs 2.22 and 2.23 now highlight the international importance of a WHS as a key material consideration in the determination of planning applications and appeals including, in the case of significant development proposals affecting WHS, the preparation of a formal environmental assessment. The formulation of specific planning policies to reflect that these sites have been designated for their outstanding universal value is also encouraged.

5.96   However, the fact of WHS designation does not preclude modern development; and nowhere within the World Heritage Convention does it state otherwise. Given some of the English designations, such as the City of Bath, any embargo would be impossible as well as inappropriate to sustain,[11] words echoed by the Secretary of State when deciding, nonetheless, to overturn his Inspector's recommendation in favour of an application to quarry coal, opencast, adjacent to Hadrian's Wall.[12] This decision is also interesting

---

[8] Letter dated January 8, 1988, from the Deputy Director of UNESCO, Michael de Bonnecourse, to Mr P.H. Denton, Heritage Sponsorship Division, DOE.

[9] Article 4 of the Town and Country Planning (General Permitted Development) Order 1995 allows restrictions to be placed on permitted development which otherwise would not require the express grant of planning permission *e.g.* the erection of telephone kiosks. See further para. 6.18 below.

[10] Lord Kennet, reported in *Hansard*, H.L., October 21, 1993, pp.690–694.

[11] Appeals by Safeway plc (Ref:APP/PO105/A/91/182135), Bath FC (Rugby) Club and Tesco Stores Limited (Ref:SW/P/5116/220/4) and British Gas plc (South Western) (Ref:APP/PO105/A/92/211437 and 213419), respectively dated March 11, 1994, all in respect of rival foodstore schemes.

[12] Appeal by Coal Contractors Limited: the former Stagshaw Colliery, Grottington,

because it led to the first High Court challenge, though unsuccessfully, that the Secretary of State had rendered his reasoning obscure by making the WHS a separate issue and holding that a different level of visual intrusion would be acceptable in relation to that designation.[13] Confirmation, through PPG 15, that WHS designation is a key material consideration, also underlines the importance of establishing the planning status of a WHS in this regard.

7. HISTORIC PARKS AND GARDENS

Since 1984, certain parks and gardens of special historic interest within England have been identified by English Heritage through its Register of Parks and Gardens. The Register is a statutory document in that it was compiled under the powers given to English Heritage under Schedule 4 of the National Heritage Act 1983 which, in turn, introduced a new section 8C to the Historic Buildings and Ancient Monuments Act 1953. This provision[14] requires English Heritage, as soon as practicable after including an entry in the Register, to notify, respectively, the owner and occupier of the garden or land, the relevant county and district planning authority and the Secretary of State (for National Heritage) of its inclusion and a copy of the entry. **5.97**

The initial Register, which is currently published as a series of 44 volumes, was assembled between 1984 and 1988. Work on updating it began in 1991 with computerisation of the Register and has yet to be completed at the time of writing. The current Register is limited to the counties of England, from (former) Avon to Wiltshire, including Greater London and Greater Manchester. In Wales, Cadw is currently working on its own register, which is expected to be completed by the end of 1996 following which consultation arrangements will be introduced similar to those for England.[15] A Register for the County of Gwent has already been prepared. **5.98**

The Historic Landscapes Panel, made up of a number of leading experts on garden history, advise English Heritage on matters of general principle. The Panel also provides a second opinion on borderline or problematic cases and acts as a referral body where there is a substantial argument over a decision reached by an Inspector. The final decision on the inclusion or grading of a site is taken by the Head of Historic Parks and Gardens. **5.99**

Only parks and gardens with historic features dating from 1939 or earlier are identified in the initial Register. Physical additions to the original site area since that date are identified but are stated not to have been taken into account in the selection of individual sites. The rationale for this particular time restriction has not been explained in the Introduction to the Register. In any event, English Heritage has now adopted a 30-year cut-off in its work on the up-dated version. Where the original layout is still in evidence most parks and gardens laid out before 1820 (particularly prior to 1750) have been included. Selection of examples from 1820 onwards is more restricted and dependent upon their individual condition and aesthetic merit. Where a **5.100**

Sandhoe, Northumberland (Ref:APP/R2900/A/91/190575).

[13] *Coal Contractors Limited v. Secretary of State for the Environment* (1993) 68 P. & C.R. 285.

[14] Historic Buildings and Ancient Monuments Act 1953, ss.8C(2), (3).

[15] Circular 9/95 (*General Development Order Consolidation 1995*), App. B, paras 5, 6.

more detailed assessment is possible or required, particular attention is paid to such matters as: whether the park or garden has been influential in the development of taste through reputation or reference in literature; whether it is a representative example of a genre of layout or of the work of a designer of national stature; any association with significant historic events or persons; its reputation or reference to it in literature; or its value as part of an integral layout or town planning scheme. However, questions of ownership, management and public accessibility are excluded from consideration of historic interest.

5.101　　The Register initially identifies each site by way of core data giving the county, district, parish and Ordnance Survey grid reference. Sites are graded as those of exceptional historic interest (Grade I), those of great historic interest (Grade II*) and those of special historic interest (Grade II). The gradings are intended to reflect the importance of the most significant features of a site in comparison with other parks or gardens within England as a whole. They are independent of any listed building within the limits of the park or garden as it is recognised that the two may not be of equal importance. Both registration and grading are comparative exercises dependent on a knowledge of garden history. A total of 1085 sites are identified in the initial Register, of which 10 per cent are classified Grade I, 30 per cent Grade II* and the remaining 60 per cent Grade II. A list of the main references used in the compilation of the description is given at the end of each entry. The level of research requires sufficient detail for the main stages of a site's development to be understood and for the existence of the surviving features to be explained. Use is made of extracts from county and local histories, articles published in journals and magazines as well as specific surveys undertaken by the Centre for the Conservation of Parks and Gardens, the County Gardens Trust. The County Sites and Monuments Record (SMR) may also provide useful information.

5.102　　The initial Register was prepared without supporting maps or plans defining the boundaries of registered sites. However, this deficiency has now been remedied with site boundary maps available from English Heritage for all existing registered sites as well as new additions.[16] They seek to show the extent of the land on which the historic layout was executed. Main buildings, including stables, lodges and follies as well as kitchen gardens, forming part of the original design are included but not normally churches or farms nor areas laid out purely for agriculture, silviculture or other economic purposes. Once these historic boundaries have been identified they are then compared with the site's present condition. Areas are then omitted which no longer include the essential character and fabric of the "designed landscape". Where, for example, parkland trees are missing, inclusion of that particular area will depend upon whether this omission amounts to complete eradica-

---

[16] The Inspector's report on completing M25 MSA proposals, affecting the setting of Grade I listed Hill Hall, Epping, Essex (with Grade II registered park) (E1/J1535/2/4/05–10), records English Heritage's admission that maps were only drawn following the hurricane in 1987 to aid grant applications for recompense. Specifically, when this was done for Hill Hall, the site may not even have been visited and the 1987/8 boundary may have been excluded due to despoilation during the construction of the M25. A boundary extension in 1993 was, nonetheless, endorsed as appropriate by the Assessor (on architectural and listed buildings issues) in his report to the SOSE.

tion, or merely loss of detail within a framework that has largely survived which, in theory, is capable of being reinstated. Where, occasionally, areas of the site exist which are regarded as being detached parts but were consciously landscaped as part of the wider design, these are then recorded in the site description and identified as "outliers" on the site boundary plan.

English Heritage readily acknowledges that the main purpose of the **5.103** Register is "to identify and draw attention to the best historic parks and gardens which constitute such an important part of the cultural heritage of England", that it does not "provide statutory protection for such sites, neither does it imply any additional powers to control development and work to them beyond normal planning powers".[17] Furthermore, the subjectivity of the assessment process is tacitly accepted by the further acknowledgements that "the accuracy of the site boundary maps depends upon good research", that both the maps and the site descriptions are open to revision as knowledge of the history of a site increases and that there may be parks or gardens which have been overlooked. Within them lies an inherent but inevitable tension between the weight that should be given to an entry in the Register and its application to a specific development control proposal; for the emphasis of the Register on the historic aspects of parks and gardens necessarily ignores the changing nature of the overall landscape both within and without the site boundary as a result of management as well as land use practices along both boundaries.[18]

No additional statutory controls follow from the inclusion of a site in the **5.104** Register; though many sites will either form part of the setting of a listed building or fall within a conservation area designation. Local planning authorities are now specifically required to consult with English Heritage on planning applications affecting Grade I and Grade II* sites.[19] An accompanying Direction also requests that all planning applications which affect sites are dealt with by the Garden History Society.[20] PPG 15 also confirms that the effect of a proposed development on a registered park or garden or its setting will be a material consideration in the determination of a planning application.[21] However, there remains a need for more specific and substantial guidance.

8. HISTORIC BATTLEFIELDS

English Heritage was persuaded to start compiling a list after the Department **5.105** of Transport won permission in 1991 to construct the A1–M1 link (now A14) affecting the site of the battle of Naseby (1645), despite opposition from conservationists and historians. The need for such a register, with boundary delineation has also been highlighted through a High Court case[22] in which

---

[17] *The Register of Parks and Gardens of Special Historic Interest in England: Notes on Compilation and Use.*

[18] See further "Historic Parks and Gardens: A review of Legislation, Policy Guidance and Significant Court and Appeal Decisions" by David Lambert and Vincent Sherlock [1995] J.P.L. 563.

[19] Town and Country Planning (General Development Procedure) Order 1995, art. 10(1), Table, para. (o) and Circular 9/95, App. B para. 4.

[20] Circular 9/95, App. B, para. 5 and App. C.

[21] PPG 15, para. 2.24.

[22] *Robert Hitchins (Builders) Limited v. Secretary of State for the Environment*

the appropriateness of a new housing site turned, in part, on whether it embraced the real battlefield of Tewkesbury (1471) or only the site of a skirmish.

5.106   In preparing the English Heritage Register, a consultant from the National Army Museum investigated 69 candidates. For each selected battlefield, a small panel of experts considered whether the fighting constituted a battle or a lesser level of engagement. Furthermore, the engagement must have involved recognised military units. They then looked at the extent of the surviving physical and documentary evidence to define the geographical area within which the battle took place. Three further criteria were then applied: the political significance of the engagement; its military historical significance; the biographical significance (*i.e.* was it the crowning glory of a military career, or was a famous leader killed or captured?) The reliability of the detailed evidence for each battle was then considered. The commentary to the Register asserts that "where the evidence of documents, archaeology, topography and landscape history was sufficient, the outer reasonable limit to the area within which the bulk of the fighting took place has been defined as the battlefield area. In those cases where the general location of the battle was known but where the evidence did not allow a boundary to be drawn, we have added the engagement to an appendix to the Register as the 'site of' a battle".[23]

5.107   Forty-three sites[24] have been included in the initial register which was published in June 1995. Each entry in the Register is said to be based on the best available evidence. It includes a map of the battlefield area showing the position of the armies and the features which were part of the original battleground. The Register goes on to state that "these maps are intended to be the starting point for battlefield conservation by identifying the most visually sensitive areas. They highlight the most valuable features that should be conserved for understanding the battle and, where appropriate, emphasised for visitors in displays or information boards. They also make clear the extent of public access".

[1995].

[23] *The Register of Historic Battlefields*, English Heritage, June 1995.

[24] (1) Maldon, Essex; (2) Stamford Bridge, North Yorks. (1066); (3) Hastings, East Sussex (1066); (4) Northallerton, North Yorks. (1138); (5) Lewes, East Sussex (1264); (6) Evesham, Hereford and Worcester (1265); (7) Myton, North Yorks. (1319); (8) Boroughbridge, North Yorks. (1322); (9) Halidon Hill, Northumberland (1333); (10) Neville's Cross, Co. Durham (1346); (11) Otterburn, Northumberland (1388); (12) Homildon Hill, Northumberland (1333); (13) Shrewsbury, Shropshire (1403); (14) Blore Heath, Staffs (1459); (15) Northampton (1460); (16) Towton, North Yorks (1461); (17) Barnet, North London (1471); (18) Tewkesbury, Glos. (1471); (19) Bosworth, Leics. (1485); (20) Stoke Field, Notts. (1487); (21) Flodden, Northumberland (1513); (22) Solway Moss, Cumbria (1542); (23) Newburn Ford, Tyne & Wear (1640); (24) Edgehill, Warwicks. (1642); (25) Braddock Down, Cornwall (1642); (26) Stratton, Cornwall (1643); (27) Hopton Heath, Staffs. (1643); (28) Adwalton Moor, West Yorks. (1643); (29) Landsdown Hill, Bath (1643); (30) Newbury, Berks. (1643); (31) Roundway Down, Wilts. (1643); (32) Winceby, Lincs. (1643); (33) Chalgrove, Oxon. (1643); (34) Cheriton, Hants. (1644); (35) Cropredy Bridge, Oxon. (1644); (36) Marston Moor, North Yorks. (1644); (37) Nantwich, Cheshire (1644); (38) Naseby, Northants. (1645); (39) Langport, Somerset (1456); (40) Rowton Heath, Cheshire (1645); (41) Stow-on-the-Wold, Glos. (1646); (42) Worcester (1651); (43) Sedgemoor, Somerset (1685).

PPG 15 now confirms that the effect of any development on a registered **5.108** site included within English Heritage's Register of Historic Battlefields will form a material consideration to be taken into account in determining planning applications such that development should be avoided except where there is no alternative.[25] Pragmatically, the commentary to the Register recognises that as the land was often farmland at the time of the battle, rarely will identifiable remains now be found due to continued agrarian activities. It states that "English Heritage does not wish to prevent such changes, nor do we advise the 'restoration' of battlefields, as for the countryside in general, continued management is both desirable and necessary". The commentary continues in this theme by stating: "Any proposal for development, of course, has to be considered in the context of the specific circumstances. Nevertheless, there are four themes which can guide the conservation of battlefields for current and future generations". These are then listed as being authenticity, visual amenity, integrity and accessibility. Whilst it is legitimate in this context to recommend that large-scale changes to battlefield topography (*e.g.* quarrying or the creation of a golf course) should be avoided the commentary then contradicts earlier remarks about the evolution of the landscape by suggesting that "cumulatively, small-scale changes can, over time, have a similarly damaging effect". Likewise, under the heading "visual amenity", the commentary recommends that buildings sited in key views, tree plantations or other barriers can be disruptive to the ability to appreciate the course of the battle; though it recognises carefully placed screening can enhance the look of battlefields and that the grouping of new buildings with existing structures can help reduce their visual impact on the landscape.

The commentary concludes that local planning authorities are the best **5.109** agents for ensuring that battlefields are conserved. Since not all battlefields are appropriately included within conservation area designation, it must be assumed that English Heritage hope that, with the guidance now found in PPG 15, the development control system will ensure that adequate protection is maintained. However, development is permissible within a conservation area provided that it does not cause harm.[26] Likewise, development is acceptable within a WHS; but unlike a WHS, the fact of battlefield designation is not a major or overriding consideration but must be weighed against other material considerations.

9. HISTORIC LANDSCAPES

At present, other than through designation as a conservation area,[27] pro- **5.110** tection of an historic landscape must rely on its intrinsic qualities. Nationally, these are recognised either by status as a National Park or an Area of Outstanding Natural Beauty.[28] At county level, the policy concept of

---

[25] PPG 15, para. 2.25.

[26] Planning (Listed Buildings and Conservation Areas) Act 1990, s.70(2); *South Lakeland DC v. SOSE* [1992] 2 W.L.R. 204.

[27] Planning (Listed Buildings and Conservation Areas) Act 1990, s.69; PPG 15, paras 4.2–4.14.

[28] National Parks and Access to the Countryside Act 1949, ss.5,87; PPG 7, paras 3.2–3.11. There are curently 10 National Parks (7 in England and 3 in Wales) and 39 designated AONBs which differ from National Parks in that the promotion of recreation is not an objective.

Special Landscape Areas[29] is now frequently used whilst at district level, recent years have seen a proliferation of "Areas of Local Landscape Significance" or "Importance". It is Government policy that "the country-side should be preserved for its own sake and that non-renewable and natural resources should be afforded protection".[30] Its status, in itself, is a material planning consideration although special statutory designations will increase the weight to be attached to its preservation[31]; though Environmentally Sensitive Areas (designated under the Agriculture Act 1986), whilst promoting policies and programmes to areas of special landscape, wildlife or historic interest, do not affect the status of the area in terms of national planning policies or development control regulations.[32]

5.111 PPG 15 encourages planning authorities to take account of the historic dimension of the landscape as a whole, rather than concentrate on selected areas,[33] through planning policies to protect the most important components and to encourage development that is consistent with maintaining its overall historic character by strengthening the rural economy through environmentally sensitive diversification.[34] PPG 15 goes on to advise that "the whole of the landscape, to varying degrees and in different ways, is an archaeological and historic artefact, the product of complex historic processes and past land-use".[35]

On the other hand, the landscape is a constantly changing feature, not least as a result of modern agricultural practices as well as through moves away from an entirely food-based approach to farming. Indeed, the Countryside Commission's Landscape Assessment Guidance[36] recognises that the term "landscape" is not just a purely visual phenomenon "because its character relies closely on its physiography and its history. Hence, in addition to the scenic or visual dimension, there are a whole range of other dimensions including geology, topography, soils, ecology, archaeology, landscape history, land use, architecture and cultural associations" which have influenced the formation of the landscape.

5.112 Landscape assessment is the general term used for the process by which a landscape is described, classified and evaluated. The descriptive process is a comparatively straightforward method of collecting and presenting information about the landscape in a systematic manner. As an example of the material to be included in a checklist of landscape elements and features, the Guidance suggests the use of historical and ecological indicators.[37] These were utilised by the Commission in its earlier Warwickshire Landscapes Project[38] to help distinguish between "ancient" and "planned" landscapes

---

[29] PPG 7, para. 2.1.

[30] *ibid.* para. 2.1.

[31] *ibid.* para. 3.1.

[32] Agricultural Act 1986, s.18; PPG 7, para. 3.18.

[33] PPG 15, para. 2.26.

[34] *ibid.* para. 2.26.

[35] *ibid.* para. 6.40

[36] (1993) known as "CCP423", pp. 4–5. See also, *Guidelines for Landscape and Visual Impact Assessment* (1995), published jointly by the Landscape Institute and the Institute of Environmental Assessment, which deals with the evaluation of specific development projects.

[37] CCP423, p.20

[38] *Assessment and conservation of landscape chartacter—The Warwickshire Landscapes Project approach*, Countryside Commision (CCP332), p.14.

arising from the use of hedges and walls to define fields in farmed landscapes. Classification requires a relatively objective recording and analysis of the intrinsic qualities of the landscape itself. Evaluation, on the other hand, involves a greater degree of subjectivity and judgment.

Perhaps it was with these considerations in mind that English Heritage stopped short of promoting the production of a register of "wider historic landscapes",[39] though Cadw, its Welsh counterpart, in collaboration with the international Council on Monuments and Sites and the Countryside Council for Wales, has committed itself to such a task in the form of Part 2 of the Register of Landscapes, Parks and Gardens of Special Historic Interest in Wales.[40] The Countryside Commission is, however, funding research into a landscape character programme that includes, amongst its aims, the identification of valuable historic landscapes. The objective is not to achieve a further category of designation but rather the provision of better information to target specific grants for landscape conservation. Although the outcome of the project will be advisory it could be used by local planning authorities to support further proposals for local landscape designations.   **5.113**

Certainly, as an emerging policy concept, the "wider historic landscape" is still in its early stages of development. It should be viewed with care by local planning authorities as a development control tool and with apprehension by the private sector as a non-statutory method of restraint. Conservation of an historic landscape depends on active land management.[41] Accordingly, future regulation will need to provide both enhancement opportunities as well as control of inappropriate development.

10. HISTORIC BUILDINGS

Archaeologists have long taken an interest in historic buildings and, in practice, would not differentiate buildings from other aspects of archaeology. After all, standing buildings are only better preserved examples of ruins or fragmentary below-ground remains, and a wide range of recording techniques and analytical methods exist.[42] However, the extensive legislation and guidance on historic buildings is outside the scope of this book and is comprehensively examined elsewhere.[43]   **5.114**

---

[39] PPG15, para. 6.40. However, a pilot project by the Cornwall Archaeological Unit and sponsored by English Heritage, has produced a series of "historic landscape maps" for the whole of Cornwall. It has been used by the County Archaeologist to guide his advice to planners to identify, within each zone, the historic processes that have shaped it, typical archaeological features, its vulnerability and its potential for amenity and research. It is also intended to provide a framework for information in the SMR. With the encouragement of English Heritage, similar maps are now in the course of preparation, including the former county of Avon, as well as smaller historic areas, such as the Gwent Levels and the leadmining region of the Peak District. However, these "historic landscape maps" will be separate from the Countryside Commision's "countryside character maps".

[40] *Protecting Our Heritage* (1996), para. 5.14. "... The Cadw approach, like buildings, lists and grades individual historic landscapes of special importance, *e.g.* the Black Mountains and the Gower Peninsula." See also draft TAN(W)5.

[41] PPG 15, para. 2.26.

[42] Wood Buildings Archaeology: Applications in Practice *(1994).*

[43] R.N. Suddards and J.M. Hargreaves, *Listed Buildings* (3rd ed., Sweet & Maxwell,

5.115   Although historic buildings have separate statutory protection under the Planning (Listed Buildings and Conservation Areas) Act 1990, some are also designated as Scheduled Ancient Monuments. These are often unoccupied buildings such as medieval barns or dovecotes, but can include bridges, urban buildings and industrial monuments and cases have arisen where scheduling has pre-dated listing procedures. As the former introduces closer controls, for example over repairs, scheduling takes priority such that listed buildings controls do not apply.[44] PPG 15 also advises that their overlap is being addressed by the Monuments Protection Programme (MPP), the current national survey by English Heritage of all known archaeological sites, the primary intention of which is to review existing schedulings and to identify further sites and monuments which may be suitable for scheduling.

5.116   Many other buildings are either of intrinsic archaeological interest or stand on ground which also contains archaeological remains. PPG 15, following the guidance in PPG 16, advises that appropriate assessment of the archaeological implications of development proposals should take place before applications are determined, including adequate arrangements for the recording of remains which would be lost in the course of subsequent building works.[45]

5.117   It should not have taken the emergence of a separate PPG to remind those concerned with the built heritage that old buildings are as much an archaeological source as buried remains. In order to manage them effectively there has to be an understanding of their individual significance relative to other examples regionally and/or nationally. Central to any programme of repair, restoration or demolition will be the recording of the main structural elements. However, account should be taken also of below-ground aspects of the building such as earlier floors and foundations or other buried remains on the site which may be affected.

11. ECCLESIASTICAL BUILDINGS

5.118   In English law, an ecclesiastical building is one which is owned and used for religious purposes. It includes all Christian religions and may include non-Christian faiths.[46] Partial use for religious purposes is sufficient.

A narrower definition is sometimes used to restrict ecclesiastical property to that owned by the Church of England. For example, a detailed definition is provided for the purposes of section 51 of AMAAA, as:

> "land belonging to an ecclesiastical benefice of the Church of England, or being or forming part of a church subject to the jurisdiction of a bishop of any diocese of the Church of England or the site of such a church, or being or forming part of a burial ground subject to such jurisdiction".[47]

5.119   An ecclesiastical building (in the wide sense) which is for the time being

---

1996).

[44] PPG 15, para. 6.34.

[45] *ibid.* para. 2.15.

[46] *Attorney-General, ex rel Bedfordshire County Council v. Trustees of Howard United Reform Church, Bedford* [1976] A.C. 363.

[47] AMAAA, s.51(5).

used for ecclesiastical purposes cannot be a monument under AMAAA.[48] It may not, therefore, become an ancient, scheduled or protected monument. Ecclesiastical buildings no longer so used, their remains or other land (even if used for ecclesiastical purposes) may, however, be monuments.

Ecclesiastical properties are subject to the planning regime and may be listed. However, church buildings of the Church of England, the Church in Wales, the Roman Catholic Church, the Methodist Church, the Baptist Union of Great Britain, the Baptist Union of Wales, the United Reform Church, the Church of Scotland, the Free Church of Scotland and the Free Presbyterian Church have the benefit of the "ecclesiastical exemption".[49] This disapplies listed building control: the need for listed building consent; powers of temporary listing; the compulsory acquisition of listed buildings, urgent works to preserve them and the offence of causing damage to listed buildings.[50] Conservation area consent, for demolitions, is not required.[51] The exemption is for churches with adequate internal rules for assessing and controlling works. A code of practice governs works benefiting from the ecclesiastical exemption.

5.120

Faculty jurisdiction

A faculty is a special licence or dispensation authorising a person to do something that could not otherwise be lawfully done. The jurisdiction extends to Church of England churches and churchyards (whether or not consecrated), consecrated burial grounds and buildings licensed for worship according to the Church of England's rites.[52]

5.121

A faculty is required before alterations are made to fabric or contents within the jurisdiction. This includes making an addition. Archdeacons may issue certificates for repairs and decorations,[53] but otherwise faculties are issued by the chancellor of the consistory court of the diocese. No applications are required for some small matters, such as minor repairs. Because of the scope of faculty jurisdiction, a faculty will normally be required for invasive archaeological investigation.

Following the report of the Faculty Jurisdiction Commission of the General Synod in 1984, *The Continuing Care of Churches and Cathedrals*, a separate regime was established for Church of England cathedrals. This was introduced by the Care of Cathedrals Measure 1990. Approval is required:

5.122

(a) for works which would materially affect the architectural, archaeological, artistic or historic character of the cathedral or of any archaeological remains[54] within its precincts;

---

[48] AMAAA, s.61(8).

[49] Planning (Listed Buildings and Conservation Areas) Act 1990, s.60; Ecclesiastical Exemption (Listed Buildings and Conservation Areas) Order 1994 (S.I. 1994 No. 1771).

[50] 1990 Act, s.60(2).

[51] *ibid.* s.75(1)(b).

[52] Care of Churches and Ecclesiastical Jurisdiction Measure 1991, s.11.

[53] Faculty Jurisdiction Measure 1964, s.12.

[54] "Archaeological remains" means "the remains of any building, work or artefact, including any trace or sign of the previous existence of the building, work or artefact in question" (Care of Cathedrals Measure 1990, s.20(1)).

(b) for the disposal of any object of architectural, archaeological, artistic or historic interest vested in the chapter of the cathedral;

(c) for any permanent addition which would materially affect the architectural, archaeological, artistic or historic character of the cathedral.[55]

5.123 Approval must be sought from the Cathedral Fabrics Commission for England for any act that involves the "disturbance or destruction of any archaeological remains within the precincts of the cathedral".[56] This would include any intrusive archaeological investigation. Other significant acts, including those that the Fabrics Commission declares are of special archaeological interest, require approval from the Fabrics Commission.[57] Other applications for approval are determined by the fabric advisory committee of the cathedral.[58]

5.124 Draft guidance entitled *The Management of Cathedral Archaeological Projects: Principles and Procedures* has been produced by the Fabrics Commission. The Fabrics Commission will balance the desirability of preserving important archaeological remains undisturbed with the desirability of supporting projects designed to further the worship and mission of the cathedral. Archaeological assessments or evaluations are required before the Fabrics Commission will determine any proposal.

The Fabrics Commission has a duty to promote co-operation with archaeological organisations in England.[59] It can also hold conferences for, amongst others, archaeological consultants.[60] Its membership must include someone with special knowledge of archaeology.[61]

5.125 Each cathedral has an archaeological consultant, unless the Fabrics Commission considers that the archaeological significance of the cathedral does not justify it.[62] The archaeological consultant and the cathedral architect produce a report every five years on the works needed to be carried out on the cathedral.[63]

---

[55] Care of Cathedrals Measure 1990, s.2(1).

[56] *ibid.* s.6(1)(a)(iii).

[57] *ibid.* s.6(1)(b).

[58] *ibid.* s.6(1). This includes archaeological recording in conjunction with the routine repair and conservation of the cathedral (*Draft Guidance on Cathedral Archaeological Projects*).

[59] Care of Cathedrals Measure 1990, s.3(2)(c).

[60] *ibid.* s.11(4)(b).

[61] *ibid.* Sched. 1, para. 3(g).

[62] *ibid.* s.12(2).

[63] *ibid.* s.14(1).

6. Development Controls

1. INTRODUCTION

The British system for controlling the use of land and buildings is one of the **6.1**
most sophisticated and complicated in the world. Its qualities and complexities arise from the ability of government, at all levels, to regulate not only
the use of land but also the form, layout and design of most of the environment in which we live. This level of control, in the public interest, requires
a balance to be maintained between competing interests. Furthermore, constraints in land supply and the consequent need for its re-use, through
re-development, make it inevitable that archaeological issues will arise.
However, in the main, archaeology will only be one consideration which will
need to be weighed in the decision-making process of granting permission. **6.2**

The bulk of the material within this chapter deals with the operation of the
planning system and the issues, both of law and practice, that directly affect
those concerned with archaeological matters. Consideration is also given, principally within the section on environmental assessment, to other projects,
such as trunk roads, where the same issues often arise. However, the same techniques of investigation and analysis will be required from the archaeologist.

2. THE PLANNING SYSTEM

"Planning control" in the legal sense is the creature of statute. Although **6.3**
limited measures already existed, the first comprehensive code was created
by the Town and Country Planning Act 1947 which introduced a uniform
and mandatory system of development control. Current legislation, for the
purposes of this book, is found in the Town and Country Planning Act 1990
(TCPA), as amended by the Planning and Compensation Act 1991, other than
in respect of listed buildings and conservation areas, which are covered by a
separate Act passed in 1990.[1] Unless statutorily exempt, all forms of
development, including changes in the use of land and buildings, will require
planning permission.

In order to achieve uniformity in decision-making, planning control is **6.4**
heavily regulated by subordinate legislation in the form of parliamentary
orders, directions, regulations and rules. It is also extensively influenced by
policy. At law, national advice, published in Circulars, Planning Policy
Guidance Notes (PPGs), Mineral Policy Guidance Notes (MPGs) and

---

[1] Planning (Listed Buildings and Conservation Areas) Act 1990.

Regional Policy Guidance Notes (RPGs), is treated as a "material consideration" in the decision-making process to which considerable weight must be attached.[2] Local planning authorities (LPAs) are also required to publish their own strategic and local policy in the form of Structure Plans, Unitary Development Plans (UDPs) and Local Plans[3] depending on the level and function of the authority in question. These plans must all be in general conformity with one another so that a tiered policy structure is achieved. Once they have been formally adopted they are known as "the development plan". Planning policy that is going through the various stages in the statutory process leading to adoption is treated as a "material consideration", the importance of which increases as it passes each stage from initial consultation to final modification.

6.5   It remains national advice that the planning system should operate on the basis that applications for development should be allowed, having regard to the development plan and other material considerations, unless the proposed development would cause demonstrable harm to interests of acknowledged importance.[4] Sections 54A and 70(2) of the TCPA require decision-makers to look first at the relevant policies contained in the development plan. Where a development plan is up-to-date and contains a specific policy dealing with a particular site there is a legal presumption that the planning decision should only be made in accordance with that policy unless there are material considerations which indicate otherwise.[5] Other "material considerations", for example, the absence of a specific policy in the development plan in respect of the application site or the existance of a rival scheme, are also weighed as part of the decision-making process.[6]

6.6   The responsibility for most planning decisions rests with the LPAs. In non-metropolitan areas within England, planning functions are split between county and district councils, the former dealing with strategic and specialist fields (e.g. minerals and waste) and the latter with all development control decisions except those relating to county matters. Statutory consultation procedures are set up between each tier to ensure that proper communication and consistency of decision-making is achieved. Metropolitan and unitary authorities (both in England and Wales), including the London boroughs, essentially fulfil both functions. National Parks and urban development areas have their own planning authorities.

6.7   The Secretary of State for the Environment ("the SOSE") and his counterpart for Wales ("the SOSW") retain overall responsibility. However,

---

[2] PPG 1 (1992), paras 20–22. The policy of other government departments is also treated as a material consideration (see e.g. Kent County Council v. SOSE [1976] P.&C.R.70—policy of DOE), provided that another department has not, in effect, dictated the planning decision (see e.g. Lavender (H) and Son Ltd v. M.H.L.G. [1970] 3 All E.R. 871).

[3] TCPA 1990, Pt. II.

[4] PPG 1, para. 5. A replacement PPG 1 was published for consultation in July 1996. Amongst the proposed changes is the removal of this presumption in favour of development.

[5] See further PPG 1, paras 25–28 for the specific applications of this principle.

[6] PPG 1, para. 23: "In principle ... any consideration which relates to the use and development of land is capable of being a planning consideration. Whether a particular consideration falling within that broad class is material in any given case will depend on the circumstances (Stringer v. MHLG 1971)". The leading practitioner's text, to which further reference should be made, is the Encyclopedia of Planning, Law and Practice (6 volumes) (Sweet & Maxwell).

because of the system of deregulation and delegation now operated they will only become involved where subordinate legislation specifically requires or gives a discretion. Accordingly, the SOSE and SOSW will usually only become the decision-maker (either through the regional Government Offices or the Welsh Office) where the planning decision concerns a project of major significance (*e.g.* the proposed Terminal Five at Heathrow Airport). This discretion to "call-in" a planning application is a wide-ranging one but based on certain published criteria that recognise not only the size but also the significance (and controversy) of the project.[7] Ordinarily, a public inquiry is held, the report and recommendation from which form the basis for the written decision by the respective Secretary of State ("the decision letter").

Where the initial decision is made by the LPA unsuccessful applicants also have a right of appeal to the SOSE, who effectively decides the application afresh, albeit with direction from both sides as to the material issues.[8] In addition a right of appeal exists for non-determination. Save with the applicant's express written agreement, the LPA is required to determine a valid planning application within eight weeks of its receipt,[9] failing which the applicant will be entitled to assume that there has been a "deemed refusal", thereby entitling him to appeal to the SOSE. Where an application is taken to appeal, there is a requirement upon the LPA to produce "sound and clearcut" reasons for refusal to explain why planning permission should not be granted; and whilst there is no "burden of proof", as in civil litigation, the LPA will be expected to defend them with appropriate evidence.[10] Equally, the appellant must pursue his case with sufficient supporting evidence. **6.8**

Whilst normally the principal parties are expected to bear their own costs, failure to fulfil the foregoing requirements can sometimes lead to an award of costs being made if the behaviour in question is considered to be unreasonable.[11] In the context of archaeology, save where the expertise is found "in house", the LPA will often be relying upon the advice of the County Archaeologist acting in the capacity of a statutory consultee. Such arrangements do not remove the responsibility of the planning officer to ensure that the reason for refusal can be fully supported at appeal as an objection to the principle of development rather than compromised, as an issue, by way of a suitable planning condition and obligation.[12] Since the publication of PPG 16 in November 1990, the majority of appeals which have raised archaeological issues, have failed due to the appellant's initial failure to follow the advice in PPG 16 to carry out a desk-top study or subsequent field evaluation to confirm the likelihood of important remains and their effects on the proposal.[13] Failure to heed written warnings, in this regard, can also put the appellant at risk as to costs.[14] **6.9**

The appeal decision is always given in written form ("the decision letter"). **6.10**

---

[7] TCPA, s.77 and Cm. 43 (1986).

[8] TCPA, s.78.

[9] Town and Country Planning (General Development Procedure) Order 1995 (GDPO), art. 20(2).

[10] *Pye (Oxford) Estates Limited v. SOSE* [1982] J.P.L. 575.

[11] See generally Circular 8/93 (*Awards of Costs incurred in Planning (etc.) Proceedings*) and *R. v. Secretary of State for the Environment, ex p. North Norfolk D.C.* [1994] 2 P.L.R. 78—"unreasonable" means unreasonable in the ordinary sense.

[12] Circular 8/93, Annex 3, paras 9–11.

[13] See paras 6.90 to 6.94, below.

[14] Circular 8/93, Annex 3, para. 6.

Members of the Planning Inspectorate, a quasi-judicial organisation that currently holds the status of a government executive agency, decide all appeals unless the determination is made by the SOSE or the SOSW, in which event it will be based on an inspector's report. The Planning Inspectorate is drawn largely from the ranks of local government officers with expertise in planning and related disciplines. An inspector's function is "inquisitorial" rather than "adversarial". In consequence, the law recognises that his or her opinion and judgment, particularly on matters of aesthetics, should prevail save in exceptional circumstances.[15] Where the application raises highly technical issues, an expert assessor will often be appointed to assist the Inspectorate. The assessor's views are usually communicated by way of a separate report. The bulk of appeals are dealt with by way of written representations.[16] Oral representations can, however, be made either by way of an informal hearing[17] or by formal public inquiry.[18]

6.11   A further right of appeal against the decision lies to the High Court under section 288(1) of the TCPA but only on a point of law. Otherwise, the validity of the decision letter cannot be questioned in any other proceedings whatsoever.[19] The statutory grounds of challenge are limited to establishing an error of law either that the decision is not within the powers of the TCPA or, more usually, that the relevant requirements were not complied with (e.g. a failure to give adequate reasons) in which event substantial prejudice must be established. Even if the grounds are made out the court has a discretion not to grant relief by quashing the decision letter unless there is a real possibility that the matter would have been decided differently.[20]

3. PERMITTED DEVELOPMENT

6.12   Planning permission is required for the carrying out of any development of land.[21] "Development" is defined by section 55(1) of the TCPA as "the carrying out of building, engineering, mining and other operations in, on, over or under land, or the making of any material change in the use of any buildings or other land".[22] For the avoidance of doubt, certain matters are expressly identified, in section 55(2), as not constituting development. These

---

[15] e.g. Rockhold Limited v. SOSE [1986] J.P.L. 130; Ainley v. SOSE [1987] J.P.L. 33.
[16] i.e. 85%; see the Town and Country Planning (Appeals) (Written Representations Procedure) Regulations 1987.
[17] Circular 10.88, Annex 2: "Planning Appeal—Code of Practice for Hearings".
[18] Town and Country Planning (Inquiries Procedure) Rules 1992; Circular 24/92, especially Annex—"Good Practice at Planning Inquiries".
[19] TCPA, s.284.
[20] Bolton M.B.C. v. SOSE [1990] 61 P. & C.R. 343; [1991] J.P.L. 598.
[21] TCPA, s.57(1).
[22] "Building operations" includes rebuilding, structural alterations of or additions to buildings, including demolition, except in certain prescribed cases and any other operations normally undertaken by a person carrying on the business of a builder" (TCPA, s.55(1A)). "Engineering operations" includes the formation and laying out of a means of access to highways. "Land" means any corporeal hereditament (i.e. landed property), including a building. "Building" includes any structure or erection of any part of a building but not plant or machinery comprised in a building (or, under the GPDO 1995, any gate, wall, fence or other means of enclosure (TCPA, s.336(1)).

include maintenance or improvement works carried out by a local highway authority to, and within the boundaries of a road, the breaking open of streets (etc.) for the inspection, repair or renewal of sewers, mains, pipes, cables (etc.) by a local authority or a statutory undertaker and the use of any building or other land within the curtilate of a dwelling house for any purpose incidental to the enjoyment of that house as a dwelling house.[23] Furthermore, certain matters are expressly stated as not requiring planning permission, for example, the resumption on the expiration of temporary permission of a previous use[24] whilst other activities, although in breach of planning control, become lawful after a period of time.[25]

Accordingly, any building operation or change of use which does not fall   **6.13** within the foregoing exceptions will require planning permission. Failure to secure planning permission carries the sanction that enforcement action may be taken by the LPA and lead, ultimately, to criminal punishment. This sanction covers not only development which is carried out without planning permission but also development which fails to comply with any condition or other limitation placed upon an existing permission.[26]

However, in order to remove the necessity of applying for planning   **6.14** permission in every instance, section 59 of the TCPA grants the Secretary of State power to make development orders granting planning permission. These regulations are currently found in the Town and Country Planning (General Permitted Development Order) 1995 (GPDO). Schedule 2 to the GPDO sets out 33 categories of development which are permitted subject to certain conditions. These include diverse uses from amusement parks to toll road facilities, minor operations and temporary uses, agricultural buildings and operations, development under local or private Acts and Orders and by statutory undertakers and other public bodies, including, for example, the National Rivers Authority, the Coal Authority and English Heritage.[27]

The term "statutory undertaker" is used now to describe a variety of   **6.15** companies and organisations which are concerned with the provision of infrastructure and transport services.[28] Whilst the programme of privatisation during the 1980s and early 1990s has led to the definition ceasing to apply to telecommunications, electricity, gas and water, the providers of these services continue to be deemed to be statutory undertakers for the

---

[23] These respective "permitted development" rights are further clarified in Pts. 1, 9–13 of the GPDO.

[24] TCPA, ss.57(2), (3), 7(5).

[25] TCPA, ss.171B(1), (2) limit the period for enforcement to four years against building, engineering, mining or other operations (from the date when the operations were substantially complete) and to use of a building as a single dwelling house. In all other cases, the period is 10 years (TCPA, s.171B(3)).

[26] See further para. 6.42 below.

[27] "Development" by or on behalf of English Heritage is permitted in respect of any building or monument under guardianship or owned, controlled or managed by them, for the following activities: (a) maintenance, repair or restoration (but no extensions); (b) erection of protective screens, fences or covers (for up to six months or such longer period as may be agreed in writing with the LPA); (c) preservation works to stabilise ground conditions by any cliff, watercourse or the coastline.

[28] A statutory undertaker is a person authorised by any enactment to carry on any railway, light railway, tramway, road transport, water transport, canal, inland navigation, dock, harbour, pier or lighthouse undertaking or any undertaking for the supplying of hydraulic power and any relevant airport operation (TCPA, s.262).

purposes of the TCPA with all the attendant advantages. However, their permitted development rights are limited to "operational land".[29] Where planning permission is not deemed to be granted then the statutory undertaker must make a planning application in the usual way.

6.16 Generally, a local authority will apply to itself for planning permission; but in so doing it cannot exclude the public from the relevant committee meeting.[30] Following consultation and publicity,[31] the Secretary of State may "call-in" the application and determine it himself if it is of particular significance or controversy. The need for an environmental assessment, where appropriate, is maintained.[32]

6.17 The Crown, which includes government departments, is not subject to the provisions of the TCPA in respect of development carried out on Crown land by itself or its agents. Whilst its buildings may be listed,[33] they are formally immune from the need for listed building consent.[34] However, it has been the practice for some years for consultation to take place with local planning authorities about development proposals, especially where land is the subject of disposal, and for planning obligations to be imposed as appropriate.[35]

6.18 Permitted development rights can be withdrawn by direction of the SOSE, or the LPA with the approval of the SOSE.[36] Colloquially known as an "article 4 direction", it can either exclude all permitted development within a particular area or specific forms anywhere within the LPA's administrative jurisdiction.[37] Certain development by statutory undertakers, principally telecommunications, cannot be so restricted nor development undertaken in an emergency.[38] The power is prospective so cannot be used to withdraw permission for development already carried out.[39] Where an application for express permission is subsequently refused or made subject to condition other than those required by the GPDO, compensation can be claimed from the LPA.[40] The use of an article 4 Direction should only be exercised in

---

[29] TCPA, s.263(1) defines "operational land" as being land which is (a) used for the purpose of carrying on the undertaking and (b) in which an interest is held for that purpose.

[30] Local Government Act 1972, s.100 and the Local Government Access to Information (Variation) Order 1992.

[31] See further Town and Country Planning Regulations 1992 and Circular 19/92 and Circular 3/95 (*Permitted Development and Environmental Assessment*).

[32] Town and Country Planning (Assessment of Environmental Effects) (Amendment) Regulations 1992.

[33] Planning (Listed Buildings and Conservation Areas) Act 1990, s.1.

[34] *ibid.* s.83.

[35] See TCPA, ss.299, 299A and Circular 18/84 (Crown Land and Crown Development). Proposed changes, following the publication of the DNH Green Paper, *Protecting our Heritage* (1996), are discussed in Chap. 8.

[36] GPDO 1995, arts 4–6. A new power has been introduced by art. 4(2) which permits the LPA, without the approval of the SOSE, to remove permitted development rights in relation to dwelling houses in conservation areas.

[37] *Thanet District Council v. Ninedrive* [1978] 1 All E.R. 703.

[38] GPDO, arts 4(3) and 4(4), see below.

[39] This consideration clearly applies to "once and for all" developments with temporary activities under "the 28 day rule" (*e.g.* game shooting) in Pt 4, Class B of the GPDO. Each day is treated as a separate use so the Article 4 Direction will have immediate effect (see *South Bucks D.C. v. SOSE* [1989] 1 P.L.R. 69).

[40] TCPA 1990, ss.107, 108.

exceptional circumstances and where there is a real and specific threat,[41] for example, inappropriate development within a WHS, as at Stonehenge. Similar considerations apply where the LPA wishes to impose a planning condition to a permission restricting or withdrawing such rights.[42]

Permitted development rights to extract minerals can also be restricted or removed under article 7 of the GPDO where the land in question is within a National Park, an AONB, a SSSI, the Broads or certain sites of archaeological interest.[43]   **6.19**

4. THE SCOPE OF PLANNING PERMISSIONS

Planning permissions come in two basic forms. An "outline" permission is where an applicant has asked only for the principle of development to be determined with details left for later submission (called "reserved matters"). Further details, in order to understand the application better (*e.g.* a desk-top archaeological study), can be sought by the LPA,[44] but this request also gives the applicant substantive right of appeal to the SOSE[45] without having to wait the minimum statutory eight-week period. A "full" or "detailed" application is a completion submission.   **6.20**

At law, the general rule is that regard may only be had to the permission itself, been including the conditions and the accompanying reasons. If the permission is subsequently challenged on the grounds that it was issued by mistake or without authority, and it incorporates the application and accompanying planning reference, these may be referred to in order to determine the scope of the permission.[46] The terms of the permission should not, however, be construed narrowly or strictly or against the LPA.[47]   **6.21**

Section 75(1) of the TCPA provides that, without prejudice to any revocation or modification, a grant of planning permission will enure for the benefit of the land and all persons for the time being interested therein.[48] However, in more instances,[49] unless the permitted development is commenced[50] within five years or such other period, whether longer or   **6.22**

---

[41] Circular 9/95, App. D, para. 1 (*General Development Order Consolidation 1995*). The procedure is set out in the GPDO, arts 5 and 6.

[42] Circular 11/95 (*The Use of Conditions in Planning Permissions*) Annex, paras. 86–88.

[43] "Site of archaeological interest" is defined by art. 1(1) of the GPDO as including scheduled monuments, land within a designated area of archaeological importance or a site registered in a county SMR. It should be noted that mineral extraction can be an exempt operation within an area of archaeological importance under the Schedule to the Areas of Archaeological Importance (Notification of Operations) (Exemption) Order 1984—see further para. 4.104 above.

[44] GDPO 1995, art. 3(2).

[45] *ibid.* art. 23(2)(c).

[46] *Wivenhoe Port Limited v. Colchester B.C.* [1985] J.P.L. 396.

[47] *Miah v. SOSE* [1986] J.P.L. 518.

[48] The case of *Pioneer Aggregates (U.K.) Ltd v. SOSE* [1985] A.C. 132 confirms that a planning permission cannot be extinguished by mere conduct alone, *e.g.* abandonment of land following cessation of mining operations.

[49] More than one permission may exist in respect of the land but they will be lost once a permission has been implemented (see also *Young v. SOSE* [1983] 2 A.C. 662).

[50] Commencement requires the execution of a "material operation" for which

shorter, as the LPA may direct the permission will lapse. Furthermore, if the development has been commenced but it appears unlikely that it will be completed within a reasonable period then a completion notice can be served by the LPA. The permission will then cease to have effect after the expiration of the further period specified in the completion notice, which will not be less than 12 months.[51] In certain limited circumstances the LPA may, subject to the approval of the SOSE, revoke a planning permission, which event gives a right to compensation.[52] This power, as with completion notices, is rarely exercised. In practice, where, for example, fresh archaeological discoveries are made during the course of the execution of a development then, as PPG 16 (para. 31) advises, "in the majority of cases it should prove possible for the parties to resolve their differences through voluntary discussion and for a satisfactory compromise to be reached".

5. ENVIRONMENTAL ASSESSMENT

6.23   Environmental assessment is an information-gathering exercise carried out by a developer which enables the LPA, or other determining body, to understand the environmental effects of a development before deciding whether or not to grant permission for that proposal. It is a technique and a process since the emphasis is upon providing an objective appreciation of the benefits and disadvantages of a particular proposal. The completed publication is known as the "environmental statement" (ES). Like the environmental assessment (EA), the ES can comprise one document or a series of documents providing the necessary information upon which the likely impact of that project can be adequately assessed.

6.24   Whilst the extent of environmental harm has always been a relevant issue in the grant of planning permission, the need for its formal and objective consideration as part of the appraisal of specific development projects was only introduced into United Kingdom law as a result of the implementation of E.C. Directive 85/337 on the Assessment of the Effects of Certain Private and Public Projects on the Environment ("the EAD"). In England and Wales, this took the form of the Town and Country Planning (Assessment of Environmental Effects) Regulations 1988 ("the EAR"). Furthermore, section 71A of the Town and Country Planning Act 1990 gives the Secretary of State for the Environment power to make regulations extending the categories of projects which are to be the subject of environmental assessment. This occurred twice during 1995 to exclude projects granted permission through "permitted development" rights and as a result of enforcement action which would otherwise come within the scope of the EAR.[53]

6.25   Separate Regulations, also published in 1988 to implement the EAD, deal with highways,[54] harbour works, afforestation projects, land drainage im-

---

planning permission would be required under the TCPA, s.56(2), *e.g.* the digging of a trench which is to contain foundations but genuinely for the purposes of carrying out the works (*Malvern Hills D.C. v. SOSE* [1982] J.P.L. 439; *Hillingdon LBC v. SOSE* [1990] J.P.L. 575; *Thayer v. SOSE* [1992] J.P.L. 264).

[51] TCPA, ss.94, 95.

[52] TCPA, ss.97–99, 107.

[53] See nn. 59, 60 below.

[54] Highways (Assessment of Environmental Effects) Regulations 1988, which inserted s.105A into the Highways Act 1980 and requires EA/ES for all highway projects

provement works and salmon farming in marine waters. However, for the purpose of section 71A and by way of general application reference should be made to the EAR and to Circular 15/88.

Given the growing requirement for environmental assessments there is **6.26** now a considerable body of material available explaining their preparation. In the context of this book the *Design Manual for Roads and Bridges*, Volume 11, Environmental Assessment ("DMRB") and the *Good Practice Guide— Prepartion of Environmental Statements for Planning Projects that Require Environmental Assessment*, published by the Department of the Environment ("the GPES") are perhaps of greatest help to archaeologists. The relevant sections dealing with cultural heritage are to be found in Appendices G and H to this book. The emphasis of this section is to highlight the legal as well as practical considerations that need to be borne in mind.

The EAR state, in broad terms, that the LPA or the Secretary of State shall **6.27** not grant planning permission in respect of an application to which the Regulations apply unless they have first taken into account the prescribed information set out in the ES. In considering whether there is a need for an EA, the EAR refer to two categories of project. Schedule 1 projects require an assessment in all cases since they relate to major projects, where environmental implications are bound to occur. These include crude-oil refineries, thermal power stations, motorways and major roads. For Schedule 2 projects, like mineral extraction, holiday villages, motorway service areas and coast protection works, an environmental assessment is not compulsory. The test is whether the project is "likely to have significant effects on the environment by virtue of factors such as their nature, size and location".[55] Questions of classification are essentially matters of fact and degree and not law, which the courts have held are primarily for the LPA to decide.[56]

Pre-application discussions and the submission of an ES, if one is deemed **6.28** to be required, after a planning application has been submitted are encouraged by the EAR. Where either the LPA or the SOSE call for an ES then the application or appeal cannot be determined until it has been received.[57] This requirement now extends to local authority applications,[58] certain categories of permitted development[59] and projects which are the subject of planning enforcement notices and require retrospective planning permission.[60]

If an ES is required or one is submitted on a voluntary basis then it must **6.29** contain sufficient detail to satisfy the requirements of Regulation 2(1) and Schedule 3 of the EAR. The specified information must include a description of the proposed development, data necessary to identify the main effects

---

involving the Secretary of State for Transport (*i.e.* trunk roads, motorways and major bridges). The Highways Agency carries out the assessments on behalf of the Secretary of State.

[55] See Circular 15/88, para. 20 for general criteria as to whether the environmental effects are likely to be "significant" and *R. v. Poole B.C., ex p. Beebee* [1991] J.P.L. 643.

[56] See also *e.g. R. v. Swale B.C. and Medway Ports Authority, ex p. RSPB* [1991] J.P.L. 39.

[57] EAR, regs 9–11.

[58] EAR, reg. 25A.

[59] Town and Country Planning (Environmental Assessment and Permitted Development) Regulations 1995 and Circular 3/95.

[60] Town and Country Planning (Environmental Assessment and Unauthorised Development) Regulations 1995 and Circular 13/95.

which that development is likely to have on the environment and a description of the likely significant effects, direct and indirect, on the environment of the development. Amongst the list of considerations are flora, fauna, landscape, material assets and cultural heritage. Archaeology falls within this last topic. In addition, where significant adverse effects are identified then a description of the proposed mitigation measures is also required. In all instances a summary in non-technical language must be provided.

6.30   In effect, the EAR shift the burden of proof on to the developer, who is required to describe and justify the environmental effects of his scheme. He must show why planning permission should be granted. If he fails to provide adequate information to show that his project is acceptable then the LPA (or the SOSE) can refuse planning permission on that ground alone. Many ESs have been criticised for being promotional statements rather than objective reports of the results of an EA. Both LPAs and planning inspectors frequently have to request additional information. Whilst the majority of planning projects dealt with at public inquiry are modified as a result of an EA many of the resulting improvements are still of a relatively minor nature and do not lead to the grant of planning permission.[61]

6.31   A systematic approach to the relevant issues is essential to the preparation of a good EA. This requires a brief to be defined for each member of the project team together with a programme and a timetable and a provisional budget. The opening section of GPES includes the obvious but necessary reminder that "in practice, the level of attention given to individual environmental topics in an EA should reflect the significance of potential impacts and their importance to the decision-making process. This, in turn, will determine the amount of background work which needs to be undertaken, the timescale for the studies, and the content, structure and length of the ES".[62] Full and early discussions with statutory consultees are also recommended.[63]

6.32   The disciplines and study identified in this chapter are equally necessary in the preparation of the archaeological input to both the EA and the ES, as the appended extracts from DMRB and GPES make clear. Investigation of the SMR, historic maps and other documents and initial consultation with the County Archaeologist will all be necessary preliminary steps.

From this initial work or "baseline studies" comes "scoping", the technique by which the focus of activity turns to the main issues and the level of detail that will be required. In an archaeological context, the scoping phase may be "pivotal" to the exclusion of any archaeological recording project[64]; for the extent of the remains, their significance, the degree of destruction and feasible mitigation measures are all issues which will need to be addressed as part of the EA.

6.33   Whilst the EAR do not require the developer to demonstrate a proven need or demand for the project in question, undoubtedly there will be some projects, for example, an extension to an airport runway, where these issues have direct links with issues affecting environmental quality as well as being "material considerations" in the decision-making process. Public consulta-

---

[61] "The Impact of Environmental Assessment on Public Inquiry Decisions" by Carys E. Jones and Christopher Wood [1995] J.P.L. 890.

[62] GPES, para. 1.4.

[63] ibid. para. 2.8.

[64] DMRB, vol. 10, section 6, para. 5.49.

tion, through open meetings and "conferences" is an important means by which a measure of support as well as identified and identifiable opposition can be established, a course presently adopted by the Highways Agency in respect of the more controversial trunk and improvement projects.

The ES is the most "visible" part of the EA process in that it draws together **6.34**
the findings of the various technical studies prior to the submission of the planning application.[65] Other than containing the prescribed information required under Schedule 3, the EAR do not lay down the form that the ES should take. Clearly, where it comprises more than one document, there will be an obvious need to identify the inter-relationship between them, their authorship and the methodology which has been utilised. GPES encourages the publication of a "method statement" so that the LPA can be informed who has written the ES, how it was prepared, what studies were undertaken to justify its conclusions, what consultation has taken place (including notes of meetings) and what guidelines, methods and techniques have been used to determine the scale and significance of the impacts.[66]

The length of the ES will not always be the best test of its quality. GPES **6.35**
suggests that for projects which involve a single site and relatively few areas of significant impact it is possible to produce a "robust" report of around 50 pages. Where more complex issues arise it suggests that the main body of the ES may extend to 100 pages or more, with a suggested maximum of 150 pages, beyond which it is likely to become cumbersome and difficult to assimilate.[67]

The Non-Technical Summary (NTS) can either be bound into the main **6.36**
report or, perhaps for easier distribution to the public, be set out in a separate document. It must describe all the conclusions of the ES including the facts and judgments on which they have been based. GPES suggests that it is good practice to write short summaries at the end of each section or chapter of the main statement, which can then be carried forward into the NTS. An overall summary table recording relative weights attached to the significance of individual impacts is also helpful.[68]

DMRB also includes helpful comments on the steps that should be taken to **6.37**
achieve adequate archaeological recording together with its timing to minimise interruption of the construction programme. Here again, project planning is a key element in the successful implementation of the findings of the EA/ES.

6. PLANNING CONDITIONS

Planning conditions are always imposed on the grant of planning permission. **6.38**
At law, a time limit for implementation must be imposed. This is normally five years for detailed permissions but the TCPA permits longer or shorter periods at the discretion of the LPA.[69] Outline permissions require the submission of reserved matters within three years and implementation

---

[65] GPES, para. 4.1.
[66] ibid. paras 4.10–4.12.
[67] ibid. para. 4.13.
[68] ibid. paras 4.17–4.20.
[69] TCPA, ss.91(1)(a),(b).

within five years or, if later, two years from the final approval of reserved matters.[70]

6.39   As well as being the subject of standard time conditions, the LPA has the power under section 72 of the TCPA to impose conditions dealing with other implementation issues. Current government advice, including model conditions, is found in DOE Circular 11/95. In the case of archaeological issues, paragraphs 53 and 54 of Appendix A to Circular 11/95 deal with fencing, the commencement of works and watching briefs. Paragraph 55 repeats the Model Condition found at paragraph 30 of PPG 16, which deals with the implementation of a permission in conjunction with a scheme of archaeological works. The preference of the Planning Inspectorate is for use of these conditions unless local circumstances dictate otherwise.[71]

6.40   There are also certain policy and legal considerations applying to the application of planning conditions based upon six tests. In summary, these require a condition to be necessary, relevant to planning, relevant to the development permitted, enforceable, precise and reasonable in all other respects.[72] It cannot, as a matter of law, seek the payment of money, nor interfere with private land ownership, nor remove statutory rights. A condition which is dependent on another's actions is not enforceable though one not allowing development to begin or occupation to occur until a specified act occurs (e.g. the formation of a junction off-site), known as a Grampian condition, is lawful.[73] An unreasonable condition does not become reasonable because an applicant suggests or consents to it, though it can be severed from a planning permission as a result of a court declaration. An application can also be made under section 73 for the removal or variation of the condition without losing the benefit of the permission itself.

6.41   Furthermore, the LPA, but not the SOSE (or the Planning Inspectorate), must also state the reason for imposing each condition.[74] Sometimes, the LPA may also wish to give guidance to an applicant in respect of other statutory consents or matters relevant to the implementation of the permission.[75] For example, the application of a "watching brief" condition would warrant a reason stating: "To safeguard the archaeological interest of the site." An appropriate informative would be: "Your attention is drawn to the need to liaise with an archaeological contractor and to allow it adequate time for site investigation and/or excavation in the building programme."

6.42   Enforcement of a planning condition, if it is merely a simple breach, can be secured by a "breach of condition" notice.[76] If the situation is more complicated, then an enforcement notice[77] and stop notice (other than use of a building as a dwelling house[78]) can be served by the LPA. Urgent breaches of

---

[70] TCPA, s.92(2).

[71] Circular 18/86 (*Planning Appeals Decided by Written Representation*), para. 34 and Circular 11/95 (*The Use of Conditions in Planning Permissions*), para. 5.

[72] PPG 1, paras 46 and 47; Circular 11/95, Annex, paras 14–42; *Newbury D.C. v. SOSE* [1981] A.C. 578.

[73] *Grampian Regional Council v. City of Aberdeen* [1984] J.P.L. 590.

[74] Town and Country Planning (General Development Procedure) Order 1995, art. 22 and Circular 11/95, Annex, para. 10.

[75] See further Circular 11/95, Annex, para. 11.

[76] TCPA, s.187A.

[77] *ibid.* s.172.

[78] *ibid.* s.183(1), (4).

planning control are now usually dealt with by court injunction under section 187B of the TCPA.[79]

7. PLANNING OBLIGATIONS

"Planning obligations", colloquially known as "section 106 agreements", **6.43** are made between the applicant/landowner/occupier and the LPA to deal with other matters, for example, financial payments and phasing of works. At appeal, a unilateral undertaking can also be given by an appellant, such as in respect of certain necessary highway works within a lump sum figure where other aspects of the draft bi-lateral agreement are still in dispute.

The scope of a section 106 agreement, depending on the capacity of "the **6.44** applicant", can be more onerous than a planning condition (*e.g.* waiving the right to enforce other permissions).[80] As a result of the development of case law on this subject, culminating in the decision of the House of Lords in the *Tesco (Witney)* case,[81] a potentially confusing difference exists between the approach which the SOSE (and the Planning Inspectorate) is obliged to take and that which an LPA can take. In the former instance, national policy advice, currently found in Circular 16/91[82] requires three tests to be satisfied before either a planning obligation or a unilateral undertaking can be accepted. In summary, the "planning benefit" must be necessary (for the development to proceed), reasonably related (to it) and fair and reasonable (in scale and kind).[83] At local level, provided the benefit serves some planning purpose and is not *Wednesbury* unreasonable[84] (*e.g.* buying or selling a planning permission through a planning gain package with no or only a nominal connection to the proposed development) then the LPA is entitled to treat the applicant's offer not only as lawful but also as a material consideration in its determination of a planning application. By the same token, if an authority decides to apply the more onerous tests currently found in Circular 16/91 then, in a public law context, it will equally not be acting unlawfully. The same considerations apply to a request made by the LPA for a "planning benefit" package.[85]

---

[79] The court has a broad discretion (*Runnymede B.C. v. SOSE* [1994] 1 P.L.R. 22) including the power to make a mandatory injunction to require the removal of an unlawful development as well as one to restrain further breaches of planning control (*Croydon LBC v. Gladden* [1994] 1 P.L.R. 30).

[80] *Good v. Epping Forest D.C.* [1994] 2 All E.R. 156.

[81] *Tesco Stores Limited v. SOSE* [1995] 2 All E.R. 636, which concerned the legality of an offer to fund a new road at Witney, Oxfordshire as part of competing superstore proposals.

[82] A Consultation Paper (*Planning Obligations*) was published in late December 1995 with a view to clarifying, but not changing, the policy on the use of planning obligations found in Circular 16/91.

[83] Circular 16/91 (*Planning and Compensation Act 1991: Planning Obligations*), Annex B, paras B7–B9; Consultation Paper, Annex A, paras 2, 9–12.

[84] *Associated Provincial Picture Houses v. Wednesbury Corporation* [1947] 2 All E.R. 680 (acting in a way in which no reasonable authority would have done, *i.e.* absurdly).

[85] See *Tesco Stores* (n. 81 above). However, the Consultation Paper (Annex A, para. 16) now seeks to bring development plan policies directly in line with national advice. It cites a policy which fails to take account of the advice in this Circular as likely to be unacceptable to the SOSE.

6.45 In the context of archaeology, a section 106 agreement can provide a useful vehicle by which the practical issues of excavation, recording and publication of results as well as funding can be dealt with. As PPG 16 points out: "Voluntary agreements are likely to provide more flexibility and be of greater mutual benefit to all the parties than could be provided for by an alternative statutory means. They have the advantage of setting out clearly the extent of the developer's commitment, thereby reducing both uncertainty over financial implications of having to accommodate any archaeological constraints and the possibility of unforeseen delays to the construction programme."[86]

6.46 The form of the section 106 agreement will, inevitably, vary to suit local circumstances and requirements. Nevertheless, there are certain issues which usually need to be taken into account when heads of terms are drawn up prior to, or as the framework for, the agreement. The following should be borne in mind:

(i) *Brief.* A brief should be issued which outlines the archaeological work to be undertaken and any other requirements. This will normally be provided by the County Archaeologist as the archaeological adviser to the LPA.

(ii) *Archaeological contractor.* A suitably qualified archaeological contractor should be employed by the developer who is also approved by the County Archaeologist.

(iii) *Specification.* The archaeological contractor should produce a specification which describes in detail how the work outlined in the brief is to be undertaken. This should be approved by the County Archaeologist.

(iv) *Finds and site records.* Agreement should be sought and arrangements made before work commences for the deposit of finds and site records in a recognised museum on completion of the project.

(v) *Monitoring.* Arrangements should be made for ensuring that all work is monitored by the County Archaeologist who should be informed of any important finds or discoveries which may require specialist treatment or a revised strategy.

(vi) *Reporting and publication.* A report on the work undertaken should be submitted for approval by the County Archaeologist within an agreed period. Where appropriate, publication in a suitable academic journal also may be required.

(vii) *Finance.* All archaeological work should be the financial responsibility of the developer.

(viii) *Responsibility.* It is the responsibility of the developer to ensure that the requirements of the brief and agreed specification are carried out to the satisfaction of the LPA to fulfil the section 106 agreement.

6.47 Enforcement of section 106 agreements can be achieved by injunction or entry onto land and execution of any works required to be carried out under the agreement. The costs can then be recovered either as a civil debt or by charging the land.

6.48 Old planning agreements (pre-1991, mainly under section 52 of the former TCPA 1971) can only be varied by application to the Lands Tribunal in the

---

[86] PPG 16, para. 26.

same way as a restrictive covenant under section 84 of the Law of Property Act 1925. New agreements can be varied after five years if circumstances permit under the power contained within section 106A of the TCPA.[87]

8. RELEVANT NATIONAL POLICY

PPG 16 (*Archaeology and Planning*), to which passing reference has already been made, was published in November 1990 as a practical (and accelerated) response by English Heritage and the Department of the Environment to the publicity and concern arising from the Rose Theatre discoveries in the early summer of 1989 and attendant litigation. In fact, the Rose Theatre "debacle" was as much about disputes between archaeologists, as they began to find themselves representing both sides of the "development process", as about the significance of the finds themselves.   **6.49**

With the appearance of a specific PPG, archaeology was firmly put into the planning system as a "material consideration". It also supplied the mechanism by which financial resources for any necessary survey, excavation or watching brief could be provided, albeit at the inevitable expense of the developer. It also promoted the presumption in favour of preserving important archaeological sites and their settings and against development adversely affecting such sites. However, this was not intended and in its application should not be treated as a blank cheque or an excuse for archaeological research but rather as a means of adding, if required, further evidence to that of existing archaeological remains.[88] Because of the importance of PPG 16 a full copy of the guidance note is provided as Appendix B to this book. The practical application of PPG 16 is considered later in this chapter.   **6.50**

In Wales PPG 16 was issued in November 1991 and took a similar form to its English counterpart. However, following a review to coincide with local government re-organisation, it was decided to depart radically from the English model. One general guidance note (PPG Wales) was published in May 1996. It devotes seven concise paragraphs to the overall archaeological strategy for Wales. These can be found in Appendix C to this book. However, paragraphs 15–31 of PPG 16 [Wales], its annexes, are still retained as specific guidance for determining planning applications. It is intended that a series of separate technical advice notes (TANs) will guide the new unitary authorities in the preparation of the specific development control policies within their UDPs. At the time of writing only a draft advice note, *Historic Buildings and Conservation Areas* (TAN(W)5) had been published.   **6.51**

PPG 15 (*Planning and the Historic Environment*), was published in England in September 1994, coinciding with the tenth anniversary of the foundation of English Heritage but, more particularly, to consolidate and strengthen the advice previously found in Circular 8/87. Whilst largely   **6.52**

---

[87] The onus is upon the applicant to show that there has been sufficient change in circumstances to warrant the modification or discharge of the agreement. A right of appeal to the SOSE is given by TCPA, s.106B.

[88] See further the article by John Pugh-Smith and John Samuels, "PPG 16: Two Years On" [1993] J.P.L. 204–210, on the practical application and outworking of the PPG following the results of a research study from Pagoda Projects commissioned by English Heritage.

dealing with listed buildings and conservation areas, PPG 15 is intended to complement PPG 16. It is directly relevant to archaeology in a number of respects, some more recognised than others. Specifically, account must now be taken of the wider historic landscape when considering the setting of listed buildings and conservation areas. World Heritage Sites, historic parks and gardens and battlefields, to which reference has already been made, are now expressly identified as material considerations to which considerable importance must be attached. However, beneath these specific matters arises the wider issue of buildings as an archaeological resource and related issues of recording before demolition or excavation takes place.[89]

6.53   In this latter context, paragraph 2.15 of PPG 15 draws attention to the fact that some historic buildings are Scheduled Ancient Monuments and that many, which are not scheduled, are either of intrinsic archaeological interest or stand on ground which contains archaeological remains. PPG 15 advises that appropriate assessment of the archaeological implications of the development proposals should take place before applications are determined, including adequate arrangements for the recording of remains which would be lost in the course of the subsequent building works. Paragraph 6.34 deals with the relationship between listing and scheduling and emphasises that the latter control takes priority. It is hoped that the current national survey of archaeological sites ("the Monuments Protection Programme") by English Heritage will avoid further overlaps and afford buildings and monuments the type of protection which is most appropriate to them.

6.54   No Welsh counterpart of PPG 15 was published. In consequence, continued reliance has been made on WO Circular 61/81 (*Historic Buildings and Conservation Areas-Policy and Procedure*) to supplement the brief references to these issues in PPG Wales (see Appendix C to this book) pending the final publication of TAN(W)5, the draft of which includes specific advice on historic parks, gardens and landscapes.

9. DEVELOPMENT PLAN POLICY MAKING

6.55   The whole of England and Wales is now covered by approved structure plans, most of which contain a general policy or policies applicable to archaeology. The requirements for UDPs for the English metropolitan areas are general policies to express broad development and land use strategy in Part I of this policy document.

6.56   However, it is at local level, where detailed proposals need to be formulated for the Local Plan or Part II of the UDP where direct archaeological input is likely to be at its greatest. Following the implementation the relevant provisions of the Planning and Compensation Act 1991[90] in February 1992 every LPA is required to prepare either a Local Plan or a UDP for its administrative areas which must contain specific policies, a reasoned justification and a proposal map.[91] Through a formal process of consultation, publication (called "deposit") and modification the plan proceeds through to adoption, at which point it has the status of the development plan.[92]

---

[89] PPG 15, paras 2.15, 3.23 and 8.5.
[90] Planning and Compensation Act 1991, Sched. 4, PPG 1, para. 18.
[91] TCPA, ss.12 and 36 and the Town and Country Planning (Development Plan) Regulations 1991, reg. 7.
[92] See para. 6.4 above.

Unresolved objections are dealt with through a public inquiry, orally or by written representation, overseen by a member of the Planning Inspectorate, whose report and recommendations form the basis of modifications. The onus is placed upon the objector to demonstrate why his proposal is better than that of the LPA or why the plan is deficient in some material respect.[93] A limited right of challenge in the High Court is given prior to formal adoption of the plan.[94]

The Secretary of State is a statutory consultee.[95] Whilst it has been stated **6.57** that he will only make an objection where plan policies are at odds with national or regional policies or where the plan is so technically defective that it would cause greater difficulties to users,[96] in practice, the extent of vetting and formal objection has been much greater since 1992. Indeed, it is clear that there is a conspicuous intention to seek consistent policy wording to mirror, so far as practicable, national guidance through the current series of circulars and PPGs. This approach applies as much to archaeological policies as, for example, to planning obligations.[97]

Apart from the statutory protection of archaeological remains as Sched- **6.58** uled Ancient Monuments under the AMAAA and historic buildings within conservation areas or as listed building under the 1990 Act,[98] LPAs are expected to take account of all other aspects of archaeology through specific planning policies.[99] Further advice to local authorities has been provided by English Heritage in *Development Plan Policies for Archaeology* (1992) and the Countryside Commission, English Heritage and English Nature joint publications, *Conservation Issues in Strategic Plans* (1993) and *Conservation Issues in Local Plans* (1996). PPG 12 (*Development Plans and Regional Planning Guidance*) (1992) provides general guidance on the formulation and procedure for making development plans.

Central to the formulation of any planning policies is the reconciliation of **6.59** the need for development with the interests of archaeology. As Local Plans and UDPs are required to deal with specific areas, whether for development allocation or restraint, it is important that the text and the proposals map clearly identify and provide policies that not only preserve but also enhance sites of archaeological interest and their settings. LPAs, either "in house" or through consultants, are required to carry out adequate survey work in the preparation of their development plans.[99a] By way of example, clear identification and differentiation between an "area of archaeological importance" and an "area of archaeological interest" on a proposals map can lead to the difference between a negotiated and well-organised programme of fieldwork and evaluation, as against confrontation and dispute, resolved in strained circumstances at appeal before a planning inspector at a public inquiry.

---

[93] *Electricity Supply Nominees v. SOSE* [1992] J.P.L. 634.

[94] TCPA, s.287(1). The power to quash is exercised only in respect of the specific policy or proposal to which the challenge relates, which leaves the remainder of the plan unaffected.

[95] TCPA, ss.13(VDPs), 33(Structure Plans), 40(Local Plans); PPG 1, para. 19.

[96] PPG 12, para. 4.17.

[97] See para. 6.44 above, especially n. 85.

[98] Planning (Listed Buildings and Conservation Areas) Act 1990.

[99] PPG 12, para. 6.8; PPG 16, paras 14–16; PPG 15, paras 1.6, 2.1–2.10.

[99a] PPG 12, paras 4.1–4.3.

10. DEVELOPMENT CONTROL PROCESS

6.60   Developers are encouraged, before making a planning application, to identify "whether the site is known or likely to contain archaeological remains".[1] This is most easily achieved by consulting the County Archaeological Officer or equivalent who is responsible for the Sites and Monuments Record (SMR). These are now held by all Shire Counties and in London by English Heritage. In fact, the quality, content and extent of SMRs varies considerably with few including all listed buildings let alone buildings of historic interest, historic landscapes, gardens, battlefields or shipwrecks and rarely distinguishing between individual finds and sites of archaeological interest. Currently, under the aegis of the RCHME there is a move to provide a more extensive and comprehensive record which will also be a National Archaeological Record. In the meantime this disparity must be taken into account when identifying whether a planning application will have archaeological implications.

6.61   Initial consultation may identify a potential archaeological interest in the area of the proposed development. In many cases, because of the lack of consultation, this is not recognised until the planning application has been submitted when time is short and a scheme is well developed; but, as with any other aspect of a planning application, the LPA can request further information under either regulation 4 of the Town and Country Planning Applications Regulations 1988 or, in the case of an outline application, article 3 of the GDPO. Article 10 of the GDPO requires the LPA to consult English Heritage where a development proposal is likely to affect the site of a scheduled ancient monument. It has been the refusal to provide any or adequate information that has led to the ultimate rejection of most planning applications with an archaeological aspect at appeal and which continues to require vigilance on the part of the authorities to enable those applications which have archaeological implications to be identified.[2]

6.62   Identification of archaeological remains is normally a two-stage process involving desk-based research followed by fieldwork where necessary.[3] Unfortunately this might seem a little confused in PPG 16 because the term "evaluation" is used for both. It would be clearer if the word "assessment" was applied to the first stage and "evaluation" to the second. General guidance as to both has been provided by English Heritage and the Institute of Field Archaeologists (see Appendices L and M to this book). Much depends upon the ability to understand and interpret the information available and from this to identify which archaeological techniques may provide the most useful information.

6.63   Having recognised the need for an assessment, its purpose is to establish the archaeological potential of the proposed development site within its national, regional and local background. The preliminary conclusions will then indicate what further action may be necessary.

6.64   The following sources of information would normally be consulted by the competent archaeologist:

(a)   *Sites and Monuments Record.* A preliminary indication of archaeolog-

---

[1] PPG 16, para. 19.
[2] *ibid.* para. 23.
[3] *ibid.* paras 20 and 21.

ical finds and sites may already exist in the SMR. However, most SMRs are multi-tiered and additional detailed information may be available including references to original sources. As the quality and range of an SMR depends upon earlier archaeological investigations and surveys, the skill to interpret the information and recognise shortcomings or other avenues of research is crucial. However, the SMR has no statutory basis at present, nor is there any duty to maintain it.[3a] Where parks, gardens and battlefields are identified reference should be made to the appropriate register compiled or in the course of compilation by English Heritage. Shipwrecks and archaeological features in river and coastal areas will be found in the National Maritime Register compiled by RCHME. Buildings of historic interest may also appear in the register of Listed Buildings.

(b) *Aerial photographs.* Evidence of archaeological sites seen as crop or soil **6.65** marks or upstanding earthworks on aerial photographs may be integrated in the SMR. Often this will include material held in the two main libraries of aerial photographs held by RCHME and the Cambridge University Committee for Aerial Photography (CUCAP). But that situation needs to be checked and if necessary those collections examined. Often the aerial photographs are treated in two stages with a general examination for the assessment followed by an enhanced analysis for the later evaluation with a more detailed plotting of archaeological evidence and land use. The latter is useful in demonstrating which fields had the right conditions to produce soil or crop marks and whether apparently blank areas such as permanent pasture need examination through other techniques.

(c) *Published sources.* References from the SMR should be followed up in **6.66** their published form as well as archaeological and historical surveys published by the RCHME, Victoria County History and others. County and locally-based historical accounts should be consulted and local nineteenth-century trades directories always provide useful background information.

(d) *Maps.* Various editions of Ordnance Survey maps should be examined **6.67** for archaeological evidence. The Geological Survey and Soil Survey maps can be useful in identifying areas of archaeological potential.

(e) *County records offices and local museums.* Unpublished documentary **6.68** sources including estate maps usually held in the County Records Office but sometimes in local museums or university libraries, can provide additional information. As with aerial photographs, these sources can be treated in two stages with a preliminary search for the assessment followed by detailed research as part of the evaluation. The necessity of the latter course will depend upon the date of the suspected archaeological remains and the scale of the proposed development.

[3a] The extent of statutory recognition of the SMR found in art. 1(1) of the GDPO 1995 which defines "site of archaeological interest" as meaning land "which is within a site registered in any record adopted by resolution by a county council and known as the County Sites and Monuments Record". The DNH Green Paper, *Protecting our Heritage* (1996), para. 4.13, proposes that a statutory duty to maintain the SMR should now be introduced as part of the package of proposed reforms. This responsibility would be undertaken by local government, the appropriate tier of which "will depend on local circumstances".

(f) *Walkover survey.* Identified archaeological sites should be visited to check recorded details. A rapid walkover survey may locate previously unrecorded remains such as earthworks and identify areas to be considered for later fieldwork such as fieldwalking, test-pitting, geophysical survey, augering, environmental sampling or trial excavations.

6.69 Having analysed the information available, it should then be clear whether "archaeological remains are known or thought likely to exist".[4] If the result is negative then no further action is required. On other sites the chances of archaeological material are sufficiently slight to warrant only a watching brief when construction work commences. Elsewhere, the assessment could show archaeological remains to be of such national importance that only total preservation could be considered.[5] Where the assessment shows the existence of archaeological remains but is unable to be precise about their nature or extent then, after discussions with the scheme's designers and the County Archaeologist, a programme of evaluation will need to be put forward.[6]

6.70 To test and refine the evidence of the assessment, several pieces of fieldwork can be carried out either selectively or together:

(i) *Fieldwalking*—methodical walking along recently ploughed fields collecting and plotting all artefacts although usually discarding material later than about 1600. Depending on the assessment and the scale of the project, this will be carried out at 10 metre or 20 metre intervals, and either each find will be individually plotted or groups plotted at regularly spaced collection points. Analysis of the material found and its distribution can indicate areas of settlement, burials or industrial activities.

6.71 (ii) *Geophysical surveys*—sensitive electrical and magnetic surveys used to locate buried features and designed to suit the scale of the project and the type of features suspected.

6.72 (iii) *Aerial photographs*—by computer-aided plotting, features already noted can be mapped to an accuracy of 3–5 metres. They can also prove an analysis of land use over the past 50 years which may not only explain the presence or absence of archaeological features but also be of assistance to other environmental disciplines. Sometimes additional aerial photography may be considered and various forms of heat-sensitive film used.

6.73 (iv) *Environmental sampling*—augering or test-pitting can recover environmental indicators such as pollen, snails and beetles as well as identify colluvial or alluvial deposits which may mask buried features.

(v) *Historical research*—detailed analysis of historical documents and maps can assist in interpreting identified archaeological remains.

6.74 (vi) *Test-pitting*—excavation of small holes down to bedrock, usually 1 metre square with either total or sample sieving of all soil. This would usually be done at regular intervals in areas of grassland not

---

[4] PPG 16, para. 19.
[5] *ibid.* para. 8.
[6] *ibid.* para. 21.

available for fieldwalking and is designed to find artefacts and environmental information.

(vii) *Trial excavations*—excavation of trenches, perhaps 2 metres by 5 metres or 10 metres but sometimes larger to test the depth of stratification, and the extent and survival of archaeological remains.

There should now be sufficient information to comment on what **6.75** archaeological remains probably exist and the effect upon them of the proposed development. Since preservation of all important archaeological features is to be desired,[7] the form of the development may need to be reconsidered to see if this can be achieved. Perhaps the site layout can be altered or different footings used. If not, then account should be taken of the significance of the remains in national, regional or local terms, and a survey or excavation proposed which will ensure that an adequate record is made of any archaeological features to be destroyed. Publication of the results in an appropriate archaeological journal should also be anticipated. PPG 16 expresses the view, only as a matter of last resort, that the LPA may need to consider refusing planning permission where developers do not seek to accommodate important remains.[8]

A watching brief may be appropriate when construction commences (PPG **6.76** 16, para. 29) and included within the planning condition recommended by Circular 11/95.[9] Contact should have been maintained with the County Archaeologist throughout the process of evaluation and his or her opinion taken in compiling the evaluation report. Indeed, by this stage it is to be hoped that the factual archaeological evidence is generally agreed even though there may be disagreement about its interpretation or the effects of the proposed development.

It is important that the impact of the proposed development upon any **6.77** archaeological remains is clearly identified. One method is to apply the non-statutory criteria used for Scheduling Ancient Monuments.[10]

Another or alternative method bases the assessment on the importance, nature and scale of the impact within the context of an environmental assessment in terms of national, regional, local or negligible importance, *i.e.*:

National. Scheduled Monuments or archaeological remains being sched- **6.78** uled and protected under the Ancient Monuments and Archaeological Areas Act 1979 or suitable for scheduling.

Regional. Sites listed in the Sites and Monuments Record (SMR) or other sources which are of a reasonably well-defined extent, nature and date and significant examples in the regional context.

Local. Sites listed in the SMR or other sources which are either of very low potential or minor importance.

Negligible. Areas in which investigative techniques have produced negative or minimal evidence of antiquity, or where large-scale destruction of deposits has taken place (*e.g.* by mineral extraction).

The nature and scale of the impact, which could range from total **6.79**

---

[7] PPG 16, paras 8, 21, 27 and 28.
[8] *ibid.* para. 28.
[9] Circular 11/95, App. A, para. 54.
[10] PPG 16, Annex 4.

destruction by the proposed development to visual or noise intrusion upon the archaeological remains can be categorised as follows:

Major. Total or substantial (50–100%) destruction of the archaeological remains or their setting.
Moderate. Significant destruction (5–49%) of the archaeological remains or their setting.
Slight. Minor destruction (1–4%) of the archaeological remains or their setting.
Negligible. Imperceptible impact upon the archaeological remains or their setting.

6.80   If further archaeological work is required by a planning condition, it is important that the developer appreciates the implications, which may be expensive and have practical and contractual consequences. PPG 16 offers a model negative condition in paragraph 30; and for both the LPA and developer it is better if the conditions are defined as closely as possible to those found in Appendix A to Circular 11/95.[11] However, it should be borne in mind that once conditions have been imposed they cannot subsequently be varied save by separate application under section 73 of the TCPA. A problem that all too often arises is where an outline permission is granted subject to a fairly modest archaeological programme. Subsequently, the LPA and/or its archaeological adviser may wish to impose more stringent conditions at reserved matters stage. At law, this is not permissible if the nature of the original permission is altered. Accordingly, sufficient care should be exercised in advance of the initial grant to ensure that any unforeseen eventualities are adequately covered.

6.81   Full-scale archaeological excavations can be labour-intensive and require a substantial amount of time. Since excavation itself is a destructive process, it is most important that the greatest care is taken and an adequate record made through written records, scale drawings and photographs. The process will involve the removal of all or substantial amounts of material down to the natural subsoil or bedrock. This can affect the design of footings for the proposed development. Subsequent analysis and conservation of artefacts and environmental samples, cataloguing, drawing and preparing a report, described by archaeologists as post-excavation work, can take as long or longer than the excavation itself.

6.82   A watching brief is designed to record anything of archaeological interest that may be discovered during the course of construction. There should be provision for the suspension of development work if the archaeologists require more time to ensure that an adequate record is made. Exceptionally this could mean an archaeological excavation, although in practice it is usually possible for the archaeological recording to take place alongside construction work. However, it is important that a timetable of work is agreed and that contractors are aware there could be delays.

6.83   Regard must also be paid to health and safety requirements. Under the Health and Safety at Work Act 1974 a general duty is owed by employers to their workmen and sub-contractors. More recently the Provision and Use of Work Equipment Regulations 1992, the Management of Health and Safety at Work Regulations 1992 and the Construction (Design and Management)

---

[11] See para. 6.39, above.

Regulations 1994 now place even more onerous duties not only on main contractors but also the management and supervising staff of archaeological sub-contractors. In effect, they must ensure not only that health and safety is formally planned well in advance but also that the design, excavation and usage, for example, of trenches are carefully worked out and regularly monitored.

The archaeological report is of the greatest importance because this is the **6.84** only record of the remains destroyed by the excavation. Usually, it is sufficient to deposit a copy of the report in the Sites and Monuments Record but with sites of importance publication in an archaeological journal will be required. Arrangements should also be made for the storage of all finds and site records in an approved museum.

11. TENDERS

All archaeological activity on a site is the responsibility of the developer. In **6.85** special circumstances some assistance may be available from a public agency, for example, English Heritage, but this will rarely be substantial. Because of the way in which field archaeology has been organised in the past, based upon regional and local rescue archaeology units, the distinction between consultancy and contracting is not always clearly defined. Furthermore, the concept of competitive tendering is only just becoming accepted. Likewise, comparing cost and quality is not easy because there are no specifically defined standards, although there is general agreement on best practice. The only absolute test is whether what is required is achievable and can be achieved at an acceptable cost.

The following points should be considered at tender stage when both **6.86** presenting and vetting tenderers:

(i) *Status.* Considering the extent to which the contractor is wholly independent of the LPA or their archaeological adviser can often save later difficulties where a conflict of interest arises.

(ii) *Range of experience.* Wide ranging and specialist knowledge is required.

(iii) *Professional qualifications.* Academic qualifications give some indication of ability. Membership of the Institute of Field Archaeologists (MIFA) is the only professional qualification available but is not always appropriate for specialist knowledge.

(iv) *Publications.* The ability to publish the results of research and views in academic journals and the media is of fundamental importance in archaeology.

(v) *Membership of Societies.* This gives an indication of involvement **6.87** in the study and development of archaeology.

(vi) *Access to specialist facilities.* Archaeology can require such a variety of facilities that no individual group can be expected to hold them all but, with good contacts and special arrangements, they should be available.

(vii) *Insurance.* Professional indemnity and public liability should be carried to an adequate level.

(viii) *Quality assurance.* Few archaeological consultancies or contractors have yet to consider applying for ISO 9001 (formerly BS 5750).

113

However, there is no reason why they should not have an internal quality assurance scheme.

(ix) *Communications skills.* If the matter is likely to prove contentious and perhaps go to public inquiry, then the ability to communicate, simply and clearly, both in writing and orally, will be essential.

(x) *Cost presentation.* Because archaeological investigation is an uncertain science sufficient contingencies should be included to cover cost variations and extensions of time. These considerations apply not only to this specialist but also to the main contractor and his sub-contractors. The lowest lump sum quotation may not always work out to be the cheapest final price.

12. PRACTICAL CONCERNS AND CONSEQUENCES

6.88

PPG 16 was implemented by the LPAs with remarkable alacrity. PPG 15 has yet to make itself felt but its ramifications are enormous. A review of PPG 16[12] considered its effects and potential future problems. Among the points of concern raised in that article were:

(i) The inconsistency in the policy wording of Local Plans and UDPs, especially with the severance of English Heritage from the DOE following the transfer of its functions to the Department of National Heritage.

(ii) Short and long term effects of the economic recession which have not allowed the implications of PPG 16 to be tested, particularly in terms of resources available to the LPAs.

(iii) The relationships of some archaeological consultants and contractors to LPAs.

(iv) The supply of suitably qualified and experienced archaeologists to meet the requirements of the public and private sector.

6.89 Discussion in that article benefited from a report on the effectiveness of PPG 16, commissioned from Pagoda Associates London by English Heritage and published in January 1992 (Pagoda I). This review had been promised by Baroness Blatch, the then Minister for Heritage, at the launch of PPG 16 in **6.90** November 1990. A further report was produced in April 1995 (Pagoda II).

Based on evidence to the end of 1993, Pagoda II differs little from the earlier report. Greater stress is laid on LPAs employing their own archaeologists (District Archaeological Officers) and an implication that the LPA should finance the maintenance of the SMR. The report recommends that the model condition in PPG 16[13] should be used in preference to section 106 agreements and that LPAs should maintain lists "of approved archaeological contractors who have experience of local archaeology". However, as before, Pagoda II draws attention to the fact that few developers undertake pre-planning application research to discover whether their plans may have archaeological implications; and still mainly on this point the report also found that developers consider the system fair.

---

[12] See n. 88, above.
[13] PPG 16, para. 30.

It was unfortunate that Pagoda II did not look at archaeological planning **6.91** appeals for the following year (1994) when the number doubled; though an equal number of successful appeals suggests a greater measure of doubt about LPA decisions on archaeological issues. Figures for planning applications and planning appeals are difficult to interpret during a period of recession and uncertainty in the building industry. Undoubtedly, there has been a clear drop in the total number of planning applications in the period 1990–94 which is reflected in a 23 per cent fall in the number of appeals. The true figure is probably much greater because it includes enforcement notices which, under the change in procedure following the introduction of the Planning and Compensation Act 1991, inflated the number of appeals from 1992. By contrast, appeals involving archaeology have increased as a proportion from 0.29 per cent in 1990 to 0.40 per cent in 1992 and 1.6 per cent by 1994.[14]

Even on the basis of Pagoda II data, that archaeology might be a significant **6.92** issue in as many as 5.4 per cent of all applications, these appear to be low figures in absolute terms. Nevertheless, experience confirms that archaeological issues are arising more often within the development control process. No doubt, because evaluations will often be the greatest expense that an applicant incurs in the early stages of a project, lack of appreciation of its effects on siting and layout will continue to result in too many appeals being dismissed on this fundamental issue.

An example from Painswick, Gloucestershire[15] illustrates the point. The **6.93** appeal concerned an outline application, with all matters reserved, for a modest residential development of four or five units on the site of a former allotment garden, flanked by modern development. The Inspector, Mr John Martin, found in favour of the appellant on the main issue, the effect of the proposed development on the character and appearance of the surrounding area and the adjoining Painswick Conservation Area. Although not part of the reasons for a refusal, a second issue, raised by Gloucestershire County Council in its consultation reply, concerned the possible effect of the proposal on the projected line of a known medieval road, recorded in the SMR, running through the eastern part of the appeal site. The Archaeology Officer felt that the development might disturb that or any settlement remains associated with it. He went on to point out that there was a further possibility of Roman and prehistoric remains associated with the precursor of the medieval road. He recommended that the appellants be requested to commission a field evaluation prior to the determination of the application.

As no action was taken in this regard, the Inspector raised the issue with **6.94** the main parties at the inquiry. Remarkably, neither of them was able to give assistance although the appellants were prepared to accept a condition requiring an evaluation to be carried out. The Inspector then comments:

"In the light of this advice, it seems to me that the balance of probability is that remains may be present under that part of the site on which it is proposed to concentrate the development, which could result in demonstrable harm to important archaeological remains. In these circumstance, paragraph 21 of PPG 16 requires that an archaeological

---

[14] Based on data provided by Compass, *Planning Magazine's* computerised database of all decision letters by the SOSE and Planning Inspectorate.

[15] T/APP/C/1625/A/94/237629/P7.

evaluation be carried out before the application or, in this case, the appeal is determined. Therefore, notwithstanding my conclusions on the planning merits of the case, I am not able to allow this appeal."

6.95   Although approaching the topic from a different angle, the same underlying tensions were addressed by Professor Martin Biddle in his opening address entitled "What future for British Archaeology?" to the Eighth Annual Conference of the Institute of Field Archaeologists at Bradford on April 13, 1994:

> "Here lie the seeds of danger. PPG 16 goes much further than the Swedish legislation because:
>
> (i)   It envisages a far greater degree and amount of preservation.
> (ii)   The full cost falls on the developer.
> (iii) It requires the developer to make arrangements for both excavation and publication, the latter (as experience has already shown) means full analytical publication; working to a post-excavation assessment and research design.
>
> It must be apparent to any disinterested person that such requirements have to be imposed with an element of constructive give and take if they are to prove acceptable, whether financially, or in economic and planning terms, or in politics. Not everyone believes that archaeology can be this important. Indeed, it has been well said that PPG 16 has survived only because we are in a recession. As we come out of recession, the strains are beginning to show and it can only be a matter of time before the whole process initiated by PPG 16 faces substantial challenge, whether in the courts or in Parliament."[16]

6.96   It has been suggested above that with the proposed doubling of the number of Scheduled Ancient Monuments within the next decade or so there will be increased challenges for Scheduled Monuments Consent. With PPG 16's advice that there should be a presumption[17] in favour of preserving all nationally "important" sites, the definition of importance is crucial.

6.97   More by implication than specific statement, PPG 16 suggests that some archaeological remains are more important than others. Reference is made[18] to remains of local importance and the *Advice Note* from English Heritage for local planning authorities[19] which suggests that there is a level of regional or county importance.

Common sense dictates that not all archaeological remains are of equal importance and a degree of pragmatism is necessary to decide which sites are of sufficient importance to merit long-term preservation, which should be excavated and which warrant either a watching brief or no further work.

6.98   A system of grading comparable to other environmental disciplines would be useful where archaeological remains can be graded in importance in terms of national, regional, local or negligible. Together with the potential impact

---

[16] Biddle, *What Future for British Archaeology?* (1994), p.6.
[17] PPG 16, para. 8.
[18] *ibid.* para. 16.
[19] *Development Plan Policies for Archaeology* (1992).

of the proposed scheme and its need, the LPA could then take an informed decision.

The case for the preservation of archaeological remains must however be assessed on the individual merits of each case, taking into account the archaeological policies in detailed development plans, together with all other relevant policies and material considerations, including the intrinsic importance of the remains and weighing these against the need for the proposed development.[20]

6.99 Pagoda II found through its interviews that "there were very few cases where developers felt that the CAO/DAO or planning authority was unreasonable."[21] Yet the report concluded that there was considerable variation in the archaeological requirements imposed on planning applicants: "We suspect that some of the variation is due to differences in practice between CAOs."[22] It would seem that this is due largely to the professional judgement of the archaeologists advising the LPAs.

6.100 Both the contest between excavation and preservation (*in situ*) and the unreasonable demands of an LPA were the subject of a four-day debate at a public inquiry in May 1995 concerning a proposal for the demolition and redevelopment of existing office premises with new office buildings at 82–90 Park Lane, Croydon.[23] The facts demonstrate the current tension in archaeological circles as to where the profession should now go in its evaluation techniques. It is also noteworthy that Professor Biddle acted as a professional witness for Croydon Borough Council.

6.101 In June 1991, full planning permission had been granted for an office development similar to the appeal scheme. That permission had been subject to an archaeological investigation of the site, which was thought to contain some of the remains of an Anglo-Saxon cemetery. An investigation carried out by the Museum of London Archaeological Service confirmed that a number of graves were located in part of the site. The appellants, supported by English Heritage, put forward a section 106 undertaking intended to secure the preservation *in situ* of the remains behind the proposed new buildings, during and after development, initially through metal mesh decking and, thereafter, by layers of terram, salt and lime free sand, polythene, dry-lean mix, mesh and bitumac. They accepted that there should be excavation within the building footprints, where the ground had already been disturbed by the construction of villas in 1893–94, when evidence of the cemetery was first discovered.

6.102 The Council's only objection to the appeal scheme proceeding was that the whole of the site should be the subject of a full excavation and recording. Supported by a number of acknowledged experts in the early Saxon period, it argued that excavation of the site was needed now in the national research interest. All three principal parties agreed that the site was of national importance but that the current rate of decay of the remains was unknown.

6.103 Ironically, the Inspector, Mr G.M. Salter, found that not only PPG 16,[24] but also the policies of the Council's Deposit Unitary Development Plan supported physical preservation *in situ* of nationally important remains. Not

---

[20] PPG 16, para. 27.

[21] Pagoda II, p.16.

[22] *ibid.* p.18.

[23] T/APP/L5240/A/245769/P2.

[24] PPG 16, paras 8 and 12.

surprisingly, he accorded considerable weight to them. He also declined to question, in his determination of the appeal, the merits of the policy in PPG 16 that nationally important remains should be preserved *in situ*. He found no clear indication that the proposed development would accelerate the current deterioration of the remains and concluded that none of the Council's arguments were so convincing as to set aside the clear presumption in favour of preserving the remains in situ and the other economic benefits of the scheme.

6.104　　Pagoda II provides comfort by stating that the relatively low number of planning appeals involving archaeology must show that developers are relatively happy with the system in operation. Yet it also states that only "about 2 per cent of all planning decisions are taken to appeal".[25] Whatever the reasons for this statistic, which must include cost and the uncertainty of success, the results are that in 1993 and 1994, 37 per cent[26] of those appeals involving archaeological issues were allowed. In most cases the Inspector recommended that planning permission be granted with a condition allowing some form of archaeological recording. Sometimes this was to be based on the model negative condition in PPG 16 (para. 30); but strangely, in a number of cases, was by use of the older Circular 1/85 condition, which provided access for archaeological work but made no provision for developer funding nor any allowance for interference with the programme of work.

6.105　　Such omissions remain unresolved in the replacement Circular 11/95 which simply repeats the same model conditions found in paragraphs 37 and 38 of Appendix A to Circular 1/85 as new paragraphs 53 and 54 of Appendix A to Circular 11/95 and reinstates, as paragraph 55, the model condition found at paragraph 30 of PPG 16. Whilst it remains the preference of the SOSE to utilise conditions rather than section 106 agreements, the extent of developer funding is likely to remain in contention.

6.106　　Several appeals have now been allowed where the Inspector was not impressed that there was sufficient evidence to justify an archaeological evaluation of the site.

An early decision letter that addressed this issue, in the context of PPG 16, concerned a proposal for two golf courses and an hotel at Staverton, Daventry, Northants.[27] The Inspector, Mr Bingley, helpfully set out the position in the following way:

> "This conclusion takes into account the advice given by English Heritage and the Royal Commission on the Historical Monuments of England brought to my attention. With regard to the former, it is a clear principle of planning control that there is a presumption in favour of development unless it would lead to demonstrable harm; the balance of evidence on the archaeological issue at the Inquiry has convinced me that no such harm has been demonstrated in this case. As far as the latter is concerned, I find nothing in the report to indicate the likelihood of further archaeological remains being found other than in the immediate vicinity of those already identified near Staverton. I am therefore of the view　that　these　documents　add　little　weight　to　the

---

[25] Pagoda II, p.19.
[26] Based on data provided by Compass (see n. 14 above).
[27] T/APP/Y2180/A/91/182424/P3.

contention that the appeal site is likely to contain significant archae-ological remains."

He went on to comment, with the presumption in favour of development **6.107** in mind, that the balance of archaeological evidence convinced him that harm had not been demonstrated nor the likelihood of further archaeological remains being found which would warrant a further and fuller evaluation of the appeal site.

At a subsequent public inquiry for a proposed petrol station, industrial **6.108** development and access roads at Henlade, Taunton, Somerset[28] the Inspec-tor, Dr D.L.J. Robins, commented:

"The remnant (railway) embankment immediately north of the site is identified in the Structure Plan as a feature of archaeological interest. However, no evidence on its significance was presented to the Inquiry but I am satisfied that any archaeological interest that there may be in the site can be adequately protected by the condition agreed by the parties."[29]

This was a standard Circular 1/85 condition.

At Hazel Farm, Ledbury, Hereford and Worcester where it was proposed to **6.109** build offices, workshop and accommodation, the same Inspector failed to recognise anything of archaeological significance on the site:

"The Council indicated in advance of the inquiry that it would not offer evidence on Nos 5 and 6 of its reasons for refusal which referred to agricultural and archaeological considerations respectively. However, it nevertheless suggested a condition to safeguard any archaeological interest in the site in accordance with a request made by the County Archaeologist.

However, I note that the County Archaeologist's post-decision rep-resentation to the Council stated that the only archaeological finds recorded were a scatter of flints and Roman and later pottery recovered in an investigation for the Ledbury bypass. As that level of finds was considered consistent with a history of manuring of fields rather than the existence of buildings I am not convinced that the archaeological interest in the site is so strong as to justify imposing the condition suggested by the Council."

Moreover, the Inspector made a grant of costs against the LPA because: **6.110**

"while the appellants had been informed that no evidence would be presented in the Inquiry the Council nevertheless requested a condition. Although the Council indicated it would impose a planning condition without pursuing the reason for refusal the appellants had a right to know in some detail the reason for its imposition, which could be unduly onerous if it was unjustified. In the event, the County Archaeologist's consultation reply, received by the Council after the issue of their decision, was only produced at my request in the Inquiry. As this reason for refusal was expressed in very general terms I consider that the appellants were put to unnecessary expense in consulting the County

---

[28] T/APP/D3315/A/94/234652/P5.
[29] T/APP/G1820/A/94/233991/P5

Archaeologist about its basis between the date of the acceptance of their appeal by the Department and the date of the Inquiry."

6.111   In two more recent appeals, the importance of the archaeological remains has been carefully balanced against the benefits of the proposed developments. At Dorney, Buckinghamshire, Eton College wished to construct a two- kilometre-long rowing lake.[30] An archaeological evaluation had identified the presence of an early Bronze Age site and other remains considered to be of regional importance. The County Structure Plan had a policy with a presumption against damaging important archaeological sites but the Inspector, Mr B.H. Smith, considered that the remains were not in a good state of preservation and the educational value of an excavation outweighed the advantages of preservation. The Secretary of State not only agreed with the Inspector's views but commented that policy objections on the basis of the Structure Plan were without merit. Additionally he balanced "the future interests of archaeology and preservation of local amenity ... and the benefits the proposals would bring to Eton College and the wider rowing community" and concluded that the benefits of the development would outweigh the other factors.

6.112   A similar discussion about balance took place at the appeal concerning the proposed construction of an opera house at Compton Verney, near Kinerton, Warwickshire.[31] However, the situation was considerably more complicated than the Eton rowing lake because the proposed development was within the Registered Parkland setting of several listed buildings and the relative importance of the archaeological remains of a possible deserted medieval village (DMV) was not agreed.

6.113   In an attempt to introduce an element of scientific appraisal the English Heritage system of scoring sites used in the Monument Protection Programme was applied to establish the site's importance. The Inspector, Mr P.J. Macdonald, commented:

> "The applicant's archaeological advisors had carried out a very impressive exercise ranking sites in the county, from which they argued that, even if the remains were accepted as those of a DMV, they were clearly of only local importance. I am inclined to think, however, that at 23 points they have under-scored the site for both historical and archaeological documentation. I also give some weight to the fact that English Heritage state that they are likely to propose scheduling in due course, and I consider that, on balance, one must proceed at present on the basis that

6.114   the remains may be of national importance.

> PPG 16 (paragraph 8) states that where nationally important remains, whether scheduled or not, are affected by proposed development there should be a presumption in favour of their physical preservation. Nonetheless, that is not determinative of the application, and the loss of the remains must be weighed against other factors. The applicants have proposed 'preservation by record', although that must clearly be a second-best option, since the remains then no longer exist for re-evaluation at some future date in the light of increased knowledge and enhanced archaeological techniques. However, the loss of the remains is a factor which must weigh against the application proposals in the overall balance.

---

[30] APP/A0400A/92/206972 and 206973.
[31] WMR/P/5398/223.

It was clear at an early stage that English Heritage had fundamental reservations about the site chosen, but that the project chose not to address those concerns. They were, of course, free to proceed in that way, but it does mean that the proposal must now stand or fall on its own merits.

The lack of any identified need for the opera house to be situated at **6.115** Compton Verney, and the failure to elevate any other sites, must also mean that the 'museum culture' argument must be treated with considerable circumspection in this case, whatever general validity it might be considered to possess.

It must, of course, be of the highest importance to the life of the nation that cultural assets are created and not merely conserved. Where creation and conservation are necessarily in conflict, hard choices have to be made. That is not the case here, however, since there is no necessity for the application proposal to be sited where it intrudes on the historic buildings and landscape of Compton Verney."

The Inspector recommended that planning permission should be refused **6.116** but noted that the Secretary of State might consider the proposal sufficiently special "to justify an exception to policy". He then went on to consider the planning balance:

"It is now necessary to look at specific aspects of the application proposals in order to consider what basis exists for an exception to normal planning policies and whether the advantages of the proposals outweigh the disadvantages.

Although the application site is within the Registered Parkland setting of a number of listed buildings, the only 'heritage' advantage claimed is the restoration of the degraded parkland. This matter has been conproposed landscaping scheme would not constitute restoration, and would make true restoration at some future time impossible.

It is important to be quite clear that no advantages to the listed **6.117** building are now claimed to flow from the application proposals. Whatever may have been the case at some stages in the past, the proposals would now make no contribution to safeguarding the mansion and ensuring its future. The future of the mansion is now likely to be as an art gallery, and its new owners have objected to the application proposals.

It is not claimed that the proposals meet a need that cannot be met on any other site. The support for the scheme shows the potential for an opera house in the Midlands. However, no other sites have ever been considered, and the choice of the present site appears to stem from the fact that at one stage the mansion belonged to one of the instigators of the Project."

The Secretary of State, however, although agreeing with the Inspector's **6.118** comments in general, reached different conclusions and considered that planning permission should be granted. On the effects on the Historic Parkland he commented:

"Considerable efforts have been made to fit the Opera House into the Parkland landscape. He has had regard to the correspondence between the Opera House Project and the Royal Fine Arts Commission on this subject. He attaches some significance to the Commission's support for the revised landscape proposals, in particular that the original shape of

Capability Brown's lake would not have to be altered. He recognises too that the proposals to restore the lake and the hillside to the north are of some importance for the Feldon Special Landscape Area as well as the historic parkland.

He considered that the proposed restoration would both benefit the parkland and landscape and enhance the Feldon Special Landscape Area."

6.119   And on the archaeological value of the site and the effects of the proposals he said:

"He recognises the arguments are highly technical and involve a great deal of professional judgment. He appreciates that there are differences between the parties on the significance of the site but he believes that no matter which interpretation is the correct one, the excavation and recording of the remains would be an acceptable alternative to their preservation *in situ*. He considers that the excavation and recording could be secured by the imposition of an appropriate condition."

This was to be based upon the model condition in PPG 16[32] amending a proposed condition to remove references to financial bonds and other mechanisms.

6.120   By contrast, at a planning appeal about a proposed housing development at Elton, Cambridgeshire[32a] which would affect the remaining traces of late medieval occupation at the edge of the village, there were conflicting opinions as to whether they were of local or national importance. The inspector, Mr P. Graham, concluded:

"In terms of the balancing excercise that I am required to carry out however, it seems to me that even if I were to accept the view that the site has only a local significance, and that the remains do not warrant preservation *in situ*, the inevitable damage that would be caused to them by the development can only weigh against the scheme."

6.121   As has already been mentioned, the majority of dismissed appeals involving archaeology since 1991 are due to the lack of evaluations carried out by developers prior to determination of the inquiry. It is also apparent that archaeological issues are becoming more complex with not only the relative importance of individual sites to be considered but also World Heritage Sites, registered historic parks and gardens, historic landscapes and registered historic battlefields. Where the application site is also within or adjacent to a Conservation Area, or sometimes an Area of Special Landscape, this would often seem to be the deciding factor against allowing the appeal.

6.122   PPG 16 together with the *Advice Note* from English Heritage (1992) have already encouraged planning authorities to state their archaeological policies in development plans. It was suggested that proposals maps could show Scheduled Ancient Monuments and areas of particular archaeological importance. Unfortunately there is resistance to this from some CAOs and a failure to understand the advantages of the planning system.[33]

6.123   Clearly stated policies, constraint maps and utilisation of existing

---

[32] PPG 16, para. 30.
[32a] T/APP/H0520/A/95/248548/P2
[33] Pagoda II, pp.2–3.

planning controls such as Conservation Areas and article 4 directions[34] will protect those archaeological sites deserving preservation and provide clear guidance to developers. This is particularly important as few developers undertake pre-application research to identify any potential archaeological implications.[35]

By contrast, "statutory undertakers" (such as the Highways Agency, the Environmental Agency, the National Rivers Authority and the water companies), who are not bound by the requirements of PPG 16, voluntarily follow its procedures from the initial assessment onwards.

Finally, the relationship between the archaeological advisers to LPAs and some archaeological contractors employed by the same bodies, was touched upon again in Pagoda II.[36] Although there has been some separation, this overlap of functions is still prevalent and brings into question the independence of advice and of contractual relationships. It is for this reason that attention has been drawn earlier in this chapter to the steps that should be taken to avoid later conflicts of interest and related difficulties.

6.124

---

[34] art. 4 of the GDPO 1995 permits the SOSE, at the request of the LPA to issue a direction either removing altogether or restricting permitted development rights within a specified area.

[35] Pagoda II, p.7.

[36] *ibid*. p.26.

7. Fiscal Considerations

1. THE UNITED KINGDOM TAX SYSTEM

The United Kingdom tax system is very complex, and becoming more so. In   **7.1**
its application to the type of receipts discussed in this book, the law is at its
most arcane. It is essential to have an awareness of how the system may
operate in each situation, both to be able to plan ahead and to avoid errors
which could result in interest charges on late-paid tax or penalties for making
incorrect returns. In this chapter it is only possible to highlight some of the
issues which must be addressed. As soon as any issue is identified, the parties
should seek specialist professional advice.

Whenever value changes hands, consideration has to be given to the   **7.2**
possible tax implications. There are also many situations in which value is
deemed to have changed hands, and these can give rise to a tax charge in
unexpected situations.

Some bodies involved in archaeological activity, *e.g.* charities, may benefit
from useful exemptions. The availability of tax exemptions may encourage
such bodies to assume they can ignore tax. This could prove to be an
expensive and an embarrassing mistake. Ancillary tax obligations may still
apply, such as registration for VAT or the operation of PAYE on the earnings
of those involved in excavations.

It is the responsibility of the recipient of any sum to determine whether,   **7.3**
and if so how, it is taxable. Unless the tax return is correctly completed,
penalties and interest may be charged. In the most serious cases, both the
Inland Revenue and H.M. Customs and Excise resort to criminal prosecution. The Inland Revenue has substantial powers to obtain information:
any attempt to avoid tax by omitting a taxable item from a return is not only
illegal but increasingly likely to be unsuccessful.

There are wide ranging areas of uncertainty and thus there is scope for   **7.4**
negotiating over the tax treatment of many transactions. Provided everything is fully declared to the Inland Revenue, it is acceptable to take a
different view to the Inspector. Any differences which cannot be resolved by
negotiation will be settled by an independent tribunal, either the Special
Commissioners or the General Commissioners. The Inland Revenue now
publishes its internal instruction manuals, which are available for viewing at
Inland Revenue offices. These will give a good indication of the line which
the Inspector is likely to take, and the reasoning for it.

Tax law is the same throughout the United Kingdom, unlike many other   **7.5**
branches of the law. For these purposes the United Kingdom includes
England, Scotland, Wales and Northern Ireland; it excludes the Isle of Man
and the Channel Islands which have their own quite distinct tax regimes.

The distinction between capital and income

7.6 The United Kingdom tax system distinguishes between capital and income (or "revenue") for both income and expenditure, and the distinction is fundamental to the tax treatment of items. A capital asset is, in general, one which is retained and benefit is taken from the ownership of it, as distinct from an asset which is owned with a view to making a profit from disposing of it. Capital expenditure is aimed at creating something of continuing benefit, as opposed to "revenue" expenditure which is generally aimed at the routine operation of a business. A sum received is capital if it is for the disposal of a capital asset, but is likely to be treated as income in other situations. The borderline is very indistinct and has been the subject of many court judgments.[1]

Why does it matter?

7.7 Since 1988, the rates at which income and capital gains tax are charged have been brought into line. Despite this, the differences in the rules make the question one of great significance. For instance, if the disposal of an asset is taxed under capital gains rules, the acquisition cost of the asset can be adjusted in line with the increase in the Retail Price Index, and no such benefit will arise if the disposal is treated as income. If the asset has been owned since before March 31, 1982 (the date to which capital gains tax was rebased), its value at that date can normally be used instead of cost if it is higher. On the other hand, there is a wider range of expenses which can be deducted if the receipt is taxed as a trading receipt.

Illegality

7.8 The fact that a transaction may be illegal does not prevent its coming within the charge to tax. For instance, the sale of an artefact illegally obtained will be subject to tax in the same way as if the object were obtained legally.

2. TAXATION OF RECEIPTS

The taxable person

Charities

7.9 Much archaeological work is carried out by charities. The owner of land of archaeological importance might consider the establishment of a charity as being an appropriate vehicle for holding the property, both to ensure its protection and to take advantage of the tax exemptions. Although charities do have tax privileges, these do not amount to a general freedom from all taxes. The trustees must understand the limitations on the exemptions to be

---

[1] *Glenboig Union Fireclay Co. Ltd v. IRC* (1921) 12 T.C. 427; *London and Thames Haven Oil Wharves Ltd v. Attwooll*, 43 T.C. 491.

sure of avoiding unpleasant surprises. In particular, there is only a very restricted exemption for trading activities carried out by charities: either the trade must be exercised in the course of the actual carrying out of a primary purpose of the charity, or the work must be carried out mainly by the beneficiaries of the charity.[2]

To avoid this problem, charities frequently set up a wholly-owned limited company to carry on trading activities (*e.g.* the provision of tourist services at an archaeological site). The company can covenant its profits to the charity. Provided the details are properly carried out, this provides a very tax-effective structure which is accepted by the Inland Revenue.   **7.10**

However the work is arranged, it is important that the trustees are alert to their obligations under the trust deed and charity law. They must avoid any arrangement or activity which could be seen by the Charity Commissioners as jeopardising the charitable status.

Pension funds

Substantial areas of land in the United Kingdom are owned by pension funds. There are exemptions from tax which reflect the privileged tax position of these funds, but this does not constitute a blanket exemption from all taxes.[3] In particular, the fund will be liable to tax if it engages in any activity which amounts to a trade. A company can be owned by the fund to carry on the activity, and this is the conventional solution to the problem. The main risk may be where a transaction is not identified in advance as giving rise to trading income. Failure to plan ahead can result in not only an unexpected (and unnecessary) tax charge, but also interest and penalties.   **7.11**

Companies and unincorporated associations

Companies and unincorporated associations (*e.g.* clubs and academic associations) pay corporation tax rather than income tax or capital gains tax, but the principles remain as described in this chapter for those taxes. These bodies may attract charitable reliefs.   **7.12**

Sources of income—the schedular system of income tax

Income is only subject to income tax if it falls within one of the schedules set out in the Income and Corporation Taxes Act 1988,[4] and expenditure is only allowed as a deduction within the specific rules which vary between the schedules. The schedules are mutually exclusive. As a result, an owner of a landed estate may have a number of sources of income which are taxed under different schedules: this can cause problems with losses arising on some ventures which cannot be offset against income arising on others. Representations to have the position improved, by among others the Country Landowners Association, have not as yet achieved any success.   **7.13**

---

[2] Income and Corporation Taxes Act 1988 (ICTA), s.505(1)(e).
[3] *ibid.* s.592.
[4] *ibid.* ss.15–20.

Activities amounting to a trade

7.14 Many of the persons involved in the processes described in this book will be carrying on an activity which amounts to a trade for tax purposes. This will include not only developers but others whose position may be less obvious, such as:

(i) Owners of historic houses and grounds who open them to the public. Although this may amount to no more than "rent" for access to the grounds by visitors, there is an agreement between the Historic Houses Association and the Inland Revenue setting out the criteria under which the activities can be treated as a trade. This can have important consequences, such as allowing relief against total income for any losses, and will usually be the preferred option for houses open to the public.

(ii) A "one-off" sale of an asset can amount to a trade if the transaction has the necessary characteristics. For instance, the fact that an asset is acquired specifically with a view to selling it at a profit will almost certainly bring it within the trading rules. Thus, the purchase and sale of an archaeological artefact can be taxed in isolation, without the need for the person to have any formally constituted business. This would also be the case where a metal detector was used to acquire artefacts for the purposes of sale.

(iii) Incidental income obtained by the owner of a historic site, such as the provision of car parking, tea-rooms, sale of guide books, etc., will be taxed as a trade.

7.15 If the activities amount to a trade, then tax is charged on the balance of profit after deducting allowable expenses. There is also a wide range of reliefs and allowances which may be available.

The practical differences between income being categorised as rents and as a trade have been somewhat reduced for individuals and trustees (not companies) by the reform of Schedule A (taxation of rents and other profits from land) in the Finance Act 1995. The computation of income for Schedule A now follows the same general principles as for a trade. In all other respects, however, the distinction remains good and care needs to be taken.

Contributions towards expenditure

7.16 Where a sum is received as a contribution towards costs, *e.g.* the costs of maintaining a property, its tax treatment will mirror that of the expenditure concerned. If the recipient is using the property in a trade, so that the expenditure is tax deductible, the contribution will be charged to tax. If the expenditure is not tax deductible, then the contribution will be free of tax.

Contributions towards expenditure qualifying for capital allowances (for instance, the construction of a new dry stone wall might qualify for Agricultural Buildings Allowance) will be deducted from the expenditure on which the allowances are given.

Grants

Grants are paid in a number of circumstances. The official approach of the   **7.17**
Inland Revenue is that it is not possible to give a blanket statement as to how
any particular grant will be treated. It all depends on the circumstances of the
case, and the tax treatment of each grant payment must be negotiated by the
individual with the local tax office. The principles to be applied are the same
as those set out below in respect of compensation receipts.

The correct treatment may depend on the status of the recipient. A farmer
who receives a grant on land or buildings used in the trade of farming may
well have to take it in as a receipt of the trade, while the same grant received
in respect of land used for commercial woodlands, from which activity the
income is tax free, may itself be tax free.

Interaction between archaeology and other grants

Quite apart from the treatment of the archaeological income itself, consider-   **7.18**
ation must be given to the impact it may have on other grants, etc., which the
landowner or occupier may be receiving, for instance:

(i)   The commencement of an archaeological dig on set-aside land may
        breach the terms of the set-aside scheme.
(ii)   Management agreements under the Wildlife and Countryside Act
        1981 contain a clause concerning the inheritance tax conditional
        exemption. These clauses do not prevent the land being subject to
        conditional exemption, but if it is, the payments made under the
        management agreement may be adjusted. The purpose is to avoid
        any "double funding" from the Treasury. Any compensatory
        payments are likely to cease, and a proportion of any lump sum
        payment may be recovered. Payments for positive works to be
        carried out (e.g. construction of fencing or the improvement of
        drainage) may continue. The position is looked at in the light of the
        facts of each individual case.
(iii)   Similar principles, aimed at preventing "double funding", apply to
        payments by the Ministry of Agriculture, Fisheries and Food under
        the Agriculture Act 1986 for farming in Environmentally Sensitive
        Areas. ESA payments will cease where the same conservation
        benefit is provided by the conditional exemption agreement. ESA
        payments may continue where they provide additional protection.
        Each case is judged on its merits.

Compensation

Previous chapters of this book indicate a number of situations in which   **7.19**
compensation may be paid, such as for refusal of scheduled monument
consent (see paras 4.73 et seq., above), orders against persons convicted of
damaging monuments (see para. 4.149, above), compensation to the possessor of goods returned to a territory from which they were unlawfully removed
(see paras 5.65 et seq., above), compensation to innocent purchasers and
compensation for revocation of planning permission (see paras 6.20 et seq.,

above). Whenever compensation is received, the tax position must be considered.

7.20 The general principle for the taxation of compensation is that it is taxed in the same way as the matter which it replaces.[5] Thus compensation for the temporary loss of trading profits will be taxed as trading profits. Compensation for the permanent deprivation of capital value will be taxed as a capital receipt. This can be an area of doubt and may need to be discussed with a professional adviser, and perhaps be negotiated with the Inspector of Taxes: it may be necessary to arrive at a split of a single sum of compensation between its various elements so that they can be taxed differently.

7.21 It is a general principle in establishing the amount of compensation to which a person is entitled that tax liabilities may be taken into account.[6] In a recent decision,[7] the High Court concluded that no deduction should be made for notional tax liabilities where both the compensation itself, and the lost profits it replaced, were liable to tax. In most of the circumstances outlined in this book, compensation will be computed without any deduction for notional tax.

7.22 Circumstances vary, and it is not possible to give a definitive statement as to how any particular compensation will be treated in any case. The following examples are given as a general illustration:

7.23 (i) A householder obtains planning consent over part of his garden, on the sale of which the gain would be exempt from capital gains tax under the principal residence rule. Consent is given to the construction of a single dwelling. While the foundations are being prepared, archaeological remains are found, the planning consent is revoked and compensation is paid.

(ii) If the land still belongs to the original owner, and the profit is not taxable on him as income because he is carrying out the development, then the compensation will be capital in his hands and will be covered by the principal residence exemption.

(iii) The same would be true if the landowner was building the new property for his own use, intending to sell the original house in due course: if the land would be covered by the principal residence exemption, then the compensation will be tax free.

(iv) If, on the other hand, a disposal of the land would not qualify for the principal residence exemption, perhaps because the garden is over 0.5 hectare in size and this part does not qualify, then the compensation will be a capital receipt, potentially liable to capital gains tax.

(v) If the land still belongs to the original owner, but he is carrying out the development himself with a view to selling the new house at a profit, then the land will have been notionally transferred to be stock of that trade and the compensation will be taxed as a receipt of the trade (possibly the only receipt, under the circumstances).

(vi) If, as may be more common, the land has been sold with planning consent to a builder, so that at the time of the revocation the land is part of the stock of the builder's trade, then the compensation will

---

[5] *Smart v. Lincolnshire Sugar Co. Ltd* (1937) 20 T.C. 643.
[6] *British Transport Commission v. Gourley*[1995] 3 All E.R. 796, H.L.
[7] *Deeny v. Gooda Walker Ltd (in voluntary liquidation) and others* [1996] S.T.C. 299.

be a "revenue" receipt and brought in as part of the income of the builder's trade.

(vii) Compensation for the refusal of scheduled monument consent will normally be taxable under capital gains tax.

Receipts under management agreements

As well as agreements for the preservation of ancient monuments under section 17 of the AMAAA, there is a wide range of other legal provisions which allow, or in some circumstances require, public bodies to enter into management agreements. These include the Wildlife and Countryside Act 1981 (general powers, for the purpose of conserving the natural beauty or amenity of land), the Agriculture Act 1986 (Environmentally Sensitive Areas), the National Parks and Access to the Countryside Act 1949 (Nature Reserves) and the Countryside Act 1968 (Sites of Special Scientific Interest).   **7.24**

These agreements vary widely in their scope and in general the Inland Revenue view receipts as being taxable. This is on the basis that the public authority is in effect paying a farmer to farm the land in a certain, restricted, way. Under the same principle as described for compensation (see para. 7.20 above), this payment is to reflect a loss of potential profit which the farmer suffers by agreeing to utilise the land in a way which is not the most profitable.   **7.25**

Alternatively, some provisions allow for a lump sum to be paid as compensation for the loss in the capital value of the land caused by the restrictions imposed. This will be treated as a capital receipt (and taxed as a "part disposal" of the land under capital gains tax) if the reduction is permanent. It is not possible to convert income receipts into capital by arranging for them to be paid as a lump sum.   **7.26**

As the agreement may commonly have a range of requirements, it may be necessary to categorise the receipts between the various items and agree the treatment of each with the Inspector of Taxes. Although most categories may be taxed as income (*e.g.* for agreement to graze the land in a particular way), others may be capital (*e.g.* for agreeing to build a car park).

Nominal payments for agreements under section 17 of the AMAAA are free of income tax. The sums involved will be small.[8] See paragraph 7.47 below on the treatment of any related direct expenditure. Any larger payments will be taxed on normal principles.   **7.27**

Care should be taken when entering into management agreements as to their impact on other matters. For instance, some agreements may be in breach of the occupier's agricultural tenancy. See also below on the possible loss of the agricultural exemption from business rates if the land is taken out of farming use. Such changes of use may also require planning consent.

---

[8] *Inland Revenue Inspectors' Manual*, para IM2272c.

Capital disposals

7.28   Where assets are owned without having been acquired for gain, a disposal is likely to be taxable as a chargeable gain. In computing the capital gain, the acquisition cost of the asset is increased in line with inflation, and there are many other rules which make the computation of chargeable gains a matter for a specialist in all but the simplest cases. An individual or trustee will be entitled to an annual exemption to set against the total gains of the tax year.

7.29   There is a general relief which can be claimed for small part disposals of land.[9] The proceeds of the sale are then deducted from the tax cost which will be allowed on the disposal of the remainder of the land, instead of being taxed at the time of the part disposal. The relief can only be claimed where:

(i)   the proceeds of the part disposal do not exceed 20 per cent of the value of the holding of land immediately before the disposal, and

(ii)   the total consideration received by the individual, for all disposals of land, in the same tax year does not exceed £20,000.

Treasure trove

7.30   The legal aspects of treasure trove are discussed at paragraphs 5.10 *et seq.* above. Where the treasure trove is retained by the Crown, the finder may be paid a reward. This sum is a gift of cash and is accepted by the Inland Revenue as being tax free.

If the object is returned to the finder, any subsequent disposal by the finder will be taxed as a capital gain. The allowable "cost of acquisition" is the market value of the object at the date the object is returned by the Crown. This may reduce the chargeable gain substantially as it may be arguable that the value at this time is close to the sale proceeds if the sale takes place soon after the gift from the Crown.

7.31   As the object will be a chattel (defined in the capital gains tax legislation as "tangible moveable property"), no gain will arise if it is sold for £6,000 or less with a marginal relief if the proceeds are slightly more."[10] In considering what is the item to which this limit applies, a "set" is treated as a single asset if it is disposed of to the same person or to persons who are acting in concert or are connected persons. This is to prevent tax being avoided by splitting up a valuable set of assets.[11] An individual or trustee will be able to set the annual exemption against the total gains of the tax year.[12]

Found objects which are not treasure trove

7.32   If an item is not treasure trove, its ownership may be a matter of dispute. Legal fees incurred in establishing title are deductible[13] in calculating the chargeable gain on a subsequent disposal. If the claimants each abandon their claim to it in return for a share in the sale proceeds, the view of the Inland

---

[9] Taxation of Chargeable Gains Act 1992 (TCGA), s.242.

[10] *ibid.* s.262.

[11] *ibid.* s.262(4).

[12] *ibid.* s.3.

[13] *ibid.* s.38(1)(b).

Revenue is that the individual's share of the proceeds derives not from the asset itself but from the agreement. This has the effect of allowing no acquisition cost to be set against the capital gain. In addition, the £6,000 chattels exemption (see above) will not be available. Whether it is worth challenging this view will depend on the circumstances of the case.

Where the object belongs to the finder, there will be no acquisition cost to **7.33** be deducted in the capital gains calculation. However, if it was found before March 31, 1982, its value at that date will be allowable.

If the object is the property of the landowner, no part of the cost of the land itself can be offset against the gain. This is because the asset, even if buried, does not form part of the land. However, if the land was owned on March 31, 1982 it follows that the buried object was also owned at that time and its value at that date will be allowed as a deduction. It will be a chattel, so the £6,000 exemption described above will apply.

Agreements with users of metal detectors

Any receipt by a landowner for granting the right to search on the land is **7.34** assessable to income tax. This will normally be under Schedule A (taxation of rent and other profits from land) but, where the owner is farming the land and the level of income is low, it may be included as a receipt of the trade and taxed accordingly.

Agreements between landowners and the users of metal detectors may allow for the finder to keep a proportion, say 50 per cent, of the value of any object found. This agreement itself constitutes a disposal of a right by the landowner, which will itself be subject to capital gains tax. The Inland Revenue's stated policy on the capital gains tax position of the landowner is as follows. If a valuable object is found and the sale proceeds are shared, two capital gains tax calculations will be required. The first relates to the disposal of a 50 per cent share in the asset to the finder at the date of the agreement, taxed at the market value on that date of the object which is later found. The second taxable gain relates to the disposal by sale of the remaining 50 per cent share in the object. This means that if the value of the object is the same at the two dates the whole of the gain is taxed on the landowner, but with the gain split between the two disposals.

This policy has been practicable in the past, but will create problems under **7.35** the new system of self-assessment which is effective from the tax year 1996–97. The landowner may be unable to submit a correct return for the year in which the agreement is entered into, as the first gain cannot be computed until the second has arisen and this is likely to be in a later tax year. It may not be practicable even to report a reasonable estimate; at the time that return has to be filed the existence of the artefact may still be unknown and its value is a key element in the calculation. The Inland Revenue may clarify its policy in due course. There are alternative views, for instance that the measure of the disposal at the time of the agreement is not related to the value of any objects eventually found, but to the value of that "expectation" at the time of the agreement; or that the disposal at that stage is not of a part of any particular asset but rather is of a legal right to share in any future proceeds.

If an alternative basis is used for the capital gains tax computation, the **7.36** following points should be borne in mind:

133

(i)   Professional help will almost certainly be needed to ensure that the chosen method is in accordance with tax law and to negotiate with the Inland Revenue over any difference of opinion.

(ii)   The fact that the calculation is not in accordance with the published Inland Revenue policy should be notified in the return.

(iii)   The split of the taxable gains between the landowner and the finder may be changed, even though the amount of the proceeds received by each remains the same.

The finder will have a gain based on his share of the sale proceeds. In calculating the taxable gain, he will be able to deduct the value of that share on acquisition, which will be the same figure taken into account as the landowner's disposal proceeds as discussed above (uplifted for any increase in the Retail Prices Index). Where the object has the same value at the two dates, this has the effect of reducing the gain taxable on the finder to nil. If the value of the object has fallen between the date of the agreement and its sale, the Inland Revenue practice would leave the finder with a loss which could only be used against capital gains arising in the same or later years (and the landowner would have a total gain exceeding the proceeds of his half share of the object).

Compulsory purchase

7.37   The acquisition of land by an authority exercising compulsory purchase powers is treated for tax like any other disposal, with the variations mentioned in the following paragraphs. The disposal will be subject to capital gains tax except in those cases where the land was stock in trade, *e.g.* of a developer or a property dealing company.

7.38   Part of the compensation may be subject to income tax as a receipt of the trade. Compensation for compulsory purchase may fall into three amounts:

(i)   for the land itself, which will be subject to capital gains tax if the land itself is a capital asset of the owner;

(ii)   for disturbance, which may be split into items taxed as income (*e.g.* for temporary loss of profits) and items taxed as capital (*e.g.* loss of goodwill);

(iii)   for severance, *i.e.* for the fall in value of other land held by the person whose land is being compulsorily acquired, which will normally be taxed as capital.

7.39   Where an authority acquires land under its compulsory purchase powers (and not by contract) the time of the transaction for tax purposes is the date the compensation is agreed.[14] This timing issue can be significant not only for the due date for the tax liability, but also for the availability of relief for losses on other transactions and for the relief mentioned in the next paragraph.

7.40   When land is disposed of to an authority with compulsory purchase powers, there is a special relief which allows any capital gain to be deferred.[15] This applies not only when the acquisition is made using the compulsory purchase powers, but on any disposal to such an authority provided that the

---

[14] TCGA, s.246.
[15] *ibid.* ss.247, 248.

landowner had not previously taken any steps to dispose of the property. Where the proceeds are invested in other land in the period from 12 months before to three years after the date of the disposal (see above), the gain on the old asset can be deducted from the acquisition cost of the new asset instead of being charged to tax. This defers the taxation of the gain until the new land is disposed of.

3. TAXATION OF EXPENDITURE

Capital/revenue distinction

The distinction between income (or "revenue") and capital (see para. 7.6   **7.41** above) applies equally to expenditure. Revenue expenditure can be deductible in arriving at income tax liability. Capital expenditure will normally only be allowed against a capital gain on the eventual disposal of the asset. Both of these are subject to many further restrictions before any deduction is allowed.

Expenditure by developers

The cost of archaeological investigations prior to an application for planning   **7.42** consent will be treated in the same way as other costs incurred in obtaining the consent. If the land belongs to the developer as stock in trade, the cost will be allowed as a deduction in computing the taxable income from the development. In other cases, the consent may be obtained by the landowner prior to sale of the site to the developer: if the land is a capital asset, the cost will be allowed as a deduction in computing the chargeable capital gain on the disposal.

If the site constitutes part of the garden or grounds of the owner's only or   **7.43** main residence, and could therefore be exempt from capital gains tax, the obtaining of planning consent will not on its own alter the tax treatment.[16] The receipt will continue to be treated as a capital matter and covered by the "main residence" exemption in appropriate cases. If the landowner does more than obtain planning consent before selling the property, he may risk being treated as a developer for tax purposes and being treated as trading, or at least losing the capital gains tax exemption on the disposal.[17]

The cost of carrying out a dig may fall on the developer. Subject to   **7.44** agreement with the Inspector of Taxes, this may be allowable as a deduction in computing the profit arising from the development, being one of the items of expenditure incurred wholly and exclusively for the purposes of earning the income. The same principle can be applied to other items of "revenue" expenditure.[18]

In other circumstances, land may be acquired by the end-user, who engages others to design and construct a building on the site (*e.g.* a supermarket company acquires a site and has a new store built for use in its trade). In this situation, the property will be a capital asset of the company: the costs of a dig

---

[16] *Inland Revenue Tax Bulletin*, August 1994, p.150.
[17] TCGA, s.224(3).
[18] ICTA, s.74(1)(a).

will not then be deductible from the profits of the trade, because they relate to a capital asset. The expenditure may be added to the cost of the property and deducted in calculating any capital gain on its eventual disposal. In cases where such expenditure is likely, and will constitute a significant cost of the project, earlier relief may be obtained if the project is planned in such a way that the construction is done, and the costs of the dig are incurred, by a development company.

7.45   The developer may donate artefacts discovered during the dig, usually to a local museum. There will be no tax deduction for the value of these, since there is no direct cost involved in the gift, as opposed to the cost of the dig.

There may be a commercial loss arising from delays in carrying out the development. While there is no specific relief from tax for such a loss, most direct expenses incurred by a developer will be tax deductible.

Expenditure by other landowners

7.46   Expenditure on establishing, preserving and defending title to land is allowable as a deduction in computing any chargeable gain arising on its eventual disposal.[19] This would extend to any costs incurred in legal action to prevent restrictions being placed on the use of the land.

Farmers and other landowners may find that there is a loss of profit involved in having monuments on the land used for the business. While there is no tax deduction for the loss of profits, much of the direct additional "revenue" expenditure will be deductible in computing the profits of the business, provided it passes the normal test of being incurred wholly and exclusively for the purposes of the business.

7.47   Where income is received tax free in the terms of an agreement under section 17 of the AMAAA (see para. 7.27 above), any related expenditure will not be tax-deductible. For instance, the agreement might require the upkeep of rabbit-proof fences. This expense would not be allowed as a deduction. In many cases, the agreement is not to do things, *e.g.* not to plant trees in a particular area, or not to deep-plough; in these cases, there would be no expenditure which was disallowed.

7.48   The schedular system of income tax (described at para. 7.13 above) prevents any deduction for an expense unless it falls within the rules of the appropriate source of income. It may therefore be important to plan matters in such a way that the income falls into the right category. A landowner can incur expenditure which is not effectively allowed for tax, particularly where an ancient monument is not located on the part of the estate used for a trade, such as farming. An ancient monument situated on land used for commercial forestry operations would be unlikely to attract any tax deduction for expenditure of a revenue nature incurred on preservation, etc.

7.49   A further area to watch is the precise ownership of the land and the capacity in which the expenditure is incurred. For example, expenditure by the freeholders of a farm which is tenanted to a family partnership (consisting of certain members of the family) would not be deductible in computing the profits of the farming business. Sometimes, ownership of "family" land-holdings is actually split between the ownership of various members of the family and family trusts.

---

[19] TCGA, s.38(1)(b).

4. CAPITAL TAXATION

Outline of United Kingdom capital taxation

Inheritance tax was introduced in 1986. It imposes a charge to tax on the estates of deceased persons. Certain lifetime transfers are also taxed, particularly those made within seven years before death. A disposal by way of gift, or otherwise "not at arm's length", will normally be subject to capital gains tax as if the full market price had been obtained unless there is a specific relieving provision which can be applied.

7.50

Landowners face particular challenges in planning to reduce the impact of capital taxation, because their assets tend to be in illiquid form which reduces the opportunities. A long-term view has to be taken: this is made more uncertain by the frequent changes in this area of taxation. Only just over 20 years have passed since estate duty was replaced with capital transfer tax, the precursor of inheritance tax.[20]

7.51

Special reliefs available in respect of heritage property

Gifts for national purposes

A transfer of any asset is exempt from inheritance tax if it is to certain bodies, listed in Schedule 3 to the Inheritance Tax Act 1984. This list includes the National Trust, the Historic Buildings and Monuments Commission for England and the equivalent Scottish bodies.[21] Capital gains tax is also excluded on gifts to these bodies.[22] Thus, if the owner of such property finds its upkeep onerous it can be transferred to such a body free of these taxes.

7.52

When property is subject to conditional exemption (which will have been agreed on a previous transfer), it can be either given or sold to such a body free of capital gains tax (see below).[23]

On a sale to the bodies mentioned above, the price paid by the public body will be somewhat less than the full market price. The principle is that the tax-saving should be shared between the parties. Normally, the price is set so that the vendor retains about 25 per cent of the tax saved. This is known as the "douceur".

7.53

Gifts for public benefit

A separate relief exempts (from both inheritance tax and capital gains tax) transfers of certain specified assets to non-profit making bodies.[24] The assets include land of "outstanding scenic or historic or scientific interest". The

7.54

---

[20] The Inland Revenue publishes a booklet entitled *Capital Taxation and the National Heritage* (IR67) which is available from Inland Revenue Reference Room at Somerset House, London WC2R 1LB, price £5.20.

[21] Inheritance Tax Act 1984 (IHTA), s.25.

[22] TCGA, s.257(1).

[23] *ibid.* ss.258(2).

[24] IHTA, s.26 and TCGA, s. 258(1).

agreement of the Inland Revenue has to be obtained before the transfer is made: power to confer this relief is given to the Inland Revenue, not the DNH or SOSE, but they do take expert advice. They will also require to be satisfied as to the continued preservation of the property and the provision of reasonable public access.

Maintenance funds for historic buildings, etc.

7.55 A qualifying maintenance fund is one which comes within the rules set out in Schedule 4 to the Inheritance Tax Act 1984.[25] The purpose is to provide funds for the maintenance of land or buildings which qualify for conditional exemption (see below). The fund attracts a variety of tax privileges, and must be held on approved trusts. A degree of flexibility is retained, as money can be withdrawn from the fund after an initial six-year period if needed for other purposes, although there will be an inheritance tax charge at this point.

Conditional exemption

7.56 The conditional exemption rules allow property to be transferred free of inheritance tax and capital gains tax.[26] The property must be designated, by the Inland Revenue. The categories include land of outstanding scenic or historic or scientific interest, buildings of outstanding historic or architectural interest, land essential for the protection of the character and amenities of such a building, and objects historically associated with such a building.[27] Scheduled monuments, and other significant archaeological remains, are specifically mentioned by the Inland Revenue as being likely to qualify.

7.57 The recipient must give undertakings as to the maintenance and repair of the property and the preservation of its character.[28] If the item is an artefact, the conditions also require it to be kept permanently in the United Kingdom, with the exception of short periods agreed in advance with the Inland Revenue. In August 1993, the Inland Revenue announced new procedures for monitoring compliance with agreements,[29] which include an annual report by the owner. A material breach of the conditions can lead to an inheritance tax and capital gains tax liability on the withdrawal of the agreement.[30]

7.58 Undertakings have also to be given for securing "reasonable access" to the public. The nature of the requirement depends on the type of asset:

    (i)   *Land.* The undertakings may involve formalising existing informal access to the land or extending or joining public paths to make a through route. New access may be needed to areas of particular landscape interest if none exists previously. For some scientific

---

[25] IHTA, ss.27, 77.
[26] *ibid.* ss.30–34, 78, 79 and TCGA, s.258(1).
[27] IHTA, s.31(1).
[28] *ibid.* s.31(2), (4).
[29] *Inland Revenue Tax Bulletin*, August 1993, p.89.
[30] IHTA, s.32(2); TCGA, s.258(5).

land it may be necessary to limit access. In the past, the degree of access required has not always been extensive, but there has in recent years been a degree of political pressure to increase it.

(ii) *Buildings*. The required access is expressed in terms of the number of days per year it is open to the public. This depends on the size of the building and may range from one day per week in Spring and Summer, plus Bank Holidays, for a small building, up to 156 days per year for a larger building capable of handling a large number of visitors.

(iii) *Works of art, and other artefacts*. These have to be made available for viewing,[31] and are entered on a register which can be purchased from the CTO, or viewed at the Victoria and Albert Museum, the National Library of Scotland, the National Museum of Wales and the Ulster Museum.[32]

If a property subject to a conditional exemption is again transferred, on death or during lifetime, a further claim to conditional exemption may be made in respect of the second transfer. If the property is sold, a charge to inheritance tax arises based on the value of the property at that time.[33] There is some uncertainty as to what constitutes a disposal bringing these provisions into play: a short tenancy for which no premium is charged will probably be outside the rules, but the grant of a long tenancy for a substantial premium will almost certainly attract the inheritance tax charge (as well as any taxes on the granting of the tenancy itself). **7.59**

Agricultural and business property relief

Many monuments are to be found on land which qualifies for agricultural or business property relief. In this case, the value of the land and buildings may be reduced for inheritance tax purposes by 100 per cent. It may often be preferable to rely on this relief to save tax where it is available, rather than entering into the restrictions imposed by conditional exemption. It is important to remember that if a charge to inheritance tax arises on a breach of the conditions (see above), agricultural or business property relief will not be available to reduce the tax charge, because there is no transfer of value at that time. **7.60**

5. VALUE ADDED TAX (VAT)

General

VAT must be charged where "taxable supplies" are made in the course or furtherance of a business.[34] It is therefore necessary to determine: **7.61**

(i) whether in VAT terms, a supply is made;

---

[31] IHTA, s.31(4).

[32] *Inland Revenue Press Release*, April 22, 1996 (a press release is issued quarterly summarising changes and highlighting noteworthy additions to the list).

[33] IHTA, s.32(3)(b).

[34] Value Added Tax Act 1994 (VATA), s.4.

(ii) whether the supply is taxable; and

(iii) whether the supply is made in the course or furtherance of a business.[35]

Business

7.62 Perhaps the most important factor in determining whether VAT liabilities arise is the question of whether or not a business is being carried on. Where there is not, there is no question of VAT becoming due. For example if an excavation is carried out on land owned by an individual in a private capacity, any payments received by the individual to compensate for the disturbance will be free of any liability to VAT.

By contrast, if the land is part of a commercial development site it will be an asset of a business and any payment received could therefore fall within the VAT net.

Supply

7.63 The word supply is very broadly defined in the VAT legislation. In brief, where anything is done for a consideration, or where a person refrains from doing something in return for a consideration, a supply is deemed to have occurred.

Taxable supplies

7.64 All supplies are deemed to be "taxable" at the standard rate of VAT unless the law deems them to be exempt or zero rated. Exemptions and zero ratings are set out in the Value Added Tax Act 1994, Scheds 8 and 9.

Transfer of property interests

7.65 The VAT legislation concerning land and property is extremely complex and the pitfalls are numerous. It is recommended that specialist advice be sought when uncertainty arises, and in all cases where large sums are involved.

In general, land and property are exempt from VAT. There are however, exceptions and it is these exceptions which create many of the difficulties. The matter is further complicated by the fact that the vendor can, in certain circumstances, choose to charge VAT by means of the so called "election to waive exemption".[36]

---

[35] VATA, s.4

[36] VATA, Sched. 10.

Compensation

It is commonly held that compensation is outside the scope of VAT. This is a   **7.66**
misconception and VAT liabilities can arise where the recipient of a
compensation payment is obliged to do something or to refrain from doing
something in return for the payment.

This matter has been the subject of a number of disputes between
taxpayers and the VAT authorities and a cautious approach is advisable. In
some cases it may be necessary to obtain agreement with the local VAT office
as to whether or not VAT is due.

Admission fees

Admission fees will be standard rated for VAT assuming the person making   **7.67**
the charge is registered or registerable for VAT. The current VAT registration
limit is £47,000 and Customs and Excise must be notified if taxable supplies
exceed this figure in a 12-month period or if there are grounds for believing
the limit will be breached in the next 30 days. Voluntary registration is
possible below this limit.

Disposal of artefacts

There is no general relief for archaeological artefacts so their sale by a   **7.68**
business will, in principle, be subject to VAT at the standard rate. There is,
however, a special scheme for second hand items which would include such
artefacts. The scheme is widely used by dealers in antiques and collectors
items and in brief, it allows for the VAT charge to be limited to the profit
margin achieved on the item sold.

The scheme only applies if certain record-keeping requirements are   **7.69**
complied with and the seller does not reclaim VAT on the purchase of the
item. If these conditions are not met, VAT must be charged on the full sale
price.

If artefacts are donated by a business VAT will be due on the cost of each
item unless its cost was less than £10 or the business did not reclaim any
VAT charged on the purchase of the item. Where the artefact is found on the
land owned by a business both of the above tests can be satisfied and no
liability would arise where the item is donated to say, a local museum.

Imported artefacts

There is a 14.29 per cent reduction in the value of certain archaeological   **7.70**
artefacts from outside the European Union, for the purpose of VAT on
importation. This reduces the effective rate of VAT on importation to 2.5 per
cent. For imports before May 1, 1995, the rate was nil. This treatment
extends to "collectors' pieces of zoological, botanical, mineralogical,
anatomical, historical, archaeological, paleontological or ethnographic
interest".[37]

---

[37] VATA, s.21(4)–(6).

7.71   The importation of "second hand goods", from outside the European Union, with a view to sale by auction is free of VAT on importation. The same treatment applies to "works of art" imported for exhibition with a view to sale, but few archaeological artefacts will come within the definition of "works of art" for these purposes.[38]

6. OTHER TAXES AND DUTIES

Uniform business rates

7.72   Any non-domestic property (other, generally, than that occupied by the Crown) is liable to the non-domestic rate. There are a number of exemptions which may be relevant in an archaeological context.

Charities

7.73   Land occupied by a charity, and used for charitable purposes, is liable to rates at 20 per cent of the amount which would otherwise be due. The charging authority has discretion to reduce this, even to nil.[39]

Agricultural land and buildings

7.74   No rates are payable on agricultural land and buildings.[40] It will be a question of fact whether land containing an ancient monument or other archaeological site remains within the definition of "agricultural land and buildings". If the land is taken into some other use, *e.g.* by being fenced off and opened to the public, it is likely that the exemption will be lost.

Unoccupied property—listed buildings and scheduled monuments

7.75   Where property is unoccupied and is either a listed building or a scheduled ancient monument no rates are payable.[41]

Valuation

7.76   Rates are charged according to the rateable value of the property, which is based on a notional rent. Where the commercial value of land is significantly reduced by the presence of a scheduled monument or other archaeological remains, this will in principle be reflected in the rateable value of the property.

The list is revised every five years (the latest list came into effect on April 1, 1995). A ratepayer can make a proposal to have the value amended where

---

[38] VAT (Treatment of Transactions) Order 1995 (S.I. 1995 No. 958).
[39] Local Government Finance Act 1988 ss.43(6), 45(6) and 47(1).
[40] *ibid.* Sched.5, para. 1.
[41] S.I. 1989 No. 2261, reg. 2(2)(d)(e).

there has been a "material change in circumstances", which includes the "mode or category of occupation of the property". The proposal may be made at any time until one year after the next valuation list comes into force. Any reduction in rateable value is back-dated to the date of the change in circumstances.[42]

Stamp duty

Duty is payable, by the transferee, on certain legal documents. For the purposes of archaeology, the principle charges will be on documents transferring a freehold, or granting a tenancy. There is no duty on gifts.[43]   **7.77**

A number of documents are exempted, and as stamp duty is payable by the transferee it is the status of that party which governs the position in many cases. The exemptions include certain transfers to a maintenance fund for historic buildings[44] and transfers to charities.[45]

Customs duties

Import duty will be nil in respect of archaeological artefacts imported. See   **7.78**
above for the VAT position on imports. There is no export levy charged by the United Kingdom, but exporters will need to consider the position in the other country, especially if this is outside the European Union.

---

[42] S.I. 1993 No. 291, regs 3, 4A(1)(b), 4B(1).

[43] Stamp Duty (Exempt Instruments) Regulations 1987, (S.I. 1987 No. 516).

[44] Finance Act 1980, s.98.

[45] Finance Act 1982, s.129.

8. Epilogue

The legislation and guidance concerning archaeology is extensive and **8.1**
complex. About 13,000 sites are currently protected as scheduled ancient
monuments and other specific types of site, such as ecclesiastical buildings,
military remains and shipwrecks, have their own individual legislation.
Changes are expected imminently to the law on treasure trove in England
and Wales; but although archaeologists will continue to debate the issues
about the morality of excavating human remains, the activities of metal
detectorists and even the need for licences to undertake archaeological
excavations, no immediate changes in legislation are expected.

Some public utilities are charged under their own legislation to have regard **8.2**
to archaeological remains. However, for the bulk of known archaeological
sites, in excess of 600,000, their only protection is through the planning
system as "a material consideration" following government guidance in PPG
16 issued in 1990 and PPG 15 in 1994. Additional non-statutory designations
have been produced to deal with other site types: world heritage sites and
English Heritage's respective registers of historic parks and gardens and
historic battlefields.

No changes are anticipated to the Ancient Monuments and Archaeological **8.3**
Areas Act 1979 now that the system for achieving scheduled monument
consent for certain cases has been made more efficient through the Ancient
Monuments (Class Consents) Order 1994. However, it is expected that the
protection of scheduled ancient monuments will be policed more strongly,
with English Heritage prepared to instigate punitive proceedings against
landowners and individuals who cause damage to monuments or use metal
detectors within the designated areas.

The setting of scheduled ancient monuments is becoming a more **8.4**
recognised cause for concern although it can be difficult to define. Broadly
speaking the setting is taken as being what can be seen and heard to or from
the monument and this is becoming a major issue in planning decisions at
appeal. If the legislation itself is not going to change certainly its effects will
be felt more widely; for English Heritage intend to increase the number of
scheduled ancient monuments from 12,500 in 1984 to about 60,000 by 2007
or 2008.[1] However, although the proposed target figures appear to have fallen
behind predictions[2] leading to a shortfall of nearly 5,000 by 2008, the increase
still represents more than a doubling of the number of scheduled ancient

---

[1] H.C. Committee of Public Accounts, *Twenty-ninth Report: Protecting and Managing England's Heritage Property* (1993), p.viii.
[2] Olivier, *Archaeology Review 1993–1994* (1994), p.10.

monuments in 1994. Since there is no appeal against a monument being scheduled, the only recourse for the landowner will be to apply for scheduled monument consent and, if this is refused, a public inquiry.

8.5   Although five cities had areas of archaeological importance designated under the Ancient Monuments and Archaeological Areas Act 1979, it is recognised that this part of the legislation has significant shortcomings. Not least of them is the fact that the areas are not protected and, although construction work may be delayed while an archaeological excavation takes place, the funding is not the responsibility of the developer. In these circumstances either the local authority or English Heritage must foot the bill.

8.6   In May 1996, the Government published two discussion documents[3] which, if adopted, will affect the implementation of the existing Ancient Monuments' legislation and the role of LPAs. In terms of planning control, the specific issues are the repeal of the areas of archaeological importance (AAI), delegation of scheduled monument controls to local authorities, a statutory duty of LPAs to maintain sites and monuments records, lifting of the requirements for scheduled monument consent beneath Church of England places of worship and alterations to Crown immunity. Only five Areas of Archaeological Importance were designated in England under the AMAAA 1979 and were designed to prevent areas of archaeological interest being damaged without record. However, there was no provision for the financing of any archaeological investigation nor for their preservation. Later guidance through PPG16 in England and Wales and NPPG5 in Scotland has superseded the effectiveness of the AAIs, hence the proposal for their abolition.

Under the AMAA Act 1979 all works to scheduled monuments required scheduled monument consent (SMC) from the Secretary of State. This was modified slightly by the Ancient Monuments (Class Consents) Order 1994 for certain minor works. Recognising that the number of scheduled ancient monuments is being radically increased, it is now proposed that LPAs might have the expertise and machinery to deal more appropriately with such applications.

8.7   At present all county councils in England and some in Scotland have a sites and monuments record (SMR); but although recognised in subordinate planning legislation,[4] the SMR has no statutory foundation and so no legal requirement for its maintenance. It is proposed that in England local government should be required to maintain the SMRs, although in each case the relevant authority tier will depend upon the local situation. In Scotland, although it is proposed to make the SMR a statutory obligation on local authorities, this may be achieved with government assistance. In Wales, where the SMRs are maintained by the Welsh Archaeological Trusts in conjunction with the Royal Commission on the Ancient and Historical Monuments of Wales, the Government does not intend any change.

---

[3] *Protecting Our Heritage* (published jointly by the Department of National Heritage and the Welsh Office) and *Protecting the built heritage: A Green Paper* (published by Historic Scotland with the Scottish Office)(1996).

[4] The extent of statutory recognition of the SMR is found in art. 1(1) of the GPDO 1995, which defines "site of archaeological interest" as meaning land "which is within a site registered in any record adopted by resolution by a County Council and known as the County Sites and Monuments Record".

In England and Wales it is expected that SMRs will contain information **8.8** about scheduled and unscheduled monuments which will encourage concern about not only the preservation of ancient monuments but also their setting.

The Government considers that, in England, where cathedrals and **8.9** churches of the Church of England may be affected by the dual controls of ecclesiastical and ancient monument legislation, the requirement for SMC may be lifted for scheduled monuments beneath places of worship. A similar arrangement may be considered for other denominations which have satisfactory internal controls.

Whilst Government statements on Crown immunity have already made it **8.10** clear that the statutory requirements for scheduled monuments will be followed, enforcement procedures will be by informal negotiations "and any disputes resolved through normal machinery of Government procedures".

If enacted through legislation, the proposals represent a major shift in the **8.11** protection of national monuments from central to local government and, to a much lesser extent, the Church of England. Of even greater significance to local authorities in England will be the obligation to maintain the SMRs. The demise of AAIs, which has been expected, will make no difference in practice. It also emphasises the success of PPG16. Crown immunity, whilst recognising the desire to follow the appropriate procedures, is essentially left intact.

Undoubtedly, a major change of attitude has taken place towards the **8.12** developer under PPG 16, which considers that the financial and preservation implications are the responsibility of those who threaten them. In effect the launch of PPG 16 in November 1990 opened up developers' funds for archaeology. No longer is the cost of rescue archaeology the burden of English Heritage and the more caring local authorities but placed firmly on the shoulders of those who are to damage the archaeological remains.

PPG 16 is not a legislative requirement but only government guidance. **8.13** Nevertheless the responsibility for its implementation has been handed to local planning authorities who know, at first hand, the balance to be drawn between the requirements for development and its impact upon archaeological remains. This weighty PPG 16 has been further bolstered by PPG 15 in 1994, which now directly links the guidance with historic buildings, historic parks and gardens, historic battlefields, world heritage sites and historic landscapes.

Despite these issues the outlook for archaeology as a registered discipline **8.14** within the planning system is optimistic. After all, the profession has undergone a revolution within five years and has shown that it can provide a suitable response. The legislation is clear and government guidance has been consistent. Not surprisingly, there has been an increase in planning applications with archaeological implications and an increase in appeals. It is to be hoped that the variations in archaeological requirements for planning applications will even out; though the decisions made at appeal appear to be consistent even if the issues are becoming more complex. To some extent archaeology has always been about debate. Now it is on a different stage with a wider audience. It is for archaeologists to present their case in a manner which can be understood by others.

Appendix A

THE ANCIENT MONUMENTS (CLASS CONSENTS) ORDER 1994 (S.1. 1994 NO. 1381)

The Secretary of State, after consultation with the Historic Buildings and **A.1** Monuments Commission for England, as respects England, and the Secretary of State for Wales, as respects Wales, in exercise of the powers conferred on them by sections 2, 3 and 60 of the Ancient Monuments and Archaeological Areas Act 1979,[1] and of all other powers enabling them in that behalf, hereby make the following Order:

Citation, commencement, interpretation and extent

1.—(1) This Order may be cited as the Ancient Monuments (Class **A.2** Consents) Order 1994 and shall come into force on 14th June 1994.
(2)   In this Order, unless the context otherwise requires—
"the Act" means the Ancient Monuments and Archaeological Areas Act 1979;
"carried out lawfully" means carried out in accordance with the terms of a consent granted by order under section 3 of the Act, or which would have been so carried out if during the period in question the monument had been a scheduled monument;
"the Commission" means the Historic Buildings and Monuments Commission for England;
"consent" means scheduled monument consent;
"domestic gardening works" includes works carried out in the non-commercial cultivation of allotments;
"horticultural works" includes domestic gardening works; and
"ploughed land" means land on which ploughing has been carried out lawfully within the period of six years immediately preceding the works in question.
(3)   This Order applies to England and Wales.

---

[1] 1946 c.59; section 36(2) was amended by the Opencast Act 1958 (c.69), section 46(1); the Coal Industry Act 1977 (c.39), Schedule 4, paragraph 1(5) and the Coal Industry Act 1987 (c.3), section 1(2) and Schedule 1, paragraph 1.

Scheduled monument consent granted by this Order

A.3   2.—(1) Subject to the provisions of this article, consent is hereby granted under section 3 of the Act for the execution of works of any class or description specified as permitted works in the Schedule to this Order.

(2)   The consent granted is subject to any condition specified in the said Schedule in relation to works of a particular class or description.

(3)   Nothing in this article shall operate so as to grant consent contrary to any limitation or condition specified in a consent granted under Part I of the Act otherwise than by this Order.

Revocation and saving

A.4   3.—(1) Subject to the provisions of this article, the Ancient Monuments (Class Consents) Order 1981[2] ("the 1981 Order") and the Ancient Monuments (Class Consents) (Amendment) Order 1984[3] ("the 1984 Order") are hereby revoked.

(2)   The 1981 Order and the 1984 Order shall continue to be effective in respect of works commenced before this Order comes into force and any limitation or condition specified in this Order shall be disregarded in the application of article 2(3) of the 1981 Order.

SCHEDULE   Article 2(1) and (2)

A.5   CLASSES OR DESCRIPTIONS OF WORKS FOR THE
        EXECUTION OF WHICH SCHEDULED MONUMENT CONSENT
              IS GRANTED BY ARTICLE 2 OF THIS ORDER

CLASS 1. AGRICULTURAL, HORTICULTURAL AND
FORESTRY WORKS

Permitted works: Agricultural, horticultural and forestry works of the same kind as those previously carried out lawfully in the same location and on the same spot within that location within the period of six years immediately preceding the date on which the works commence; but excluding works falling into one or more of the following categories—

Works not permitted: (a) in the case of ploughed land, any works likely to disturb the soil of any part of that land below the depth at which ploughing of that part has previously been carried out lawfully;

(b) in the case of land other than ploughed land, any works likely to disturb the soil below the depth of 300 millimetres;

---

[2] 1979 c.46; sections 2 and 3 were amended by the National Heritage Act 1983 (c.47), Schedule 4, paragraphs 27 and 28.
[3] S.I. 1981/1302.

(c) sub-soiling, drainage works, the planting or uprooting of trees, hedges or shrubs, the stripping of top soil, tipping operations, or the commercial cutting and removal of turf;

(d) the demolition, removal, extension, alteration or disturbance of any building, structure or work or of the remains thereat;

(e) the erection of any building or structure;

(f) in the case of works other than domestic gardening works, the laying of paths, hardstandings or foundations for buildings or the erection of fences or other barriers.

CLASS 2. WORKS BY BRITISH COAL MINING OPERATIONS[4]

Permitted works: Works executed more than 10 metres below ground level [by any licensed operator (within the meaning of the Coal Industry Act 1994)]: by the British Coal Corporation, or any person acting pursuant to a licence granted by the Corporation under section 36(2) of the Coal Industry Nationalisation Act 1946.

CLASS 3. WORKS BY BRITISH WATERWAYS BOARD

Permitted works: Works executed by the British Waterways Board, in relation to land owned or occupied by them, being works or repair or maintenance, not involving a material alteration to a scheduled monument, which are essential for the purpose of ensuring the functioning of a canal.

CLASS 4. WORKS FOR THE REPAIR OR MAINTENANCE OF MACHINERY

Permitted works: Works for the repair or maintenance of machinery, being works which do not involve a material alteration to a scheduled monument.

CLASS 5. WORKS URGENTLY NECESSARY FOR SAFETY OR HEALTH

Permitted works: Works which are urgently necessary in the interests of safety or health provided that:—

(a) the works are limited to the minimum measures immediately necessary; and

---

[4] S.I. 1994/2576.

(b)   notice in writing justifying in detail the need for the works is given to the Secretary of State as soon as reasonably practicable.

CLASS 6. WORKS BY THE COMMISSION

Permitted works: Works executed by the Commission.

CLASS 7. WORKS OF ARCHAEOLOGICAL EVALUATION

Permitted works: Works of archaeological evaluation carried out on or on behalf of a person who has applied for consent under section 2 of the Act being works carried out—
(a)   in order to supply the Secretary of State with information required by him for the determination of that application;
(b)   under the supervision of a person approved for that purpose in writing by the Secretary of State or the Commission; and
(c)   in accordance with a written specification approved for that purpose by the Secretary of State or the Commission.

CLASS 8. WORKS CARRIED OUT UNDER CERTAIN AGREEMENTS CONCERNING ANCIENT MONUMENTS

Permitted works: Works for the maintenance or preservation of a scheduled monument or its amenities being works executed in accordance with the terms of a written agreement between the occupier of the monument and the Secretary of State or the Commission under section 17[5] of the Act.

CLASS 9. WORKS GRANT AIDED UNDER SECTION 24 OF THE ACT

Permitted works: Works for the preservation, maintenance or management of a scheduled monument being works executed in accordance with the terms of a written agreement under which the Secretary of State or the Commission defray, or contribute towards, the cost of those works pursuant to their powers under section 24[6] of the Act.

---

[5] Section 17 was amended by the National Heritage Act 1983 (c.47), Schedule 4, paragraph 43.
[6] Section 24 was amended by the National Heritage Act 1983 (c.47), Schedule 4, paragraph 48.

CLASS 10. WORKS UNDERTAKEN BY THE ROYAL COMMISSION ON THE HISTORICAL MONUMENTS OF ENGLAND OR THE ROYAL COMMISSION ON ANCIENT AND HISTORICAL MONUMENTS OF WALES

Permitted works: Works consisting of the placing of survey markers to a depth not exceeding 300 millimetres for the purpose of measured surveying of visible remains undertaken by the Royal Commission on the Historical Monuments of England or by the Royal Commission on Ancient and Historical Monuments of Wales.

Appendix B

PLANNING POLICY GUIDANCE: ARCHAEOLOGY
AND PLANNING (PPG 16 DEPARTMENT OF THE
ENVIRONMENT (1990))—PRINCIPAL TEXT AND
ANNEX 4

Introduction

1. This guidance is for planning authorities in England, property owners,   **B.1**
developers, archaeologists, amenity societies and the general public. It sets
out the Secretary of State's policy on archaeological remains on land, and
how they should be preserved or recorded both in an urban setting and in the
countryside. It gives advice on the handling of archaeological remains and
discoveries under the development plan and control systems, including the
weight to be given to them in planning decisions and the use of planning
conditions. (Separate controls exist for scheduled monuments—see Annex
3.) The guidance pulls together and expands existing advice, within the
existing legislative framework. It places no new duties on local authorities,
and should not place any significant additional burden on local authorities.

2. The guidance is arranged as follows:
    A – **The importance of archaeology:** a general introduction (paragraphs
    3–14)
    B – **Advice on the handling of archaeological matters in the planning
    process:**
        – Development plans (paragraphs 15–16)
        – Sites and Monuments Records—SMRs (paragraph 17)
        – Planning applications (paragraphs 18–26)
        – Planning decisions (paragraphs 27–28)
        – Planning conditions (paragraphs 29–30)
        – Discovery of archaeological remains during development (paragraph
        31)
    Annex 1 – **Key bodies and organisations.**
    Annex 2 – **Contact Addresses for County Archaeological Officers and SMRs.**
    Annex 3 – **Legislative arrangements:** scheduling of ancient monuments,
    control of scheduled monuments and their management; Offences;
    Metal Detectors; Areas of Archaeological Importance (AAIs); Envi-
    ronmental Assessment; Simplified Planning Zones (SPZs).
    Annex 4 – **Secretary of State's criteria for scheduling.**
    Annex 5 – **Ancient Monuments (Class Consent) Order 1981.**

THE IMPORTANCE OF ARCHAEOLOGY

B.2 3. Archaeological remains are irreplaceable. They are evidence—for prehistoric periods, the only evidence—of the past development of our civilization.

4. Today's archaeological landscape is the product of human activity over thousands of years. It ranges through settlements and remains of every period, from the camps of the early hunter gatherers 400,000 years ago to remains of early 20th century activities. It includes places of worship, defence installations, burial grounds, farms and fields, and sites of manufacture.

5. These remains vary enormously in their state of preservation and in the extent of their appeal to the public. "Upstanding" remains are familiar enough—the great stone circles, the castle and abbey ruins of the Middle Ages or abandoned coastal defence systems. But less obvious archaeological remains, such as ancient settlements and field systems, are also to be found across large parts of the country. Some prehistoric sites in wetland areas contain important wood and organic remains. Many buildings in older towns lie on top of Roman, Anglo-Saxon or medieval structures.

6. **Archaeological remains should be seen as a finite, and non-renewable resource, in many cases highly fragile and vulnerable to damage and destruction. Appropriate management is therefore essential to ensure that they survive in good condition. In particular, care must be taken to ensure that archaeological remains are not needlessly or thoughtlessly destroyed. They can contain irreplaceable information about our past and the potential for an increase in future knowledge. They are part of our sense of national identity and are valuable both for their own sake and for their role in education, leisure and tourism.**

7. The present century has been a period of striking environmental changes. Some changes, like the erosion of coastal areas, have occurred naturally. But much archaeological heritage has been destroyed by human activity—for example, by modern construction methods in urban development and expansion of the road network, by modern agricultural techniques (in particular deep ploughing or drainage of wetlands), and by mineral extraction.

B.3 8. With the many demands of modern society, it is not always feasible to save all archaeological remains. The key question is where and how to strike the right balance. **Where nationally important archaeological remains, whether scheduled or not, and their settings, are affected by proposed development there should be a presumption in favour of their physical preservation.** Cases involving archaeological remains of lesser importance will not always be so clear cut and planning authorities will need to weigh the relative importance of archaeology against other factors including the need for the proposed development (see also paragraph 27). Regardless of the circumstances, taking decisions is much easier if any archaeological aspects of a development site can be considered early on in the planning and development control process. This is discussed in Section B.

9. Archaeological records for England currently contain around 600,000 sites and monuments. some 13,000 nationally important cases enjoy special protection as "scheduled monuments", under the Ancient Monuments and

Archaeological Areas Act 1979. English Heritage have embarked on a survey programme which is expected to result in significant additional numbers being given this statutory protection (see Annex 3).

10.   Scheduling archaeological remains ensures that the case for preservation is fully considered given any proposals for development or other work which might damage the monument. The planning system, as paragraph 18 emphasizes, is equally in a position to consider the desirability of preserving archaeological remains, and the various options open to planning authorities for dealing with archaeological remains are considered in Section B. Much can be achieved within the wider planning process when developers are prepared to enter into discussions with archaeologists and consider fully the needs of archaeology. This voluntary approach to considering the needs of archaeology is a well-established and growing practice and has been formalized in Codes of Practice by the British Archaeologists' and Developers' Liaison Group (BADLG) (see paragraph 26; also Annex 1, paragraph 9), and the Confederation of British Industry (CBI) Code for Mineral Operators.

11.   Archaeological issues are often important in minerals planning, particularly in the extraction of sand and gravel. River valleys have provided an attractive place for man to settle but at the same time these areas often contain valuable sand and gravel resources. Minerals can clearly only be worked where they are found so they often differ from other forms of development in that there is not the same flexibility of choice of location. The CBI's revised Code of Practice for Mineral Operators on archaeological investigations provides advice on how minerals operators should consult archaeological interests in formulating planning applications, to ensure that archaeological factors are fully taken into account in the planning decision process.

12.   The key to informed and reasonable planning decisions, as emphasized in paragraphs 19 and 20, is for consideration to be given early, before formal planning applications are made, to the question of whether archaeological remains exist on a site where development is planned and the implications for the development proposal. When important remains are known to exist or when archaeologists have good reason to believe that important remains exist, developers will be able to help by preparing sympathetic designs using, for example, foundations which avoid disturbing the remains altogether or minimise damage by raising ground levels under a proposed new structure, or by the careful siting of landscaped or open areas. There are techniques available for sealing archaeological remains underneath buildings or landscaping, thus securing their preservation for the future even though they remain inaccessible for the time being.

13.   If physical preservation *in situ* is not feasible, an archaeological excavation for the purposes of 'preservation by record', may be an acceptable alternative (see also paragraphs 24 and 25). From the archaeological point of view this should be regarded as a second best option. The science of archaeology is developing rapidly. Excavation means the total destruction of evidence (apart from removable artefacts) from which future techniques could almost certainly extract more information than is currently possible. Excavation is also expensive and time-consuming, and discoveries may have to be evaluated in a hurry against an inadequate research framework. The

preservation *in situ* of important archaeological remains is therefore nearly always to be preferred.

14. Positive planning and management can help to bring about sensible solutions to the treatment of sites with archaeological remains and reduce the areas of potential conflict between development and preservation. Both central government and English Heritage have important roles to play (see Annex 1). **But the key to the future of the great majority of archaeological sites and historic landscapes lies with local authorities, acting within the framework set by central government, in their various capacities as planning, education and recreational authorities, as well as with the owners of sites themselves. Appropriate planning policies in development plans and their implementation through development control will be especially important.**

B: ADVICE ON THE HANDLING OF ARCHAEOLOGICAL MATTERS IN THE PLANNING PROCESS

Development plans

B.4   15. **Development plans should reconcile the need for development with the interests of conservation including archaeology. Detailed development plans (i.e. local plans and unitary development plans) should include policies for the protection, enhancement and preservation of sites of archaeological interest and of their settings. The proposals map should define the areas and sites to which the policies and proposals apply. These policies will provide an important part of the framework for the consideration of individual proposals for development which affect archaeological remains and they will help guide developers preparing planning applications.**

16. Although the surviving numbers of archaeological remains are finite and irreplaceable, obviously not all of them are of equal importance. Planning authorities may therefore wish to base their detailed development plan policies and proposals on an evaluation of the archaeological remains in their area. **Archaeological remains identified and scheduled as being of national importance should normally be earmarked in development plans for preservation. Authorities should bear in mind that not all nationally important remains meriting preservation will necessarily be scheduled; such remains and, in appropriate circumstances, other unscheduled archaeological remains of more local importance, may also be identified in development plans as particularly worthy of preservation.**

Sites and Monuments Records—SMRs

B.5   17. All shire counties now maintain Sites and Monuments Records (SMRs) staffed by at least one professional officer, usually employed by the County Council. In London the SMR is maintained by English Heritage. In ex-Metropolitan county areas centralised SMRs are jointly maintained by Metropolitan Boroughs. An increasing number of non-metropolitan District Councils now employ archaeological staff within their planning departments. **All planning authorities should make full use of the expertise of County Archaeological Officers or their equivalents** (see Annex 1 paragraphs

4–6). English Heritage is ready to advise on the archaeological policies proposed for inclusion in draft plans. Consultation with English Heritage, as suggested by DOE Circular 22/84 (Annex C, paragraph 1), may be of particular help in urban areas where important archaeological remains may not be adequately identified by scheduling.

Planning applications

18.   **The desirability of preserving an ancient monument and its setting is a**   **B.6**
material consideration in determining planning applications whether that monument is scheduled or unscheduled. Developers and local authorities should take into account archaeological considerations and deal with them from the beginning of the development control process. Where local planning authorities are aware of a real and specific threat to a known archaeological site as a result of the potential exercise of *permitted development rights* (as set out in Schedule 2 to the Town and Country Planning General Development Order 1988) they may wish to consider the use of their powers under Article 4 of that Order to withdraw those rights and to require specific planning permission to be obtained before development can proceed. Most such directions require the Secretary of State's approval, either before they come into effect or within six months of being made, unless they relate solely to a listed building. Further advice on the use of Article 4 Directions is given in Appendix D to DOE Circular 22/88.

(a)   The first step: early consultations between developers and planning authorities

19.   The needs of archaeology and development can be reconciled, and   **B.7**
potential conflict very much reduced, if developers discuss their preliminary plans for development with the planning authority at an early stage. Once detailed designs have been prepared and finance lined up, flexibility becomes much more difficult and expensive to achieve. In their own interests, therefore, prospective developers should in all cases include as part of their research into the development potential of a site, which they undertake before making a planning application, an initial assessment of whether the site is known or likely to contain archaeological remains. The first step will be to contact the County Archaeological Officer or equivalent who holds the SMR, or English Heritage in London. The SMR provides information about the locations where archaeological remains are known or thought likely to exist. Where important remains are known to exist or where the indications are that the remains are likely to prove important, English Heritage are also ready to join in early discussions and provide expert advice. Special notification requirements apply in designated Areas of Archaeological Importance—see Annex 3, paragraphs 19–20.

20.   These consultations will help to provide prospective developers with advance warning of the archaeological sensitivity of a site. As a result they may wish to commission their own archaeological assessment by a professionally qualified archaeological organisation or consultant. This need not involve fieldwork. Assessment normally involves desk-based evaluation of existing information: it can make effective use of records of previous

discoveries, including any historic maps held by the County archive and local museums and record offices, or of geophysical survey techniques.

(b) Field evaluations

B.8 21.   Where early discussions with local planning authorities or the developer's own research indicate that important archaeological remains may exist, it is reasonable for the planning authority to request the prospective developer to arrange for an archaeological field evaluation to be carried out before any decision on the planning application is taken. This sort of evaluation is quite distinct from full archaeological excavation. It is normally a rapid and inexpensive operation, involving ground survey and small-scale trenching, but it should be carried out by a professionally qualified archaeological organisation or archaeologist. The Institute of Field Archaeologists (see Annex 1 for address), publishes a Directory of members, which developers may wish to consult. Evaluations of this kind help to define the character and extent of the archaeological remains that exist in the area of a proposed development, and thus indicate the weight which ought to be attached to their preservation. They also provide information useful for identifying potential options for minimising or avoiding damage. On this basis, an informed and reasonable planning decision can be taken.

22.   Local planning authorities can expect developers to provide the results of such assessments and evaluations as part of their application for sites where there is good reason to believe there are remains of archaeological importance. If developers are not prepared to do so voluntarily, the planning authority may wish to consider whether it would be appropriate to direct the applicant to supply further information under the provisions of Regulation 4 of the Town and Country Planning (Applications) Regulations 1988 and if necessary authorities will need to consider refusing permission for proposals which are inadequately documented. In some circumstances a formal Environmental Assessment may be necessary. For further details see Annex 3, paragraphs 21 and 22.

(c) Consultations by planning authorities

B.9 23.   When planning applications are made without prior discussion with the local planning authorities, the authorities should seek to identify those applications which have archaeological implications, and to assess their likely archaeological impact by consulting the County Archaeological Officer or equivalent and the County Sites and Monuments Record. When it is evident that a particular development proposal is likely to affect archaeological remains, applicants may need to be asked to provide more detailed information about their scheme—for example, the type of foundations to be used—or they may be asked to carry out an evaluation. Planning authorities should also ensure that they are fully informed about the nature and importance of the archaeological site and its setting. They should therefore seek archaeological advice, normally from the County Archaeological Officer or equivalent who in turn may wish to consult locally based museums and archaeological units and societies. In the case of a development proposal that is likely to affect the site of a scheduled ancient monument Article 18(1) of the Town and Country Planning General Development Order 1988, requires local planning authorities to consult

English Heritage. Local planning authorities may find it helpful to consult more generally with English Heritage. Local planning authorities may find it helpful to consult more generally with English Heritage on applications for development that affect non-scheduled sites. Existing information about a site is often sufficient to allow authorities to make planning decisions which take into account all material considerations.

(d) Arrangements for preservation by record including funding

24. The Secretary of State recognises that the extent to which remains can   **B.10** or should be preserved will depend upon a number of factors, including the intrinsic importance of the remains. Where it is not feasible to preserve remains, an acceptable alternative may be to arrange prior excavation, during which the archaeological evidence is recorded.

25. **Planning authorities should not include in their development plans policies requiring developers to finance archaeological works in return for the grant of planning permission.** By the same token developers should not expect to obtain planning permission for archaeologically damaging development merely because they arrange for the recording of sites whose physical preservation *in situ* is both desirable (because of their level of importance) and feasible. **Where planning authorities decide that the physical preservation *in situ* of archaeological remains is not justified in the circumstances of the case and that development resulting in the destruction of the archaeological remains should proceed, it would be entirely reasonable for the planning authority to satisfy itself before granting planning permission, that the developer has made appropriate and satisfactory provision for the excavation and recording of the remains. Such excavation and recording should be carried out before development commences, working to a project brief prepared by the planning authority and taking advice from archaeological consultants. This can be achieved through agreements reached between the developer, the archaeologist and the planning authority (see following paragraph). Such agreements should also provide for the subsequent publication of the results of the excavation. In the absence of such agreements planning authorities can secure excavation and recording by imposing conditions (see paragraphs 29 and 30).** In particular cases where the developer is a non-profit making community body, such as a charitable trust or housing association, which is unable to raise the funds to provide for excavation and subsequent recording without undue hardship, or in the case of an individual who similarly does not have the means to fund such work, an application for financial assistance may be made to English Heritage.

26. Agreements covering excavation, recording and the publication of the results may take different forms. For example, developers or their archaeological consultants and local planning authorities may wish to conclude a voluntary planning agreement under section 106 of the Town and Country Planning Act 1990 or other similar powers. The Secretary of State is pleased to note the increasing number of agreements being reached within the terms and spirit of the British Archaeologists' and Developers' Code of Practice. Model agreements between developers and the appropriate archaeological body regulating archaeological site investigations and excavations can be obtained from the British Property Federation. These agreements can provide for the excavation and recording of sites before development work starts.

Voluntary agreements are likely to provide more flexibility and be of greater mutual benefit to all the parties than could be provided for by alternative statutory means. They have the advantage of setting out clearly the extent of the developer's commitment, thereby reducing both uncertainty over the financial implications of having to accommodate any archaeological constraints and the possibility of unforseen delays to the construction programme.

Planning decisions

B.11 27.   Once the planning authority has sufficient information, there is a range of options for the determination of planning applications affecting archaeological remains and their settings. As stated in paragraph 8, where nationally important archaeological remains, whether scheduled or not, and their settings, are affected by proposed development there should be a presumption in favour of their physical preservation *in situ* i.e., a presumption against proposals which would involve significant alteration or cause damage, or which would have a significant impact on the setting of visible remains. **The case for the preservation of archaeological remains must however be assessed on the individual merits of each case, taking into account the archaeological policies in detailed development plans, together with all other relevant policies and material considerations, including the intrinsic importance of the remains and weighing these against the need for the proposed development.**

28.   There will no doubt be occasions, particularly where remains of lesser importance are involved, when planning authorities may decide that the significance of the archaeological remains is not sufficient when weighed against all other material considerations, including the need for development, to justify their physical preservation *in situ*, and that the proposed development should proceed. As paragraph 25 explains, planning authorities will, in such cases, need to satisfy themselves that the developer has made appropriate and satisfactory arrangements for the excavation and recording of the archaeological remains and the publication of the results. If this has not already been secured through some form of voluntary agreement, planning authorities can consider granting planning permission subject to conditions which provide for the excavation and recording of the remains before development takes place (see following section). Local planning authorities may, as a matter of last resort, need to consider refusing planning permission where developers do not seek to accommodate important remains.

Planning conditions

B.12 29.   **Planning authorities should seek to ensure that potential conflicts are resolved and agreements with developers concluded before planning permission is granted. Where the use of planning conditions is necessary, authorities should ensure that, in accordance with DOE Circular 1/85, they are fair, reasonable and practicable.** It is however open to the local planning authority to impose conditions designed to protect a monument and to ensure that reasonable access is given to a nominated archaeologist—either to hold a "watching brief" during the construction period or specifically to carry out archaeological investigation and recording in the course of the permitted operations on site. Conditions on these lines help to ensure that if remains of archaeological significance are disturbed in the course of the work, they can be recorded and, if necessary, emergency salvage undertaken.

30. **In cases when planning authorities have decided that planning permission may be granted but wish to secure the provision of archaeological excavation and the subsequent recording of the remains, it is open to them to do so by the use of a negative condition i.e. a condition prohibiting the carrying out of development until such time as works or other action, e.g. an excavation, have been carried out by a third party. In such cases the following model is suggested:**

> **"No development shall take place within the area indicated (this would be the area of archaeological interest) until the applicant has secured the implementation of a programme of archaeological work in accordance with a written scheme of investigation which has been submitted by the applicant and approved by the Planning Authority."** (Developers will wish to ensure that in drawing up a scheme, the timetable for the investigation is included within the details of the agreed scheme).

The use of this model is also advocated in the CBI Code of Practice for Mineral Operators. The advice on the use of the above condition should be regarded as supplementary to that contained in DOE Circular 1/85 relating to archaeology.

Discovery of archaeological remains during development

31. The preceding guidance (paragraphs 19 and 20 in particular) has been **B.13** framed to minimise occasions when totally unexpected problems arise while development is in progress. Nevertheless, and in spite of the best pre-planning application research, there may be occasions when the presence of archaeological remains only becomes apparent once development has commenced. Developers may wish to consider insuring themselves against the risk of a substantial loss while safeguarding the interest of historic remains unexpectedly discovered on the site. Conflicts that may otherwise arise between developers and archaeologists may not be easy to solve although English Heritage, who have a great deal of experience in handling these situations, are ready to offer practical advice, as is the British Archaeologists' and Developers' Liaison Group. Where fresh archaeological discoveries are deemed by the Secretary of State, on English Heritage's advice, to be of national importance, in accordance with his published criteria (see Annex 4), the Secretary of State for National Heritage has power to schedule the remains. In that event developers would need to seek separate scheduled monument consent before they continue work. It is also open to a planning authority or the Secretary of State to revoke a planning permission if deemed necessary, in which case there is provision for compensation. In the majority of cases, however, it should prove possible for the parties to resolve their differences through voluntary discussion and for a satisfactory compromise to be reached.

ANNEX 4

SECRETARY OF STATE'S CRITERIA FOR SCHEDULING ANCIENT MONUMENTS

B.14 The following criteria (which are not in any order of ranking), are used for assessing the national importance of an ancient monument and considering whether scheduling is appropriate. The criteria should not however be regarded as definitive, rather they are indicators which contribute to a wider judgment based on the individual circumstances of a case.

(i) *Period*: all types of monuments that characterise a category or period should be considered for preservation.

(ii) *Rarity*: there are some monument categories which in certain periods are so scarce that all surviving examples which still retain some archaeological potential should be preserved. In general, however, a selection must be made which portrays the typical and commonplace as well as the rare. This process should take account of all aspects of the distribution of a particular class of monument, both in a national and a regional context.

(iii) *Documentation*: the significance of a monument may be enhanced by the existence of records of previous investigation or, in the case of more recent monuments, by the supporting evidence of contemporary written records.

(iv) *Group Value*: the value of a single monument (such as a field system) may be greatly enhanced by its association with related contemporary monuments (such as a settlement and cemetery) or with monuments of different periods. In some cases, it is preferable to protect the complete group of monuments, including associated and adjacent land, rather than to protect isolated monuments within the group.

(v) *Survival/Condition*: the survival of a monument's archaeological potential both above and below ground is a particularly important consideration and should be assessed in relation to its present condition and surviving features.

(vi) *Fragility/Vulnerability*: highly important archaeological evidence from some field monuments can be destroyed by a single ploughing or unsympathetic treatment; vulnerable monuments of this nature would particularly benefit from the statutory protection which scheduling confers. There are also existing standing structures of particular form or complexity whose value can again be severely reduced by neglect or careless treatment and which are similarly well suited by scheduled monument protection, even if these structures are already listed historic buildings.

(vii) *Diversity*: some monuments may be selected for scheduling because they possess a combination of high quality features, others because of a single important attribute.

(viii) *Potential*: on occasion, the nature of the evidence cannot be specified precisely but it may still be possible to document reasons anticipating its existence and importance and so to demonstrate the justification for scheduling. This is usually confined to sites rather than upstanding monuments.

Appendix C

PLANNING GUIDANCE (WALES): PLANNING POLICY, WELSH OFFICE (1996)—EXTRACTS

Conservation Areas (Paras 122–129, 130 omitted)

131.　No additional statutory controls follow from the inclusion of a site in the World Heritage List or on the Register of Landscapes, Parks and Gardens of Special Historic Interest in Wales. However, local planning authorities should protect registered parks and gardens and take full account of the historic landscape in preparing their development plans and in determining planning applications. Once the parks and gardens section of the Register is complete, arrangements for statutory consultation on planning applications affecting sites on the Register will be introduced. In the meantime voluntary arrangements exist where individual sections of the Register have already been published.

132.　The inclusion of a site in the World Heritage List highlights the outstanding international importance to be taken into account by local planning authorities in determining planning applications and listed building consent applications, and by the Secretary of State in determining cases on appeal and following call-in.

133.　It is generally preferable for both the applicant and the planning authority if related applications for planning permission and for listed building or conservation area consent are considered concurrently.

Archaeology

134.　Where nationally important archaeological remains, whether scheduled or not, and their settings are affected by proposed development, there should be a presumption in favour of their physical preservation. Cases involving lesser archaeological remains will not always be so clear cut and planning authorities will need to weigh the relative importance of archaeology against other factors including the need for the proposed development.

135.　Archaeological remains identified and scheduled as being of national importance should normally be earmarked in development plans for preservation. Authorities should bear in mind that not all nationally important remains meriting preservation will necessarily be scheduled: such remains and, in appropriate circumstances, other unscheduled archaeological remains of more than local importance, may also be identified in development plans as particularly worthy of preservation.

136.   The needs of archaeology and development can be reconciled, and potential conflict very much reduced, if developers discuss their preliminary plans for development with the planning authority at an early stage. In certain circumstances, this may involve the developer in commissioning an archaeological assessment (sometimes as part of a wider environmental assessment) before submitting a planning application. If important remains are thought to exist at the development site, it is reasonable for the planning authority to request the prospective developer to arrange for an archaeological field evaluation to be carried out before any decision on the planning application is taken.

137.   Planning authorities should not include in their development plans policies requiring developers to finance archaeological works in return for the grant of planning permission. By the same token, developers should not expect to obtain planning permission for archaeologically damaging development merely because they arrange for the recording of sites whose physical preservation in situ is both desirable (because of their level of importance) and feasible.

138.   Where planning authorities decide that physical preservation in situ of archaeological remains is not justified in the circumstances of the case and that development resulting in the destruction of the archaeological remains should proceed, it would be entirely reasonable for the planning authority to satisfy itself, before granting planning permission, that the developer has made appropriate and satisfactory provision for the excavation and recording of the remains and the publication of the results of that work.

139.   In cases when planning authorities have decided that planning permission may be granted but wish to secure the provision of archaeological excavation and the subsequent recording of the remains, it is open to them to do so by the use of a negative condition, *i.e.* a condition prohibiting the carrying out of the development until such time as works or other action, *e.g.* an excavation, have been carried out by a third party.

140.   Scheduled ancient monuments are exempt from conservation area control; Scheduled Monument Consent for proposed works to a scheduled ancient monument must be sought from the Secretary of State. Planning permission alone is not sufficient to authorise the works.

Appendix D

PLANNING POLICY GUIDANCE: PLANNING AND
THE HISTORIC ENVIRONMENT (PPG 15,
DEPARTMENT OF THE ENVIRONMENT AND
DEPARTMENT OF NATIONAL HERITAGE
(1994))—EXTRACTS

2. DEVELOPMENT PLANS AND DEVELOPMENT CONTROL

2.1   The principal Act (as amended) requires development plans to include **D.1**
policies for 'the conservation of the natural beauty and amenity of the land'
and for 'the improvement of the physical environment'. The Town &
Country Planning (Development Plan) Regulations 1991 require authorities
to have regard to environmental considerations in preparing their plan
policies and proposals. The protection of the historic environment, whether
individual listed buildings, conservation areas, parks and gardens, battlefields or the wider historic landscape, is a key aspect of these wider
environmental responsibilities, and will need to be taken fully into account
both in the formulation of authorities' planning policies and in development
control.

Development plans

2.2   Structure, local, and unitary development plans are the main vehicle for **D.2**
ensuring that conservation policies are co-ordinated and integrated with
other planning policies affecting the historic environment. Imaginative
planning policies can not only reduce threats to it, but increase its
contribution to local amenity. By including suitable policies in their plans,
local authorities can give encouragement to the satisfactory reuse of
neglected historic buildings, particularly where major groups of buildings
need to be tackled comprehensively, and where other planning factors, such
as traffic problems, may be discouraging reuse.

2.3   Section 54A of the principal Act provides that where, in making any
determination under the Planning Acts, regard is to be had to the development plan, the determination must be made in accordance with the
development plan unless material considerations indicate otherwise. It is
therefore important that plans include all the criteria on the basis of which
planning decisions will be made. Plans should set out clearly all conservation

policies relevant to the exercise of an authority's development control functions, and also policies which are relevant to cases where development and conservation issues are linked and will need to be addressed together.

2.4   The Courts have accepted that section 54A does not apply to decisions on applications for listed building consent or conservation area consent, since in those cases there is no statutory requirement to have regard to the provisions of the development plan. However, authorities should ensure that aspects of conservation policy that are relevant, directly or indirectly, to development control decisions are included—for instance, policies for alterations or extensions to listed buildings that also constitute development (to which section 54A will directly apply). In view of the statutory requirements that authorities should have special regard to the desirability or preserving any listed building or its setting, or any features of special architectural or historic interest which it possesses, and should pay special attention to the desirability of preserving or enhancing the character or appearance of any conservation area in exercising their development control functions, plans should also include policies for works of demolition or alteration which, while not in themselves constituting development, could affect an authority's decision on a related application for planning permission.

2.5   There may be some detailed conservation policies which have no bearing on issues of development control—for instance, policies for the treatment of some internal features of listed buildings where this would not affect consideration of planning applications but might require listed building consent. Other examples may relate to certain types of alteration, repairs, maintenance or decoration. These policies should be presented as supplementary guidance rather than included in the plan itself. Such guidance will carry greater weight to the extent that it has been the subject of public consultation, has been formally adopted by the authority, and is published in a format which gives clear advice and is readily available to the public. Development plans should contain a reference to such policies in the reasoned justification, together with a clear indication of where those policies may be seen in full.

2.6   Full guidance on the preparation of plans is given in *PPG 12*. Structure plans and the first part of unitary development plans provide a statement of the overall strategy for a county, borough or metropolitan district area, and should include conservation of the historic environment as one of their key topics, taking account of any broad strategic regional planning guidance. The structure plan should provide a broad planning framework, guiding the approach to be adopted in local plans to such issues as the capacity of historic towns to sustain development, the relief of pressure on historic central areas by the identification of opportunities for growth elsewhere, and the provision of transport infrastructure which respects the historic environment.

2.7   Local plans and the second part of unitary development plans should set out more detailed development control policies for an authority's area: they should include both the policies which will apply over the area as a whole, and any policies and proposals which will apply to particular neigh-bourhoods. Both policies and proposals should be illustrated on the proposals map (see paragraph 7.14 of *PPG12*).

2.8   Local plans should set out clearly the planning authority's policies for the preservation and enhancement of the historic environment in their area, and the factors which will be taken into account in assessing different types of planning application—for example, proposals for the change of use of particular types of historic building or for new development which would affect their setting. It is important that clear policies are formulated for cases where new development is proposed in order to provide income for the upkeep of historic buildings (see Department of the Environment *Circular 16/91*). Plans should also include a strategy for the economic regeneration of rundown areas, and in particular seek to identify the opportunities which the historic fabric of an area can offer as a focus for regeneration. Excessively detailed or inflexible policies concerning individual buildings or groups of buildings should be avoided.

2.9   Plans which should set out authorities' broad criteria for the designation of new conservation areas and for the review of existing conservation area boundaries; and, where possible, which particular areas are in mind for both. The process of assessment, detailed definition or revision of boundaries, and formulation of proposals for individual conservation areas (as required by Section 71 of the Act) should involve extensive local consultation and should be pursued separately from the local plan process itself. But the plan should provide a policy framework, making clear to the public how detailed assessment documents and statements of proposals for individual conservation areas relate to the plan, and what weight will be given to them in decisions on applications for planning permission and conservation area consent. (See also paragraphs 4.3–4.7, 4.10 and 4.15). Designation strategies should take account of the fact that authorities now have general powers to control the demolition of dwelling houses outside conservation areas (see Department of the Environment *Circular 26/92*).

2.10   English Heritage is a statutory consultee of draft plans, but is also able to offer specialist advice at preparation stage. In conjunction with the Countryside Commission and English Nature, it is also issuing guidance on conservation in strategic and local plans. There can often be advantage in consultation at an early stage in plan preparation with other statutory agencies and with the national amenity societies and local conservation bodies, as well as wider public consultation at the formal deposit stage.

Development control

2.11   The Secretary of State attaches particular importance to early consultation with the local planning authority on development proposals which would affect historic sites and structures, whether listed buildings, conservation areas, parks and gardens, battlefields or the wider historic landscape. There is likely to be much more scope for refinement and revision of proposals if consultation takes place before intentions become firm and timescales inflexible. Local planning authorities should indicate their readiness to discuss proposals with developers before formal planning applications are submitted. They should expect developers to assess the likely impact of their proposals on the special interest of the site or structure in question, and to provide such written information or drawings as may be required to understand the significance of a site or structure before an

D.3

application is determined. The principle of early consultation should extend to English Heritage and the national amenity societies on cases where a formal planning or listed building consent application would be notifiable to them by direction or under the GDO.

2.12 It is generally preferable for both the applicant and the planning authority if related applications for planning permission and for listed building consent are considered concurrently. Authorities are required by section 66(1) of the Act, in considering whether to grant planning permission for development which affects a listed building or its setting, to have special regard to the desirability of preserving the building or its setting or any features of architectural or historic interest which it possesses. It is unlikely that they will be able to do so effectively unless the planning application is accompanied by a listed building consent application (where the development in question requires one) or at least contains an equivalent amount of information. If an authority is asked to consider a planning application in isolation, a decision on that application cannot be taken as predetermining the outcome of a subsequent application for listed building consent. Authorities are also required by section 72 of the Act, in the exercise in a conservation area of their powers under the Planning Acts (and Part I of the Historic Buildings and Ancient Monuments Act 1953), to pay special attention to the desirability of preserving or enhancing the character or appearance of that area. In the case of unlisted buildings in conservation areas, the Courts have held that consent for the demolition of a building may involve consideration of what is to take its place (see paragraph 4.27).

2.13 Local planning authorities are urged to ensure that they have appropriately qualified specialist advice on any development which, by its character or location, might be held to have an adverse effect on any sites or structures of the historic environment. The need for environmental assessment of major development proposals affecting historic areas should be considered in the light of the advice given in Department of the Environment *Circular 15/88*. Authorities should ensure that the Royal Fine Art Commission is consulted on all planning applications raising conservation issues of more than local importance, and should take the RFAC's views fully into account in reaching their decisions.

2.14 The design of new buildings intended to stand alongside historic buildings needs very careful consideration. In general it is better that old buildings are not set apart, but are woven into the fabric of the living and working community. This can be done, provided that the new buildings are carefully designed to respect their setting, follow fundamental architectural principles of scale, height, massing and alignment, and use appropriate materials. This does not mean that new buildings have to copy their older neighbours in detail: some of the most interesting streets in our towns and villages include a variety of building styles, materials, and forms of construction, of many different periods, but together forming a harmonious group. Further general advice on design considerations which are relevant to the exercise of planning controls is given in Annex A to *PPG 1*.

2.15 Some historic buildings are scheduled ancient monuments, and many which are not scheduled are either of intrinsic archaeological interest or stand on ground which contains archaeological remains. It is important in such cases that there should be appropriate assessment of the archaeological implications of development proposals before applications are determined; and that, where permission is to be granted, authorities should consider whether adequate arrangements have been made for recording remains that would be lost in the course of works for which permission is being sought. Further advice on archaeology and planning is given in *PPG 16*.

World Heritage Sites

2.22   Details of World Heritage Sites in England are given in paragraph 6.35. No additional statutory controls follow from the inclusion of a site in the World Heritage list. Inclusion does, however, highlight the outstanding international importance of the site as a key material consideration to be taken into account by local planning authorities in determining planning and listed building consent applications, and by the Secretary of State in determining cases on appeal or following call-in.   **D.4**

2.23   Each local authority concerned, taking account of World Heritage Site designation and other relevant statutory designations, should formulate specific planning policies for protecting these sites and include these policies in their development plans. Policies should reflect the fact that all these sites have been designated for their outstanding universal value, and they should place great weight on the need to protect them for the benefit of future generations as well as our own. Development proposals affecting these sites or their setting may be compatible with this objective, but should always be carefully scrutinised for their likely effect on the site or its setting in the longer term. Significant development proposals affecting World Heritage Sites will generally require formal environmental assessment, to ensure that their immediate impact and their implications for the longer term are fully evaluated (see paragraph 2.13 above).

Historic parks and gardens

2.24   Again no additional statutory controls follow from the inclusion of a site in English Heritage's Register of Parks and Gardens of Special Historic Interest (see paragraph 6.38), but local planning authorities should protect registered parks and gardens in preparing development plans and in determining planning applications. The effect of proposed development on a registered park or garden or its setting is a material consideration in the determination of a planning application. Planning and highway authorities should also safeguard registered parks or gardens when themselves planning new developments or road schemes.   **D.5**

Historic battlefields

2.25   A similar non-statutory Register of Historic Battlefields is being prepared by English Heritage (see paragraph 6.39). This will not entail additional statutory controls, but, when consultation with landowners and others on the content of the Register is complete, it too will need to be taken into account by local planning authorities. The effects of any development   **D.6** on the limited number of registered sites will form a material consideration to be taken into account in determining planning applications.

The wider historic landscape

D.7 2.26 Conservation of the wider historic landscape greatly depends on active land management, but there is nevertheless a significant role for local planning authorities. In defining planning policies for the countryside, authorities should take account of the historical dimension of the landscape as a whole rather than concentrate on selected areas. Adequate understanding is an essential preliminary and authorities should assess the wider historic landscape at an early stage in development plan preparation. Plans should protect its most important components and encourage development that is consistent with maintaining its overall historic character. Indeed, policies to strengthen the rural economy through environmentally sensitive diversification may be among the most important for its conservation.

Relationship between listing and scheduling

D.8 6.34 Some buildings are scheduled as ancient monuments as well as listed. These are for the most part unoccupied buildings, such as medieval barns or dovecotes, some bridges, and some urban buildings (eg. guildhalls) and industrial monuments. Some areas of overlap reflect the fact that scheduling pre-dated the listing legislation. Where a building is scheduled and listed, scheduling—which introduces closer controls (eg. over repairs) than does listing—takes priority and listed building controls do not apply. For the future, the policy will be to accord buildings and monuments the type of protection which is most appropriate to them, and where possible to avoid overlaps between listing and scheduling. The overlap is being addressed in the current national surveys of archaeological sites (the Monuments Protection Programme) being carried out by English Heritage, to evaluate all known archaeological sites in England, review existing schedulings, and identify further sites and monuments which may be suitable for scheduling.

World Heritage Sites

D.9 6.35 The World Heritage Convention (adopted by UNESCO in 1972) was ratified by the United Kingdom in 1984. The Convention provides for the identification, protection, conservation and presentation of cultural and natural sites of outstanding universal value, and requires a World Heritage List to be established under the management of an inter-governmental World Heritage Committee, which is advised by the International Council on Monuments and Sites (ICOMOS) and the World Conservation Union (IUCN). Individual governments are responsible for the nomination of sites, and for ensuring the protection of sites which are inscribed in the List. There are, at present, ten World Heritage Sites in England:

> Durham Cathedral and Castle
> Fountains Abbey, St Mary's Church and Studley Royal Park
> Ironbridge Gorge

Stonehenge, Avebury and associated sites
Blenheim Palace and Park
Palace of Westminster and Westminster Abbey
City of Bath
Hadrian's Wall Military Zone
The Tower of London
Canterbury Cathedral (with St Augustine's Abbey and St Martin's Church).

6.36 Full details of the operation of the World Heritage Convention, including the selection criteria for cultural and natural sites, are contained in the *Operational Guidelines for the Implementation of the World Heritage Convention*.

6.37 The significance of World Heritage designation for local authorities' exercise of planning controls is set out in section 2 (paragraphs 2.22–2.23). Local planning authorities are also encouraged to work with owners and managers of World Heritage Sites in their areas, and with other agencies, to ensure that comprehensive management plans are in place. These plans should:

— appraise the significance and condition of the site;
— ensure the physical conservation of the site to the highest standards;
— protect the site and its setting from damaging development;
— provide clear policies for tourism as it may affect the site.

ICOMOS can provide advice and assistance in carrying forward this work.

Historic parks and gardens

6.38 The Register of Parks and Gardens of Special Interest in England is maintained by English Heritage, to whom all enquiries about its compilation should be made. Sites of exceptional historic interest are assessed as grade I, those of special historic interest as grade II*. The grading of these sites is independent of the grading of any listed building which falls within the area. The Register is under review, with the aim of extending its coverage of parks and gardens deserving protection. (See also paragraph 2.24.) **D.10**

Historic battlefields

6.39 English Heritage's draft Register of Historic Battlefields, which will be comparable in status with the Parks and Gardens Register, is shortly to be the subject of public consultation. The proposed Register identifies a limited number of areas of historic significance where important battles are sufficiently documented to be located on the ground. They will not be graded. The Register will be periodically reviewed by English Heritage, to whom all enquiries about compilation and content should be addressed. (See also paragraph 2.25.) **D.11**

173

The wider historic landscape

D.12 6.40 Suitable approaches to the identification of the components and character of the wider historic landscape are being developed by the Countryside Commission (see its *Landscape Assessment Guidance*) and English Heritage (as part of current research on methodology for historic landscape assessment). Appraisals based on assessment of the historic character of the whole countryside will be more flexible, and more likely to be effectively integrated with the aims of the planning process, than an attempt to define selected areas for additional control. It is unlikely therefore to be feasible to prepare a definitive register at a national level of England's wider historic landscape. The whole of the landscape, to varying degrees and in different ways, is an archaeological and historic artefact, the product of complex historic processes and past land-use. It is also a crucial and defining aspect of biodiversity, to the enhancement of which the Government is committed. Much of its value lies in its complexity. regional diversity and local distinctiveness, qualities which a national register cannot adequately reflect.

Appendix E

CIRCULAR 11/95 (THE USE OF CONDITIONS IN PLANNING PERMISSIONS)—EXTRACTS

Sites of archaeological interest

E.1 80. Scheduled ancient monuments are protected by Part I of the Ancient Monuments and Archaeological Areas Act 1979, and investigation for archaeological purposes is provided for in designated areas by Part II of that Act. Where these provisions apply, their effect should not be duplicated by planning conditions (cf. paragraphs 21–23 above), although authorities granting planning permission in such circumstances are advised to draw the attention of the applicant to the relevant provisions of the 1979 Act.

81. Where, however, planning permission is being granted for development which might affect a monument which has not been scheduled, or which might affect land in an area which is considered to be of archaeological interest but which has not been formally designated as such under section 33 of the 1979 Act, the local planning authority may wish to impose conditions designed to protect the monument or ensure that reasonable access is given to a nominated archaeologist—either to hold a "watching brief" during the construction period or specifically to carry out archaeological investigation and recording before or in the course of the permitted operations on the site. (For further advice on archaeology and planning conditions see paragraphs 29 and 30 of PPG 16: Archaeology and Planning or PPG 16 (Wales), and model conditions 53–55).

Sites of archaeological interest (not scheduled or designated under 1979 Act)

E.2 53. No development shall take place until fencing has been erected, in a manner to be agreed with the local planning authority, about [insert name of monument]; and no works shall take place within the area inside that fencing without the consent of the local planning authority (paragraphs 80–81).

54. The developer shall afford access at all reasonable times to any archaeologist nominated by the local planning authority, and shall allow him to observe the excavations and record items of interest and finds (paragraphs 80–81). Conditions should not require work to be held up while archaeological investigation takes place, though some developers may be willing to give such facilities.

55. No development shall take place within the area indicated (this would be the area of archaeological interest) until the applicant, or their agents or successors in titles, has secured the implementation of a programme of archaeological work in accordance with a written scheme of investigation which has been submitted by the applicant and approved in writing by the local planning authority.

Developers will wish to ensure that in drawing up a scheme, the timetable for the investigation is included within the details of the agreed scheme.

Appendix F

ENGLISH HERITAGE ADVICE NOTE FOR LOCAL
PLANNING AUTHORITIES: DEVELOPMENT PLAN
POLICIES FOR ARCHAEOLOGY (ENGLISH
HERITAGE (1992))

Introduction

Underlying both PPG 16 and this leaflet are three main principles of **F.1**
conservation archaeology.

**The value, variety and vulnerability of England's archaeological remains
justifies a presumption in favour of the physical preservation in situ of the
most important sites, buildings, and remains.*

**The archaeological heritage is part of the wider historic environment,
whose care is a major element of environmental conservation in town and
countryside.*

**Accurate expert information, on the condition and significance of the sites
affected by development proposals, is essential for decision-making on
planning and land-use issues.*

The national importance of archaeological sites and the need for their
conservation is underlined by the Department of the Environment's Planning Policy Guidance Note 16, Archaeology and Planning. It codifies an
framework for protecting such sites, emphasising the important part played
by the statutory planning system, through the incorporation of appropriate
policies in development plans. (PPG 16, paragraphs 14–16). More recently,
the Planning and Compensation Act 1991 has required the preparation of
district-wide local plans, and introduced a presumption in favour of
proposals which are in accord with the development plan. The legislation is
amplified in PPG 1 (March 1992) and PPG 12 (February 1992).

For many years English Heritage and its predecessors have been advising
planning authorities on draft development plans. This leaflet has been
produced by English Heritage, in the light on PPG 16, to offer more detailed
advice to planning authorities on including archaeological policies in
development plans. It has been produced in conjunction with the Association of County Archaeological Officers, following current practice
throughout the country, and is concerned with the archaeological content of

Regional Planning Guidance, Structure and Local Plans, parts I and II of UDPs, and mineral and waste plans.

This leaflet refers to existing structures, procedures, and responsibilities in local government. It takes into account recent changes in the development planning system, but a revised edition will be produced if significant changes to the structure of local government takes place as a result of the work of the Local Government Commission. It is likely, however, that any future administrative arrangements will need similar kinds of policies and close working partnerships between Sites and Monuments Records (SMRs), conservation archaeologists, and local planning authorities.

A framework for archaeology in development plans

F.2 *Because plan policies should normally be drafted to suit the distinctive circumstances of the plan area, this leaflet offers broad guidance, although it should be able to provide the raw material for policies. English Heritage can supply examples of well-drafted policies drawn from plans already in use: ring 0171 937 3049 for details of the relevant English Heritage office. Planning authorities and county archaeological officers are asked to help us keep our list up to date by forwarding new approved policies.*

Plans at all levels need general policies to reiterate the presumption of PPG 16 (paragraphs 8 and 27) in favour of the preservation of important archaeological sites and their settings, and against development adversely affecting such sites. Some important archaeological sites may already be scheduled as of national importance, or will be scheduled during the Monuments Protection Programme (MPP), but others are likely to remain unscheduled, and plan policies will need to reflect this. Guidance on the significance of unscheduled sites can be obtained from county archaeological officers (CAOs) and the specialist officers of some district councils. In some important cases, English Heritage advice is also available.

Policies are also required to set out the general approach to development control. Applicants should be required to provide information on the impact of their proposals on any archaeological remains and their settings. Permission should normally be refused for development adversely affecting important archaeological sites. Where refusal would not be justified or disturbance by development is unavoidable, the local planning authorities will require applicants to undertake an agreed programme of mitigation, if necessary by prior recording.

Regional planning guidance

F.3 The primary function of regional guidance is to provide the framework for the preparation of structure plans. Regional guidance will generally cover those issues which need a wider geographical coverage than individual structure plans. It provides opportunities for integrating archaeological conservation with other environmental interests at the strategic level. Archaeology ought to be taken into account as a constraint or as an asset when considering infrastructure projects, such as motorways or industrial development, as well as their indirect effect of generating consequential development. The nature and distribution of archaeological sites varies across the country, and regional planning guidance should seek to reflect the individual character and importance of a region's archaeology.

Structure plans and part I of UDPs

The definition of special historic landscapes is currently under consider- **F.4**
ation, following the government White Paper This Common Inheritance
(1990). Such areas might contain both visible and buried components,
ranging in date from earliest times to modern post-industrial landscapes.
This combination will require parallel conservation and management
techniques from the strategic to the local level. A preliminary policy
statement by English Heritage was published in Conservation Bulletin 14
(June 1991).

The Department of the Environment's PPG 12, *Development Plans and Regional Planning Guidance* (February 1992), identifies conservation of the natural and built environment as one of nine key topics for structure plans (paragraph 5.9). The main function of structure plans in setting out general policies and strategic proposals is covered in PPGs 1 and 12. PPG 12 (paragraph 6.5) makes clear that conserving the archaeological heritage should be given high priority when development plans are drawn up. In addition, part A of PPG 16 (paragraph 6) emphasises that 'care must be taken to ensure that archaeological remains are not needlessly or thoughtlessly destroyed' and, in paragraph 8, that 'where nationally important archaeological remains, whether scheduled or not, and their settings are affected by proposed development there should be a presumption in favour of their physical preservation'. At the strategic level, structure plan policies should set out a presumption in favour of preserving scheduled ancient monuments and other nationally important archaeological sites, and their settings, in coordination with other conservation interests. The buried or otherwise obscured nature of many remains also requires that decisions take into account advice about their character and condition.

Detailed policies relating to the management of archaeological sites will normally be set out in local plans. Structure plans could also include a broadly-framed policy setting out the local authority's commitment to promote where practicable the appropriate management, understanding, and enhancement of ancient monuments and archaeological sites.

The identification of wider landscapes whose historic qualities deserve conservation and enhancement can also be a strategic issue, especially where one or more adjacent plan areas may be involved. Structure plan policies relating to major designations, such as Areas of Outstanding Natural Beauty, should ensure that historical aspects are taken into account alongside other conservation issues. We encourage county councils to consider a general strategic approach to historical landscape conservation. English Heritage can offer advice and assistance in preparing a framework.

Local plans and part II of UDPs

F.5 *Planning decisions should take into account the archaeological policies in detailed development plans, together with all other relevant policies and material considerations, including the intrinsic importance of the remains, weighing these against the need for the proposed development.*

The Planning and Compensation Act 1991 has placed an increased emphasis on the development plan as the basis for development control. This is reflected in PPG 12, and therefore local plans should contain policies covering archaeological sites. Archaeology deserves presentation in the plan as a local resource of social value worthy of good stewardship. Policies should cover identification, preservation and enhancement, and recording in advance of destruction. They will also need to reflect the guidance set out in PPG 16 (paragraph 27), repeating the presumption against proposals for significant alteration, damage, or significant impact on settings, while emphasising that preservation must be assessed on the merits of the individual case.

It is important that plans provide sufficient guidance for developers preparing planning applications (for example, designated and other major constraints) but it is neither necessary nor desirable to define all currently-known archaeological sites on the proposals map. Such an approach might well mislead potential developers through omitting as yet unknown sites, understating the importance of imperfectly known sites, or risking premature and incorrect assessments of importance. A two-fold approach is therefore often appropriate. The proposals map should show ancient monuments scheduled at the time the plan is adopted, and it could also indicate easily definable areas of particular importance or vulnerability. However, the plan policies should be clear that in order to take account of previously unknown or undervalued sites, the established procedures of consultation, desk-top assessment, and field evaluation, as described in PPG 16, should also be followed in the earliest stages of preparing development proposals. The plan will therefore need to explain the policies, procedures, and criteria each authority will use to identify the existence of a site, and assess its importance when determining a planning application. Conservation archaeologists can define and keep under review areas of potential significance for the constraints maps used in development control. Recognition that an application affects such an area can generate a specialist consultation, which in turn will initiate further processes of site assessment. Problems may arise where land has been made the subject of plan proposals for specific uses, such as housing or industry. The reasoned justification for such 'allocations' should carry a caveat alerting potential developers that such allocation or definition does not obviate the need to follow the procedures laid down by PPG 16.

PPG 16 (paragraph 15) states that the proposals map of detailed development plans should define the areas and sites to which policies and proposals apply. This requirement needs interpretation in the context of archaeological sites and other remains. The basic difficulty is that archaeological knowledge is not static: new sites are discovered and known ones reassessed as a result of the MPP. This is illustrated by the accepted need for detailed evaluation of buried archaeological sites and deposits against a specific development proposal. At that stage the importance of an archaeological site, and thus the weight given to it, can be most accurately assessed in order to make a defensible planning decision. The basic source of up-to-date information will be the SMR, together with the Secretary of State's non-statutory criteria of national importance set out in PPG 16, and any additional factors needed to define regional and county significance.

Policies for protection

Local Plan policies expressing the presumption in favour of preserving important sites ought to make clear that development which adversely affects sites or settings of scheduled ancient monuments and other nationally important remains will not be permitted. For certain archaeological sites, authorities may wish to extend this policy to sites and monuments of especial local importance. **F.6**

Policies for the protection and conservation of areas as well as sites of special archaeological interest should also be considered where appropriate. Such areas may be archaeological in character or potential, or they may be designated for another reason, such as scenic beauty. In either case, special policies for protection and enhancement ought to be devised, tailored to the qualities and needs of the area.

Policies for development control

PPG 16 codifies a widely accepted set of principles for giving appropriate consideration to archaeological matters during development control, both before and after deciding an application. These ought to be described in the reasoned justification for plan policies, with specific policies supporting the following key stages: **F.7**

Evaluating the importance of archaeological remains

The buried and often invisible nature of archaeological remains justifies a policy reinforcing the local planning authority's right to require information from an applicant about the impact of a proposed development. This information, including the results of evaluation by fieldwork, is necessary to assess the potential impact of the applicant's proposals. **F.8**

Assessing the archaeological impact of development

A preliminary assessment will already have been made from the SMR, but additional information from fieldwork evaluation will often be needed for a fuller assessment which may be sufficient to refuse planning permission at this stage. **F.9**

Mitigating development impact

Plans should include a policy establishing the planning authority's intention to ensure mitigation of the impact of development proposals on important archaeological remains and their settings. Mitigation can be achieved by **F.10** encouraging suitable designs, modifying them to increase physical preservation, or not permitting development to commence until as a last resort a programme of archaeological investigation and recording has been agreed and implemented. The mechanisms for reconciling development with the archaeological interest need to be stated clearly. It is normally preferable to avoid archaeological disturbance. Where this is not already achieved by the applicant's proposal, local authorities' will seek mitigation by amendment of the proposal by re-siting, redesign, or alternative foundation methods. On other cases and where the balance of other factors is in favour of granting permission, mitigation might take the form of archaeological investigation and recording of evidence before its destruction.

Implementing the proposal

F.11 This would include any mitigation of archaeological impact, achieved by use of planning conditions or section 106 agreements.

Monitoring and enforcement

F.12 This would comprise supervision to ensure that planning permissions, conditions, and related agreements or undertakings were implemented as agreed.

Review of procedures

F.13 The effectiveness of these procedures needs to be kept under continual review, both as part of the process of development control, and to promote the conservation and improved general understanding of the local archaeological heritage.

Policies for management

F.14 The intrinsic cultural value of important archaeological sites and their potential contribution to public understanding and enjoyment, justifies measures to ensure their long-term preservation in good condition. This can be achieved through good management within the context of countryside strategies and other non-statutory documents. Where resources permit authorities may also wish to include a general policy in the development plan explaining that the local planning authority will encourage and, where practicable, assist owners of important archaeological sites to maintain them in good condition and to adopt sympathetic land management regimes.

Local authorities should be in a position to set an example to private owners and other public bodies through management of sites in their ownership. In cases where important archaeological sites or monuments may be threatened, or appropriate care and management is not assured, local authorities may wish to consider acquisition or guardianship. They could also make partnership arrangements for the beneficial management of ancient monuments, with private landowners, conservation trusts, or other public bodies.

The key to successful preservation and enhancement is the preparation and implementation of a site management plan. This has been discussed nationally by English Heritage in *Ancient Monuments in the Countryside*

(1987), and will be the subject of more detailed technical papers. Detailed policies and plans or agreements covering specific sites should be prepared to encourage improved public access, and better understanding through presentation.

When detailed advice relating to specific sites or areas would be helpful to those preparing proposals, this guidance could take the form of planning briefs or design guides, to supplement the plan. Countryside strategies can be effective vehicles to integrate conservation policies for archaeological sites with those covering other environmental interests.

Sources of advice

Successful conservation archaeology depends upon the information **F.15** contained in SMRs , and the expertise of the archaeologists who manage them. Together with English Heritage's regional conservation teams and the officers of some district councils, these are at present the main sources of specialist advice for planning authorities. English Heritage can also provide advice and support in matters of positive site management, subject to the availability of resources, and CAOs and other professional archaeological staff will also be able to assist.

Appendix G

STAGES OF ARCHAEOLOGICAL ASSESSMENT
DESIGN MANUAL FOR ROADS AND BRIDGES, VOL.
11, SECTION 3, PART 2 (CULTURAL HERITAGE),
CHAP. 8 (REVISED 1994)

8.1 Archaeological assessments should become increasingly detailed as a   G.1
scheme develops, and in accordance with the archaeological importance of
the land likely to be affected. It is also particularly important that, as the
archaeological assessment becomes more detailed, it both informs and takes
account of the development of mitigation measures. Assessment and design
are part of an iterative process.

8.2 The following are the key stages in the assessment process. The
terminology used reflects common usages among archaeologists and to avoid
confusion should be employed in all correspondence on archaeological
matters.

Stage 1

8.3 The objective at this stage is to undertake sufficient assessment to   G.2
identify the archaeological constraints with particular broadly defined roles,
or corridors, as developed by the Design Organisation and agreed with the
Overseeing Department's Project Manager. The Design Organisation should
employ someone with experience of archaeological assessment to carry out
the work associated with this Stage.

IN ENGLAND AND NORTHERN IRELAND

8.4 The steps to take are:-   G.3

   (i)   contact the County Archaeologist or ES : HMB as appropriate and
        obtain, from the SMR or MBR in Northern Ireland, information on
        the location of designated sites and other recorded sites within the
        study area. Data should also be obtained from the relevant NMR.

  (ii)   identify any potential archaeological constraints associated with
        route corridors. These will include all Scheduled Ancient Monu-
        ments, other notable individual recorded remains, or groups of
        remains of lesser importance. Sites of previous finds should also be

noted where they might indicate that an area could contain potentially important buried remains.

8.5 The result of the archaeological assessment at this Stage, to be described in the Stage 1 Report, should consist of:-

(a) a map of the study area showing route corridors, all designated sites and areas, and all areas where, based on a study of the SMR and NMR or MBR, there might be potentially important remains.

(b) a statement on the archaeological content of the study area and the archaeological constraints associated with route corridors. If possible, it should also give a provisional indication of which areas would require additional surveys, how detailed those surveys would need to be in each case, and whether there were particular timing constraints (for example, a walkover survey would need to be done before crops were planted in ploughed soil).

IN SCOTLAND

G.4 The following procedures apply:

8.6 SOID Roads Directorate will consult HS (along with other statutory consultees) on the Project Brief. HS will advise at this stage on the need for a formal desk assessment of the route corridor, its estimated costs and timescale.

8.7 SOID Roads Directorate will commission through HS, the production by an external archaeological consultant of 'A desk top archaeological assessment of historic sites and buildings' within the route corridor. HS will oversee its production. The consultant will identify all recorded archaeological constraints, including both scheduled and unscheduled sites, using information available in the National Monuments Record of Scotland. (Information on listed buildings and designed landscapes will also be included at this stage). HS will arrange to consult Regional Archaeologists, where appropriate, to incorporate any additional information from local SMRs. Using this information the consultant will colour code the route corridor in the way described in The Scottish Office discussion document *Roads, Bridges and Traffic in the Countryside* (SO 1992):-

Red	(area)	scheduled monument
	(cross)	listed buildings
Yellow	(area)	other known archaeological site
		designed landscape
Green		insufficient information:
		more work needed
Blue		probably archaeologically sterile

8.8 The results of the archaeological assessment at this Stage, to be described in the Stage 1 Report, should consist of:

— a single sided A3 map based, factual report identifying the position and, as far as possible, the extent of all recorded archaeological and built heritage features;

— a covering letter from HS assessing the information presented and clearly stating HS' position. This will assess, as far as possible at this stage, the relative importance of both individual sites and any important groupings; it will indicate whether preservation is mandatory in each case or whether other forms of mitigation might be possible; it will attempt to identify any clear gaps in the archaeological record and give a provisional indication of where further field work or documentary study might be necessary to better define the archaeological resource, what methods might be appropriate and any timing constraints.

8.9   These documents will be forwarded to SOID Roads Directorate who will in turn supply a copy to the Design Organisation undertaking the Stage 1 study. The archaeological and built heritage information and advice will be incorporated into their Stage 1 Assessment Report. HS will be sent a copy of this report to verify the archaeological and built heritage content.

IN WALES

The following apply: **G.5**
8.10   The procedures are in line with those recommended by PPG 16 for the consideration of development proposals by local authorities.

8.11   The objective at this stage is to identify the known archaeological constraints within a route corridor to ensure that proper regard is given to the potential archaeological resource during route selection. The responsibility for commissioning this appraisal will form part of the brief given to the consultants appointed by the Overseeing Department to undertake the initial route planning.

8.12   The basis of this appraisal will be as follows:

   (i)   The collation of all data held in the regional SMR;
   (ii)   a review of readily available vertical and oblique aerial photographic information;
   (iii)   a review of first edition Ordnance Survey maps and other readily available historic maps;
   (iv)   field visits to determine the present condition of all known archaeological sites;
   (v)   a review of the present land-use, soil and topographical conditions to show how these might suggest the location and density of as yet unknown archaeological remains within the route corridors.

8.13   The result of the archaeological appraisal at this Stage, to be described in the Stage 1 Report, should consist of:

   (i)   a map of the study area showing route corridors and all designated sites and areas, and all areas where, based on a study of the SMR and NMR, there might be potentially important remains;
   (ii)   a statement on the archaeological content of the study area and the archaeological constraints associated with route corridors;
   (iii)   a statement which includes the Design Organisation's recommendations on any areas or sites within the study area which should be regarded as a constraint or where mitigation would have to be considered. The statement should indicate where additional

archaeological survey work is required, what those surveys should consist of and whether there were particular timing constraints (for example, intensive field walking would need to be done before crops were planted in ploughed soil, and ground and geophysical survey undertaken whilst crops were not growing in the fields).

Stage 2

IN ENGLAND AND NORTHERN IRELAND

G.6   8.14   The objective at this stage is to undertake sufficient assessment to identify the archaeological factors, and the effects upon them, to be taken into account by the Design Organisation in developing and refining route options, in agreement with the Overseeing Department's Project Manager.

8.15   The steps to be taken are:-

(i)   check with the County Archaeologist or ES : HMB as appropriate that, since the Stage 1 assessment, there have been no additions to the number of designated sites or areas, or recorded remains on the SMR and NMR, or MBR in Northern Ireland;

(iia) where the Stage 1 desk study and the subsequent verification of its results show that there is no evidence that any significant archaeological remains will be affected by a route option, contact EH or ES : HMB and ask for confirmation that further work is not required;

DETAILED DESK TOP ASSESSMENT

G.7   (iib) where the desk study indicates that significant archaeological remains may be affected by route options, the Design Organisation should commission a study from an experienced archaeologist. Its aim should be to identify and evaluate all remains within the study area recorded on the county SMR, the NMR or the MBR in Northern Ireland, or in other published sources and to assess the likely impacts of route options. This assessment will be based on the information produced at Stage 1, but will be more detailed and will focus on the route options. It should include an assessment of aerial photographs, where available. The study should also consider the evidence gathered in the light of past/current land use in order to provide an assessment of the documented information. This will involve a consideration of possibly significant gaps in the documentary evidence;

PRELIMINARY WALKOVER SURVEY

G.8   (iii) in some cases, the desk study may not provide sufficient information on the possible impacts of route options. This may be the case in areas where archaeological sites are masked by later deposits such as alluvium, colluvium or peat; where site detection has been made difficult by current land use such as pasture, parkland, woodland or existing structures; or where there are clear gaps in the recorded information due to a lack of fieldwork in the past. In such circumstances and with the agreement of the Overseeing Department's Project Manager, a preliminary walkover survey of the relevant area(s) should be undertaken. Advice about surveys is given in paragraphs 8.28–8.38. It is important to note that surveys at this stage should be conducted to meet the objective of assessment at Stage 2, and are likely to be less detailed than those undertaken after the selection of a preferred route. It should be remembered that walkover surveys may need to be carried out on bare ground *i.e.* after crops have been harvested;

(iv)   EH or ES : HMB should be consulted on the scope of the survey brief which should be agreed with the Overseeing Department's Project Manager before being finalised. It is also important to bear in mind the need not to cause undue public anxiety and property blight;

(v)   prepare a statement which sets out the findings of the detailed desk top study (and the preliminary walkover survey where appropriate) and assess the probable impacts of the route options on archaeological remains;

(vi)   obtain EH's or ES : HMB's 'in confidence' views on the impacts of route options on archaeological remains.

8.16   The result of the archaeological assessment at this Stage, to be described in the Stage 2 Report, should consist of:

(a)   an updated version of the map of the study area produced at Stage 1 showing the route options, all designated sites and areas, and all other areas where there might be potentially important remains (based on a study of the SMR, NMR and MBR, other documentary material and, where applicable, the preliminary walkover survey;

(b1)   (where the detailed desk top study indicated that there was no need for a walkover survey), a statement which describes the archaeological value of the study area including any constraints, and assesses the significance of the possible impacts of route options. The statement should also set out the reasons why a survey was not considered necessary and should indicate whether EH or ES : HMB agrees with this procedure.

(b2)   (where a walkover survey has been conducted), a statement which describes the archaeological value of the study area, and assesses the significance of the possible impacts of route options, taking account of agreed mitigation measures. The statement should set out the criteria used to define levels of significance, and should describe the archaeological survey techniques employed, and the results of the survey, as well as the results of the desk study. The statement should indicate clearly any areas or sites within the study area which should be regarded as a constraint. The Overseeing Department's Project Manager should be informed if it would be valuable to send a copy of the survey results to the local SMR, NMR or MBR in Northern Ireland.

(c) a separate statement of the 'in-confidence' views of officers of EH or ES : HMB, on the implications of route options for archaeological remains.

IN SCOTLAND

G.9 The following procedures apply:

8.17 SOID Roads Directorate will advise HS of the route options selected for further assessment. HS will check the desk assessment prepared at Stage 1 to confirm that no further sites have come to light since its preparation. This will be particularly significant if there has been any considerable delay between completion of the Stage 1 study and undertaking the Stage 2 Route Option Assessment.

8.18 As part of the Route Option Assessment HS will agree with SOID Roads Directorate an appropriate programme of archaeological evaluation, including an estimate of costs and timescale for both further documentary and/or field research which might be necessary in order to determine fully the archaeological impact of the various route options. This programme of work will build upon the provisional recommendations made in the Stage 1 Assessment Report, but will concentrate on the areas covered by the specific routes selected for further assessment. Further archaeological evaluation may be necessary at this stage where, for example, the precise limits of recorded sites or their significance is uncertain or in areas where there has been little previous field work but where topography suggests that early settlement may have been likely, or in areas where early archaeological features may be masked by later deposits or features of more modern land use. A full assessment of the survival of such features at this stage should lead to better informed decisions on the selection of the preferred route and minimise archaeological work required in advance of road construction itself.

8.19 SOID Roads Directorate will commission, through HS, the agreed programme of archaeological evaluation. This work will be undertaken by an appropriately qualified archaeological consultant, selected by tender and working to an archaeological assessment brief drawn up by HS. The work will be managed by HS.

8.20 The archaeological assessment brief will generally require a factual report of the results of the further work undertaken including details of all sites researched and, if possible, an assessment of their relative significance. The archaeologist consultant should also provide an assessment of the relative impact of the various route options on the archaeological resource and recommendations for mitigation measures which would be required on all the routes under consideration. They will also update the archaeological desk assessment report drawn up at Stage 1, adding the route options to the maps along with all additional archaeological information arising out of this work.

8.21 The results of an archaeological assessment at this Stage, to be described in the Stage 2 Report, should consist of:

— an updated version of the A3 map-based archaeological assessment report produced at Stage 1, to include the various route options under assessment and all additional information resulting from the Stage 2 archaeological evaluation.

— a copy of the consultants report on the Stage 2 archaeological work.

— a covering letter from HS giving HS assessment of the impact of the various route options on the archaeological and built heritage. Where possible this will state HS preferences and will detail mitigation measures, with an estimate of likely costs for all route options. It will clearly identify any options where the impact on the archaeological and built heritage would be unacceptable to HS.

8.22 These documents will be forwarded to SOID Roads Directorate who will in turn supply a copy to the Design Organisation undertaking the Stage 2 Assessment Report. The information and advice these contain will be incorporated into their report on the preferred route.

IN WALES

The following apply: **G.10**

8.23 Where archaeological constraints are a significant factor in route selection, it may be necessary to develop the appraisal report before going to Public Consultation. There may be the need for additional field survey to plan accurately the archaeological remains or to develop other aspects of appraisal given in paragraph 8.13. The relative merits of the individual archaeological sites identified will have to be evaluated by a qualified archaeologist on the basis of the information gathered.

8.24 The statement describing the archaeological appraisal and any other relevant information will be deposited with the regional SMR, following the approval of the Overseeing Department's Project Manager.

8.25 Cadw will be consulted by the Overseeing Department on the recommendations of the appraisal report and advise on the impact of possible route options on archaeological remains.

Stage 3

Note: The principles outlined below which apply to this stage of assess-   **G.11**
ment are generally applicable in England, Wales, Northern Ireland and Scotland. Minor differences are noted in the text. The only major departure is that in Scotland HS will continue to advise SOID Roads Directorate on all archaeological work required at this stage.

8.26 The objective at this stage is to undertake sufficient assessment to identify the significant archaeological impacts likely to arise from construction of the preferred route, and to identify the location, type and importance of the archaeological constraints associated with that route.

8.27 In some cases, a sufficiently comprehensive survey of the preferred route will have been undertaken at Stage 2, and, after consultation with EH, Cadw, HS or ES : HMB as appropriate there will be no need for field surveys. The only action required in these cases will, therefore, be:-

(i)   confirmation that the detailed desk study (and any walkover survey) already undertaken provides comprehensive information on the preferred route's impacts on archaeological remains;

(ii)   assessment of the preferred route's probable impacts on archaeological remains;

(iii) consideration of whether any work to mitigate adverse impacts will be required before construction;

(iv) confirmation of the views of EH, Cadw, HS or ES : HMB as appropriate on the impacts on archaeological remains of the preferred route.

FIELD SURVEY

G.12   8.28 In other cases, the desk study conducted at Stage 2 will need to be supplemented by further survey work commissioned by the Design Organisation from an experienced archaeologist or archaeological organisation. In Wales it will be necessary, in most cases, to commission a programme of investigative, on-site survey work along the preferred route. Before commissioning a field survey, it is important to note the limitations on the Overseeing Department's powers of entry under section 289(1) of the Highways Act 1980, or section 140 of the Roads (Scotland) Act 1984. The Overseeing Department's powers to enter privately owned land to conduct surveys for the preparation of a road scheme can be used to conduct an archaeological survey which does not involve breaking the surface of the ground. Whilst there is no reason why soil samples obtained under section 289(1); or Section 140 for engineering purposes cannot also be used for in the archaeological assessment, where practicable, the Overseeing Department has no powers to conduct archaeological surveys which break the ground surface. It is therefore reliant on the goodwill of landowners to allow access for the conduct of such surveys. Where the need for such surveys has been agreed with the Overseeing Department's Project Manager, agreements should be sought with the landowner to allow access and the necessary excavation or boring.

8.29 Before undertaking any field survey, the Overseeing Department's Project Manager, in conjunction with the Design Organisation, should write to the landowner and explain what work is necessary. Landowners should be fully informed of their right not to allow surveys which in any way damage the surface of the ground. Suggested specimen letters for different types of archaeological survey in England and Wales are at Annex III (the Overseeing Department's Project Manager should consider the need for formal notices of intention to enter land or for wayleave agreements). If a landowner refuses permission for a survey which breaks the ground surface, EH or the County Archaeologist in England, or Cadw in Wales, should be consulted on whether it would be realistic to conduct the survey in adjoining land by agreement, if this could be obtained. Outside England and Wales, further advice should be sought from HS or ES : HMB as appropriate.

8.30 A landowner may ask for information on rights of ownership over any finds made during a survey. As a general rule, archaeological finds become the property of the owner of the land in or on which they are found unless the original owner of the object can be ascertained.

8.31   However, if the items found are of gold or silver, or a reasonable   **G.13**
proportion of either, the finder must report the find to the local Coroner. He
or she will then hold an inquest to discover if the items were deliberately
hidden with the intention to retrieve, and should thus be considered
Treasure Trove. If they are not so considered, then they will revert
immediately to the finder. If they are so considered, and a museum in this
country wishes to acquire them, then the items are referred to the Treasure
Trove Reviewing Committee for a fair market valuation to be offered to the
finder, in return for the objects entering the collection of a particular
museum. Overseeing Departments should therefore consider entering into
an agreement with the owner of the land which they are surveying so that any
finds are shared with the landowner.

8.32   Scots Law of Treasure Trove is different. Under Scots law any object to
which no clear line of ownership can be determined belongs to the Crown.
Therefore, if during the course of site works, building operations or
archaeological excavations an object of undetermined ownership is found it
must be declared by the funder of the archaeological excavation or by the
person who found it.

8.33   As the funder of many archaeological excavations Historic Scotland
reports such objects directly to the Crown Office. Members of the public
should declare such objects to their local museum, or the National Museums
of Scotland or directly to the police or Procurator Fiscal, who in turn hand it
over to the Crown Office. If they are of sufficient importance pending
assignation to a museum, objects remain in Crown ownership. However,
more commonly for objects recovered from excavations sponsored by HS
ownership would be transferred by the Crown to the Secretary of State for
Scotland, on whose behalf HS would subsequently act. HS is advised by the
Find Disposal Panel, which includes a representative of local museum
interests and of the Royal Museum on "disposal" to a museum.

8.34   Where a field survey is undertaken, its primary objective should be to
discover the location and importance of all remains which could be affected,
and to assess how significant the preferred route's impact on them would be.
The advice of the relevant statutory body should be sought on the extent of
the survey.

8.35   It may be possible to achieve the assessment objective at this stage by a
combination of field-walking, and geophysical survey techniques (which can
help identify underground remains by measuring, for example, the resistivity, magnetism or electro-magnetism of the ground surface). However, it
should be noted that it is an offence under section 42 of the Ancient
Monuments and Archaeological Areas Act, 1979 to use geophysical equipment in a protected place (any place which is either the site of an Ancient
Monument or any monument in the care of a local authority, the statutory
bodies or the Secretary of State) without prior consent from EH, Cadw, HS or
ES : HMB as appropriate.

8.36   In some cases, it may be necessary to consider excavation survey
techniques, such as limited trial trenching and test pitting. These techniques
may be needed where the location, type and significance of any important
archaeological remains and how they might be affected by a preferred route
are not known with reasonable certainty, or where more information is

desirable to help finalise agreed mitigation measures. The need for these methods to be used should be discussed with the appropriate statutory body.

G.14   8.37   If it is already apparent that a full excavation of a site will be required before start of works, excavation surveys at this stage may well be unnecessary and could impair the results of the later on-site work. However a survey of the site is usually valuable where full excavation is proposed. This helps to establish information on site preservation and potential, which is essential for production of a satisfactory brief including accurate estimates of time and resources required. The scale of any excavation survey must also take account of the fact that the Overseeing Department is dependent on the goodwill of landowners to conduct such surveys (see paragraphs 8.28–29, above). EH in England, and Cadw in Wales, should be consulted before excavation survey techniques are employed. A suggested specimen letter to a landowner asking permission to conduct a survey in England or Wales involving trial trenches or test pits is at Annex III. In Scotland advice should be sought from HS.

8.38   Where a preferred route's impact on palaeoenvironmental evidence (see paragraph 3.3) is likely to be significant (*i.e.*, if the construction of the route would destroy a significant part of the palaeoenvironmental evidence in the locality), provision should be made for special soil samples to be taken and analysed. This can be done at any time up to start of works although opportunities may be limited by growing crops. Soil samples for engineering purposes are unlikely to be adequate for palaeoenvironmental analysis, although it may help the Design Organisation to see those samples as well. Where it is likely that a preferred route will affect significant archaeological remains, it is important that the agreed mitigation measures should recognise that palaeoenvironmental evidence should be collected simul-taneously. This will enable any remains to be dated more accurately, and put into their historical context.

8.39   In addition to the desk study, walkover survey or field survey, in the exceptional circumstances where aerial photographs are needed and existing ones are inadequate, it might be necessary to take aerial photographs of part or all of a route. The statutory bodies should be consulted first. If aerial photographs are being proposed for another purpose, the Design Organisation in England and Wales, or HS in Scotland, should be consulted to see if it is possible to produce photographs which will fulfil a dual role. Before aerial photographs are commissioned approval should be obtained from the Overseeing Department's Project Manager.

8.40   In England, Wales and Northern Ireland, where a field survey has been completed, the Design Organisation should produce a statement which describes the survey techniques employed, the results of the field survey, any earlier walkover survey and the desk study. It should assess the archaeolog-ical value of remains along the preferred route, the significance of likely impacts on them, taking account of agreed mitigation and recording measures. The latter should incorporate details of any proposed excavations or other archaeological work to be undertaken after the Overseeing Depart-ment has taken entry of the land, including a description of the purpose and location of the excavations, methods, duration, any post-excavation reports and the costs of the excavation and analysis. The Overseeing Department's Project Manager should also be informed if it would be valuable to publish the results in an archaeological journal, and/or send a copy of the report to the local SMR the NMR, or MBR in Northern Ireland. In Scotland HS, as archaeological manager on behalf of SOID Roads Directorate, will advise on report requirements and their publication.

8.41   EH's views on the archaeological impacts of the preferred route should also be obtained, for English road schemes. In Wales Cadw will advise the Overseeing Department of their views on the recommendations included in the assessment report and draw up a brief for a programme of fieldwork to be undertaken before construction work begins.

8.42   The results of the assessment at this stage should be described in the Environmental Statement and should consist of:

(a)   a map of the preferred route showing all designated sites and areas, and all other areas where there are potentially important remains;

(b)   a statement on the archaeological constraints taking account of the results of any surveys, aerial photographs, and noting the comments of statutory consultees. The statement should describe the archaeological constraints, and state their relative value. It should also assess the significance of the impacts on them arising from the possible construction of the preferred route taking account of agreed mitigation measures. The statement should set out the criteria used to define levels of significance;

(c)   where relevant a description of the results of any field surveys and the techniques used.

Appendix H

PREPARATION OF ENVIRONMENTAL
STATEMENTS FOR PLANNING PROJECTS THAT
REQUIRE ENVIRONMENTAL ASSESSMENT—
A GOOD PRACTICE GUIDE: APPENDIX 10
(CULTURAL HERITAGE/MATERIAL ASSETS)
(CONSULTATION DRAFTS) (1995[1])

APPENDIX 10—CULTURAL HERITAGE/MATERIAL ASSETS

1 'Cultural Heritage' is the collective term used to describe aspects of the **H.1**
environment which reflect the history of human activities, ideas and
attitudes. It is not limited to material and economic aspects of life, but also
reflects spiritual and intellectual value. The term embraces the subject areas
of history, archaeology, architecture and urban design, and in many cases is
closely tied to the rural or urban landscape. For the purpose of this Guide,
'cultural heritage' and 'material assets' are treated as a single topic area.

2 It is important that cultural heritage is adequately covered during an EA,
since it is generally irreplaceable, and should be viewed in the same light as
other finite or non-renewable resources.

EXISTING INFORMATION AND LEGISLATION

Archaeology

3 Although archaeological remains are a fundamental part of our heritage, **H.2**
development and other human activities continue to result in damage or loss
of archaeological sites. It is essential therefore that any archaeological
remains should be identified before development on a given site takes place.
For England and Wales, PPG 16—*Archaeology and Planning*— gives advice
on handling archaeological remains and other discoveries under planning
procedures. It stresses the importance of early consultations between local
authorities, archaeologists and developers and places the onus on local
authorities, through their development plan policies, to promote the

---

[1] In Scotland NPPG5 (Archaeology and Planning) and Planning Advice Note 42
(Archaeology) apply.

protection, enhancement and preservation of sites of archaeological interest and on developers to fund appropriate archaeological works prior to development. Where nationally important archaeological remains (whether scheduled or not), and their settings are affected by proposed development there is a presumption in favour of their physical preservation.

4   The National Monuments Record held by the Royal Commission on the Historical Monuments of England provides a national overview of records available for the cultural heritage, both archaeology and buildings, and includes the national archaeological record of sites and monuments in England and the national library of air photographs. Similar information can be obtained from the Royal Commissions on Ancient and Historical Monuments of Scotland and Wales. The National Records and local 'Sites and Monuments Records' (SMRs), usually held by county councils in England, by four regional archaeological trusts in Wales, and in Scotland by regional and island councils, should provide a catalogue of known archaeological sites. The records are continually being updated as significant new sites are identified and some are given statutory protection as 'Scheduled Monuments' under the Ancient Monuments and Archaeological Areas Act 1979. Local authorities may also designate their own policy areas, such as 'Areas of Archaeological Significance', in development plans.

5   The national importance of a monument and the appropriateness of scheduling is assessed according to eight criteria, although selection is also designed to ensure a representative sample of each 'class' of monument. These criteria provide a useful framework within which to judge both nationally important and locally important archaeological remains. They are period, rarity, documentation, group value (importance may be enhanced by association with other monuments), survival and condition, fragility or vulnerability, diversity and potential (where the importance of remains cannot be precisely known but there is good evidence to anticipate it).

6   Designations provide a useful, but not yet exhaustive schedule of sites. Some sites are outside the scope of current legislation and many await the completion of the Monuments Protection Programme. The absence of scheduled sites from an area must not be taken as evidence that it is devoid of sites or landscapes of archaeological importance. In addition, sites and landscapes of more regional or local importance have a contribution to make. In some cases they will contribute to the local distinctiveness of an area. Early consultation with the county archaeologists or English Heritage in England, the Archeological Trust or Cadw in Wales and the Regional/Islands Archaeologist or Historic Scotland in Scotland should help identify the cultural importance of the site or area.

Maritime archaeology

H.3   7   The 'cultural heritage' is not confined to land. Historic shipwrecks may be designated under the Protection of Wrecks Act 1973. Any survey, excavation or development proposals affecting such sites may be subject to the granting of a licence for that purpose from the Secretary of State for National Heritage or the Secretary of State for Scotland and Wales. While development below the low watermark is not generally subject to planning control the consent of the relevant Government Department may be required and EA may be required as part of the consent procedure, as, for example, with applications for licences to extract marine minerals. It may also be the case that a development on land may have an impact on underwater sites, which would need to be taken into account when assessing an EA. The Royal Commissions listed in paragraph 4 should be consulted on the archaeological potential of the proposed area of development.

World Heritage Sites

8   There are at present 10 World Heritage sites in England and four in Wales. No additional statutory controls follow from the inclusion of sites in the UNESCO World Heritage List, but inclusion does highlight the outstanding international importance of the sites as a key material consideration to be taken into account. Information aboout World Heritage Sites in England is given in PPG 15.

Historic buildings

9   Buildings of special architectural or historic interest make an important   **H.4** contribution to the quality and character of the built environment. Under the Planning (Listed Buildings and Conservation Areas) Act 1990 the most important historic buildings are 'listed' and are afforded statutory protection.

10   Listed buildings in England and Wales[2] are classified in 3 grades to show relative importance: Grade I (only about 1.4% of listed buildings are in this category); Grade II* (some 4% of listed buildings); and Grade II.

The current principles for selecting buildings to be listed are:

- All buildings built before 1700 which survive in anything like their original condition;
- Most buildings built between 1700–1840, though selection is necessary;
- Buildings constructed between 1840–1914. In this category only buildings of definite quality and character are listed;
- Only selected buildings from the period after 1914 are listed;
- Buildings which are less than 30 years old are normally only listed if they are of outstanding quality. Buildings which are less than 10 years old are not listed.

11   The following are the main criteria which the Secretary of State applies in deciding which buildings to include in the statutory lists:

- **architectural interest**: the lists are meant to include all buildings which are of importance to the nation for the interest of their architectural design, decoration and craftmanship; also important

---

[2] In Scotland buildings of special architectural or historical interest are listed under the Town and Country Planning (Scotland) Act 1972. The criteria for selection and listing are different to those set out in paragraphs 9 and 10. For amendments which apply in Scotland please see Historic Scotland, Longmore House, Salisbury Place, Edinburgh EH9 1SH.

examples of particular building types and techniques, *e.g.* buildings displaying technological innovation or virtuosity, and significant plan forms;

- **historic interest**: this includes buildings which illustrate important aspects of the nation's social, economic. cultural or military history;

- **close historical associations** with nationally important people or events;

- **group value**, especially where buildings comprise together an important architectural or historical unity or a fine example of planning, *e.g.* squares, terraces or model villages.

A particular building may qualify for listing under more than one of these criteria.

Conservation Areas

12   Areas of special architectural or historical interest, the character or appearance of which it is desirable to preserve or enhanced, may be designated as Conservation Areas. This designation recognises the importance of securing the protection of groupings of buildings. Conservation Areas may be centred on listed buildings and may also include pleasant groups of other buildings, open spaces, trees, an historic street pattern, a village green or features of historic or archaeological interest. These should all contribute to the special character of an area.

13   In addition to listed buildings and Conservation Areas there are many more buildings and settlements which, while unprotected, are also valuable contributors to the rural and urban scene. Consideration should be given to the contribution these may make to the character, appearance, fabric, and archaeological, historic or architectural integrity of an area in and around a proposed development site.

Historic landscapes

H.5   14   Historic landscapes are also an integral part of cultural heritage and are an increasingly scarce and threatened resource. Historic landscapes may be valued as:

- works of art in their own right, based on their aesthetic quality;

- providing a significant historical record;

- providing a setting for buildings or monuments of architectural or archaeological importance;

- making a particular contribution to the variety of scenery in the countryside;

- containing valued habitats for wildlife.

They may occur in an industrial, urban or rural location.

15   Historic landscapes may be afforded special protection as part of a larger

designated landscape (such as a National Park or AONB), but, unlike scheduled ancient monuments and listed buildings, are not currently provided with statutory protection. Nevertheless, they make an important contribution to the character of the landscape generally in conjunction with many factors including archaeological features and historic buildings. Other landscape resources are mentioned in Appendix 9.

Parks and gardens

16   English Heritage maintain the Register of Parks and Gardens of special **H.6** historic interest in England. Local authorities should have copies of the volumes of the Register relating to their area. Sites of exceptional historic interest are assessed as Grade I, those of great historic interest as Grade II*, and those of special historic interest as Grade II. (The grading of these sites is independent of the grading of any listed building which falls within the area.) Inclusion on the register is a material consideration when planning permission is sought for development that would affect the character of a registered park or garden. In Scotland the Inventory of Gardens and Designed Landscapes is maintained by Scottish Natural Heritage and copies are held by planning authorities. The Secretary of State has to be consulted when they may be affected by a development proposal.

17   In Wales, Cadw (Welsh Historic Monuments Executive Agency) is preparing a register of Historic Parks and Gardens in the principality which is expected to be completed by the end of 1996.

Historic battlefields

18   English Heritage introduced a Register of Historic Battlefields in England in 1995 which identifies a limited number of areas of historic significance where important battles are sufficiently documented to be located on the ground. They are not graded. Further information may be obtained from English Heritage. In Scotland, details of historic battlfield sites are kept by Historic Scotland.

POTENTIAL IMPACTS

19   Developments of many different types and in many different locations **H.7** have the potential to cause direct and indirect impacts on cultural heritage. These are often likely to be negative unless attention has been given to them during the design process. The following summary is not intended to be exhaustive, but merely to illustrate the range of potential impacts. It should be clear from these that the impacts can be complex and need not be direct. Further guidance of the position in England is given in PPG15—Planning and the Historic Environment. In Scotland information is available in the Memorandum of Guidance on Listed Buildings and of Conservation Areas published by Historic Scotland, in NPPG 5 and in PAN 42.

20   **Loss/destruction**: The most dramatic potential negative impact is the

direct loss or destruction of an element of cultural heritage. This, for example, may include the demolition of an historic building or the disturbance of an archaeological feature during the construction of a development.

21 **Visual intrusion**: This is a potentially important impact in both urban and rural settings. An unsympathetic development may impinge on the character and appearance of an area through inappropriate siting or design—directly affecting Conservation Areas, historic buildings, ancient monuments, areas of archaeological importance, historic landscapes and settlements.

22 **Physical damage**: There are a number of impacts which may potentially cause damage to the physical fabric of archaeological remains, historic buildings or historic landscapes. These include:

- *air pollution*: which may cause damage to historic buildings and ancient monuments;

- *vibration*: which may cause damage to historic buildings, ancient monuments and archaeological remains. This may be a potential impact during construction, or during the operation of certain developments;

- *recreation pressure*: which may occur as a result of improved access or by directly attracting visitors. This may cause physical damage and change the intrinsic character of the feature;

- *ecological damage*: there are a number of potential impacts which may affect flora and fauna as a result of a particular development. These impacts may also affect cultural heritage, as flora and fauna is an important component of heritage features, particularly historic landscapes. Potential impacts outlined in Appendix 5 on flora and fauna may therefore be relevant to cultural heritage.

ASSESSMENT OF EFFECTS ON CULTURAL HERITAGE

H.8 23 **Scoping**: At the outset it is important to establish the potential value of the development site with regard to the three main components of cultural heritage: namely archaeology, historic buildings and historic landscapes. Where the site is well documented or contains listed structures or features, this importance can usually be established quite quickly. However, lack of information does not mean that a site is devoid of interest; it may yet require investigation, especially with regard to archaeology and historic landscape features. In these instances, a site visit, combined with discussions with appropriate individuals or organisations, should help clarify the position.

24 The scoping phase should end with identification of any requirements for further information to be collected during the baseline studies. These should focus on the potential types of impact which the development could have at any phase, and the potential cultural value of the site.

25 **Baseline surveys:** Any further baseline studies should be undertaken by

an expert in cultural heritage. Additional work required to describe the existing situation may consist of:

- archive research, including study of old maps and paintings of the site;

- field study by a trained archaeologist and geophysical surveys where appropriate;

- trial excavations by a trained archaeologist.

26 **Prediction of impacts**: Like the baseline studies, the prediction of impacts and an evaluation on their significance will need to be undertaken by an expert in cultural heritage. During this assessment it will be important to consider not only direct impacts such as loss or damage of important features but also indirect impacts such as changing water table levels which can affect the preservation of archaeological features in situ.

27 **Mitigation of impacts**: By adopting good practice and certain mitigation measures it may be possible to address many of the potential impacts of a development on cultural heritage. The primary method of mitigating adverse impacts is to recognise the site or monument early in the planning and site selection process and avoid it (preservation in situ), leaving a suitable buffer zone around the site. In the case of nationally important monuments, buildings and landscapes this may be the most appropriate course of action, unless it can be shown that the need for a particular development in a sensitive location is unavoidable and outweighs the significance of the heritage feature.

28 If avoidance is not a possible alternative, amelioration can be achieved by reduction of the potential impacts and the preservation of heritage features, which could involve physically relocating a monument. In the case of visual intrusion affecting the character of cultural heritage, reduction of the degree of exposure of the development can be achieved by siting, screening and detailed design.

29 In the case of archaeological remains where destruction is unavoidable, appropriate provisions may be necessary to excavate and record remains before development commences (rescue excavation) depending on the merits of individual sites. In urban situations where archaeological remains are in deep stratified layers spanning centuries of occupation, construction design sympathetic to the preservation of archaeological deposits in situ may be required. If the site is 'unpredictable' in its archaeological potential, it may be necessary to arrange for the construction stage to be overseen by an archaeologist.

30 The need to reconcile archaeology and development and to avoid potential conflicts has led to the production of two codes of practice for land based archaeology produced by the British Archaeologists and Developers Liaison Group and the Confederation of British Industry (specifically for mineral operators). For developments below the low water mark, the Crown have published the Joint Nautical Archaeology Policy Committee Code of Practice for Seabed Developers in 1996. If these codes are followed, along with the guidance in PPG 16, conflicts and impacts can be largely mitigated.

Appendix I

MANAGEMENT OF ARCHAEOLOGICAL PROJECTS (ENGLISH HERITAGE (1991)) (MAP 2)

1 Introduction

1.1   This is the latest in a series of documents dealing with archaeological **I.1** project management. Its contents have been substantially influenced by the documents which preceded it. In particular *Principles of Publication in Rescue Archaeology*. a report by a working party of the Ancient Monuments Board for England Committee for Rescue Archaeology (1975), commonly referred to as the Frere report after the working party chairman, and *The Publication of Archaeological Excavations*, a report of a joint working party of the Council for British Archaeology and the Department of the Environment (1982), referred to as the Cunliffe report, have been of fundamental importance in developing approaches to the management of projects and the dissemination of their results. These two reports have given rise to a set of archaeological management concepts and terms which have achieved a wide currency. It is appropriate briefly to review these reports to put the present document in context.

1.2   The Frere report was particularly concerned to address the problem of how to publish an ever-increasing quantity of archaeological data. The report put forward a model for archaeological projects which saw data management at a series of levels. With hindsight the principal problem with the model was with the concept of the Level 3 report: this was to contain all the data recovered, prepared to a standard equal to that required for publication. Although the report stated that 'refined' publication at Level 4 should be the objective in the future, the need for the prior preparation of a Level 3 report separate from the production of a report text for publication, meant that achieving publication was still time-consuming and expensive.

1.3   In addressing this problem the Cunliffe report stressed the need for the critical selection of data. Particular emphasis was put on the research design as a means of exercising this selectivity. The need for 'well defined thresholds for review and forward planning' was identified as an appropriate mechanism for implementing this. Although the model put forward in the Cunliffe report has been of great value, putting it into practice has been difficult. One of the principal purposes of the present document is to develop the concept of regular critical review as the key to successful archaeological project management, and to suggest how this might be achieved.

1.4 A previous version of this document has been issued (*Management of Archaeology Projects*, 1989—subsequently referred to as *MAP* 1989). This addressed two aspects of project documentation: first it gave a fuller definition of the terms set out in the Frere and Cunliffe reports; it also set out the role that documentation should play in an archaeological project. The purpose of the present document is to revise and expand *MAP* 1989, as a result of experience gained through using it, and in particular to re-examine and define more fully the management process which leads to the production of project documentation, which was not covered in *MAP* 1989.

1.5 This revised document puts forward and describes in detail a model for the management of archaeological projects. The most innovative part of this model is identified as 'assessment of potential for analysis' (phase 3, figure 1) and this has received detailed treatment because the importance of a formal post-excavation review phase has become evident. It is intended that this management framework will operate side by side with a framework of academic priorities which will help to estimate archaeological value. These priorities will of necessity change as the successful completion of well planned projects contributes to the growth of the academic database.

1.6 The opportunity has also been taken to revise the definitions made in *MAP* 1989 and to produce sample specifications of key project documents (appendices 2 to 6). There is currently a need for the standardisation of terms in use within the profession, and it is hoped that this document will contribute to this.

2 Summary

I.2 2.1 Archaeological projects are set up to collect specified data within time and cost constraints. The academic justification for the project must be clearly formulated and expressed at the outset. The end result should be a publication which reflects the significance of the data collected, and the creation of an archive deposited in an appropriate place for continuing curation and legitimate access.

2.2 For any project, a team with the appropriate knowledge and skills must be appointed. It is a basic principle of good management practice, and fundamental to project's success, that all the principal members of the team have a common understanding of the project objectives and communicate effectively with each other.

2.3 To be managed effectively an archaeological field project of any size must be organised in phases. These phases are:

- phase 1 — project planning
- phase 2 — fieldwork
- phase 3 — assessment of potential for analysis
- phase 4 — analysis and report preparation
- phase 5 — dissemination

Each of these phases should have clearly defined objectives and be appropriately resourced in terms of staff, equipment, time and costs.

2.4 Regular review of a project's results is essential if academically acceptable objectives are to be consistently pursued and appropriately resourced. The purpose of such review is to establish the significance of the results at each phase and to define the work needed as a consequence in the subsequent phase. This is achieved through sequential and phase-related project documentation:

- phase 1 — project design, which defines the objectives of the whole project and gives an outline of the overall resources likely to be necessary to achieve these
- phase 2 — site archive, which records all the primary data collected during fieldwork
- phase 3 — assessment report, which states the academic potential of the data in the site archive
  - — updated project design which sets out the further work considered necessary to fulfil this academic potential
- phase 4 — research archive, which records the data resulting from the analysis phase and forms the basis of the final report
  - — report text for publication, which reflects the importance of the results of the project and their contribution to archaeological knowledge
- phase 5 — publication
  - — project archive for deposition

2.5   The process during each stage of a project will usually be externally monitored. The level of external monitoring will have to be agreed in advance with the project sponsor. Any changes to the design of a project may have to be negotiated as part of the project monitoring undertaken by the project sponsor, but in any case they must be recorded and communicated to all concerned. A system of quality control must also be in place to ensure that work is carried out to an acceptable professional standard.

3   A model for the management of archaeological projects

3.1   In any project, a team is appointed to carry out a number of linked tasks   **I.3**
to achieve predetermined objectives. These tasks will be planned to occur in a specific order within cost and time constraints. The purpose of project management is to ensure that the tasks undertaken are organised and monitored to achieve the required outcome. For archaeological projects the successful outcome is defined as a published report which accurately reflects the archaeological significance of the results, supported by a properly curated and accessible archive.

3.2   To set up and run any project effectively it is necessary:

- to formulate clearly defined objectives and standards
- to establish soundly based estimates of the resources required to achieve the objectives
- to appoint a project manager who can motivate and coordinate the team
- to appoint a team with appropriate knowledge and skills

- to establish and maintain effective communication between all team members and external people involved
- to establish and operate a system of quality control
- to monitor progress and address any problems revealed as soon as possible

These activities are fundamental to the model of archaeological project management which follows. Their specific application during each project phase is discussed in sections 4 to 8.

3.3   In order to perform these activities successfully it will be necessary to employ a wide range of project management techniques. Detailed discussion of these is outside the scope of this document. Some of the techniques most relevant for archaeological project management are summarised at appendix 1.

3.4   Experience in English Heritage of archaeological project management has shown that the definition and consistent pursuit of objectives can be difficult. It is this problem which the proposed project management model is intended particularly to address. Objectives for archaeological projects must be defined and justified not only in practical, but also in academic terms. This academic justification must make clear the issues that the work will address, and the framework of academic priorities into which the project will fit. Due to the difficulty of predicting the potential of archaeological evidence, the original academic objectives may well need to be refined more than once during the life of a project. To ensure that this redefinition is possible it is necessary to identify phases within a project, at the end of each of which the priorities of the project can be reconsidered and resources redirected appropriately. (These points are what the Cunliffe report called 'thresholds for review and forward planning').

3.5   This document identifies five principal phases through which a large archaeological field project would normally pass (see figure 1, p. 209):

- phase 1   —   project planning
- phase 2   —   fieldwork
- phase 3   —   assessment of potential for analysis
- phase 4   —   analysis and report preparation
- phase 5   —   dissemination

These phases, with the possible exception of phase 3, are familiar components of archaeological projects. However the emphasis on following a similar staged approach in each phase, culminating in a critical review at the end of each phase, is new.

3.6   As figure 2 (see p. 210) shows, these stages form a repeated cycle of activities:

- Proposal: a proposal is put forward, defining and justifying the objectives to be met—this should give due consideration to the relevant academic priorities as well as practical considerations, and show the estimated cost of undertaking the work
- Decision: following consideration of the proposal as set out above, a decision is made as to whether or not the project should move to the data-collection stage. Where a positive decision is taken a budget should be set and appropriate resources made available
- Data-collection: will implement the decision to proceed and result

Figure 1

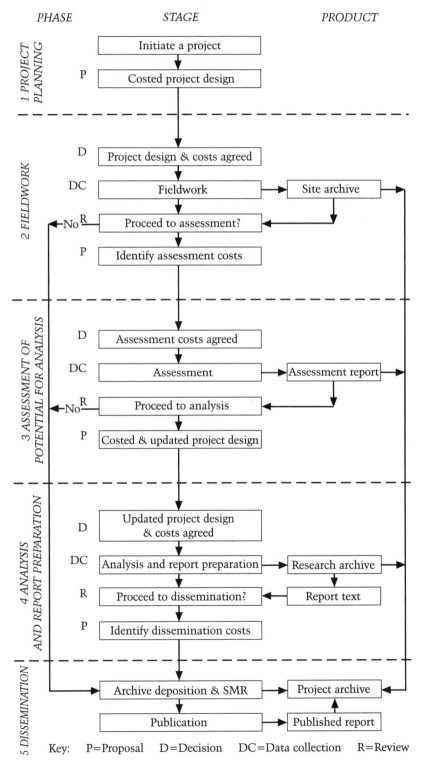

PHASE   STAGE   PRODUCT

1 PROJECT PLANNING

P — Initiate a project / Costed project design

2 FIELDWORK

D — Project design & costs agreed
DC — Fieldwork → Site archive
No R — Proceed to assessment?
P — Identify assessment costs

3 ASSESSMENT OF POTENTIAL FOR ANALYSIS

D — Assessment costs agreed
DC — Assessment → Assessment report
No R — Proceed to analysis
P — Costed & updated project design

4 ANALYSIS AND REPORT PREPARATION

D — Updated project design & costs agreed
DC — Analysis and report preparation → Research archive
R — Proceed to dissemination? ← Report text
P — Identify dissemination costs

5 DISSEMINATION

Archive deposition & SMR → Project archive
Publication → Published report

Key: P=Proposal   D=Decision   DC=Data collection   R=Review

in the collection of appropriately documented data. The term data is here and throughout used in a broad sense to include site records, materials recovered from the site, and any results obtained from subsequent analysis

- Review: assesses the significance of the data collected, and gives consideration to the most appropriate next step.

The end result of each cycle may be the formulation of new or modified proposals, thus initiating another cycle at the next project phase. A proposal is the first stage of any project phase: however a phase will only begin once a positive decision to fund the work has been made. In practice therefore in phases 2, 3 and 4 the proposal is the final stage. Figure 1 (see p. 209) has been drawn to reflect this.

Figure 2

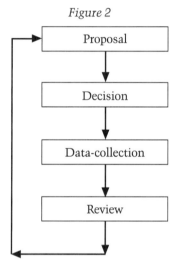

3.7   Three review stages are identified in figure 1. At each of these the relevant project documentation is reviewed, allowing objectives to be redefined, the subsequent phase to be planned, and appropriate costs identified.

3.8   This cyclical process of data-collection and review, followed by selection, further study, and ultimately dissemination, is fundamental to the structure of an archaeological project. Formalising this process is important and will ensure that:

- projects are carried out to consistent standards
- project proposals are well presented and carefully justified, so that they satisfy project sponsors, those responsible for the care of archaeological sites, and the ultimate consumers of the results
- archaeological projects are managed in a professional manner

3.9   The system of regular review and follow-up will probably cause some hiatus in the execution of a project. This will, however be offset by the improved end-product, and the reduction of misdirected effort. With careful planning disruption can be reduced or mitigated. The following general principles should always be considered:

- an outline plan of the whole project should exist at the outset

- the needs of the next phase in a programme should always be kept in view: for example the assessment phase can be initiated relatively quickly after the completion of fieldwork if the site archive (the ordering and review of which has to precede assessment) has been compiled to a high standard
- sponsors and all participants in a project should be made aware of the timetable to which a project is running, and should be consulted well in advance about their participation
- organisations running several projects should ensure that project review stages are timetabled so as not to coincide.

3.10   The funding of archaeological projects can vary. Ideally funding would be made available in blocks related to one or more of the five project phases. In practice, however, funding will be dependent on the internal policy of the project sponsor. Project budgets may be established on a once-and-for-all basis at the beginning of the fieldwork. Where this is the case the staged approach to project planning should still apply. Regular reviews will ensure that at each phase the balance of the project's fund is allocated appropriately.

4   Phase 1: project planning

Evaluation projects

4.1   The project management model described begins to operate at the point **I.4** when a decision has been taken to initiate a project (see figure 1, p. 209). Large archaeological field projects, however, may have been preceded by one or more preliminary phases of evaluation. These evaluations may have formed projects in their own right and will have followed the cycle of activities described at 3.6. The results of these evaluation projects will be critical in defining the objectives of any subsequent field project, and in estimating the resources necessary to achieve the objectives once defined. It should be appreciated that evaluation may produce results of sufficient significance to merit assessment, analysis and publication in their own right (see sections 6.7 and 8), even if the result of evaluation is a decision not to initiate a further project.

4.2   Evaluation will almost invariably commence with a desk top study. In those cases where such study yields insufficient information, rapid and limited fieldwork may follow. The purpose of such fieldwork is to define, as far as possible, the likely nature and extent of the archaeological deposits under consideration.

4.3   The evaluation report produced will present a digest of information on the character and significance of the deposits under review. This report will form the basis of the proposal on appropriate further action.

4.4   A copy of the evaluation report must be lodged with the commissioning body (*e.g.* developer) and an entry made in the relevant sites and monuments record (SMR hereafter). It is also important that a note be published recording that an evaluation has taken place, summarising its results, and stating where the archive can be consulted. This is also necessary where the evaluation results are negative, or when there is to be a time lag between the completion of the evaluation and the start of any resultant project. Material collected during evaluation should be accessible in the interim to archaeologists and other related professionals.

Formulating the project design

I.5   4.5 The end-product of the initial planning stage is the project design, a specification for which is given in appendix 2. This defines the objectives of the whole project and outlines the overall resources likely to be necessary to achieve them. The project design will provide the framework for the execution of the project through to completion. Even if the funding is agreed in phase-related blocks (see 3.10) it is necessary to have an overview of the aims and anticipated costs at the outset. The project design will also give more specific details of the strategies and resources appropriate to the fieldwork phase.

4.6 Work on the project design can only begin when the project manager and core team have been assigned to the project. This core team will include representatives of all relevant specialisms (*e.g.* environmentalists, technologists, conservators, illustrators, surveying/dating specialists, documentary historians, artefact specialists, etc). The project manager and core team will together formulate the project design, although it is the project manager's responsibility to ensure that all potential areas of enquiry are considered and appropriate resources allocated.

4.7 Once the composition of the project team has been established team members will wish to ensure that contact has been made with other organisations which have an interest in the project, including the museum or other body which will become the eventual recipient of the project archive. Consideration should also be given at this stage to seeking any additional academic guidance needed.

4.8 The compilation of a project design is essentially a four stage process and should be carried out in the following sequence:

- Background: sufficient relevant background information should be studied to allow a reasoned estimate to be made of the nature of the data which will be gathered, for example their type, quantity, condition, and significance. This may draw on the results of a prior evaluation project (see 4.1 to 4.4)
- Aims and objectives: consideration of the potential character of the data, as identified above, will assist in formulating specific project objectives. These will include the academic objectives of a project, termed the research design
- Methodology: the proposed data collection methods should be described, making clear why those advocated are the most appropriate and will best ensure that the data collected can fulfil the project's aims as set out above. No archaeological report is better than the data upon which it is based: establishing appropriate recording and recovery strategies is crucial to a project's success
- Resources and timetable: the recording and recovery strategies defined above will affect the character and quantity of the data collected, and form the basis of the justification for the timetable, staffing, equipment, and funding level proposed

Planning for fieldwork

4.9   The aim in undertaking a programme of fieldwork should be to produce **I.6** a comprehensive site archive as defined in appendix 3. This can only be properly achieved if the resources needed for fieldwork are correctly estimated and deployed. Where this is done, time will not be wasted at a later stage attempting to solve problems which were not properly addressed during excavation. An appropriate level of resourcing will ensure maximum efficiency and allow the subsequent assessment phase to go ahead with the minimum of delay. Particular attention should be paid to the following areas:

- Records: adequate time should be allowed to ensure that records are checked and internally consistent. A system for detecting errors should be established, and particular effort should be made during fieldwork to rectify errors as soon as possible. The use of computer-based recording systems can be an invaluable aid in this respect
- Artefacts: specialists should be asked to identify work which needs to be carried out on site, and their advice should be sought on how this should be done. Basic artefact sorting and identification such as spot-dating can help to inform decisions on fieldwork strategy, and raise fresh questions in time for them to be appropriately addressed. Arrangements should be made for the proper cataloguing and storage of artefact. It may well be appropriate to involve a museum professional in this stage of the planning process. Allowance should be made in the project timetable and budget for any occasional visits by conservators and other specialists which may prove necessary
- Archaeological science: specialists need to be asked to identify any work which should be carried out on-site, and their advice should be sought on how this should be done. While some material will always be best handled under laboratory conditions, some environmental samples, for example, can more efficiently be dealt with on-site. Material should be properly catalogued and stored, following appropriate professional advice, and allowance should be made in both the project timetable and budget for any necessary occasional site visits by archaeological scientists.

4.10   The site archive is a primary resource and must be properly curated and stored so that it can be consulted in the future. The project manager should ensure that appropriate advice on conservation needs is available to the project team. Long term storage is a museum responsibility, and it is essential that contact with a museum professional is made at a sufficiently early stage. Museum requirements must be established and appropriate resources allocated. The United Kingdom Institute for Conservation (UKIC)'s *Guidelines for the preparation of excavation archives for long term storage* (Walker, 1990) and the Museums and Galleries Commission's *Standards in the museum care of archaeological collection* (in prep), in particular the section headed 'Standards for the preparation and transfer of archaeological archives' should be referred to when planning for curation.

213

5 Phase 2: fieldwork

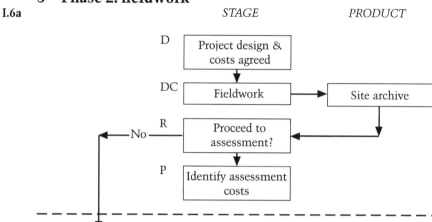

STAGE   *PRODUCT*

Figure 3

Key: P=Proposal   D=Decision   DC=Data-collection   R=Review

Decision-making

I.7   5.1 When the project design is complete, approval will have to be sought from the project sponsor and those responsible for the care of the site to be excavated. The fieldwork phase cannot commence until the proper approval has been given. Agreement to proceed may include provision for progress monitoring by the project sponsor.

Data-collection

I.8   5.2 It is likely to be at this point that the full project team will be brought together. This will consist of the core team (see 4.6) plus the site staff and relevant consultants. It is essential that data-collection does not commence until the project manager has ensured that all involved are thoroughly acquainted with the project design. Particular attention should be paid to ensuring that:

- there is a common understanding of the objectives of fieldwork and of each individual's role in it
- individuals are clear about their own role and their relationship to other team members
- recording and recovery policies and on-site procedures are explained, and any necessary collective or individual training undertaken

5.3 There is a potential danger during data-collection, the funds allocated to creating a high quality ordered site archive may be diverted to intensifying fieldwork. The project design will however have specified the expected level of resourcing needed for different aspects of the fieldwork, and particular attention should be paid to ensuring that resources remain appropriately allocated within that framework. If any area of a project is not conforming to the agreed project design steps should be taken either to bring the project back on course, or where necessary, to revise the project design. Any changes in priorities, methodologies or timetabling should be discussed and agreed with other members of the project team, as they may have implications for other aspects of the project. Any alterations to the project design should be made by authorised staff and should be recorded: they should also be reported to the project sponsors, especially if they have not been involved in their formulation.

Review

5.4   The site archive comprises the excavation records and any materials   **I.9**
recovered. It should be quantified, ordered, indexed, and internally consistent. It should also contain a site matrix, a site summary (a short report giving a preliminary account of the discoveries), and brief written observations on the artefactual and environmental data.

5.5   Once the site archive has been completed it will be possible to move on to the review stage to see if the original or redirected project objectives have been achieved, and whether it is necessary to proceed to a formal 'assessment of potential for analysis' as the next phase of the project. The speed and efficiency with which this can be done will be directly dependent on the resources given to on-site recording and storage.

5.6   In some cases review of the quality, character, and significance of the data-collection may indicate that a formal assessment phase is unnecessary. In such cases a certain level of published information should be regarded as an irreducible minimum (see appendix 7). Steps must be taken to complete an SMR entry, arrange for the deposition of the archive, and publish a brief report summarising the results of the project.

5.7   Where the review indicates that a formal assessment phase is required, an interval to plan this assessment work programme will be needed. At this stage steps must be taken to make an initial entry into the SMR.

Planning for assessment

5.8   The project team is responsible for formulating a programme for the   **I.10**
assessment phase. Different types of material will require different assessment methods. It is consequently most important that the views of all the relevant specialist contributors as well as team members should be sought when estimating costs and preparing a timetable.

5.9   The most time-consuming and costly aspect of the assessment phase is likely to be supplementary data-collection (see 6.6 to 7). As far as possible the need for supplementary data must be identified and estimated for when planning the assessment phase.

5.10   The internal programming of the assessment phase is critical. Most assessments will involve a sequence of events which must be identified and appropriately timetabled. For example, if money and time are not to be wasted bulk sample processing and sorting has to wait for the pottery specialist to decide, in collaboration with the team member assessing the site stratigraphy, which contexts are worthwhile; bone assessment has to wait until the bulk samples have been sorted; work on the fish bones has to wait until they have been extracted from the mammal bones; and integration of assessment results must wait until all the individual specialist assessments are ready. Consequently all relevant staff have to be consulted before a programme for this phase can be finalised.

I.11   6   Phase 3: assessment of potential for analysis

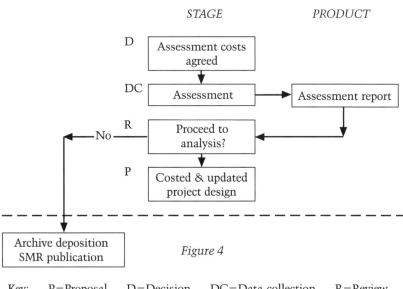

Figure 4

Key: P=Proposal   D=Decision   DC=Data-collection   R=Review

The nature and purpose of assessment

I.12

6.1   Some of the most challenging problems facing those managing archaeological projects centre on post-excavation work, in particular the widely acknowledged need to be selective when planning this work. It is therefore crucial that academic and archaeological objectives are carefully defined before any work takes place. This is essential to ensure that appropriate selection is made and a publication produced which accurately reflects the value of the data-collection (see 1.5, 3.4). It has become clear that, to ensure post-excavation funding is allocated to best effect, and post-excavation planning decisions are firmly based, there is a need for a formal review phase, here termed 'assessment of potential for analysis'.

6.2   The assessment phase is a pivotal point in the execution of an archaeological project. Its purpose is to evaluate the potential of the data-collection to contribute to archaeological knowledge and to identify the further study necessary. The complexity of the assessment phase and the amount of time required will vary; for example deeply stratified urban sites will probably require more detailed work on the stratigraphy than rural sites with a limited occupation span. It should however be stressed that any work undertaken should be directed towards allowing decisions to be made about the potential of the data and the nature of the future programme: no detailed analytical study should be undertaken until the assessment phase has been completed. Considerable breadth of academic knowledge is needed to make the necessary judgements: the best available staff should be used for assessment. Alternative sources of expert advice should be sought if not available within the project team.

6.3   A key aspect of this assessment phase, which deserves emphasis at the outset, is the need for a co-ordinated approach. the importance of integrating artefact and environmental evidence with the stratigraphic record has long been acknowledged, but not always fully exploited. Too often programmes of analysis have been initiated on related groups of data with insufficient contact between the specialists concerned and no cross-reference made until the final stages of publication preparation. The assessment phase must establish the full potential of the properly integrated data as early as is practical

6.4   The end-product of the assessment phase is an assessment report, the contents of which are more fully defined in appendix 4. This report will include all the information necessary to make decisions about the future direction of the project. It is formed of three principal parts:

- a factual summary, characterising the quantity and perceived quality of the data contained in the site archive
- a statement of the archaeological potential of the data contained in the site archive
- recommendations on the storage and curation of the data contained in the site archive, and the timescale on which this should be achieved. (An appropriate museum professional should be involved in this aspect of the assessment)

Decision-making

6.5   Costs and a timetable for the assessment phase must be agreed with the project sponsor before work can commence. If appropriate these may also be presented to those responsible for the care of the excavated site for their approval. Agreement to proceed may include provision for progress monitoring by the project sponsor.   **I.13**

Data-collection

6.6   The data to be collected at this stage are specified in more detail in appendix 5. In some cases the value of the material being assessed will be self-evident. If, for example, a large collection of securely stratified environmental data from a previously unresearched context type is recorded in the site archive, its potential can easily be characterised because it is known to be unique. Equally, a small collection of highly fragmented pottery from a site with high residuality and a long occupation span can be identified as having no apparent potential without supplementary records being necessary.   **I.14**

6.7   In other cases further work will be needed to establish the archaeological potential of the material. The methods used will vary according to the type of material and the extent to which it is already understood. For example collections of pottery largely represented in existing regional type series may be rapidly scanned to achieve an adequate assessment, whereas for environmental material such as parasite eggs or pollen a sample of the material may need to be studied in detail to estimate its potential. It must be stressed, however, that any processing and recording should only be done to demonstrate that a particular research topic has potential. It is important that those responsible for managing and monitoring the project during this stage should ensure that this is the case.

6.8 Before the bulk of the environmental and artefactual data is assessed it is important that all contexts containing residual or contaminated material are identified. In order to do this, initial artefact dating (*e.g.* ceramic, glass, clay pipes) should be integrated with the site matrix (see appendix 3). This will inform those working on material where contamination or residuality cannot be observed, of contexts for which further study may be unprofitable.

6.9 It is of crucial importance that all assessors of material are adequately briefed. It is the project manager's responsibility to ensure that all those involved are provided with the material for assessment in a suitably ordered and accessible manner, and with the relevant background and contextual data.

6.10 Artefact and environmental specialists should be provided with:

- an up to date copy of the project design
- a copy of the site, environmental, and finds summaries (see appendix 3)
- specific information on the individual contexts from which the material referred to them for assessment comes including:
  * context type
  * position in the stratigraphic sequence, and/or relationship to major structures
  * approximate date where known, or details of how this is to be derived
  * degree of contamination or residuality
  * recovery method
- sufficient data to allow contexts to be grouped together to provide useful and appropriate analytical units for study. Analysis work depends to a great extent on such groupings, rather than on the deductions that can be drawn from a single context. Groupings are likely to be defined primarily by chronology (*e.g.* by provisional phases or groups of similar phases), and secondarily by structural context or context type
- details of any questions the project manager wants the specialist to consider

6.11 Artefact and environmental specialists should liaise closely with conservators during this stage to ensure that appropriate recommendations can be made on both immediate and long-term conservation requirements.

6.12 Assessment and selection of artefactual and environmental material for further study is now widely practised, but assessment of structural data is less commonly undertaken. More rigorous consideration must be given to justifying the degree of stratigraphic analysis proposed. For example proposing a forward programme which does little more than reiterate context descriptions and relationships that exist in the records and matrix of the site archive cannot be justified. Structural analysis should be directed towards establishing an interpretation of the site record and describing why a particular phasing or interpretation is suggested. Assessment should identify the need for further work on the stratigraphic records in these terms.

6.13   Once assessments have been made of the individual classes of data, the results should be integrated. This is the stage at which all the strands of evidence can be brought together for the first time and their combined potential considered. For example, in isolation a group of pottery from a pit may be of limited significance, but in conjunction with the study of plant remains and animal bone the potential of all the elements may be greatly increased. To be successful this will need a period of intense communication between all the specialists involved. This should be achieved principally through regular meetings of the project team. It is essential that the project manager makes all the material category assessment reports available to all members of the project team, so that the full potential of the site archive can be explored.

Review

6.14   The end-product of the data-collection stage of the assessment phase will be an assessment report. Once this assessment report is written, the project team should review its contents to establish whether it is appropriate to proceed to analysis.   **I.15**

6.15   In some cases this review of the assessment report will reveal that an analysis phase is not appropriate. However, it will still be necessary to prepare a report accurately reflecting the significance of the results for publication (see appendix 7), complete an SMR entry, and arrange for the deposition of the archive.

6.16   Where assessment does demonstrate that the site archive contains material which has the potential to contribute to the pursuit of local, regional or national research priorities, appropriate data should be identified for analysis. When identifying such data it should be borne in mind that such work should be directed towards the final product of a project, the publication. Review should isolate:

- material crucial for interpreting the site which should be published
- material which merits publication for its intrinsic archaeological value outside the context of the site report, for example artefact or environmental studies
- material considered to have no present archaeological potential or relevance

The data identified as appropriate for analysis should be worked up into a formal proposal, which will be expressed as an updated project design.

Planning for analysis: updating the project design

6.17   The purpose of this stage is to put forward proposals for work to be carried out in the analysis phase. These proposals will be expressed as an updated project design, which will define the objectives on the analysis phase and the strategies and resources necessary to achieve them. This process is more fully described in appendix 5. The format of the updated project design is the same as that for the original project design (see 4.8 and appendix 2) with   **I.16** an additional section, 'Summary of potential', which summarises those aspects of the data-collection selected for analysis during the assessment phase.

6.18 All the project team members to be involved in the analysis phase should contribute to the formulation of the updated project design. Some materials will need to be worked on sequentially by more than one specialist. It is critical that such sequences be identified at a sufficiently early stage in consultation with all concerned, so that an achievable and agreed programme can be formulated.

6.19 Additional guidance external to the project team may be sought at this stage, both to focus and fine tune the formulation of research objectives, and consider the available report format options. Academic and editorial comment can more usefully be canvassed at this stage than at a later stage in the preparation of a report text, when alteration is more difficult and more expensive.

6.20 Planning for the analysis phase should bear in mind the two objectives to be met, namely the production of a research archive and of a report for publication. Analysis should be planned with the publication firmly in view, and the research archive should only contain data which derive from the analysis of material intended for publication. The urge to accumulate data not specified in the updated project design as part of the research archive or publication must be resisted.

6.21 When establishing the resources needed for analysis therefore, allowance must be made for the cost of synthesizing the research archive and of producing a report for publication. The scope of the report will have been defined in the updated project design as a publication synopsis. Preparation of a report to publication standard requires the performance of a wide range of related tasks which can be easily overlooked when planning for analysis: it is most important that these are identified at an early stage (see 7.6 and appendix 7). Contact should be established at this stage with the proposed publication outlet to establish cost implications of editorial or reprographic requirements.

6.22 It must be borne in mind that transfer of the report draft to an editor for publication is not the end of the process. Consideration must be given to the need for provision, once the editorial processes are underway, of time for team members to answer queries, correct proofs, and act as general liaison in the period between delivery to the publishing body and the eventual appearance of a printed report. The timescale on which this will be done will depend on priorities established by the publishing body, who should be consulted about the likely timescale and editing needs.

6.23 Any additional resources necessary to complete the project archive (see 8.2) must also be identified at this stage. The assessment report will have identified any material in the site archive for which special arrangements for long term curation need to be made. Discussion with the museum or other archive recipient will have been held earlier in the project (see 4.10), and it may now be necessary to re-establish contact and make a formal agreement on a mutually acceptable transfer date for the project archive.

7 Phase 4: analysis and report preparation

Figure 5 **I.17**

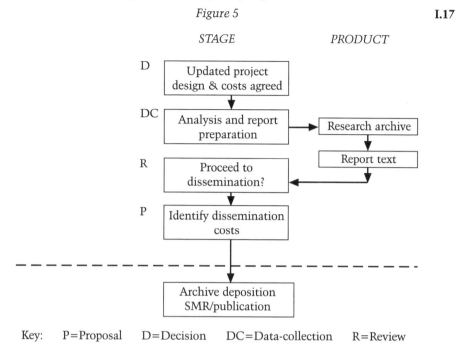

Key: P=Proposal D=Decision DC=Data-collection R=Review

Decision-making

7.1 When the updated project design document is complete, approval of the **I.18** project design should be sought from the project sponsor and those responsible for the care of the excavated site. Analysis cannot commence until the updated project design has been approved. Agreement to proceed may include provision for progress monitoring by the project sponsor.

7.2 A copy of the publication synopsis should be sent to the appropriate editor at this stage to ensure that it conforms to requirements.

Data-collection and report preparation

7.3 At this stage it is essential that all members of the project team are fully **I.19** briefed. The project manager should ensure that all those involved have contributed to the formulation of the updated project design and are thoroughly acquainted with it. Particular attention should be paid to ensuring that:

- there is a common understanding of the objectives of the analysis phase
- individuals are clear about their own role and their relationship to other team members
- recording and analytical strategies are explained and any necessary additional collective or individual training undertaken

7.4 Data-collection should be approached in two stages:

- compilation of the research archive, involving detailed work on the stratigraphy, artefacts and environmental data and the production of catalogues, illustrative material, and draft report text
- selection of data from the research archive to produce an integrated report text for submission to editors

Assessment will have removed many of the uncertainties about the results of analysis, but until the work has been done the exact content of the publication cannot be finalised.

7.5 It will be important to ensure that resources for analysis are directed towards achieving the stated academic objectives and not towards other interesting areas of enquiry outside the scope of the planned publication. It is also important that classes of material which cannot fulfil the potential predicted at assessment are identified at an early stage to allow modification of the work plan and allow re-allocation of resources. Any changes in priorities, methodologies or timetabling should be discussed and agreed with other members of the project team, as they may have implications for other aspects of the project. Any alterations to the project design or report contents should be made by authorised staff and should be recorded: they should also be reported to the project sponsors and if substantial enough to alter significantly the planned publication, editorial approval should also be sought.

7.6 The report should be submitted in a completed state containing all the evidence, analysis, and synthesis the author considers necessary to fulfil the project design. All aspects of text, tables, artwork and other illustrative material, figure and contents lists, list of contributors, camera ready copy (CRC) for fiche, bibliography, appendices, and any other items for inclusion, should be fully integrated and cross-referenced. In effect the submitted report should be in a sufficiently final state for the author to be willing to allow it to be publicly distributed in manuscript. If specific guidelines are not supplied the appropriate British Standards Institute conventions (BS 4148, BS 5261) or the English Heritage Academic and Specialist Publications Branch guides *Preparing your text for publication (1991)* and *Preparing your illustrations for publication (1991)* can be used (see also appendix 7).

Review

I.20 7.7 Once a completed text for publication has been produced it should be sent to the project sponsor and other parties for their approval. The advice of an independent academic referee may well be sought by the project team or required by the project sponsor or publishing body at this stage. Referees may be asked for their opinion on the quality of the report and to comment specifically on all or any of the following:

- How far the publication reflects the stated aims of the project design
- whether the publication meets general archaeological and academic standards and priorities
- whether the proposed publication meets the requirements of the publishing body
- whether publication of the report is warranted and whether it meets professional standards

When establishing the suitability of a report for publication, reference can be made to appendix 7.

7.8   At this stage the opportunity should also be taken to review the success of the project as a whole. Consideration should be given to:

- the objectives it has been possible to achieve
- the standard of the work attained
- the accuracy of the time/cost forecasts

Such a review will provide essential feedback for estimating and decision making on other projects.

Planning for publication

7.9   Once the content of the publication text has been agreed the cost of **I.21** publication must be established. When calculating costs allowance must be made for proof-reading (galleys and page proofs generally, or if typesetting from disc, equivalent but different proofing stages) which will already have been calculated as a project cost (see 6.22).

7.10   A breakdown of the costs of publication and a production schedule should be made in consultation with the relevant editor/publishing body. The production costs incurred by the publishing body will in general include:

- typesetting
- origination of CRC of both text and illustrations, including page make-up
- printing
- marketing/distribution

8   Phase 5: dissemination

8.1   Before the publication is printed there will be a period during which **I.22** appropriate members of the project team will liaise with the editorial team about matters of content and presentation, such as dealing with queries and checking proofs. Dissemination may result in a number of different types of publications: a project sponsor may require a more general account of a project's results for example. The need for such publications will have been identified in the project design, and arrangements for their dissemination should also be made at this point.

8.2   Once the final draft report has entered the editorial phase the project archive can be transferred to the recipient museum. The project archive will contain:

- the project design
- the site archive

Depending on the work undertaken after fieldwork it may also contain:

- the assessment report
- the updated project design
- the research archive
- a copy of the report draft submitted for publication
- a copy of the published report

- original artwork, CRC, fiche origination material, plates and any other items used by the printer in producing the printed paper.

8.3   The record of the project results previously made in the SMR (see 5.7) should now be updated.

Appendix 1: project management techniques

(see also main text para 3.3)

I.23   Project management is a large subject with a literature of its own. some relevant topic headings are listed below, and those responsible for managing archaeological projects may usefully pursue these and other management skills further.

A1.1   Teams and team meetings

I.24   A1.1.1   It is essential that a team with appropriate knowledge and skills is appointed to undertake a project. Once the team and its manager have been appointed the success of a project will largely depend on how effectively its members communicate with one another.

A1.1.2   Representatives of the project team should be selected to attend regular meetings. All relevant areas of interest should be represented (*e.g.* archaeological scientists, artefact specialists, etc). Project sponsors may also be invited to attend team meetings.

A1.1.3   The purpose of team meetings is:

- to maintain a constant critical view of the project's objectives and make any necessary adjustments to the project design
- to ensure that progress and expenditure accord with the forecast
- to involve all members of the project team in making any necessary adjustments to priorities, methodologies, timetabling, or budget
- to inform all members of the project team of progress in areas outside their own particular concern
- to ensure that work is carried out to an appropriate professional standard.

A1.1.4   Records should be kept of the progress reported and the decisions made at team meetings for circulation to all concerned.

A1.2   Estimating

I.25   A1.2.1   It is of fundamental importance to establish accurate forecasts of time and costs required. In order to achieve accuracy:

- adequate time should be devoted to forward planning
- representatives of each specialist area within a project should be adequately consulted
- reference should be made to records of time and cost performance of previous projects

A1.3 Controlling time and money: the work plan

A1.3.1 It is necessary to formulate a work plan to ensure that a project **I.26** operates effectively within its time and cost constraints. The work plan will detail:

- the projected start date
- the projected finish date
- the tasks to be performed
- the order in which they must be performed
- the projected start and finish dates for individual tasks

A1.3.2 There are a number of different ways of representing the work plan for example Gant Charts, Pert Charts. The size and complexity of the project will dictate the best methods of record and display.

A1.3.3 Regular review will be necessary and should be undertaken to ensure that the work plan is adhered to. The effects of planned or unplanned deviation must be considered and steps taken either to return to the original plan or make agreed necessary adjustments.

A1.3.4 Adjustments may necessitate rescheduling or reallocation of resources. The work plan must always be updated to reflect any changes made, and when necessary approval for this must be sought.

A1.4 Resource accounting

A1.4.1 Expenditure of time and money can only be successfully controlled **I.27** if it is recorded. All members of a project team should maintain an appropriately detailed record of time spent on project tasks. It should be the project manager's responsibility to define the task headings under which activities are recorded, and the appropriate level of record, so that task records can be grouped and general trends observed. Tasks will range from project specific activities to more general headings, for example attending team meetings.

A1.4.2 The project manager should also be responsible for ensuring that an appropriate record is kept of cash-flow.

A1.5 Monitoring

A1.5.1 Project sponsors may well wish to satisfy themselves that a project **I.28** is being run efficiently and to the agreed specification. The level of monitoring will vary in accordance with the sponsor's requirement and the needs of specific projects. The level and form of monitoring should be agreed between the sponsors and the project manager at an early stage. Monitoring may be carried out by a representative of the sponsor attending some or all team meetings, by regular contact with the project manager, or by more or less detailed involvement.

A1.5.2 The purposes of monitoring at every phase are:

- to ensure that the objectives and methodologies defined in the project design are being adhered to
- to discuss and agree necessary changes to the project design
- to ensure that the work is being carried out to an appropriate professional standard

- to ensure that progress accords with the time/cost forecast
- to discuss any aspect of the project of legitimate concern to the sponsor

A1.5.3 Monitoring of an archaeological project will principally take place during phases 2 to 4 (fieldwork, assessment, analysis, and report preparation). In order to monitor a project effectively the project monitor must have at each stage:

- the current project design
- the current work plan
- details of the budget for the current stage and overall
- the opportunity to discuss and examine work in progress

A1.5.4 If monitoring reveals that any of the necessary criteria are not being fulfilled, steps must be taken to establish the reasons for this. Consideration must be given to whether or not the project design is still valid, and where appropriate adjustments must be made to the work programme to ensure that the re-defined targets can be met.

A1.5.5 Records of monitoring should be kept and circulated to all concerned.

A1.6 Project management packages

I.29

A1.6.1 A large number of project management software packages are now available. These packages provide an effective tool for planning, controlling and adjusting project programmes.

Appendix 2: project design specification

(see also main text paras 4.8 and 6.17)

A2.1 Background

I.30

A2.1.1 Description of the area/site to be examined:

    i) location including grid reference, abbreviated if necessary to protect the site from unauthorised interference
    ii) map/location plan
    iii) the period and type of site
    iv) the condition of the site, and the anticipated state of preservation of its deposits

A2.1.2 Previous work:

    i) a short synopsis of previous archaeological work
    ii) the location of existing site archives, and the extent to which they have been consulted
    iii) the results of any evaluation fieldwork undertaken

A2.1.3 Reasons for and circumstances of the project:

    i) the threat or other justification for carrying out the proposed work

ii)   the legal status of the site

iii) the timing of the project

iv)   arrangements for access agreed with landowners and site occupiers

v)   proposed reinstatement (after excavation)

A2.1.4   Archive deposition:

i)   where it is intended that the excavated material and records should be deposited and curated. This must be discussed and agreed with landowners, museum authorities, and other relevant bodies

ii)   any specific recording requirements resulting from the decision on final location of the material

iii) any specific environmental or other conditions anticipated to be necessary for the optimum storage of site data

A2.2   Aims and objectives

A2.2.1   Academic or research design: I.31

The following should be described and justified:

i)   the contribution the project is expected to make to archaeological knowledge, in the context of the current framework of local, regional and national research priorities. For all projects (not just those funded by English Heritage) reference may usefully be made to English Heritage funding criteria (1991). In summary the following attributes of a site should be considered:
  * survival/condition
  * period
  * fragility/vulnerability
  * documentation
  * potential

ii)   the potential for integrating a project with existing archaeological research for example funded by the Science and Engineering Research Council (SERC) or a university

iii) opportunities for integrating aspects of a project with related non-archaeological research for example if the site is within a Site of Special Scientific Interest (SSI)

iv)   likely possibilities for future research which may emerge from the project

v)   opportunities for experimental work

A2.2.2   Publication and presentation:

i)   the likely scale of the published report (eg monograph, article or note) and the intended place of publication. The relevant editor or editorial committee must be consulted

ii)   arrangements made for display and public information, including possibilities for community involvement or liaison with museums, schools etc

A2.3   Methods statement

I.32   A2.3.1   Particular attention should be paid to the relationship between the data which it is anticipated will be gathered, the methodological approach to be applied to these data and the project's objectives (as expressed in A2.2). The statement should make clear how the methods advocated are those best suited to ensuring that the data collected will fulfil the stated aims of a project. The following should be considered in the formulation of a method statement:

    i)   the components of a site which will be investigated and those which will not

    ii)   the different types of data-gathering methods to be used, for example documentary research, survey, photogrammetry, excavation, environmental sampling

    iii)   the recovery and recording strategies which it is intended to employ during fieldwork, for example sampling of selected deposits, on-site flotation and sieving, finds recovery and processing programmes, and discard policies. These should be related to the different classes of data anticipated from the site, for example structural data, artefacts, environmental material

    iv)   in those cases where a suitable methodology does not appear to exist, consideration should be given to the necessity for development work

A2.4   Resources and programming

I.33   A2.4.1   Staffing and equipment:

    i)   details should be given of the structure and size of the project team and the levels of experience represented by its component members. The need for any collective or individual pre-fieldwork training should be identified

    ii)   all the tasks identified in the methods statement should be listed and related to the individual members of the project team

    iii)   information should be given of the materials and equipment needed to fulfil the tasks defined in the methods statement (*e.g.* the hire of heavy plant, flotation equipment)

    iv)   details, compiled in association with a conservator and relevant museum professional, of materials and equipment needed to ensure that the archaeological data collected (*e.g.* records, artefacts, environmental material) are appropriately stored and curated.

    v)   details of premises hire, security provision, health and safety provision

A2.4.2   Timetable:

    i)   details should be supplied of the projected programme of the project through to completion. This should include fieldwork, assessment, analysis and dissemination

    ii)   the programme should be expressed on a cascade chart or by some similar form of graphic representation. The cascade chart should show:

         ∗   all the tasks to be undertaken in the correct sequence

  * the inter-relatedness and interdependence of tasks
  * time-critical elements
  * the length of time allocated to each task
  * the personnel (or grade) allocated to each task
  * agreed monitoring points

A2.4.3 Budget:

  i)   the costs of undertaking the work programme described should be
       presented making clear the basis of the calculation, for example
       salary scales, allowance for inflation and any other adjustments
  ii) once the tasks directly related to fulfilling the projects objectives
       have been costed, allowance should be made for other legitimate
       costs, for example general administrative and managerial tasks,
       participation in project team meetings, employers liability insur-
       ance, compliance with health and safety legislation, monitoring,
       staff holidays, training etc
  iii) cashflow and detailed cost projections should be shown in
       conjunction with the timetable shown on the cascade chart

Appendix 3: site archive specification

(see also main text paras 4.9, 6.8 and 6.10)

The site archive will contain all the data gathered during fieldwork and must   I.34
be quantified, ordered, indexed, and internally consistent. The site archive
represents the original record of the project's results and must not be
amended, even when subsequent research suggests interpretations and
conclusions different from those set down at the time of fieldwork. If at this,
or any subsequent stage in a project, material is discarded from the site
archive, this fact must be recorded (see also A4.3.2).

A3.1   Materials and records

A3.1.1   The first objective in assembling the site archive is to preserve the   I.35
integrity of the primary field record. It must be maintained in optimum
conditions to ensure the physical survival of the records, ecofacts, artefacts
and other specimens. It will contain where relevant the following elements:

  • copies of correspondence relating to fieldwork
  • survey reports (eg borehole, geophysical, documentary)
  • site notebooks/diaries
  • original photographic records
  • site drawings (plans, sections, elevations)
  • original context records
  • artefacts, ecofacts and any other sample residues
  • original finds records (eg registered finds, bulk finds, artefact dating
    catalogues)
  • records of conservation and x-rays undertaken during fieldwork
  • original sample records
  • original skeleton records
  • computer discs and printout

A3.1.2   When compiling the site archive, the need for good images for security copying should be borne in mind. It is possible, for example, to fiche directly from drawings if the correct materials, letter and number size etc are used and staff are trained appropriately.

A3.2   Matrix and summaries

I.36   A3.2.1   In addition to these elements the site archive should also contain a brief objective statement summarising the nature and quantity of the various classes of data collected, which completes the task of observation and prepares for review without moving into the areas to be covered by the assessment and analysis phases. This summary should be compiled by those most closely involved with the fieldwork as soon after fieldwork has been completed as is possible. The following documentation should be produced:

   i)   a full site matrix: all stratigraphic relationships should be cross-checked and the stratigraphic sequence of the site firmly established. It may be supplemented by annotated lists of contexts or sketch plans as appropriate

   ii)   a summary account of the context record: not at this stage an exhaustive descriptive account of the site, but rather a short report describing the site and synthesizing the context record (say 2–5 pages of text). The site summary and matrix together represent a mechanism for taking forward an understanding of a site while acknowledging that interpretation may well change as work proceeds through the succeeding assessment and analysis phases

   iii)   a summary of the artefact record: a brief statement of the range, quality, condition and any other pertinent details of the artefact collection

   iv)   a summary of the environmental record: a brief statement of the range, quality, condition and any other pertinent details of the environmental material collected

Appendix 4: assessment report specification

(see also main text paras 6.4 and 6.6)

A4.1   Factual data

I.37   A4.1.1   For each component of the project (eg stratigraphic/structural, artefactual, environmental) there should be a statement setting out:

   i)   the quantity of material and or records

   ii)   the provenance of material: this should include comment on provisional dating, and evidence for contamination or residuality

   iii)   the range and variety of material: this should include comment on any bias observed due to collection and sampling strategies

   iv)   the condition of material: this should include comment on the extent to which an assemblage is likely to be affected by preservation bias, and comment on its potential for long-term storage

   v)   the existence of primary sources or relevant documentation which may enhance the study of site data

A4.1.2   The means of collecting the data listed at A4.1.1 should be briefly described (eg rapid scanning, 10% sample recorded, pilot study based on x-radiography).

A4.2   Statement of potential

A4.2.1   This should comprise a considered statement on the value of the   **I.38**
data listed at A4.1. The statement should be addressed at two levels:

i)   For each material category consideration should be given to:
  *   questions posed in the project design which the data-collection has the potential to answer
  *   new research questions resulting from the data-collection
  *   the potential value of the data-collection to local, regional, and national research priorities

ii)   The significance of an individual material category may be greatly enhanced by considering its study with that of inter-related material. The contents of all the material category assessment records should be considered in this light before an integrated assessment report is prepared. This should summarise:
  *   site specific questions posed in the project design which the data-collection has the potential to answer
  *   potential new research topics resulting from the recovery of the data-collection
  *   the potential value of the site to local, regional and national research priorities

A4.3   Storage and curation

A4.3.1   This section should be compiled following consultation with   **I.39**
conservators and the appropriate museum professional and should contain:

i)   comment on both immediate and long-term conservation and storage requirements for the data held in the site archive
ii)   recommendations about discarding material from mixed, contaminated or unstratified contexts, where there is no apparent purpose in retention.

A4.3.2   In formulating a discard policy due regard must be given to the views of the eventual recipient of the archive, the legal owners of the material, and those responsible for the care of the excavated site (see A3.4).

Appendix 5: updated project design specification

(see also main text para 6.17)

A5.1   Background

A5.1.1   The following should be provided: **I.40**

i)   a summary of the original academic objectives of the project, as expressed in the original project design
ii)   a summary of the results of the project to date

A5.2 Summary statement of potential

A5.2.1 Review of the assessment report will have identified:

  i) material of critical importance for interpreting the site
  ii) material which merits publication for other stated reasons outside the context of a site report

A5.2.2 The perceived academic potential of the data represented by i) and ii) if such material is proposed for analysis, should be briefly explained. The extent to which original objectives may be fulfilled, and new questions have been posed, should be made clear.

A5.3 Aims and objectives

I.41 A5.3.1 Academic or post-excavation research design. The following should be described and justified:

  i) the specific research aims to be addressed during analysis, and the contribution which they are expected to make to archaeological knowledge, in the context of the current framework of local, regional and national research priorities
  ii) details of the specific elements of the data-collection which will be the subject of analysis, and the academic objectives to which they are expected to contribute
  iii) the potential for integrating a project with existing archaeological research for example funded by the SERC or a university
  iv) opportunities for integrating aspects of a project with related non-archaeological research (it may be necessary to obtain outside advice on this)
  v) likely opportunities for future research which may emerge from the project
  vi) opportunities for experimental work

A5.3.2 Publication and presentation

  i) a publication synopsis should be prepared, giving the proposed format, structure, and content of the published report. It should include:
      * a short summary explaining how the report has been planned to reflect the archaeological significance of the project as expressed in A5.3.1
      * a chapter by chapter breakdown of the report, giving a summary of the contents of each and indicating the different methods of presenting the information (*e.g.* published text, tables, line drawings, half tones, colour plates, and fiche)
      * the anticipated length of the text sections and proposed number of illustrations, tables etc
  iii) those aspects of a site which could support a more popular treatment should be identified

A5.4   Methods statement

A5.4.1   The methods statement should make clear how the methods   **I.42**
advocated are those best suited to ensuring that data-collection will fulfil the
stated aims of the project. The following issues should be considered in the
formulation of the methods statement:

    i)   the recording strategies which it is intended to employ during
analysis, for example a basic quantification of all stratified
ceramics, with detailed fabric analysis undertaken on identified
key groups only. The treatment to be accorded to each type of data
should be described, for example structural data, human bone.

    ii)   in those cases where a suitable methodology does not appear to
exist consideration should be given to the necessity for develop-
mental work

A5.5   Resources and programming

A5.5.1   Staffing and equipment   **I.43**

    i)   details should be supplied of the size of the project team and the
levels of expertise represented

    ii)   all the tasks identified in the methods statement should be listed
and related to the role and responsibilities of the individual
members of the project team and the need for any collective or
individual training identified

    iii)   details should be given of the materials and equipment needed to
fulfil the tasks defined in the methods statement

A5.5.2   Timetable

    i)   details should be supplied of the projected programme of the
project through to completion, ie analysis and dissemination

    ii)   the programme should be expressed on a cascade chart or by some
similar form of graphic representation. The cascade chart should
show:

        * all the tasks to be undertaken in the correct sequence
        * the inter-relatedness and interdependence of tasks
        * time-critical elements
        * the length of time allocated to each task
        * the personnel (or grade) allocated to each task
        * agreed monitoring points

A5.5.3   Budget

    i)   the costs of undertaking the work programme described should be
presented

    ii)   once the tasks directly related to fulfilling the project's objectives
have been costed, allowance should be made for other legitimate
costs, for example general administrative and managerial tasks,
participation in project team meetings, monitoring, training,
holidays etc (see also appendix 1)

    iii)   cashflow and detailed cost projections should be shown in
conjunction with the timetable shown on the cascade chart

Appendix 6: research archive specification

(see also main text para 6.20)

Catalogues and other records

I.44 A6.1.1 The research archive will be derived from the work done during the analysis phase and will comprise: stratigraphical/structural, artefact, environmental, and other catalogues and all other records as well as details of the methods and selection strategies used in each case. Each separate data group should be cross-referenced to related data groups, to the final publication, and if necessary to a general context concordance. These should be supplemented by indices to allow users maximum accessibility to the contents. The archive will contain some or all of the following elements:

- context information: recording (on duplicate copies) any amendments to original field records resulting from analysis
- photographic catalogue: details of all photographs taken as part of analysis
- photographs: photographs taken as part of analysis
- stratigraphic drawings: any amended versions (on copies) of original site plans and sections cross-referenced to earlier versions
- object catalogues: details of items selected for analysis, publication and record drawings, and the location of objects
- object drawings: object drawings undertaken as part of analysis either as record drawings or for publication
- x-ray catalogue: details of all x-rays taken as part of analysis cross-referenced to object catalogue
- x-rays: x-rays taken as part of analysis, cross-referenced to objects
- conservation records: details of conservation undertaken during analysis, cross-referenced to objects conserved
- sample catalogue: details of samples selected for analysis
- human bone catalogues: details recorded for analysis
- animal bone catalogues: details recorded for analysis

A6.2 Analytical reports

I.45 A6.2.1 Report text derived from the above material, and which will form the basic text from which the final publication will be prepared, comprising:

i) site narrative: an interpretive structural and stratigraphic history of the site, illustrated by maps/plans/elevations and sections. It should be possible to relate this back to the site records listed above

ii) artefact reports: the full text, accompanying data, and illustrations relating to those artefacts selected for analysis. It should be possible to relate this back to the object catalogues, and to the final publication text, especially where individual reports are not reproduced in full

iii) environmental reports: the full text, accompanying data, and illustrations relating to environmental data selected for analysis. It should be possible to relate this back to the environmental catalogues and to the final publication

Appendix 7: guidelines for the preparation of published reports

(see also main text paras 5.6, 6.15, 6.21, 7.6 and 7.7)

A7.1 Minimum requirements

A7.1.1 The published report of an archaeological project should always **I.46** contain the following information:

i)   the research objectives as expressed in the project design and the updated project design where applicable

ii) circumstances and organisation of the work and the date at which it was undertaken

iii) identity of the individuals/organisation by whom the work was undertaken

iv) summary account of the results of the project

v)   summary of the contents of the project archive, where it is housed and how it may be consulted

A7.1.2 Reports of fieldwork projects should additionally give:

i)   the national grid reference (suitably abbreviated if publication of the exact site location is not in the general interest, or if it is necessary to restrict public access)

ii) the parish

A7.2 Report-writing criteria

A7.2.1 When writing up the results of a project consideration should be **I.47** given to the following:

i)   the report should appropriately reflect the importance of the results of the project and deal adequately with the site's social, political, and historical context

ii)   the interpretation of the site should be justified by the evidence presented. Ambiguities in the data base should be discussed, and where more than one interpretation is possible the alternatives should be presented (at least in summary)

iii) the report should present information about what was found in a well balanced, logical, accessible, and structured way. It should be immediately intelligible to and usable by those who know nothing about the site

iv)   the extent to which the objectives of the project have been fulfilled should be discussed, including a critical assessment of the methodologies employed

v)   the report should be written clearly and concisely, and should make appropriate, consistent, and economical use of other methods of data presentation for example tables, plans, or photographs (it is important to consult the publication editor if innovative presentation methods are necessary, as publication costs may be increased)

vi)   specialist reports and their supporting data should be carefully chosen and given their proper value. Specialist contributors must

235

be involved in or informed of editorial decisions affecting the
presentation of their work in print

vii) all the constituent parts (text, figures, photos, and specialist
reports) should cross-refer adequately. Readers should be able to
find their way around the report without difficulty

viii) attention should be drawn to areas of future study potential which
it has not been possible to explore fully within the limits of the
agreed project design

A7.3   Production criteria

I.48   A7.3.1   Consideration will have been given in producing figures and
typescript to any notes for authors supplied by the publishing body. As part of
the process of producing the report draft consideration must be given to the
following:

i) wordprocessing must be competently done and output checked
by the contributor responsible for the original work. This is
especially important as much work can be saved by accuracy at
this stage, particularly as typesetting from disc is used increasingly to produce archaeological reports and accuracy avoids extra
re-keying and correction stages

ii) good quality clear prints of half tones and colour negatives for
colour plates should be selected at an early stage in the preparation of the report draft as they must be available to the editor
with the rest of the report draft

iii) the presentation of line drawings and tables should also be
discussed and agreed at an early stage in report preparation, and
the art work must be available to the editor at the same time as the
report draft

iv) figure, table and photograph captions should also be drafted at an
early stage, and should in general be supplied as text to be typeset,
not as Letraset or stencil lettered directly onto the figure artwork

v) the bibliography should be complete, checked, integrate all
contributors' bibliographic contributions, observe BSI, and use
conventions compatible with the house style of the publishing
body

vi) errors are the responsibility of the authors and should, so far as
possible be identified and rectified before the editorial processes
begin

vii) text supplied to the editors should incorporate all revision
necessary as a consequence of internal and external refereeing. It
must be established with the publishing body at an early stage in
the production processes what their refereeing requirements are,
as these may differ from those of the sponsors, and incompatibil-
ity is best anticipated and resolved at an early stage

viii) it is more cost effective to agree on format and presentation of
material with editors at an early stage. Alteration of report
presentation during the editorial process is uneconomical and
leads to production delay

ix) in-house editing by the project team can save time, but should
only be done after consultation with the publishing body, and

must take due consideration of the style and format of the published report if it is not to waste time and resources

x) indexing is a specialist skill, best done by a trained professional. Where required they cannot be produced until the report is at page proof stage, and are generally commissioned by the publisher. Special requirements, or a wish to be involved, should be discussed at an early stage in the editorial processes

Appendix J

MODEL BRIEFS AND SPECIFICATIONS FOR
ARCHAEOLOGICAL ASSESSMENTS AND FIELD
EVALUATIONS (ASSOCIATION OF COUNTY
ARCHAEOLOGICAL OFFICERS (1993))

Introduction

Information on the potential archaeological impact of an application for **J.1** planning permission to develop land must be available prior to determination so that it may be taken fully into account as a material consideration. This accords with DoE's Planning Policy Guidance Note 16 on Archaeology and Planning, and with policies in the Structure and Local Plans prepared by local planning authorities.

The Assessments and Field Evaluations which may be required to provide that information must be designed and specified within the context of Briefs issued by the archaeological adviser to the local planning authority (the planning archaeologist). These are the members of ACAO together with some District Archaeologists, and, prospectively, their equivalents in the new unitary authorities.

This advisory note offers a generalised framework for a **Brief as the basis for a subsequent Specification**, or for a **Brief incorporating a Specification**.

In drawing upon examples already in use, it intends to provide a firm basis for the production of models which reflect local needs in town and countryside. The principles and procedures are generally applicable to all proposals for ground disturbance with a potential archaeological dimension, including works outside planning control or evaluations initiated after determination of an application. An Appendix comments on issues arising from the involvement of archaeology in the planning process. The advice is primarily concerned with England and Wales.

In recognising that model briefs and specifications can be valuable and time-saving devices for planning archaeologists, consultants and contractors, ACAO would also stress that they are no more than a framework for a wide variety of individual cases, the design of each needing to address particular problems and circumstances. Unresponsive use of models could produce poor results that might undermine the credibility of evaluation as a process, as well as inhibit its technical development. This topic is rapidly evolving: ACAO welcomes comments on matters that might be considered in a future edition, and the booklet has been designed to facilitate marginal annotation.

*The **Association of County Archaeological Officers** was founded in 1973. It has members or observers representing all the counties of England and Wales. Their responsibilities include the provision of planning advice, the maintenance of Sites and Monuments Records, and, in some cases, fieldwork investigation and recording.*

Definitions

J.2   Terminology follows the five-stage sequence for integrating archaeological aspects within the development process as defined by English Heritage following Darvill and Gerrard (1990). These are Appraisal, Assessment, Field Evaluation, Strategy Formulation and Strategy Implementation. This document focuses upon the first three stages.

An *Appraisal* is a rapid reconnaissance of site and records to identify whether a development proposal has a potential archaeological dimension requiring further clarification.

An *Assessment* is a thorough review of all existing archaeological information relating to an area potentially affected by proposals for development, stopping short of further data collection and synthesis through primary research including fieldwork.

A *Field Evaluation* is a programme of intrusive and/or non-intrusive fieldwork designed to supplement and improve existing information to a level of confidence at which planning recommendations can be made.

According to the scale and circumstances of a case, some of the stages of *Appraisal, Assessment* and *Field Evaluation* may be run together as a sequence. Some may begin with a *Field Evaluation* incorporating work that in other cases would have been done earlier in an *Assessment*. Always, it is important to:

(a)   ensure applicants provide adequate information
(b)   keep the stages of work required of them as simple as possible
(c)   keep archaeological requirements made of a developer reasonable and necessary.

A *Brief* is defined as an outline framework of the planning and archaeological situation which has to be addressed, together with an indication of the scope of works that will be required.

A *Specification* is a schedule of works in sufficient detail to be quantifiable, implemented and monitored.

In preparing a Brief (or Brief and Specification), consideration should be given to the following elements.

1 Summary of brief

This will be a short 'plain language' summary, intelligible to a lay recipient **J.3**
and suitable for copying by a planning archaeologist or applicant's consultant
to non-archaeological colleagues or employers who need to know about it. It
should identify the location of the SMR, the planning archaeologist and the
local registered museum.

2 Site location and description

This will accurately identify the site on a map extract at an appropriate scale. **J.4**
Normally the author will make a site inspection as the basis for describing
matters such as altitude, current land use, vegetation cover and any other
relevant factors. It should include any readily available information about
possible physical constraints upon investigations known to the developer or
planners, while not absolving others from taking any necessary precautions
over underground services, overhead lines, basements, etcetera.

3 Planning background

This will describe the proposal, and include any local planning authority **J.5**
reference number. It may describe any significant planning history and refer
to relevant planning policies (PPG 16 may also be cited). Information may be
provided about other environmental matters the planning authority may
need to take into consideration, such as ecology and rights of way. Any need
for scheduled monument consent in order to carry out evaluation by
fieldwork will be indicated.

4 Archaeological background

This will summarise what is known already about the archaeological **J.6**
potential of the land affected by the proposal, and, as far as is relevant, the
surrounding area. In the case of town sites it should indicate whether deep
strata are known to survive locally. The level of detail must be sufficient to
support a recommendation for evaluation. Technical terms such as
'neolithic' should be explained. Any available information about the likely
state of preservation should be provided, or the lack of such information
indicated. Grid references should be provided for sites mentioned but not
shown on a plan. If the brief is for an *Assessment*, this section will
incorporate an *Appraisal* of SMR information. If it is for a *Field Evaluation*
this section will incorporate the results of any earlier *Appraisal* or *Assessment*, together with an indication of the completeness and reliability of the
information obtained.

5 Requirement for work

Against the planning and archaeological background this section will **J.7**
indicate why an assessment or evaluation is required. Its purpose will be to
enable the local planning authority to make an informed and reasonable
decision on the planning application. In general terms its scope will be to
gather sufficient information to establish the presence/absence, extent,

241

condition, character, quality and date of any archaeological deposits within the whole area potentially affected by development. This section can be supplemented by a preliminary comment on the potential of known or suspected deposits for addressing research themes relevant to local and regional archaeological understanding, as an explanation why it is necessary to clarify whether they ought to be preserved.

6 Stages of work and techniques

J.8 6.1 In the case of a **Brief for a separate Specification**, this will outline the range of available investigative techniques, and require justification for those selected in the light of local geology and land-use. It may indicate the sequence or combination of different techniques in a 'nested' approach, with the detailed design of one stage arising from the accumulating results of previous stage(s). It will provide any general information about strategy and timetable. The Brief will also be the planning archaeologist's yardstick for validating any detailed project design or specification.

6.2 In the case of a **Brief incorporating a detailed Specification**, the investigative techniques and the stages of work will be identified. They will be described in sufficient detail

(a) for time and cost to be estimated by a contractor
(b) to provide a fair basis for seeking competitive quotations
(c) to facilitate validation of contractors' methodological proposals by the planning archaeologist.

6.3 Some of the investigative techniques will apply only to an *Assessment*, others only to a *Field Evaluation*, and some to both, but at different intensities. All techniques should be considered but the following are the most commonly applicable:

(a) *Completion/Review of Desk-Top SMR Assessment*
(b) *Comprehensive Site Inspection/Topographical Survey*
Visual inspection of the entire site; examination of available exposures such as geological test pits (or records) and recently cut field ditches; presented in a standardised output
(c) *Documentary Research*
Examination of available maps and other documentary sources (printed and manuscript), and other relevant background material relating to the site and its environs (such as field names), either to assess potential for additional full research on specific issues, or to carry it out at that stage.
(d) *Aerial photography/survey*
Examination and plotting of all relevant photographs for the site and its environs; commissioning any new photography
(e) *Earthwork survey*
Survey of earthworks in pasture; detection and planning of residual earthworks in arable and woodland
(f) *Assessment of artefact content of topsoil*
This will involve measuring the surface distribution of artefacts through collection by some or all of these techniques, taking account of prevailing ground conditions,
(i) general line walking of all/part of the site

(ii) detailed collection on part of the site
(iii) sampling of soil from trial trenching
(g) *Geophysical prospection/ground radar*
    With appropriate methodology according to ground conditions; and a
    sampling strategy based on the type of information to be gathered
(h) *Trial trenching/Auguring/boreholes*
    A programme of hand-dug/machine cut and hand cleaned trial trench-
    ing; appropriate locations and proportions of the whole development
    site should be based on information accumulated from previous
    activities; areas of no known archaeology should not necessarily be
    ignored; positioning and sampling strategy may need to be defined in
    agreement with the planning archaeologist.
(i) *Volumetric sampling of test pits for artefacts*
(j) *Palaeoenvironmental assessment*
    For which a detailed and site-specific design will be required.

7 Methods

7.1 The proposed methodologies for the investigative techniques listed J.9
above must be validated by the planning archaeologist. They can be
expressed

(a) either in association with each specified technique as relevant
(b) or through a set of standard statements provided separately by the
    planning archaeologist as required policy for work in the area in
    question, to which archaeological contractors are expected to adhere
(c) or through standard statements about techniques provided by the
    contractor and approved by the planning archaeologist.

7.2 A projected *timetable* must be agreed for the various stages of work, so
that provision can be made for monitoring.

7.3 *Staff structure*, including specialist sub-contractors, must be agreed,
through a list of key project staff with qualifications and experience. IFA
membership together with IFA's Codes of Conduct and formally adopted
guidelines are yardsticks of competence and good operating practice.
Consequently it is normally prudent to disallow the use of unwaged staff as
likely to affect standards adversely (but see appendix E viii, E ix).

7.4 *Health and safety* matters (including site security) must be primarily a
matter for the contractor. However, in the name of general responsibility and
for the protection of the planning archaeologist as task monitor, it is
reasonable to require evidence of conformity to the Health and Safety at
Work Act.

7.5 *Field Survey techniques* can be specified or approved so that there is
compatibility with other work carried out in the area, as long as this pays due
regard to the needs of the particular project. Matters to be covered can
include:

(a) earthwork survey: level of recording—sketch, identification, analytical;
    scales and conventions (hachure/contour)
(b) standards and protocols for use of metal detectors
(c) transect and collection intervals for general and detailed fieldwalking

243

(d) standards of representation (including scales) for results of general reconnaissance, plotting of aerial photographs, geophysical prospection, etcetera.

(e) methods for preparing fieldwalking statistics in order to maintain consistency within an area

(f) *pro formae* for outputs from structured walkovers.

7.6 *Excavation* is a potentially destructive evaluation technique. The brief should ensure clear and enforceable guidelines for work on machine-opened trenches, such as:

(a) An appropriate machine must be used, with an appropriate bucket, usually a wide toothless ditching blade. Choice should be influenced by prevailing site conditions, and the machine must be able to carry out a clean job.

(b) All machine work must be carried out under the direct supervision of an archaeologist.

(c) All topsoil or recent overburden must be removed down to the first significant archaeological horizon in successive level spits. The continued use of machinery beyond this point should only take place when specifically agreed with the planning archaeologist as necessary for the particular type of evaluation.

(d) The top of the first significant archaeological horizon may be cleared by the machine, but must then be cleaned by hand and inspected for features.

(e) Sufficient of the archaeological features and deposits identified must be excavated by hand through a specified or agreed sampling procedure to enable their date, nature, extent and condition to be described. No archaeological deposits should be entirely removed unless this is unavoidable. It is not necessarily expected that all trial trenches will be fully excavated to natural subsoil, but the depth of archaeological deposits across the whole site must be assessed. The stratigraphy of all trial trenches should be recorded even where no archaeological deposits have been identified.

(f) All excavation, both by machine and by hand, must be undertaken with a view to avoiding damage to any archaeological features or deposits which appear to be worthy of preservation *in situ*.

(g) Any human remains which are encountered must initially be left *in situ*. If removal is necessary this must comply with relevant Home Office regulations.

7.7 *Recording systems* must be specified or approved. The format of recording forms is less important than the existence of relevant fields. Matters for consideration include:

(a) structure for site record and media to be used with special reference to archival curation needs

(b) recording forms/context sheets

(c) plans, sections/profiles of significant contexts and scales

(d) photographic formats and coverage

(e) finds collection policies

(f) finds recording systems, including bulk processing arrangements and immediate conservation arrangements for 'small' finds. For these, reference should be made to the IFA Guidelines for Finds Work.

244

(g)   environmental sampling strategies

7.8   Where records or material needing further work are generated, *post-field requirements* can be specified or approved, covering matters such as:

(a)   assessment of potential for reporting and further analysis
(b)   preparation of the archive of field records and material, including measures for security, packaging and conservation
(c)   archive deposition.

7.9   A standard variation clause will allow the specification to be varied by agreement in response to significant discoveries during the evaluation process.

8   Monitoring arrangements

8.1   This will state the need for arrangements to monitor the progress and   **J.10** effectiveness of the evaluation to ensure proper execution of the specification and therefore conformity to the brief. The arrangements will include an agreement of stages at which monitoring is appropriate and indicate the possibility of random inspection. If not provided for elsewhere, they will indicate how the monitoring of a phased programme will allow agreement on the results of a previous phase to trigger the design and commencement of the subsequent one.

8.2   Any officially approved rates of cost per visit to be charged for monitoring should be stated so that the applicant/developer will be aware of the need to make financial provision.

9   Reporting requirements

9.1   For many evaluation projects the preparation of a report will be   **J.11** relatively simple, following on directly from the fieldwork and achieved within a standard format. The Brief will ensure that reporting conforms to general requirements on content and format.

9.2   For more extensive and complicated evaluation projects, the procedures outlined in English Heritage's *Management of Archaeological Projects* 2nd Edition 1991 (MAP2) should be followed for immediate post-field archive preparation and initial assessment. Agreement can then be reached about what aspects need to be taken forward to provide a report in the required format containing the information needed for planning purposes.

9.3   The general requirements on content and format will cover:

(a)   the components and general level of detailed information and illustration for the report: normally these should include
   (i)   plans of trenches and features
   (ii)   tables summarising features and artefacts by trench together with their interpretation
   (iii)   plans of actual deposits, and, where appropriate, extrapolated to indicate potential deposits
(b)   consideration of evidence within the wider landscape setting
(c)   whether details and styles can be determined by the contractor; any need to conform to established local systems or formats for local publications
(d)   any requirement for a critical review of the effectiveness of the methodology to provide a confidence rating for the results

(e) any requirement for a separate interpretation of the significance of the results, in archaeological or planning terms, and in what format

(f) any recommendations for further evaluation if necessary

(g) any timescale for report production so that it can meet development control deadlines

10 Archive deposition

J.12 10.1 This will ensure that the results of the evaluation, the site archive (records and any materials recovered) will be placed in a suitable form in a registered museum within an agreed timetable. The planning archaeologist should indicate the availability to contractors of guidelines prepared by potential recipient bodies, including full explanation of the legal situation regarding finds, so that any requirements for security copying and storage grants are taken into account when estimates are prepared. It is appropriate to recommend that archives be prepared in accordance with established guidelines (UKIC 1990, MGC 1992).

10.2 Consideration should be given to the following points:

(a) content and format of archive: this should be prepared to the minimum acceptable standard defined in MAP2 (5.4 & Appendix 3). The integrity of the archive should be maintained.

(b) ownership of material: every effort should be made to ensure transfer of ownership to an appropriate museum; if it is to remain with the landowner, provision should be made for a full record of the material

(c) repository: in some circumstances this may be indicated in the Brief, the Specification should summarise the agreement with the appropriate repository.

(d) submission of a summary report and details of archive deposition to the SMR and the NMR

(e) expected time limits for deposition of archive.

11 Publication and dissemination

J.13 This will indicate requirements for public availability of the evaluation report at a given interval after production (usually a maximum of 6 months) through the SMR, NMR and any other standard local source such as the local registered museum. It should also deal with publication requirements if no further work is envisaged. These, which may have a cost implication, at the minimum require the submission of a summary of results to the local County Journal or equivalent publication, including one-line reports on work done with negative results.

12 Other Factors

J.14 This will indicate any other factors relevant to the applicant or potential contractors.

Appendix

A The importance of explaining purpose

(i) The requirement for evaluation must be substantiated and expressed in **J.15** sufficiently robust terms and in sufficient detail to resist challenge on archaeological and legal grounds.

(ii) The complexities of procedure and methodology for evaluation can easily distract attention from the reasons for doing it. It is important to stress the basic purpose in seeking to conserve the heritage, namely to improve understanding of a finite and non-renewable cultural resource that can serve a wide range of social uses, now and in the future.

(iii) Clarity about the detailed requirements for a properly conducted process of evaluation is equally important. Applicants need to know what the local planning authority's archaeological adviser considers sufficient for the purpose, and will want to quantify the costs to their development. Applicants and their consultants need to be aware of the stages and processes involved. Archaeological organisations tendering for contracts to provide the information also need to be clear about requirements.

B Initial appraisal

(i) PPG 16 (para 19) which discusses early consultations between developer **J.16** and local planning authority, provides the framework for the first stage of archeological work in the development process. This will require reference to the SMR, and, if not already cross-referenced, to the records of the local museum together with a brief check of the main published literature, and normally a site visit. It can be done by the planning archaeologist in response to a preliminary enquiry or a submitted application, or by an applicant's consultant as part of a preliminary enquiry discussed with the planning archaeologist.

(ii) The objective is to provide an informed answer to the question whether there is an archaeological dimension to be considered in the determination of any application, and whether this needs to be clarified through further investigation. A positive answer will lead to a Brief and Specification for the next stage, the Assessment, or, in simpler cases, lead straight into it.

(iii) Appraisals will need careful consideration by the planning archaeologist, especially when offered by the applicant, if the Sites and Monuments Record is relatively underdeveloped. Some assessment work may have to be undertaken as a matter of routine: this would apply if aerial photographic holdings were not up to date and sketch plotted, and if no systematic survey of historical map documentation had been undertaken. This may also apply to large area sites where nothing in particular is known or no adjacent sensitivities have been identified.

C Assessment

(i) This will review and validate what has already been noted in the **J.17** Appraisal, and supplement it with any other available material. It is essentially a desk-top study with a relatively small non-intensive field component. In smaller cases it may follow from and form part of the planning archaeologist's Appraisal. In larger scale cases it may be undertaken or commissioned by the developer's consultant for validation by the planning archaeologist.

(ii) The objective of Assessment is to see whether there is sufficient information to enable the local planning authority to consider properly the proposal's archaeological implications, and, if not, whether further information can reasonably be required through implementing a Field Evaluation. In already well-documented areas no further work may be necessary. It also has the potential, if carried out at the right stage in the design of proposals, to influence them so that archaeological impact is minimised.

(iii) Larger scale Assessments will require their own Brief and Specification. These will indicate the types of sources relevant to the case. They are likely to include the SMR, aerial photographs from all sources, relevant Museums, the County Record Office and local history collections, historical maps (from which a map regression exercise may be required), local experts and societies, and extensive visual inspection of the site, and, for urban sites, collection of information on basements.

(iv) The product of the Assessment will be a report that:

(a) assembles, summarises and orders the available evidence
(b) synthesises it and places it in the local and/or regional context
(c) comments on its quality and reliability and indicates how it might need to be supplemented by Field Evaluation to provide the information required for planning purposes.

(v) The Assessment ought to provide a basis for indicating whether further work will need to involve land adjacent to the application site.

D Field evaluation—brief and specification

J.18 (i) The Appraisal/Assessment is the basis for a brief which must:

(a) indicate what further information is likely to be required to evaluate the archaeological dimension for planning purposes
(b) provide an outline methods statement covering the means of obtaining it, listing relevant activities

(ii) The Brief will be prepared by the planning archaeologist or, exceptionally, drafted by an applicant's consultant for approval by the planning archaeologist. There should always be scope for dialogue over its content between the planning archaeologist and a consultant or contractor. Use of a model brief is strongly recommended for tailoring to particular circumstances, and as guidance for others. This will provide opportunities for ensuring that county policies for the historic environment and local knowledge are taken fully into account. The brief must provide the framework for a more precise specification of work, which is the mechanism for

(a) ensuring that the required information will actually be produced
(b) allowing the applicant to estimate the likely costs
(c) providing a basis for 'level-playing-field' tendering by contractors

(iii) The Specification will elaborate how the methods outlined in the brief are to be applied. From the viewpoint of the planning archaeologist, clarity about methodology is needed to ensure the specification is capable of producing the information that is required, and with minimum impact upon the archaeological resource. This ought not to be confused with the role of specifications in regulating client-contractor relationships, though there will inevitably be a considerable overlap between the two. The ultimate test of a specification is that it is sufficiently detailed and precise to ensure that the effectiveness and quality of work by a contractor selected through competition on price can be verified by the planning archaeologist.

(iv)   There is a range of opinion and practice about the responsibility for writing specifications.

(a)   Some regard this as part of the curatoral function insofar as it is a means of safeguarding the archaeology of a locality and ensuing a level playing-field for competing contractors. This approach depends upon the production of specifications having an economy and effectiveness that will be acceptable to the applicant.

(b)   Others feel the writing of specifications is a matter for the contractor, either on principle, or because they lack the resources to do it themselves. This means that specifications written by a consultant or a contractor need to be approved by the planning archaeologist for commendation to the local planning authority, in response to a brief. That may require negotiation on technical matters, which may prove difficult with a contractor already selected competitively and on the basis on an unapproved specification.

(v)   Many planning archaeologists currently prefer, in smaller scale cases, to combine the brief, outline methods statement and detailed specification for evaluation work in the same document. This ought to be organised clearly into sections to facilitate and clarify any necessary discussion between the parties involved about the various stages of work.

(vi)   The term 'Project Design' is sometimes used in the context of briefs and specifications. Its current primary derivation is from English Heritage's MAP2, which is concerned with archaeological research projects *per se*, rather than as components of the development process. It is likely to be most relevant to exceptionally large-scale evaluations and to post-consent recording projects. Here, when required of contractors, the Project Design provides an opportunity to assess the quality of their response to the brief. It also facilitates the conduct of such work within the framework of MAP2 with its inbuilt review procedures.

(vii)   The planning archaeologist needs to ensure that the recording system to be used by a contractor will be generally applicable to the task in hand, by reference to a known standard or by verification of a proposed system. It need not mean conformity to a particular field recording system or sheet, providing what is used contains the required fields of information. Methods statements in specifications can require reporting of fieldwork results in terms of established local databases for finds and structures (see I below). This requirement will be relatively undemanding in evaluations which generally locate and characterise archaeological deposits rather than excavate them extensively.

E Field evaluation—implementing and monitoring

J.19 (i) The specification must provide for notification of the planning archaeologist when the contractor commences, and at the start of agreed stages thereafter. The planning archaeologist must be prepared to make spot visits to fieldwork in progress, in order to

(a) ensure that the specified work is being carried out properly, in relation to securing the required information with minimal intervention (but not policing any contractual arrangements between applicant, consultant and contractor)

(b) agree with the applicant and his contractor any proposals for amending the specification in the light of emerging results

(c) acquire familiarity with the field situation about which recommendations will have to be made to the local planning authority.

(ii) Problems may arise, especially in larger and more sensitive evaluation schemes, where the applicant employs a consultant who has a significant input to the preparation of the brief issued by the planning archaeologist, and perhaps writes the specification. Monitoring of fieldwork by the planning archaeologist may be resisted on the grounds that the consultant is capable of providing quality control and the applicant will decide when to give the required information to the planning archaeologist as adviser to the local planning authority. In such circumstances it must be made clear that the planning archaeologist needs not only to have the required information but also to see the methods through which it has been obtained. Model briefs and specifications will facilitate this process, but in the final analysis it is reasonable for the local planning authority to require facilities for monitoring the applicant's contractor. Not least, it will help discussion between the planning archaeologist and the consultant and/or contractor on the implications of unexpected discoveries for extra work, or absences for reduced work.

(iii) The need to monitor compliance extends to all types of fieldwork.

(a) It is particularly important in fieldwalking to ensure conformity to the transect plan and collecting strategy.

(b) The implementation of necessary data-enhancement techniques for remote sensing survey output needs to be ensured.

(c) Test pitting or trial trenching by machinery must demonstrably avoid under- and over-digging, and there will need to be arrangements for agreeing what is a 'significant archaeological deposit' and a 'deposit worthy of preservation' (7.6 above). Machining of some types of archaeological deposits can be justified exceptionally but under no circumstances should the machine be used to cut arbitrary trenches down to natural deposits. Machining down to natural subsoil, for example through deep ditches to obtain a section, should not be undertaken unless specifically agreed.

(iv) Monitoring must be properly documented and a standard form is recommended. This will help deal with situations

(a) where the information may have to be rejected as inadequate due to shortcomings in implementing the agreed specification

(b) where the interpretation of the evidence becomes a key issue in a Public Inquiry into a refusal of consent for an archaeological reason

(c)   where monitoring of fieldwork recording required by a condition on a consent shows serious deficiencies, and evidence may be needed to support formal enforcement proceedings or even a prosecution.

(v)   Planning archaeologists must ensure that they posess, or have access to, the kind of technical skills needed to monitor fieldwork (and post-fieldwork) effectively. Generalised indicators may provide a foundation for monitoring, such as contractors'

(a)   membership of IFA bringing with it personal adherence to the IFA Bylaw *Code of Approved Practice for the Regulation of Contractual Arrange-ments in Field Archaeology.*

(b)   adherence to a locally adopted manual of procedures or to one offered and validated.

(vi)   Monitoring is not deemed to have been completed before the archive has been deposited and a suitable report or publication agreed.

(vii)   It must be remembered that clear examples of non-compliance by a contractor need communicating by the planning archaeologist to an appli-cant or his consultant within a reasonable time in order to safeguard against liability claims.

(viii)   The use of local societies in development-related fieldwork raises complex issues on which there is a range of views. On the one hand it is difficult to see how this can be achieved realistically in most cases given the time constraints, technical problems and confidentiality associated with commercially commissioned evaluation work. On the other hand, some experienced groups have demonstrated competence in smaller scale eval-uation or recording work whose commercial cost might also be burdensome to many private individuals, such as small house extensions in areas of general sensitivity. Additionally, some societies possess local knowledge of a kind that does not easily find its way into site-specific SMRs and ought to be consulted in appropriate circumstances by those involved in the archaeology of the development process. Whether or not local societies become involved in this kind of work, its controlling framework must always be properly drafted briefs and specifications, their effective monitoring, and the IFA Codes of Conduct (IFA 1986, 1990). All organisations carrying out work in the context of development must be able to meet timetables and quality standards.

(ix)   Those codes explicitly exclude the use of volunteers as a cheap substitute for skilled professional staff or the use of unemployed pro-fessionals on a voluntary basis. However, there may be scope for the use of 'traditional' volunteers on development-related excavations with a training element having developer sponsorship specifically for that purpose, pro-viding the voluntary/training element is ancillary to the core project staffing, and properly supervised.

F   Field evaluation: production of report

(i)   Reporting arrangements for fieldwork evaluations will need to form part of the brief and/or specification. The purpose of the report is to provide information which will enable a planning application to be determined by the local planning authority.   **J.20**

251

(ii) The fieldwork will have been commissioned by the applicant, so the report is the applicant's, as the means of providing the required information, however much the planning archaeologist may have been involved in earlier discussions. The report is therefore initially a private document to the applicant from his contractor who also needs to be able to give independent advice to his client, initially at least on a confidential basis. In cases of commercial sensitivity where the applicant is also using a local authority based contractor, the planning archaeologist must not seek or obtain information prematurely before the formulation of report and recommendations, except through agreed monitoring procedures.

(iii) In some circumstances a programme of evaluation may, in answering the questions posed, also raise others. Every attempt should be made to deal with the problem by agreed modification of the specification while fieldwork is in progress. There is a case for evaluation specifications containing a standard variation clause providing a contingency arrangement for extra machining, trial trenching or geophysics to answer particular problems which arise during fieldwork. These can be closely specified, costed and controlled. Where this is not possible for logistical reasons, or the applicant is unwilling, the necessary further evaluation must be strongly recommended to the local planning authority. If the case is clear enough, and clearly documented, failure to respond will justify a recommendation of refusal on grounds of insufficient information.

(iv) The information provided by an evaluation will ultimately be deposited in the SMR and may also be fed into other local and national data systems. This will be ensured through the terms of the specification. However, the commercial sensitivity of information about archaeological constraints on land which applicants are competeing to acquire for development can cause problems.

(a) An applicant will not want to make it available to competitors, either at all or free of charge, yet this ought not to keep it out of the public domain indefinitely. There should be a standard requirement for deposit in a public archive within 6 months of notification of results to the LPA. In any case, the evaluation information provided in support of a planning application will be a public document as a committee background paper.

(b) Of more concern is the scenario of several developers wishing to evaluate a site independently, making a cumulative impact on its archaeology. The planning archaeologist may be justified in asking the vendor to provide a single generally available evaluation whose cost would be passed on to the eventual purchaser.

(c) Deposition of an archive in a registered museum automatically places it unconditionally in the public domain.

G   Making assessments and evaluations of value for preservation

J.21   (i) Ultimately the planning archaeologist has to form a view of the significance of the results from assessment and/or evaluation so that a recommendation can be made to the District or County Planning Officer.

(ii) It is good practice to ensure specifications address this issue explicitly, *either* by debarring such expressions of view entirely from a contractor's report, *or* by requiring it in a separate statement which may in turn be linked to recommendations for further work.

(iii) Planning archaeologists seeking the latter must bear in mind the potential interest of the contractor, though both are expected to work to a presumption in favour of preservation. The Secretary of State's non-statutory criteria for scheduling in PPG 16 Annex IV provide a general method for assessing the importance of what has been discovered.

(iv) The synthesis which is a key factor in assessing importance for preservation can be more easily provided by an established local contractor than by a non-local one. There will need to be careful monitoring to ensure that locally important sites are not devalued by non-local contractors who may lack the time or inclination to do the necessary research.

H   Evaluations and full recording projects

(i) The advice offered in this document is primarily concerned with pre-consent evaluations. The planning process also regulates field recording carried out as a condition of a consent. The larger scale and greater intensity of such work may impose extra regulatory burdens and raise other procedural issues, but the overall process will be similar.   **J.22**

(ii) The reason for the recording action and its objectives must be spelt out in a brief which draws upon any evaluation results and outlines the broad methods to be adopted. The implementation of that brief will need to be specified at a level of detail which permits monitoring and control of works by the planning archaeologist. The brief ought to provide or require the equivalent of a Project Design.

(iii) Reporting procedures will need attention, bearing in mind the common misconception amongst developers that their enforceable responsibilities end with the actual fieldwork. As far as possible, the approach advocated in English Heritage's MAP2 should be followed. It represents the best available approach to estimating total project costs (and therefore developer liabilities), and a reasonable guarantee of securing the minimum necessary post-excavation programme to report results adequately.

(iv) Monitoring compliance in the post-consent phase of archaeological work may present difficulties. For large and complex recording projects it may be beyond the capabilities or resources of the planning archaeologist. In such cases it is essential to devise verifiable mechanisms of inspection and control, whether by agreement with the developer's consultant or by using a contractor hired by the local planning authority.

(v) Compliance also covers the implementation of development, to ensure that agreed measures for preservation are properly implemented, and that no unplanned destructive ground works take place.

I   Post-excavation work: reporting into local systems

(i) It is reasonable to ensure through requiring particular methods in specifications that the output of fieldwork is in a format conforming to existing local data systems. The principle is already established by requirements for report to the SMR and deposit in the local Museum.   **J.23**

(ii) The purpose of such requirements is to ensure that the data recovered are presented in formats which will facilitate comparison and synthesis without the need for a further stage of basic data preparation after the developer's obligations have been discharged. This presupposes the existence of local systems for storing data on ceramics, other finds, structures etcetera, (in addition to the SMR).

(iii) Recipient systems for data storage will have to be devised with sufficient simplicity, breadth and flexibility to be readily acceptable to contractors. They must be generally compatible with the most widely used field recording systems and be capable of dynamic response to new information rather than act as interpretative straight-jackets.

(iv) Such systems will be maintained as part of the local archaeological provision. Input to them will need to be seen as part of the reporting process, to be undertaken by either the developer's contractor or by the maintainers of the systems as sub-contractors. Project estimation must allow for both data preparation and data inputting.

J Post-excavation work: reporting and synthesis/research

J.24 (i) The developer's obligations for post-fieldwork analysis include reporting into the public domain. It will be reasonable to require considered comment on how the results relate to the archaeological reasons for undertaking the work, especially if those reasons were originally expressed in terms of a research framework for the project.

(ii) If the requirements of PPG 16 are not to be challenged as unduly onerous, restraint must be exercised in seeking full research-based syntheses for what has been presented and justified as a rather simpler recording exercise. This is not to make an artificial distinction between the recording process and the academic considerations which ought always to inform it, but to try and draw a line between basic and further research, a boundary likely to vary from case to case.

(iii) On the other hand, the risk inherent in over-restraint of the research element is that data recovery will be more readily portrayed as rubbish collection, despised by 'real' archaeologists and incomprehensible to the wider public (including the developers) in whose name it is being done. The risk is exacerbated by the nature of evaluations which tend to identify and characterise the presence of archaeological evidence, without subjecting it to any destructive analysis.

K Services combining roles for planning advice and fieldwork implementation

J.25 (i) Local authority archaeologists who have managerial responsibility for a service with separate functions for planning and fieldwork need to approach the issues discussed above openly, and with care. Distinguishing the two roles is essential for a process which is usually development-driven and developer-funded, in order to minimise the risk of conflicts of financial interest. English Heritage urges that daylight be visible between the two functions. In concurring, ACAO also urges that sight must not be lost of the basic purpose behind conservation archaeology, to increase understanding of the local historic environment.

(ii) That basic purpose depends upon local organisations of sufficient minimum critical mass to cover the range of subjects and tasks in the locality. In the sizes of localities now existing and likely to be produced by the local government review, that coverage may in practice not be obtainable in some places without a size of organisation that incorporates both roles. In such cases the local authority managing archaeologist will need to identify carefully the financially sensitive stages of archaeological involvement in the development process. In appraising the impact of a development proposal upon types of evidence, the planning archaeologist ought to be able to seek the academic advice of fieldwork colleagues, and also in drawing up particular briefs and specifications where expert detailed local knowledge can be an important consideration. Planning archaeologists however will always assimilate acquired information from whatever source in order to be able to offer independent planning advice.

(iii) In situations where one part of a service can undertake work arising from the advice of the other part, planning archaeologists must have explicit systems of internal monitoring appropriate to local circumstances, in addition to any operated by a developer's consultant. This would involve peer group review either between parts of the service or within the fieldwork organisation. It is essential that such systems

(a) are agreed with an applicant's agent or consultant before fieldwork begins
(b) and are sufficiently robust to withstand challenges of fieldwork results or planning recommendations.

L   Manuals and model statements

(i)   Manuals of procedures and model statements can clarify publicly what is generally required within the area of a local planning authority. They can also facilitate separation of roles in bilateral services and ameliorate some difficulties associated with competitive tendering.   **J.26**

(ii)   Planning archaeologists are advised to produce model versions of briefs, specifications and methods statements which will provide a 'level playing field' for potentially competitive contractors. The development of such documents and their citation in briefs will allow those planning archaeologists who wish to retain an involvement in the drafting of specifications to withdraw from the most detailed levels.

(iii)   In an area with a bilateral service, for the planning archaeologist to require that specifications conform with the local procedures manual may appear to give the local fieldwork arm a competitively 'unfair' advantage, but in practice a good manual will actually help level the playing field for the archaeology. An effective manual of procedures will reflect common practices familiar to competent professional units.

References

Darvill T and Gerrard C 1990.   **J.27**
Evaluating archaeological sites: the Cotswold Trust Approach
Cotswold Archaeological Trust Annual Review 2 (1990)

English Heritage 1991

Management of Archaeological Projects. 2nd Edition

English Heritage 1991
Development Plans for Archaeology

IFA 1986
Institute of Field Archaeologists:
Code of Conduct

IFA 1990
Institute of Field Archaeologists:
Code of Approved Practice for the Regulation of Contractual Arrangements in Field Archaeology

IFA 1992
Institute of Field Archaeologists: *Guidelines for Finds Work*

MGC 1992
Museums and Galleries Commission:
Standards in the Museum care of archaeological collections

PPG16
Planning Policy Guidance Note 16: Archaeology and Planning Department of the Environment, November 1990

SMA 1992.
Society of Museum Archaeologists
Guidelines on the Selection Retention and Display of Archaeological Collections (Draft).

UKIC 1990
United Kingdom Institute for Conservation:
Guidelines for the Preparation of Excavation Archives for long-term storage

Appendix K

CODE OF CONDUCT (INSTITUTE OF FIELD ARCHAEOLOGISTS (1994))

INTRODUCTION

The object of the Code is to promote those standards of conduct and **K.1** self-discipline required of an archaeologist in the interests of the public and in the pursuit of archaeological research.

Archaeology is the study of the nature and past behaviour of human beings in their environmental setting. It is carried out through the investigation and interpretation of the material remains of human activities, which together constitute the archaeological heritage. The archaeological heritage is a finite, vulnerable and diminishing resource.

The fuller understanding of our past provided by archaeology is part of Society's common heritage and it should be available to everyone. Because of this, and because the archaeological heritage is an irreplaceable resource, archaeologists both corporately and individually have a responsibility to help conserve the archaeological heritage, to use it economically in their work, to conduct their studies in such a way that reliable information may be acquired, and to disseminate the results of their studies.

Subscription to this *Code of Conduct* for individuals engaged in archaeology assumes acceptance of these responsibilities. Those who subscribe to it and carry out its provisions will thereby be identified as persons professing specific standards of competence, responsibility and ethical behaviour in the pursuit of archaeological work.

The Code indicates the general standard of conduct to which members of the Institute are expected to adhere, failing which its governing body may judge them guilty of conduct unbecoming to a member of the Institute and may either reprimand, suspend or expel them. The Institute from time to time produces written standards and guidance for the execution of archaeological projects, which members are advised to respect in the interests of good professional practice; a full list of the IFA 'Standard and Guidance' documents published to date will be found in the 'Further Reading' section appended to the Code.

The *Code of Conduct* was formally ratified and adopted as a By-Law of the Institute at the Annual General Meeting held on 3rd June 1985, and amended

257

by Ordinary Resolutions passed at Annual General Meetings held on 12th September 1988, 17th September 1993 and 14th October 1994. It should be read in conjunction with the *Memorandum and Articles of Association, Code of Approved Practice for the Regulation of Contractual Arrangements in Field Archaeology, Disciplinary Regulations* and 'Standard and Guidance' documents. (By-Law enacted under Article 45, pursuant to Clause 3 of the Memorandum.)

PRINCIPLE 1

K.2   The archaeologist shall adhere to the highest standards of ethical and responsible behaviour in the conduct of archaeological affairs.

Rules

1.1   An archaeologist shall conduct himself or herself in a manner which will not bring archaeology or the Institute into disrepute.

1.2   An archaeologist shall present archaeology and its results in a responsible manner and shall avoid and discourage exaggerated, misleading or unwarranted statements about archaeological matters.

1.3   An archaeologist shall not offer advice, make a public statement, or give legal testimony involving archaeological matters, without being as thoroughly informed on the matters concerned as might reasonably be expected.

1.4   An archaeologist shall not undertake archaeological work for which he or she is not adequately qualified. He or she should ensure that adequate support, whether of advice, personnel or facilities, has been arranged. (See Note on Rule 1.4)

1.5   An archaeologist shall give appropriate credit for work done by others, and shall not commit plagiarism in oral or written communication, and shall not enter into conduct that might unjustifiably injure the reputation of another archaeologist.

1.6   An archaeologist shall know and comply with all laws applicable to his or her archaeological activities whether as employer or employee, and with national and international agreements relating to the illicit import, export or transfer of ownership of archaeological material. An archaeologist shall not engage in, and shall seek to discourage, illicit or unethical dealings in antiquities. (See Notes on Rule 1.6)

1.7   An archaeologist shall abstain from, and shall not sanction in others, conduct involving dishonesty, fraud, deceit or misrepresentation in archaeological matters, nor knowingly permit the use of his or her name in support of activities involving such conduct.

1.8   An archaeologist, in the conduct of his or her archaeological work, shall not offer or accept inducements which could reasonably be construed as bribes.

1.9   An archaeologist shall respect the interests of employees, colleagues, and helpers. He or she shall give due regard to the welfare of employees in terms of pay, conditions, security of employment, equal opportunities and career development. (See Note on Rule 1.9)

1.10 An archaeologist shall not reveal confidential information unless required by law; nor use confidential or privileged information to his or her own advantage or that of a third person. (See Note on Rule 1.10)

1.11 An archaeologist shall take account of the legitimate concerns of groups whose material past may be the subject of archaeological investigation.

1.12 An archaeologist has a duty to ensure that this Code is observed throughout the membership of the Institute, and also to encourage its adoption by others.

PRINCIPLE 2

The archaeologist has a responsibility for the conservation of the archaeological heritage.   K.3

Rules

2.1 An archaeologist shall strive to conserve archaeological sites and material as a resource for study and enjoyment now and in the future and shall encourage others to do the same. Where such conservation is not possible he or she shall seek to ensure the creation and maintenance of an adequate record through appropriate means of research, recording and dissemination of results. (See Note on Rule 2.1)

2.2 Where destructive investigation is undertaken the archaeologist shall ensure that it causes minimal attrition of the archaeological heritage consistent with the stated objects of the project. (See Note on Rule 2.2)

2.3 An archaeologist shall ensure that the objects of a research project are an adequate justification for the destruction of the archaeological evidence which it will entail.

PRINCIPLE 3

The archaeologist shall conduct his or her work in such a way that reliable information about the past may be acquired, and shall ensure that the results be properly recorded.   K.4

Rules

3.1 The archaeologist shall keep himself or herself informed about developments in his or her field or fields of specialisation.

3.2 An archaeologist shall prepare adequately for any project he or she may undertake.

3.3 An archaeologist shall ensure that experimental design, recording, and sampling procedures, where relevant, are adequate for the project in hand.

3.4 An archaeologist shall ensure that the record resulting from his or her work is prepared in a comprehensive, readily usable and durable form.

3.5 An archaeologist shall ensure that the record, including artefacts and specimens and experimental results, is maintained in good condition while in his or her charge and shall seek to ensure that it is eventually deposited where it is likely to recieve adequate curatorial care and storage conditions and to be readily available for study and examination.

3.6 An archaeologist shall seek to determine whether a project he or she undertakes is likely detrimentally to affect research work or projects of other archaeologists. If there is such a likelihood, he or she shall attempt to minimise such effects.

PRINCIPLE 4

K.5 **The archaeologist has responsibility for making available the results of archaeological work with reasonable dispatch.**

Rules

4.1 An archaeologist shall communicate and co-operate with colleagues having common archaeological interests and give due respect to colleagues' interests in, and rights to information about sites, areas, collections or data where there is a shared field of concern, whether active or potentially so.

4.2 An archaeologist shall accurately and without undue delay prepare and properly disseminate an appropriate record of work done under his or her control. (See Notes on Rules 2.1 and 4.2)

4.3 An archaeologist shall honour requests from colleagues or students for information on the results of research or projects if consistent with his or her prior rights to publication and with his or her other archaeological responsibilities. (See Note on Rule 4.3)

4.4 An archaeologist is responsible for the analysis and publication of data derived from projects under his or her control. While the archaeologist exercises this responsibility he or she shall enjoy consequent rights of primacy. However, failure to prepare or publish the results within 10 years of completion of the fieldwork shall be construed as a waiver of such rights, unless such failure can reasonably be attributed to circumstances beyond the archaeologist's control. (See Note on Rule 4.4)

4.5 An archaeologist, in the event of his or her failure to prepare or publish the results within 10 years of completion of the fieldwork and in the absence of countervailing circumstances, or in the event of his or her determining not to publish the results, shall if requested make data concerning the project available to other archaeologists for analysis and publication.

4.6 An archaeologist shall accept the responsibility of informing the public of the purpose and results of his or her work and shall accede to reasonable requests for information for dispersal to the general public. (See Note on Rule 4.6)

4.7 An archaeologist shall respect contractual obligations in reporting but shall not enter into a contract which prohibits the archaeologist from including his or her own interpretations or conclusions in the resulting record, or from a continuing right to use the data after completion of the project. (See Note on Rule 4.7)

APPENDIX A: NOTES ON THE RULES

The following Notes explain particular applications of the Rules; further **K.6** explanations may be added as needs arise.

Rule 1.4 It is the archaeologist's responsibility to inform current or prospective employers or clients of inadequacies in his or her qualifications for any work which may be proposed; he or she may of course seek to minimise such inadequacies by acquiring additional expertise, by seeking the advice or involvement of associates or consultants, or by arranging for modifications of the work involved; similar considerations apply where an archaeologist, during the course of a project, encounters problems which lie beyond his or her competence at that time.

It is also the archaeologist's responsibility to seek adequate support services for any project in which he or she may become involved, either directly or by way of recommendation.

Rule 1.6
(a) The archaeologist should also consider his or her position in respect of seeking or accepting financial benefit on his or her own behalf or that of relatives in relation to the recovery or disposal of objects or materials recovered during archaeological work.
(b) Archaeologists working on the foreshore and underwater may at times find themselves in difficulty regarding their association with commercial salvors and others engaged in exploiting the underwater cultural heritage. The underlying principles are 1) conserving the seabed heritage, 2) using it economically and in such a way that reliable information may be acquired, 3) dissemination of the results and 4) professional permanent curation of the total site archive.

It may be a legitimate part of the archaeologist's duty to work with commercial salvage organisations or individuals, in respect of recording sites and material, including possible museum acquisitions, and assessing sites and the work that takes place on them. In such dealings, however, archaeologists must ensure that:-
1) they do not knowingly permit their names or services to be used in a manner which may promote the recovery of archaeological material unless the primary objective of their work is to preserve the scientific integrity of the total site archive in a permanent professionally curated and publicly accessible collection, and unless provision is made for its study, interpretation and publication.
2) they do not enter into any contract or agreement whereby archaeological or curatorial standards may be compromised in deference to commercial interests
3) so far as excavated material is concerned, they do not encourage the purchase of objects in any case where they have reasonable cause to believe that their recovery involved the deliberate unscientific destruction or damage of archaeological sites, and that they discourage the sale and consequent dispersal of excavated material

4) they do not encourage the purchase of objects where there is reasonable cause to believe that recovery involved the failure to disclose the finds to the proper legal or governmental authorities.

Rule 1.9 Particular attention is drawn to the application of labour legislation and laws, regulations and advice which might have a bearing on the health and safety of people involved in or potentially affected by archaeological projects, and to the maintenance of adequate insurance cover, both for persons and for property.

Rule 1.10 The archaeologist should also exercise care to prevent employees, colleagues, associates and helpers from revealing or using confidential information in these ways. Confidential information means information gained in the course of the project which the employer or client has for the time being requested be held inviolate, or the disclosure of which would be potentially embarrassing or detrimental to the employer or client. Information ceases to be confidential when the employer or client so indicates, or when such information becomes publicly known. Where specifically archaeological information is involved, it is however the responsibility of the archaeologist to inform the employer or client of any conflict with his or her own responsibilities under Principle 4 of the Code (dissemination of archaeological information) and to seek to minimise or remove any such conflict.

Rules 2.1 and 4.2 Dissemination in these Rules is taken to include the deposition of primary records and unpublished material in an accessible public archive.

Rule 2.2 Particular attention should be paid to this injunction in the case of projects carried out for purposes of pure research. In all projects, whether prompted by pure research or the needs of rescue, consideration should be given to the legitimate interests of other archaeologists; for example, the upper levels of a site should be conscientiously excavated and recorded, within the exigencies of the project, even if the main focus is on the underlying levels.

Rule 4.2 This rule carries with it the implication that an archaeologist should not initiate, take part in or support work which materially damages the archaeological heritage unless reasonably prompt and appropriate analysis and reporting can be expected. Where results are felt to be substantial contributions to knowledge or to the advancement of theory, method or technique, they should be communicated as soon as reasonably possible to colleagues and others by means of letters, lectures, reports to meetings or interim publications, especially where full publication is likely to be significantly delayed.

Rule 4.3 Archaeologists recieving such information shall observe such prior rights, remembering that laws of copyright may also apply.

Rule 4.4 It is accepted that the movement of archaeologists from one employment to another raises problems of responsibility for the publication of projects. This ultimate responsibility for publication of a piece of work must be determined either by the contract of employment through which the work was undertaken, or by agreement with the original promoter of the work. It is the responsibility of the archaeologist, either as employer or employee, to establish a satisfactory agreement on this issue at the outset of work.

Rule 4.6 The archaeologist should be prepared to allow access to sites at suitable times and under controlled conditions, within limitations laid down by the funding agency or by the owners or the tenants of the site, or by considerations of safety or the wellbeing of the site.

Rule 4.7 Adherence to this Rule may on occasion appear to clash with the requirements of Rule 1.10. A client employer may legitimately seek to impose whatever conditions of confidentiality he or she wishes. An archaeologist should not accept conditions which require the permanent suppression of archaeological discoveries or interpretations.

APPENDIX B: FURTHER READING

IFA Constitutional Documents

The Institute of Field Archaeologists: Memorandum and Articles of Associ- **K.7**
ation.
Revised edition, October 1993. [The *MAA* were originally subscribed in 1985. This revised edition incorporates amendments to the Articles approved at Annual General Meetings of the Institute held on 7.7.86, 14.9.87, 16.9.89, 17.9.90, 16.9.91, 14.9.92 and 17.9.93, and at the Extraordinary General Meeting held on 8.4.87.]

By-Laws of the Institute of Field Archaeologists: Code of Approved Practice for the Regulation of Contractual Arrangements in Field Archaeology.
Revised Edition, October 1994. [The *CAPRCAFA* was formally ratified and adopted as a By-Law of the Institute at the Annual General Meeting held on 17.9.90. This revised edition incorporates amendments to the By-Law approved at Annual General Meetings of the Institute held on 17.9.93 and 14.10.94.]

By-Laws of the Institute of Field Archaeologists: Disciplinary Regulations.
Revised Edition, October 1993. [The *DR* were formally ratified and adopted as a By-Law of the Institute at the Annual General Meeting held on 7.7.86. This revised edition incorporates amendments to the By-Law approved at Annual General Meetings of the Institute held on 16.9.91, 14.9.92 and 17.9.93.]

IFA Standard and Guidance Documents

Institute of Field Archaeologists: Standard and Guidance for Archaeolog- **K.8**
ical Desk-Based Assessments.
August 1994. [The *SGADBA* was formally adopted as 'IFA-approved practice' at the Annual General Meeting of the Institute held on 14.10.94.]

Institute of Field Archaeologists: Standard and Guidance for Archaeolog-
ical Field Evaluations.
August 1994. [The *SGAFE* was formally adopted as 'IFA-approved practice' at the Annual General Meeting of the Institute held on 14.10.94.]

Institute of Field Archaeologists: Standard and Guidance for Archaeolog-
ical Watching Briefs.

August 1994. [The *SGAWB* was formally adopted as 'IFA-approved practice' at the Annual General Meeting of the Institute held on 14.10.94.]

Institute of Field Archaeologists: Draft Standard and Guidance for Archaeological Excavations.
August 1994. [The *DSGAE* was adopted on a one year interim basis at the Annual General Meeting of the Institute held on 14.10.94.]

Appendix L

IFA STANDARD AND GUIDANCE FOR ARCHAEOLOGICAL DESK-BASED ASSESSMENTS (INSTITUTE OF FIELDS ARCHAEOLOGISTS (1994))

STANDARD

An Archaeological Desk-Based Assessment will determine, as far as is **L.1**
reasonably possible from existing records, the nature of the archaeological
resources within a specified area using appropriate methods of study which
satisfy the stated aims of the project, and which comply with the Codes of
Practice of the Institute of Field Archaeologists.

DEFINITION OF DESK-BASED ASSESSMENT

Archaeological Desk-Based Assessment is defined as an assessment of the **L.2**
known or potential archaeological resource within a specified area or site on
land or underwater, consisting of a collation of existing written and graphic
information in order to identify the likely character, extent, quality and
worth of the known or potential archaeological resource in a local, regional,
national or international context as appropriate.

PURPOSE

The purpose of Desk-Based Assessment is to gain information about the **L.3**
known or potential archaeological resource within a given area or site,
including its presence or absence, character and extent, date, integrity, state
of preservation and relative quality, in order to make an assessment of its
worth in the appropriate context leading to:

- the formulation of a strategy to ensure the recording, preservation or
  management of the resource
- the formulation of a strategy for further investigation, whether or not
  intrusive, where the character and value of the resource is not sufficiently
  defined to permit a mitigation strategy or other response to be devised
- the formulation of a proposal design for further archaeological investigation within a programme of research.

OCCURRENCE

L.4   Desk-Based Assessments may occur:

● in response to a proposed development which threatens the archaeological resource;
   as part of the planning process (within the framework of appropriate national planning policy guidance notes) and/or development plan policy;
   as part of an Environmental Assessment (see 3.1 below);
   or outside the planning process (e.g. ecclesiastical development, agriculture and forestry, works by statutory undertakers).
● within a programme of research not generated by a specific threat to the archaeological resource.
● in connection with the preparation of management plans by private, local or national bodies.

Desk-Based Assessments may therefore be instigated or commissioned by a number of different individuals or organisations, including Local Planning Authorities, national advisory bodies, government agencies, private landowners, developers or their agents, archaeological researchers, etc.

GUIDANCE

1   INTRODUCTION

L.5   **1.1**   This guidance seeks to define best practice for the execution of Desk-Based Assessments and concomitant reporting, in line with the By-laws of the Institute of Field Archaeologists (in particular *The Code of Practice and The Code of Approved Practice for the Regulation of Contractual Arrangements in Field Archaeology*). It seeks to expand and explain general definitions in the Codes.

1.2   The Standard and guidance apply to all types of preliminary research on land or underwater, whether generated by academic research, by local interest, through the planning process, by management proposals or by any other proposals which may affect the archaeological resource within a specified area.

1.3   In addition the guidance seeks to amplify that given in *Planning Policy Guidance Note 16* (PPG 16; Dept. of Environment 1990) and its equivalents (see Appendix 7) and to be compatible with current guidelines issued by regulatory authorities.

1.4   The terminology used follows PPG 16, guidance issued by the Association of County Archaeological Officers (ACAO 1993) and English Heritage (1991), with amplifications where necessary. It tries to take account of differences in terminology, legal and administrative practice in different parts of the UK. A glossary of terms used may be found in Appendix 1.

1.5   This document provides guidance for work carried out within the British Isles. Whilst general guidance is given, this document cannot be exhaustive, particularly in its treatment of legislative issues; archaeologists working in the different countries must ensure that they are familiar with the specific legislation and common law pertinent to those areas.

2   PRINCIPLES: THE BY-LAWS OF THE INSTITUTE OF FIELD ARCHAEOLOGISTS

2.1   An archaeologist undertaking archaeological Desk-Based Assessments   **L.6**
must adhere to the four principles enshrined in the Institute of Field Archaeologist's Code of Conduct and the rules governing these principles

1   The archaeologist shall adhere to the highest standards of ethical and responsible behaviour in the conduct of archaeological affairs.
2   the archaeologist has a responsibility for the conservation of the archaeological heritage.
3   The archaeologist shall conduct his or her work in such a way that reliable information about the past may be acquired, and shall ensure that the results be properly recorded.
4   The archaeologist has responsibility for making available the results of archaeological work with reasonable dispatch.

2.2   Further, the *Code of Approved Practice for the Regulation of Contractual Arrangements in Field Archaeology* specifically addresses professional conduct in situations where work is sponsored or commissioned on a contractual basis, especially as part of development controlled by the planning process. It provides guidance on professional behaviour where more than one individual or body are competing for the same piece of work, and seeks to ensure that the terms and conditions for all work are clearly defined, normally by contract.

3   PROCEDURES

3.1   Project Identification

3.1.1   *Within the planning framework* in England, Wales and Scotland the   **L.7**
desirability of preservation of archaeological deposits is now a material consideration, and consequently "developers and local authorities should take into account archaeological considerations and deal with them from the beginning of the development control process" (Planning Policy Guidance Note 16 and Scottish Office Environment Department 1994).

3.1.2   As the desirability of preservation of archaeological remains is now a material consideration in the planning process, local authorities can reasonably request an applicant to provide further information on archaeological matters so that 'an informed and reasonable planning decision can be taken' (PPG 16, section 21). Under this guidance, requests for Desk-Based Assessment will generally be made by the planning archaeologist or curator.

3.1.3   *Within the planning framework* an Appraisal of the proposal area will be carried out to determine whether further information is required

(ACAO 1993). This will normally have been undertaken by the planning archaeologist or curator (*e.g.* county, District or Regional Archaeological Officer), but may also have been carried out by the applicant or their agent.

3.1.4 On occasion, however, a Desk-Based Assessment may be commissioned in advance of submission of a planning application by the applicant or through their agent or advisor. It should be stressed that in this circumstance it is appropriate for any proposals for Desk-Based Assessment to be agreed with the planning archaeologist in advance, so that the aims and methodology are agreed and excessive cost not incurred. In such circumstances matters of confidentiality will need to be carefully considered by all parties involved. The planning archaeologist may also be best positioned to offer advice to applicants on project designs, should the applicants be unfamiliar with archaeological matters.

3.1.5 Current practice has been further defined by the Association of County Archaeological Officers (ACAO; 1993, appendix C) to lead to a product that will be a report that:

a) assembles, summarises and orders the available evidence
b) synthesises it and places it in the local and/or regional context
c) comments on its quality and reliability and indicates how it might be supplemented by Field Evaluation to provide the information required for planning purposes.

3.1.6 Certain developments fall within special regulations or statute different from or additional to the standard planning process (*e.g.* some projects initiated by Statutory Undertakers, Crown Commissioners, Ministry of Defence etc). Certain of these organisations subscribe to codes of practice (*e.g.* the Water Companies) or agreements (formal or informal) with the lead national archaeological bodies to take into consideration the affects of development proposals on the archaeological resource.

3.1.7 *Environmental Assessment* (EA) applies to projects potentially having significant environmental effects (as defined in Council Directive 85/337 EEC, and as implemented in the UK), and requires a systematic analysis of such effects before a decision to permit the project is taken. The 'developer' is again required to provide information for the deciding agency to consider in the decision-making process, and further give bodies with relevant environmental responsibilities an opportunity to comment before consent is given. Certain information also has to be given to the public. EA is mandatory in relation to certain projects and may be extended to others. Appraisal and Desk-Based Assessment are inevitable; field evaluation may also be required (see Appendix 1 for definitions; and IFA Standard and Guidance on Field Evaluation).

3.1.8 In EA projects Desk-Based Assessment is usually initiated by the 'developer' or through their advisors, rather than the local planning authority. It is still appropriate for any requirements for Field Evaluation to be discussed and agreed with the relevant planning archaeologist or curator in advance, to avoid needless damage to the archaeological resource.

3.1.9   *In a research context* the area for potential investigation or study will have been selected by the archaeologist with regard to specific aspects or themes relating to their own defined research interests. This could include work undertaken through universities, central government agencies, local authorities, museums, independent trusts, private companies or private individuals.

3.1.10 *Management proposals by private landowners or others* may also result in Desk-Based Assessments, to obtain information in order to enhance the environmental or archaeological resource.

3.1.11 The commissioning of Desk-Based Assessments therefore depends on the circumstances of the project, and may be by developers, government agencies, private bodies or others.

3.1.12 **Whether or not the Desk-Based Assessment has arisen through the planning or Environmental Framework, from research or management proposals, an archaeologist should only undertake an archaeological *Desk-Based Assessment* which is governed by a written *Specification* or *Project Design*, agreed with all relevant parties, as this is the tool against which performance, fitness for purpose and hence achievement of standard can be measured.**

3.1.13 The *Specification* or *Project Design* is therefore of critical importance.

3.2   Briefs, Specifications and Project Design

3.2.1   The planning stage of any project is key in its success. The following statements assume that *Briefs* (or *Project Outline* in Scotland) and *Specifications* are issued by those requiring work done (planning archaeologists or curators, developers or their agents, etc; whilst *Project Designs* can either be a response to the *Brief/Project Outline* or *Specification*, or be initiated, for example, as part of a research proposal (*cf.* English Heritage 1991).   **L.8**

3.2.2   A *Brief* is a simple outline framework of the situation to be addressed, with an indication of the scope of works that will be required (IFA By-Law; ACAO 1993). It does not provide sufficient detail to form the basis for a measurable standard; but it could form the basis for a *Specification* or a *Project Design*.

3.2.3   A *Specification* sets out a schedule of works in sufficient detail for it to be quantifiable, implemented and monitored (ACAO 1993). It should be sufficient to form the basis of a measurable standard (Appendix 3).

3.2.4   A *Project Design* also sets out a schedule of works in sufficient detail to be quantifiable, implemented and monitored, and therefore also forms the basis for a measurable standard. However, a *Project Design* may include additional information which covers contractual details such as staffing levels or cost relevant to the commissioning but not necessarily the monitoring body. A *Project Design* may be prepared in response to a *Brief/Project Outline* or *Specification*; or it may be a research proposal generated independently of the planning framework (Appendix 4; and English Heritage 1991, appendix 2).

3.2.5   A *Brief/Project Outline* or *Specification* may form the basis for a *Project Design*. For Desk-Based Assessments within the planning framework, the *Brief* or *Specification* will usually be prepared by the planning archaeologist or curator and issued by the commissioning body (the developer or their agent) to selected tenderers, who respond with a costed *Project Design*. The *Brief/Project Outline* or a *Specification* may be prepared by the applicant or their agent, but it is essential that the planning archaeologist has agreed the proposals, so that they have been accepted as 'fit for purpose'.

3.2.6   *Briefs/Project Outlines, Specifications* and *Project Designs* must be prepared by suitably qualified and experienced persons, utilising specialist advice and appropriate sources where necessary.

3.2.7   The *Specification* and/or *Project Design* must identify the objectives, scope, geographical area, methodology and, wherever possible, means of dissemination of the results of the assessment.

3.2.8   In the case of Environmental Assessment, the *Brief/Project Outline* or *Specification* will usually have been prepared by the developer or their agent, and issued to tenderers who again respond with a costed *Project Design*. This may also apply to management proposals.

3.2.9   Proposals for Desk-Based Assessments in research work will take the form of a *Project Design*, prepared by the researching archaeologist, and agreed with any sponsoring body. If there is no external sponsor there must nevertheless be a *written* design so that the validity of any models or questions posed can be properly assessed.

3.2.10 No *Desk-Based Assessment* should take place on the basis of a *Brief/Project Outline* alone, as it could not achieve the appropriate standard (there being nothing to measure performance against).

3.2.11 The *Specification* or *Project Design* must be agreed by all parties concerned before work commences.

3.2.12 The *Specification* or *Project Design*, particularly the requirement for evaluation within the planning and EA framework, must be expressed in sufficiently robust terms and in sufficient detail to withstand challenges on archaeological and legal grounds.

3.2.13 Any archaeologist preparing a *Specification* or *Project Design* must be fully appraised of all relevant legislation, and must abide by it.

3.2.14 The *Specification* or *Project Design* should contain, as a minimum, the following elements:

- Site location (including map) and description
- Context of the project
- Geological and topographical background
- Archaeological and historical background
- General and specific aims of study
- Proposed study methodology (including specified sources)
- Field visit (purpose)

- Report preparation (method)
- Copyright
- Archive deposition
- Publication and dissemination proposals
- Timetable
- Staffing
- Health & Safety Statement
- Any other specific necessary reference to legislation
- Monitoring procedures

3.2.15 The contents, and different weighting of detail between *Specification* and *Project Design* contents are further amplified in Appendices 3 and 4. *Briefs/Project Outlines* and *Specifications* are also discussed in detail in ACAO 1993.

3.2.16 An archaeologist responding to a tender which includes a *Brief/Project Outline* or *Specification* may refer to these elements in the *Project Design* if they are set out in sufficient detail, rather than repeat them. Any variation to the *Project Design* or *Specification* must be agreed in writing with the sponsor and all relevant parties.

3.3 Sources and Data Collection (including field visits)

3.3.1 All work undertaken must conform to the agreed *Specification* and/or **L.9** *Project Design*. Variations must be confirmed in writing by all relevant parties.

3.3.2 All techniques must comply with relevant legislation and be demonstrably fit for the defined purpose(s).

3.3.3 Full and proper records (written, graphic, digital and photographic as appropriate) should be made for all work.

3.3.4 All staff, including sub-contractors, must be suitably qualified and experienced for their project roles, and employed in line with IFA Codes and practices. The manager should preferably be a member of IFA.

3.3.5 All staff, including sub-contractors, must be fully briefed and aware of the work required under the specification, and must understand the projects aims and methodologies.

3.3.6 Sufficient and appropriate resources (staff, equipment, accommodation etc.) must be used to enable the project to achieve its aims, the desired quality and timetable, and to comply with all statutory requirements. It is the role of the archaeologist undertaking the work to define appropriate staff levels.

3.3.7 The archaeologist undertaking an archaeological Desk-Based Assessment shall consider, in the light of the *Brief* and/or *Specification*, the need to examine appropriate sources. All sources actually consulted should be listed in the report (whether or not they have been productive); and all other known sources which have not been consulted but which are thought to be of potential relevance should also be listed in the report. The reasons for non-consultation should be given. The Assessment report should contain a full discussion of the likely implications of the choice of sources actually consulted to the reliability of the conclusions reached.

3.3.8 The range of sources containing potential archaeological information that need to be studied in undertaking a Desk-Based Assessment will vary according to a number of factors:

- The size and location of the land subject to a proposal for development, landuse change, alternative management strategy, archaeological intervention or any other relevant future effect upon the archaeological resource
- The intensity of previous archaeological investigation
- The exact purpose and requirements of study

(A list of sources of potential archaeological information is provided in Appendix 2; this is by no means exhaustive.)

3.3.9 In most cases the archaeologist undertaking a Desk-Based Assessment shall, unless access is restricted, visit the study area in order to assess possible factors, such as existing or previous landuse, that may have affected the survival or condition of known or potential archaeological sites. All assessments should include an explicit statement as to whether or not a visit has taken place and, if so, a description of the procedures used and any constraints to observation encountered.

3.3.10 The requirements of Health and Safety cannot be ignored no matter how imperative the need to record archaeological matters. All archaeologists undertaking fieldwork must do so under a defined Health and Safety Policy. Archaeologists undertaking fieldwork must observe all safe working practices, whether required by their own policies or those of the principal development contractor; the Health and Safety arrangements must be agreed and understood by all relevant parties before work commences. Risk Assessments must be carried out and documented for every field project. For further guidance refer to the bibliography (Appendix 7).

3.3.11 All equipment must be suitable for the purpose and in sound condition and comply with Health and Safety Executive recommendations. It should be noted that diving equipment in particular is subject to statutory controls under the Diving Operations at Work Regulations, over and above the suitability for purpose and sound condition.

3.4 Monitoring

L.10 3.4.1 All work must be monitored, by the archaeological organisation undertaking the work (*i.e.* tracking), and if appropriate by the planning archaeologist and commissioning body, or their nominated representatives (see for example Darvill in Hunter and Ralston 1993, 169ff). The guidance below is directed in general at monitors from outside the organisation undertaking the work. However, many of the points apply equally to internal monitors or managers (*e.g.* 3.4.2).

3.4.2 A monitor should be suitably experienced and qualified, or have access to appropriate specialist advice, in order to monitor properly.

3.4.3 Monitoring must be undertaken against the written *Specification* and/or *Project Design*.

3.4.4 Monitors, where not representing the commissioning body, must be careful not to instruct the archaeologist undertaking the work to vary the agreed *Specification* or *Project Design* without consultation with all relevant parties, particularly if this will result in a variation of contract and cost.

3.4.5 Monitors, where not representing the commissioning body, should bear in mind the need for flexibility, within the stated parameters, in contractual matters such as staff numbers, budgets or timetable.

3.4.6 All monitoring visits must be documented by both parties.

3.4.7 Non-compliance with the agreed *Specification* or *Project Design* must be pointed out by the monitor to the archaeologists undertaking the work, and their client if appropriate, at the earliest opportunity (see ACAO 1993, section E(vii), 17).

3.4.8 Monitors should be aware of their legal duties, particularly regarding Health and Safety and the reporting and advising against bad and unsafe practice.

3.4.9 All monitoring arrangements must be mutually agreed at the outset of the project; the archaeologist undertaking fieldwork must inform the planning archaeologist or other monitor of the commencement of work with reasonable notice.

3.4.10 Whilst the monitor may choose to visit at any time, normally they should inform the archaeologist undertaking the work of any intended visits in advance. Monitors must respect reasonable requests from the client commissioning the work to attend only at pre-arranged times and, if necessary in the company of the client's representative.

3.4.11 Any costs for monitoring to be charged by the planning archaeologist or other monitor must be agreed at the outset of the project.

3.5 Reports

3.5.1 All reports should be written in a clear, concise and logical style; **L.11** technical terms should be explained if the report is for a non-archaeological audience. Consideration should be given during the preparation of the report to the requirements of Public Inquiries if appropriate.

3.5.2 The content of archaeological Desk-Based Assessment reports will vary according to the scope of the proposals and the complexity or otherwise of the information available from existing sources; presentation may also be determined by the requirements of the body or person commissioning the work.

3.5.3 Reports should contain as a minimum:

- Non-technical summary
- Introductory Statements

- Aims and purpose of the assessments
- Methodology
- An objective statement of results
- Conclusion, including a confidence rating
- Supporting illustration at appropriate scales
- Supporting data, tabulated in appendices
- Index and location of archive
- References

The contents are discussed in more detail in Appendix 5.

3.5.4 Where the project is carried out within the planning process, the report must contain sufficient data to enable 'an informed and reasonable decision to be made'. Further guidance on this is contained in ACAO 1993.

3.5.5 Subject to any contractual requirements on confidentiality, copies of the report must be submitted to the appropriate county Sites and Monuments Record within six months of completion of report.

3.6 Other considerations

L.12 3.6.1 In many circumstances Desk-Based Assessments will occur before development proposals are in the public domain. The archaeologist undertaking this type of work, therefore, has a duty of confidence to the client commissioning the work. At the same time all archaeologists have a duty to disseminate the results of their work with reasonable dispatch. In these circumstances a period of confidentiality (excluding legal obligations) must be agreed in advance of work commencing that is acceptable to both parties; this period should not exceed 12 months from the submission of the report to the client. The archaeologist should also recognise that, excluding archaeological matters, some information given by the client in order to assist the progress of the assessment may remain confidential *in perpetuo*.

3.6.2 It is advisable that most Desk-Based Assessment projects are governed by a written contract to which the agreed *Specification* is attached (see IFA Technical Paper no. 8, 1991). They should be dated and signed by both parties and include reference to area of study outlined on an attached map, reference to the *Specification*, permission for access for visual inspection, completion of report, method and timetable of payment and/or retention, and copyright arrangements.

3.6.3 Unless otherwise agreed in a contract, the copyright of any written or graphic or photographic records and reports rests with the originating body (the archaeological organisation undertaking the work), who will licence their use in relation to the specific project by the client or sponsoring body. Such agreements on copyright should be agreed with the sponsoring body at the outset of the project (see Appendix 6).

3.6.4 Material copied or cited in reports should be duly acknowledged; and all copyright conditions (such as those for Ordnance Survey maps) observed.

3.6.5 All aspects of publicity must be agreed at the outset of the project between the commissioning body and the archaeological organisation or individual undertaking the project.

3.6.6 All archaeologists undertaking work must respect the sponsor's or client's requirements over confidentiality, but the archaeologist must emphasise their professional obligation to make the results of archaeological work available to the wider archaeological community within a reasonable time (see 3.5.5).

3.6.7 An archaeologist or archaeological organisation undertaking such projects must ensure that they have adequate insurance policies, Public Liability, some relevant form of civil liability or Professional Indemnity.

3.6.8 Statutory requirements regarding archaeological matters vary within the United Kingdom, commissioning bodies and others may therefore find it useful to consult the relevant documents listed in Appendix 7 and can obtain further guidance from the appropriate advisory bodies listed in Appendix 8.

APPENDIX 1: GLOSSARY OF TERMS USED

Appraisal a rapid reconnaissance of site and records to identify **L.13** (within the planning framework) whether a development proposal has a potential archaeological dimension requiring further clarification (ACAO 1993, 4); **or** a rapid reconnaissance of site and records to identify whether a particular project or study area has potential for further academically-oriented research involving non-intrusive or intrusive methods

Assessment (Desk-Based) an assessment of the known or potential archaeological resource within a specified area or site (land-based, inter-tidal or marine), consisting of a collation of existing written and graphic information, in order to identify the likely character, extent and relative quality of the actual or potential resource. (See also *Standard and Guidance for Archaeological Desk-Based Assessments.*)

Brief/Project Outline an outline framework of the archaeological circumstances which may have to be addressed, together with an indication of the scope of works that will be required. In Scotland the Brief may be referred to as a Project Outline (see Historic Scotland 1993), which has to be addressed, together with an indication of the scope of works that will be required.

Client the individual or organisation commissioning and funding the project

Curator a person or organisation responsible for the conservation and management of archaeological evidence by virtue of official or statutory duty, including for

	example County or District Archaeological Officers, Regional Archaeology Officers, national bodies such as English Heritage and Cadw.
Environmental Assessment	a systematic analysis of a project's potential effects on all aspects of the environment including cultural heritage, in order to provide information for the deciding agency to consider in the decision-making process, and further give bodies with relevant environmental responsibilities the opportunity to comment before consent is given. EA applies to projects having significant environmental effects as set out in Directive 86/337/EEC and as implemented in the UK, which came into effect in July 1988.
Evaluation	a limited programme of non-intrusive and/or intrusive fieldwork which determines of the presence or absence of archaeological features, structures, deposits, artefacts or ecofacts within a specified area or site; and, if present, defines their character and extent, and relative quality. It enables an assessment of their worth in a local, regional, national or international context as appropriate. (See IFA Standard and Guidance on Archaeological Field Evaluations)
Planning archaeologist	see curator.
Project Design	a written statement on the project's objectives, methods, timetable and resources, forming the framework for the execution of the project through to completion, set out in sufficient detail to be quantifiable, implemented and monitored. Normally prepared by an archaeologist or organisation undertaking the fieldwork, frequently in response to a Brief or Specification.
Specification	a written schedule of works required for a particular project (by a curator, planning archaeologist or client), set out in sufficient detail to be quantifiable, implemented and monitored. Normally prepared by or agreed with the relevant curator.

APPENDIX 2: SOURCES OF ARCHAEOLOGICAL INFORMATION

Archaeological Databases

L.14	Source Type	Archaeological Excavation and Survey Records, National Monuments Records, National Buildings Records, Regional and Local Sites and Monuments Records, Listed Building Lists, Scheduled Ancient Monuments Lists, Regional Inventories, Public & Private Collections of Artefacts and Ecofacts.

Source Location	National Heritage Bodies, Royal Commissions, Local Authorities, Museums, Archaeological Trusts and Units, Universities, Ordnance Survey, Local Archaeological and Historical Societies.

Historical Documents

Source Types	Charters, Registers, Manuscript Collections (Secular and Ecclesiastical), Deeds, Wills, Estate Papers, Electoral Rolls, Contemporary Published Accounts (eg County and Agricultural Surveys), Industrial Investigations.
Source Location	Public Record Office, Parish Records, Estate Collections, Museums, National and Local Libraries, County and District Archives, Study Centres, Press Libraries, Ordnance Survey, British Library.

Cartographic & Pictorial Documents

Source Type	Early Maps, Prints and Paintings, Tithe Maps, OS Maps, Estate Plans, Admiralty Charts.
Source Location	Public Record Offices, Parish Records, Estate Collections, Museums, National and Local Libraries, County and District Archives, Ordnance Survey, Press Libraries, Private Collections, MoD Hydrographic Office, Local Archaeological and Historical Societies.

Aerial Photographs

Source Type	Aerial Photographs
Source Location	National Registers of Aerial Photographs (including RAF and OS flights), Museum Collections, National Heritage Bodies, Sites and Monuments Records, University Collections, Private Collections (in some instances a flight may be commissioned as part of the study).

Geotechnical Information

Source Type	Borehole and Test Pit Logs, Site Surveys Geological Maps, Offshore Surveys.
Source Location	Clients Engineers Records, Ordnance Survey, British Standards Institute, British Geological Survey Publications, Commercial Offshore Survey Companies, University Oceanographic Departments.

Secondary and Statutory Sources

Source Type	Regional and Period Archaeological Studies, Landscape Studies, Local Knowledge, Dissertations, Policy Statements and Research Frameworks, Legislative Documents, European Directives, Local Development Plans, Unitary Development Plans, Constraints Maps.
Source Location	Libraries, Local Landowners, Local and National Museums, Universities, Academic Journals, Monographs and Other Publications, Local Archaeological and Historical Societies.

APPENDIX 3: PREPARATION OF SPECIFICATION

L.15   The Specification should contain, as a minimum, the following elements:

- Non-technical summary (intelligible to the lay reader)
- Site location and description (NGR, size, geology, landuse, topography, physical constraints)
- Planning Background (proposal details, planning policies, other environmental matters, Scheduled Monument constraints, Protected Wrecks etc)
- Archaeological and Historical Background (including plan or NGR, site status)
- Purpose/aims of work (clearly stated in both general and specific aims)
- Methodology (sources with justification for selection; field visit)
- Report preparation, contents and distribution
- Copyright
- Archive deposition (including finds ownership, recipient museum)
- Publication and dissemination
- Timetable, if appropriate
- Staffing—in general terms only—eg the site director should be a member of the Institute of Field Archaeologists, but **not** the number of staff
- Health and Safety statement
- Monitoring procedures required by the curator, including any charges

APPENDIX 4: PROJECT DESIGN CONTENTS

L.16   The Project Design should contain, as a minimum, the following elements:

- Non-technical summary (intelligible to the lay reader)
- Site location and description (NGR, size, geology, landuse, topography, physical constraints)
- Planning Background (proposal details, planning policies, other environmental matters, Scheduled Monument constraints, Protected Wrecks), if appropriate
- Geological and topographical background
- Archaeological and Historical Background (including built landscape and technical, plan or NGR, site status)
- Purpose/aims of work (clearly stated in both general and specific aims)

- Methodology (sources selected, with justification for selection; field visit including any constraints)
- Report preparation and contents
- Copyright
- Archive deposition (including field finds ownership, recipient museum)
- Publication and dissemination proposals
- Timetable
- Staffing
- Health and Safety policies and implementation, including Risk Assessment
- Insurances
- Monitoring procedures (internal, curatorial, contractual)
- Costs (or these may be presented in a covering letter)

A contracting archaeologist responding to a tender with specification may refer to these elements if defined in a *Brief* or *Specification* set by curator or client, rather than repeat them in a *Project Design*.

APPENDIX 5: REPORT CONTENTS

Non-technical summary
This should outline in plain, non-technical language, the principle **L.17** reason for the work, its aims and main results, and should include reference to authorship and commissioning body.

Introduction
This should outline the circumstances leading to the commission of the report, any restrictions on reporting or access to relevant records, size, surface geology and topography of the study area.

Aims and Objectives
These should reflect or reiterate the aims set in the *Project Design* or *Specification*.

Methodology
The methods used and an outline of sources consulted, including any variation to the agreed *Project Design* or *Specification*, should be set out carefully, and explained as appropriate.

Summary of Archaeological Results
This should outline, as a series of objective statements organised clearly in relation to the methods used, the known and potential archaeological interests by period and/or type and indicate their significance with reference/inclusion of supporting evidence as appropriate.

Development or other Impact (if appropriate)
This should outline the likely effect of the development and other factors on the known or potential archaeological resource. If the precise impact cannot be evaluated, this should be stated.

Conclusions
It may be appropriate to include a section which summarises and interprets the results, and puts them into context (local, national or otherwise). Other elements could include a confidence rating or statement on the reliability of sources used, or limitations imposed by particular factors. Recommendations on further work may also be

required, but in most circumstances within the planning framework this will be the responsibility of the relevant planning archaeologist or curator.

Appendices

These should consist of essential technical and other detail to support 1–4 above and may consist of a copy of the *Brief/Specification* for the work, summaries of sources of evidence consulted with reference to location, catalogue nos etc, transcripts or copies of documents (where copyright permissions exist or are attainable), project archive catalogue, list of consultees, index to site codes.

Figures & Plates

Most archaeological desk-based reports will need the inclusion of at least one figure showing known or potential archaeological interests within or affecting the development area. The figure should be clearly numbered and easily referenced to the National Grid. Other figures and plates should be included as appropriate.

References and Bibliography

A list of all primary and secondary sources used, as well as those not consulted must be given.

Other

Contents List, Acknowledgements

APPENDIX 6: COPYRIGHT

L.18   Under the *Copyright, Designs and Patents Act* 1988 the organisation or person undertaking field and reporting work retains the copyright to the written and graphic material, unless this has been varied in the contract for the work. This position should be made clear to all relevant parties at the outset of work.

The circumstances under which the report or records can be used by other parties should be made clear at the inception of the project. For example one of these clauses could be incorporated into the *Specification* or *Project Design*:

The .... [name of organisation carrying out the work] shall retain full copyright of any commissioned reports, tender documents or other project documents, under the *Copyright, Designs and Patents Act* 1988 with all rights reserved; excepting that it hereby provide an exclusive licence to the client for the use of such documents by the client in all matters directly relating to the project as described in the Project Specification.

or

The .... [name of organisation] will assign copyright to the client upon written request but retains the right to be identified as the author of all project documentation and reports as defined in the *Copyright, Designs and Patents Act* 1988 (Chapter IV, s.79).

In the last instance a further letter actually granting copyright needs to be sent to the client.

The proposals for distribution of the report must be made clear to all parties at the outset of the field project.

Appendix M

STANDARD AND GUIDANCE FOR
ARCHAEOLOGICAL FIELD EVALUATIONS
(INSTITUTE OF FIELD ARCHAEOLOGISTS (1994)

STANDARD

A Field Evaluation will determine as far as is reasonable possible, the nature **M.1**
of the archaeological resource within a specified area using appropriate
methods and practices which satisfy the stated aims of the project, and
which comply with the By-laws of the Institute of Field Archaeologists.

DEFINITION OF FIELD EVALUATION

Archaeological Field Evaluation is defined as a limited programme of **M.2**
non-instrusive and/or intrusive fieldwork which determine presence or
absence of archaeological features, structures, deposits, artefacts or ecofacts
within a specified area on land or underwater. If such archaeological remains
are present Field Evaluation defines their character and extent, and quality;
and it enables an assessment of their worth in a local, regional, national or
international context as appropriate.

PURPOSE OF FIELD EVALUATION

The purpose of Field Evaluation is to gain information about the archaeolog- **M.3**
ical resource within a given area or site, including its presence or absence,
character and extent, date, integrity, state of preservation and relative
quality, in order to make an assessment of its worth in the appropriate
context, leading to:

- the formulation of a strategy for the preservation or management of those
  remains; and/or
- the formulation of an appropriate response or mitigation strategy to
  planning applications or other proposals which may affect adversely such
  archaeological remains, or enhance them; and/or
- the formulation of a proposal for further archaeological investigation
  within a programme of research

OCCURRENCE

M.4   Field Evaluations may occur:

- in response to a proposed development which threatens the archaeological resource;
  as part of the planning process (within the framework of appropriate national planning policy guidance notes and development plan policy;
  as part of an Environmental Assessment (see 3.1 below);
  or outside the planning process (*e.g.* ecclesiastical development, agriculture and forestry, works by statutory undertakers
- within a programme of research not generated by a specific threat to the archaeological resource.
- in connection with the preparation of management plans by private, local or national bodies.

Field Evaluation may therefore be instigated or commissioned by a number of different individuals or organisations, including Local Planning Authorities, national advisory bodies, government agencies, private landowners, developers or their archaeological researchers, etc.

GUIDANCE

1   INTRODUCTION

M.5   1.1   This guidance seeks to define best practice for the execution of Field Evaluations and concomitant reporting, in line with the By-laws of the Institute of Field Archaeologists (in particular *The Code of Conduct* and *The Code of Approved Practice for the Regulation of Contractual Arrangements in Field Archaeology*). It seeks to expand and explain general definitions in the Codes for the practice of fieldwork and reporting.

1.2   The Standard and guidance apply to all types of preliminary field investigations land-based, inter-tidal and underwater, whether generated by academic research, by local interest, through the planning process, by management proposals or by any other proposals which may affect the archaeological resource within a specified area.

1.3   In addition, the guidance seeks to amplify that given in *Planning Policy Guidance Note* 16 (PPG 16; Dept. of Environment 1990) and its equivalents (see Appendix 7), and to be compatible with current guidelines issued by regulatory authorities.

1.4   The terminology used follows PPG 16, guidance issued by the Association of County Archaeological Officers (ACAO) and English Heritage (1991), with amplifications where necessary. It tries to take account of different terminology, legal and administrative practice in different parts of the U.K. A glossary of terms used may be found in Appendix 1.

1.5   This document provides guidance for work carried out within the British Isles. Whilst general guidance is given, this document cannot be exhaustive, particularly in its treatment of legislative issues; archaeologists working in the different countries must ensure that they are familiar with the specific legislation and common law pertinent to those areas.

2   PRINCIPLES: THE BY-LAW OF THE INSTITUTE OF FIELD ARCHAEOLOGISTS

2.1   An archaeologist undertaking archaeological field evaluations must   **M.6**
adhere to the four major principles enshrined in the Institute of Field Archaeologists' By-law, the *Code of Conduct* and the rules governing those principles:
  1   The archaeologist shall adhere to the highest standards of ethical and responsible behaviour in the conduct of archaeological affairs.
  2   The archaeologist has a responsibility for the conservation of the archaeological heritage.
  3   The archaeologist shall conduct his or her work in such a way that reliable information about the past may be required, and shall ensure that the results be properly recorded.
  4   The archaeologist has the responsibility for making available the results of archaeological work with reasonable dispatch.

2.2   Further, the *Code of Approved Practice for the Regulation of Contractual Arrangements in Field Archaeology* specifically addresses professional conduct in situations where work is sponsored or commissioned on a contractual basis, especially as part of development controlled by the planning process. It provides guidance on professional behaviour where more than one individual or body are competing for the same piece of work, and seeks to ensure that the terms and conditions for all work are clearly defined, normally by contract.

3   PROCEDURES

3.1   Project identification

3.1.1   *Within the planning framework* in England, Wales and Scotland the   **M.7**
desirability of preservation of archaeological deposits is now a material consideration, and consequently "developers and local authorities should take into account archaeological considerations and deal with them from the beginning of the development control process" (*Planning Policy Guidance Note 16* and Scottish Office Environment Department 1994).

3.1.2   As the desirability of preservation of archaeological remains is now a material consideration in the planning process, local authorities can reasonably request an application to provide further information on archaeological matters so that 'an informed and reasonable planning decision can be taken' (PPG 16, section 21). On occasion it may be deemed sufficient to carry out a desk-based Assessment, in order to provide information to make an informed and reasonable decision; on other occasions it will not.

3.1.3   *Within the planning framework* an Appraisal of the proposed area will be carried out to determine whether further information is required

(ACAO 1993). This will normally have been undertaken by the planning archaeologist or curator (*e.g.* County, District or Regional Archaeological Officer), but may have been carried out by the applicant or their agent. Under this guidance, requests for Field Evaluations will generally be made by the planning archaeologist or curator.

3.1.4 On occasion, however, a Field Evaluation may be commissioned in advance of submission of a planning application by the applicant or through their agent or advisor. It should be stressed that in this circumstance it is appropriate for any proposals for Field Evaluation to be agreed with the planning archaeologist in advance of intrusive fieldwork, so that the archaeological resource is neither needlessly interfered with nor damaged, nor inappropriate or excessive cost incurred. In such circumstances matters of confidentiality will need to be carefully considered by all parties involved. The planning archaeologist may also be best positioned to offer advice to applicants on project designs, should the applicants be unfamiliar with archaeological matters.

3.1.5 Certain developments fall within special regulations or statute different to the standard planning process (*e.g.* some projects initiated by Statutory Undertakers, Crown Commissioners, Ministry of Defence etc). Certain of these organisations subscribe to codes of practice (*e.g.* the Water Companies) or agreements (formal or informal) with the lead national archaeological bodies to take into consideration the affects of development proposals on the archaeological resource.

3.1.6 *Environmental Assessment* (EA) applies to projects potentially having significant environmental effects (as defined in Council Directive 85/337 EEC, and as implemented in the UK via the various Statutory Instruments etc), and requires a systematic analysis of such effects before a decision to permit the project is taken. The 'developer' is again required to provide information for the deciding agency to consider in the decision-making process, and further give bodies with relevant environmental responsibilities an opportunity to comment before consent is given. Certain information also has to be given to the public. EA is mandatory in relation to certain projects, and may be extended to others. Appraisal and Desk-based Assessment are inevitable; Field Evaluation may also be required (see Appendix 1 for definitions; and IFA Standard and Guidance for Desk-Based Assessments).

3.1.7 In EA projects Field Evaluation is usually initiated by the 'developer' or through their advisors, rather than the local planning authority. It is still appropriate for any requirements for Field Evaluation to be discussed and agreed with the relevant planning archaeologist or curator in advance, to avoid needless damage to the archaeological resource.

3.1.8 *In a research context*, areas or sites for Field Evaluation will have been identified and selected by an archaeologist based on specific aspects of themes relating to their own defined research interests. This could include work undertaken through universities, central government agencies, local authorities, museums, independent trusts, private companies or private individuals.

3.1.9 *Management proposals by private landowners or others* may also result in Field Evaluations to obtain information in order to enhance the environmental or archaeological resource.

3.1.10 The commissioning of Field Evaluations therefore depends on the circumstances of the project; and may be by developers, government agencies, private bodies or others.

3.1.11 **Whether the Field Evaluation has arisen through the planning framework (including Environmental Assessment), from research interests, or management proposals, an archaeologist should only undertake a Field Evaluation which is governed by a written *Specification* or *Project Design* prepared in consultation with or approved by the relevant planning archaeologist or curator, as this is the tool against which performance, fitness for purpose, and hence achievement of Standard can be measured.**

3.1.12 the *Specification* or *Project Design* is therefore of critical importance.

3.2   Briefs/Project Outlines, specifications and project designs

3.2.1 The planning stage of any project is key in its success. This section addresses the initial design stages of a field project, after Appraisal has determined the need for further work, in whatever circumstances. The following statements assume that *Briefs/Project Outlines* and *Specifications* are issued by those requiring work done (planning archaeologists or curators, developers or their agents etc); whilst *Project Designs* can **either** be a response to the *Brief/Project Outline* **or** *Specification, or* be initiated, for example as part of a research proposal (*cf* English Heritage 1991). This may be summarised as follows:

M.8

Root Documents (from originator)	Specification (for negotiation/ tendering etc; usually from originator	Full Details (for reference/ monitoring etc)
Brief ⟶	Specification ⟶	Project Design
Mitigation ⟶	Specification ⟶	Project Design
Research Outline ('Brief'/ 'Project Outline') ⟶		Project or Research Design

3.2.2 A *Brief/Project Outline* is a simple outline framework of the situation to be addressed, with an indication of the scope of works that will be required (IFA By-Law; ACAO 1993). It does not provide sufficient detail to form the basis for a measurable standard; but it could form the basis for a *Specification* or a *Project Design*.

3.2.3 A *Specification* sets out a schedule of works in sufficient detail for it to be quantifiable, implemented and monitored (ACAO 1993). It should be sufficient to form the basis for a measurable standard (Appendix 3).

3.2.4 A *Project Design* also sets out a schedule of works in sufficient detail to be quantifiable, implemented and monitored, and therefore also forms the basis for a measurable standard. However, a *Project Design* may include additional information which covers contractual details such as staffing levels or cost relevant to the commissioning but not necessarily the monitoring body. A *Project Design* may be prepared in response to a *Brief/Project Outline* or *Specification*; or it may be a research proposal generated independently of the planning framework. (Project Designs and their contents are further addressed in Appendix 4 and English Heritage 1991, appendix 2.)

3.2.5 A *Brief/Project Outline* or a *Specification* may form the basis for a *Project Design*. For Field Evaluations within the planning framework, the *Brief/Project Outline* or *Specification* will usually be prepared by the planning archaeologist or curator and issued by the commissioning body (the developer or their agent) to selected tenderers, who respond with a costed *Project Design*. The *Brief/Project Outline* or a *Specification* may be prepared by the applicant or their agent, but it is essential that the planning archaeologist has agreed the proposals, so that they have been accepted as 'fit for purpose'.

3.2.6 *Briefs/Project Outlines, Specifications* and *Project Designs* must be prepared by suitably qualified and experienced persons, utilising specialist advice where necessary.

3.2.7 The *Specification* and/or *Project Design* must identify the objectives, scope, geographical area aethodology and, wherever possible, means of dissemination of the results of the assessment.

3.2.8 In the case of Environmental Assessment, the *Brief/Project Outline* or *Specification* will usually be prepared by the developer or their agent, and issued to tenderers who again respond with a costed *Project Design*. This may also apply to management proposals.

M.9 3.2.9 Proposals for Field Evaluation in research work will take the form of a *Project Design*, prepared by the researching archaeologist, and agreed with any sponsoring body. If there is no external sponsor there must nevertheless be a *written* design so that the validity of any models or questions posed can be properly assessed.

3.2.10 No Field Evaluation should take place on the basis of a *Brief/Project Outline* alone, as it could not achieve the appropriate standard (there being nothing to measure performance against).

3.2.11 When preparing either a *Specification* or a *Project Design* an archaeologist must give full consideration to all available practicable methods of evaluation (listed below in Appendix 2) and decide upon the most appropriate and best available to meet the purpose of the work, seeking specialist advice where necessary.

3.2.12 The archaeologist must be mindful that the purpose of evaluation is to determine the presence, or not, of archaeological deposits and to assess their nature, extent etc, and must not unnecessarily interfere with archaeological remains. The archaeologist must make every effort to ensure that Field Evaluation is minimally-intrusive and minimally-destructive to archaeological remains in both the design and execution of work.

3.2.13 It followes that evaluation projects may be properly terminated (as long as the resource is left in a stable condition) before all requirements of a *Specification* are fulfilled, when some master criterion is met, such as recognition of such a significant constraint as to render proposed development impractical (such recognition should be formally agreed with the sponsor before termination).

3.2.14 The *Specification* or *Project Design* must be suited to the project under consideration; any methods advocated (such as percentage samples) must reflect the type of archaeology likely to occur and should not become inflexible irrespective of site; standard templates should therefore be used with care. Other considerations include 'reasonableness' in relation to scale of proposal, presence of buildings, landuse etc. The principle of BATNEEC—Best available techniques not entailing excessive cost—as enshrined in guidance on Environmental Assessment (Hughes 1992, 326ff) should be utilised.

3.2.15 The *Specification* or *Project Design*, particularly the requirement for evaluation within the planning and EA framework, must be expressed in sufficiently robust terms and in sufficient detail to withstand challenges on archaeological and legal grounds.

3.2.16 Any archaeologist preparing a *Specification* or *Project Design* must be fully appraised of all relevant legislation, and must abide by it.

3.2.17 When preparing a *Specification* or *Project Design* consideration should be given to the need to include appropriate contingency arrangements with respect to field procedures (and thus often to resourcing). In many cases it may prove impossible to conserve the resource and/or to meet the project objectives without a reasonable degree of flexibility to apply professional judgment in the field. Sponsors should be helped to understand that rigid requirements may unavoidably result in a failure to meet their own objectives, and thus waste their resources. Contingency arrangements should not be 'blank extras' but should be properly specified in their own right as a function of prior knowledge of the site, the physical context of the site and the primary objectives of the evaluation. Contractors must be in a position to justify in detail the eventual implementation of contingency arrangements.

3.2.18 The *Specification* or *Project Design* must be agreed by all parties concerned before work commences.

3.2.19 The *Specification* or *Project Design* should contain, as a minimum, the following elements:

- Site location (including map) and description
- Context of the project
- Geological and topographical background

- Archaeological and historical background
- General and specific aims of fieldwork
- Field methodology
- Report preparation, contents and distribution
- Copyright
- Archive deposition
- Publication and dissemination proposals
- Timetable
- Staffing
- Health and Safety statement
- Any other specific necessary reference to legislation
- Monitoring procedures
- Contingency arrangements (if appropriate)

3.2.20 The contents, and different weighting of detail between *Specification* or *Project Design* contents are further amplified in Appendices 3 and 4. *Briefs/Project Outlines* and *Specifications* are also discussed in detail in ACAO 1993.

3.2.21 An archaeologist responding to a tender which includes a *Brief/ Project Outline* or *Specification* may refer to these elements in the *Project Design* if they are set out in sufficient detail, rather than repeat them. Any variation to the *Project Design* or *Specification* must be agreed in writing with the sponsor and all relevant parties.

3.3 Fieldwork

M.10   3.3.1 All fieldwork undertaken must conform to the agreed *Specification* and/or *Project Design*. Variations must be confirmed in writing by all relevant parties.

3.3.2 All techniques used must comply with relevant legislation and be demonstrably fit for the defined purpose(s).

3.3.3 Full and proper records (written, graphic, digital and photographic as appropriate) should be made for all work, using pro forma record forms and sheets appropriate to the work.

3.3.4 All staff, including sub-contractors, must be suitably qualified and experienced for their project roles, and employed in line with IFA Codes and practices. The site director and/or manager should preferably be a member of IFA.

3.3.5 All staff, including sub-contractors, must be fully briefed and aware of the work required under the specification, and must understand the projects aims and methodologies.

3.3.6 Sufficient and appropriate resources (staff, equipment, accommodation etc) must be used to enable the project to achieve its aims, the desired quality and timetable, and to comply with all statutory requirements. It is the role of the archaeologist undertaking the work to define appropriate staff levels.

3.3.7 All equipment must be suitable for the purpose and in sound condition and comply with Health and Safety Executive recommendations. It should be noted that diving equipment in particular is subject to statutory controls under the Diving Operations at Work

Regulations, over and above the suitability for purpose and sound condition.

3.3.8 Artefact and environmental data collection is a standard element of any intrusive field evaluation. Project collection and discard policies, strategies and discard policies must be fit for the defined purpose, and understood by all staff and sub-contractors. (See also *Guidelines for Finds Work*, IFA 1992 and *Standard and Guidance for Finds and Ecofact Studies and Curation*, IFA forthcoming.)

3.3.9 The requirements of Health and Safety cannot be ignored no matter how imperative the need to record archaeological information; hence Health and Safety will take priority over archaeological matters. All archaeologists undertaking fieldwork must do so under a defined Health and Safety Policy. Archaeologists undertaking fieldwork must observe all safe working practices, whether required by their own policies or those of the principal development contractor; the Health and Safety arrangements must be agreed and understood by all relevant parties before work commences. Risk Assessments must be carried out and documented for every field project. For further guidance refer to the bibliography (Appendix 7).

3.4 Monitoring

3.4.1 All work must be monitored, by the archaeological organisation **M.11** undertaking the work (*i.e.* tracking), and if appropriate by the planning archaeologist and commissioning body, or their nominated representatives (see for example Darvill in Hunter and Ralston 1993, 169ff). The guidance below is directed in general at monitors from outside the organisation undertaking the work. However, many of the points apply equally to internal monitors or managers (*e.g.* 3.4.2).

3.4.2 A monitor should be suitably experienced and qualified, or have access to appropriate specialist advice, in order to monitor field and post-field work properly.

3.4.3 Monitoring must be undertaken against the written *Specification* and/or *Project Design*.

3.4.4 Monitors, where not representing the commissioning body, must be careful not to instruct the archaeologist undertaking the work to vary the agreed *Specification* or *Project Design* without consultation with all relevant parties, particularly if this will result in a variation of contract and cost.

3.4.5 Monitors, where not representing the commissioning body, should bear in mind the need for flexibility, within the stated parameters, in contractual matters such as staff numbers, budgets or timetable.

3.4.6 All monitoring visits must be documented by both parties.

3.4.7 Non compliance with the agreed *Specification* or *Project Design* must be pointed out by the monitor to the archaeologists undertaking the work, and their client if appropriate, (see ACAO 1993, section E(vii), 17).

3.4.8 Monitors should be aware of their legal duties, particularly regarding

Health and Safety and the reporting and advising against bad and unsafe practice.

3.4.9 All monitoring arrangements must be mutually agreed at the outset of the project; the archaeologist undertaking fieldwork must inform the planning archaeologist or other monitor of the commencement of work with reasonable notice.

3.4.10 Whilst the monitor may choose to visit at any time, normally they should inform the archaeologist undertaking the work of any intended visits in advance. Monitors must respect reasonable requests from the client commissioning the work to attend only at pre-arranged times and, if necessary in the company of the client's representative.

3.4.11 Any costs of monitoring to be charged by the planning archaeologist or other monitor must be agreed at the outset of the project.

3.5   Post-fieldwork analyses and reports

M.12   3.5.1 All retained artefacts and ecofacts must be cleaned, conserved and packaged in accordance with the requirements of the recipient museum and/or national guidelines.

3.5.2 The project archives must be prepared in accordance with the requirements of the recipient museum and national guidelines.

3.5.3 All analytical and assessment work must be carried out by suitably qualified and experienced staff.

3.5.4 All staff, including sub-contractors, must be fully appraised of the *Specification* or *Project Design* before commencing work, and should fully understand the work required of them.

3.5.5 The level of recording and analysis of artefacts and ecofacts should be appropriate to the aims and purpose of the project, and should not exceed the requirements of the *Specification* or *Project Design* unless variation has been agreed.

3.5.6 All reports must address the aims and purposes of the evaluation.

3.5.7 All reports should be written in a clear, concise and logical style; technical terms should be explained if the report is for a non-archaeological audience. Consideration should be given during the preparation of the report to the requirements of Public Inquiries if appropriate.

3.5.8 Reports should not include recommendations unless required by the planning archaeologist or project *Specification/Project Design*. However, it would be reasonable for the client to seek independently the contractor's opinion. Contractors should be careful to note whether or not the provision of such advice is a *contractual* requirement.

3.5.9 Reports should contain as a minimum:

- Non-technical summary
- Introductory statements
- Aims and purpose of the evaluation

- Methodology
- An objective summary statement of results
- Conclusion, including a confidence rating
- Supporting illustrations at appropriate scales
- Supporting data, tabulated or in appendices, including as a minimum a basic quantification of all artefacts and ecofacts (number and weight), and structural data
- Index to and location of archive
- References

The contents are discussed in more detail in Appendix 5.

3.5.10 Where the project is carried out within the planning process, the report must contain sufficient objective data to enable 'an informed and reasonable decision to be made'. Further guidance on this is contained in ACAO 1993.

3.5.11 Subject to any contractual requirements on confidentiality, copies of the report must be submitted to the appropriate county Sites and Monuments Record within six months of completion of report.

3.5.12 Copies of a site summary (see English Heritage 1991) must be submitted to the appropriate Sites and Monuments Record, the National Archaeological Record and, where appropriate the central government conservation organisation within 6 months of completion of the fieldwork.

3.5.13 In Scotland the primary product of fieldwork is the Data Structure Report (Historic Scotland 1993) with a costed assessment for further fieldwork and/or post-excavation and publication. This report does not have a broad equivalent elsewhere in the UK (see Appendix 1).

3.6 Archives, ownership and deposition

3.6.1 The requirements for archive preparation and deposition must be **M.13** addressed at the outset of the project.

3.6.2 The proposed recipient museum or other repository must be contacted at the project planning stage, and particular project arrangement for the deposition of the site archive should be detailed in the *Specification* and/or *Project Design*.

3.6.3 Archive deposition must take account of the requirements of the recipient museum or repository, and the relevant sections of the Museums and Galleries Commissions Guidelines relating to the preparation and transfer of archives or the appropriate national guidelines. A copy of the paper archive should be lodged with the appropriate national archaeological record, in accordance with their specific requirements.

3.6.4 In Scotland, the paper archive is lodged with the National Monuments Record of Scotland although finds are deposited in a museum; a second copy of all or parts of the paper archive should be made available to the museum receiving the finds.

3.6.5 The site and research archives (English Heritage 1991, appendices 3 and 6) generated during fieldwork and post-fieldwork should be deposited with the recipient museum or other repository in the required format. Artefacts and environmental data form part of those archives.

3.6.6 In England, Wales, Northern Ireland the Isle of Man ownership of objects rests with the landowner, except where other law overrides this (*e.g.* Treasure Trove; *Burials Act* 1857). The archaeologist undertaking the fieldwork or the planning archaeologist must make this clear at the inception of the project (in the *Brief/Project Outline, Specification* or *Project Design*).

3.6.7 It should be noted that the different areas have, *inter alia*, differing reporting procedures for Treasure Trove, differing requirements for finds deposition, and the material cannot be exported from the Isle of Man without a licence. A licence is required for excavation work in the Isle of Man and Northern Ireland. Archaeologists unfamiliar with the procedures in any area should seek guidance from the appropriate authorities (see Appendices 7 and 8).

3.6.8 Except in Scotland, it is the responsibility of the archaeologist undertaking the fieldwork to endeavour to obtain the consent of the landowner in writing for finds' donation and deposition with the recipient museum where this is appropriate.

3.6.9 Except in Scotland, in the event that the landowner is unwilling, for whatever reason, to donate the finds to the appropriate recipient museum, the archaeologist undertaking the fieldwork must endeavour to ensure all artefacts and ecofacts are recorded, safely packaged and conserved where appropriate before transfer to the owner, and that their location/ownership is stated in the site archive and public record. It should be noted that the owner's explicit (written) permission is required before entering such personal information in the public record (*cf. inter alia* the *Data Protection Act* 1984).

3.6.10 In Scotland all newly-discovered ancient objects, whether precious metal or not, may be claimed as on behalf of the Crown, if their owner cannot be traced. The law applies no matter where, or on whose property, objects may be found and whether such objects may be hidden or lost. All finds should be reported to the Procurator Fiscal and Queen's and Lord Treasurer's Remembrancer. The ownership of artefacts from excavations undertaken by central government, where the Crown does not claim them as Treasure Trove, is passed to the Secretary of State for Scotland. Ownership is then passed, on the recommendation of the Finds Disposal Panel, to the appropriate museum (Historic Scotland 1993).

3.6.11 The rules of ownership applicable to material which has come from a vessel (*i.e.* all those classified as a 'wreck') differ from those applicable to material on land and material found on the seabed which is not a wreck. Under the *Merchant Shipping Act* 1894 original owners have one year in which to claim ownership, after which the material is sold with the proceeds going to the Crown. The Act is implemented such that ownership of historic wreck maybe passed to the salvor in lieu of a salvage award. The Department of Transport, which administers the Act, have said that it favours the retention of material by museums, but this does not always happen. In cases of wreck material the Marine Emergency Administration Division of the Department of Transport should be contacted. (For further information see Firth 1993, 65ff.)

3.7 Other considerations

3.7.1 It is advisable for Field Evaluation projects to be governed by a written contract or agreement to which the agreed *Specification* or *Project Design* is attached. Such contracts or agreements should be dated, signed by both parties and include reference to the defines area of study outlined on a map, to the *Specification* or *Project Design*, to conditions for access, programme, method and timetable for payment (including any retentions), and copyright arrangements (see IFA Technical Paper no. 8). **M.14**

3.7.2 Unless otherwise agreed in a contract, the copyright of any written or graphic or photographic records and reports rests with the originating body (the archaeological organisation undertaking the fieldwork and analysis), who will licence their use in relation to the specific project by the client or sponsoring body. Such agreements on copyright should be agreed with the sponsoring body at the outset of the project (see Appendix 6).

3.7.3 Material copied or cited in reports should be duly acknowledged; and all copyright conditions (such as those for Ordnance Survey maps) observed.

3.7.4 All aspects of publicity must be agreed at the outset of the project between the commissioning body and the archaeological organisation or individual undertaking the project.

3.7.5 All archaeologists undertaking work must respect the sponsor's or client's requirements over confidentiality, but the archaeologist must endeavour to emphasise their professional obligation to make the results of archaeological work available to the wider archaeological community within a reasonable time (see 3.5.11).

3.7.6 An archaeologist or archaeological organisation undertaking such projects must ensure that they have adequate insurance policies, Public Liability, some relevant form of civil liability indemnity or Professional Indemnity.

3.7.7 Statutory requirements regarding archaeological matters vary within the United Kingdom, commissioning bodies and others may therefore find it useful to consult the relevant documents listed in Appendix 7 and can obtain further guidance from the appropriate advisory bodies listed in Appendix 8.

APPENDIX 1: GLOSSARY OF TERMS USED

Appraisal   a rapid reconnaissance of site and records to identify (within the planning framework) whether a development proposal has a potential archaeological **M.15**

dimension requiring further clarification (ACAO 1993, 4); **or**

a rapid reconnaissance of site and records to identify whether a particular project or study area has potential for further academically-oriented research involving non-intrusive or intrusive methods

Assessment (Desk-Based)

an assessment of the known or potential archaeological resource within a specified area or site (land-based, inter-tidal or marine), consisting of a collation of existing written and graphic information, in order to identify the likely character, extent and relative quality of the actual or potential resource. (See also *Standard and Guidance for Archaeological Desk-Based Assessments*.)

Brief/Project Outline

an outline framework of the archaeological circumstances which have to be addressed, together with an indication of the scope of works that will be required. In Scotland the Brief may be referred to as a Project Outline (see Historic Scotland 1993).

Client

the individual or organisation commissioning and funding the project

Curator

a person or organisation responsible for the conservation and management of archaeological evidence by virtue of official or statutory duty, including for example County or District Archaeological Officers, Regional Archaeology Officers, national bodies such as English Heritage and Cadw.

Data Structure Report

an initial organisation on paper, of the information retrieved from an excavation, comprising a narrative account of the site sequence, indices, or contexts, drawings, photographs, small finds, and environmental samples, and a list of project documentation. This report is relevant in Scotland and there is no broad equivilent elsewhere in the UK. Details are given in Historic Scotland 1993.

Environmental Assessment

a systematic analysis of a project's potential effects on all aspects of the environment including cultural heritage, in order to provide information for the deciding agency to consider in the decision-making process, and further give bodies with relevant environmental responsibilities the opportunity to comment before consent is given. EA applies to projects having significant environmental effects as set out in Directive 86/337/EEC and as implemented in the UK, which came into effect in July 1988.

Evaluation

a limited programme of non-intrusive and/or intrusive fieldwork which determines of the presence or absence of archaeological features, structures, deposits, artefacts or ecofacts within a specified area or site; and, if present, defines their character and extent, and relative quality. It enables an assessment of their worth in a local, regional, national or international context as appropriate.

Planning archaeologist see curator.

Project Design   a written statement on the project's objectives, methods, timetable and resources, forming the framework for the execution of the project through to completion, set out in sufficient detail to be quantifiable, implemented and monitored. Normally prepared by an archaeologist or organisation undertaking the fieldwork, frequently in response to a Brief or Specification.

Specification   a written schedule of works required for a particular project (by a curator, planning archaeologist or client), set out in sufficient detail to be quantifiable, implemented and monitored. Normally prepared by or agreed with the relevant curator.

APPENDIX 2: FIELD TECHNIQUES

There is a wide range of archaeological techniques available for field evaluation. In many instances several techniques may be valid for the requirements of the brief, and it will be necessary to explain the selection criteria. Wherever possible the first considered option should be for non-destructive survey, though in most instances this will probably not produce the necessary level of confidence in the information gained, nor result in a set of information which can be verified at, for example Public Inquiry. The methods selected **must** be fit for the purpose defined. **M.16**

This standard covers the following methods of field evaluation:

a) **Non-destructive**

- Geophysical Survey
- Remote sensing
- Geochemical Survey
- Earthwork Survey
- Field Scanning (ie observation and mapping of artefact and other distributions, but not collection of artefacts)
- Standing Building Survey

b) **Destructive Methods** (of varying destructive potential)

- Augering
- Hand-excavated test pits
- Hand-excavated trenches
- Machine-stripped and manually excavated test pits
- Machine-stripped and manually excavated trenches
- Probing (frequently used underwater)
- Surface Artefact Collection (Fieldwalking for collection as opposed to scanning)*.

*This method is destructive as it removes part of all of the archaeological resource, albeit that resource generally removed from its original context. Selective collection (eg only removing prehistoric pottery and flint tools) will bias both the remaining resource and the collected data; this method is not recommended other than non-collection of modern debris identifiable in the field (though its presence must be recorded).

Further information on selection of techniques is set out in the ACAO document 1993.

Methods such as prop wash and explosives (used occasionally for underwater exploration) are not generally acceptable. Further guidance on marine evaluation techniques is available in *Guidelines for the Assessment of the Marine Archaeological Resource* (Oxley in draft 1993, for IFA).

APPENDIX 3: PREPARATION OF SPECIFICATION

M.17 The Specification should contain, as a minimum, the following elements:

- Non-technical summary (intelligible to the lay reader)
- Site location and description (NGR, size, geology, landuse, topography, physical constrains)
- Planning Background (proposed details, planning policies, other environmental matters, Scheduled Monument constraints, Protected Wrecks etc)
- Archaeological and Historical Background (including plan or NGR, site status)
- Purpose/aims of fieldwork (clearly stated in both general and specific aims)
- Field methodology (techniques selected, with justification for selection; detailed exposition of techniques, artefact collection policies, discard policies, environmental collection strategy and implementation, recording techniques)
- Post-fieldwork methodologies (cleaning, conservation, cataloguing, packaging, dating techniques, archive preparation)
- Report preparation, contents and distribution
- Copyright
- Archive deposition (including finds ownership, recipient museum)
- Publication and dissemination
- Timetable, if appropriate
- Staffing—in general terms only—eg the site director should be a member of the Institute of Field Archaeologists, but **not** the number of staff
- Health and Safety statement
- Monitoring procedure required by the curator, including any charges

APPENDIX 4: PROJECT DESIGN CONTENTS

M.18 The Project Design should contain, as a minimum, the following elements:

- Non-technical summary (intelligible to the lay reader)
- Site location and description (NGR, size, geology, landuse, topography, physical constraints)

- Planning Background (proposal details, planning policies, other environmental matters, Scheduled Monument constraints, Protected Wrecks), if appropriate
- Archaeological and Historical Background (including built landscape and technical, plan or NGR, site status)
- Geological and topographical background
- Purpose/aims of fieldwork (clearly stated in both general and specific aims)
- Field methodology (techniques selected, with justification of selection; detailed exposition of techniques, artefact collection policies, discard policies, environmental collection strategy and implementation, recording techniques, and any measures for the conservation/reburial of surviving deposits)
- Post-fieldwork methodologies (cleaning, conservation, cataloguing, packaging, dating techniques, archive preparation)
- Report preparation and contents
- Copyright
- Archive deposition (including finds ownership, recipient museum)
- Publication and dissemination proposals
- Timetable
- Staffing
- Health and Safety policies and implementation, including Risk Assessment Insurances
- Monitoring procedures (internal, curatorial, contractual)
- Costs (or these may be presented in a covering letter)

A contracting archaeologist responding to a tender with specification may refer to these elements if defined in a *Brief* or *Specification* set by curator or client, rather than repeat them in a *Project Design*.

APPENDIX 5: REPORT CONTENTS

The specific requirements of any report will necessarily vary according to the scope of works, the nature of the results or other factors. However, the following sections will occur in most reports: **M.19**

Non-technical summary
This should outline, in plain, non-technical language the principle reason for the work, its objectives and main results; and should include reference to authorship and commissioning body.

Introductory statements
These could include acknowledgements, circumstances of the project such as planning background, the archaeological background, an outline nature of work, the site description (including size, geology and topography, location), when the project was undertaken and by whom.

Aims and Objectives
These should reflect or reiterate the aims set of in the *Project Design* or *Specification*.

Methodology
The methods used, including the detail of any variation to the agreed

Project Design or *Specification* should be set out carefully, and explained as appropriate.

Results

These should be set out as a series of summary objective statements, organised clearly in relation to the methods used, and describing both structural data and associated finds and/or environmental data recovered. Descriptive material should be clearly separated from interpretative statements. Technical terminology (including dating or period references) should be explained where necessary if the report is aimed at a largely non-archaeological audience. The results should be amplified where necessary by the use of drawings and photographs; and by supporting data contained in appendices (below).

Conclusions

It may be appropriate to include a section which sums up and interprets the results and puts them into context (local, national or otherwise). Other elements could include a confidence rating on techniques used, or on limitations imposed by particular factors (eg weather or problems of access). Recommendations on further work may also be required, but in most circumstances within the planning framework this will be the responsibility of the relevant planning archaeologist or curator.

Archive location

The final destination of the archive (records and finds) should be noted in the report. If the archive is likely to remain with the originating body for some time, that should also be noted in the report, along with the reason.

Appendices

These should contain essential technical and supporting detail, including for example lists of artefacts and contexts or details of measurements, gazetteers etc. It may also be appropriate to include the *Project Design* or *Specification* for ease of reference.

Figures & Plates

Most reports will need to include one or more illustrations for clarity; as a minimum a location plan should be included. Any plans or sections should be clearly numbered and easily referenced to the National grid and related to the specified area.

References and Bibliography

A list of all sources used should be appended to the report.

Copy of Specification

It may be helpful to include a copy of the original *Specification* in order to assess whether or not the defined aims and objectives have been met. The report can then be used for reference without recourse to other documentation.

APPENDIX 6: COPYRIGHT

M.20 Under the *Copyright, Designs and Patents Act* 1988 the organisation or person undertaking field and reporting work retains the copyright to the written and graphic material, unless this has been varied in the contract for the work. This position should be made clear to all relevant parties at the outset of work.

The circumstances under which the report or records can be used by other parties should be made clear at the inception of the project. For example one of these clauses could be incorporated into the *Specification* or *Project Design*:

The .... [name or organisation carrying out work] shall retain full copyright of any commissioned reports, tender documents or other project documents, under the *Copyright, Designs and Patents Act* 1988 with all rights reserved; excepting that it hereby provide an exclusive licence to the client for the use of such documents by the client in all matters directly relating to the project as described in the Project Specification.

or

The .... [name of organisation] will assign copyright to the client upon written request but retains the right to be identified as the author of all project documentation and reports as defined in the *Copyright, Designs and Patents Act* 1988 (Chapter IV, s. 79).

In the last instance a further letter actually granting copyright needs to be sent to the client.

The proposals for distribution of the report must be made clear to all parties at the outset of the field project.

Appendix N

STANDARD AND GUIDANCE FOR ARCHAEOLOGICAL EXCAVATIONS (INSTITUTE OF FIELD ARCHAEOLOGISTS (1994))

DRAFT STANDARD AND GUIDANCE FOR ARCHAEOLOGICAL EXCAVATIONS

STANDARD

An Archaeological Excavation will examine and record the archaeological **N.1** resource within a specified area, using appropriate methods and practices which satisfy the stated aims of the project and which comply with the Code of Conduct, Code of Approved Practice for the Regulation of Contractual Arrangements in Field Archaeology, and other relevant By-Laws of the Institute of Field Archaeologists, and which will result in an ordered, accessible archive and one or more published accounts.

DEFINITION OF EXCAVATION

Excavation is defined as a programme of controlled, intrusive fieldwork with **N.2** defined research objectives which examines and records archaeological deposits, features and structures and, as appropriate, retrieves artefacts, ecofacts and other remains within a specified area or site (on land or underwater). The records made and objects gathered during fieldwork are studied and the results of that study published in detail appropriate to the Project Design and in the light of findings.

PURPOSE OF EXCAVATION

The purpose of Excavation is to examine the archaeological resource within a **N.3** given area or site within a framework of defined research objectives, to seek a better understanding of and compile a lasting record of that resource, to analyse the findings/record and then to disseminate the results of the research.

OCCURRENCE

Excavations may occur:

N.4 • in response to a proposed development which threatens the archaeological resource: as part of the Planning Process (within the framework of appropriate national planning policy guidance notes) and/or development plan policy;
as part of an Environmental Assessment (see 3.1.1 below);
or outside the planning process (eg ecclesiastical development, agriculture and forestry, works by statutory undertakers)
• within a programme of research not generated by a specific threat to the archaeological resource
• in connection with management plans and mitigation strategies by private, local and national bodies

GUIDANCE

1 INTRODUCTION

N.5 1.1 This guidance seeks to define best practice for the execution of Excavations and concomitant reporting, in line with the By-laws of the Institute of Field Archaeologists (in particular *The Code of Conduct* and *The Code of Approved Practice for the Regulation of Contractual Arrangements in Field Archaeology*). It seeks to expand and explain general definitions in the Codes for the practice of fieldwork and reporting.

1.2 The Standard and guidance apply to all types of excavations (land-based, inter-tidal and underwater), whether generated by academic research, by local interest, through the planning process, by management proposals or by any other proposals which may affect the archaeological resource within a specified area.

1.3 In addition, the guidance seeks to amplify that given in appropriate national planning policy guidelines (see Appendix 7), and to be compatible with current guidelines issued by regulatory authorities.

1.4 The terminology used followed PPG 16, and guidance issued by the Association of County Archaeological Officers (ACAO; 1993) and English Heritage (1991), with amplifications where necessary. It tries to take account of differences in terminology, legal and administrative practice in different parts of the UK. A glossary of terms used may be found in Appendix 1.

1.5 This document provides guidance for work carried out within the British Isles. Whilst general guidance is given, this document cannot be exhaustive, particularly in its treatment of legislative issues; archaeologists working in the different countries must ensure that they are familiar with the specific legislation and common law pertinent to those areas.

2 PRINCIPLES: THE CODE OF CONDUCT AND OTHER BY-LAWS OF THE INSTITUTE OF FIELD ARCHAEOLOGISTS

2.1 An archaeologist undertaking archaeological excavations must adhere to the four major principles enshrined in the Institute of Field Archaeologists' By-laws the *Code of Conduct* and the rules governing those principles:　　　　**N.6**

1 The archaeologist shall adhere to the highest standards of ethical and responsible behaviour in the conduct of archaeological affairs.
2 The archaeologist has a responsibility for the conservation of the archaeological heritage.
3 The archaeologist shall conduct his or her work in such a way that reliable information about the past may be required, and shall ensure that the results be properly recorded.
4 The archaeologist has the responsibility for making available the results of archaeological work with reasonable dispatch.

2.2 Further, the *Code of Approved Practice for the Regulation of Contractual Arrangements in Field Archaeology* specifically addresses professional conduct in situations where work is sponsored or commissioned on a contractual basis, especially as part of development controlled by the planning process. It provides guidance on professional behaviour where more than one individual or body are competing for the same piece of work, and seeks to ensure that the terms and conditions for all work are clearly defined, normally by contract.

3 PROCEDURES

3.1 Project identification

3.1.1 *In response to a proposed development within the planning process* an Appraisal of the proposed area will have been carried out, normally by the planning archaeologist or curator. The desirability of preservation of archaeological remains is now a material consideration in the planning process, local authorities can reasonably request further information about archaeological matters so that 'an informed and reasonable planning decision can be taken' (PPG 16, section 21); such information is normally provided through carrying out a Desk-based Assessment and/or a Field Evaluation. (For further details see the IFA Standards & Guidance for Archaeological Desk-based Assessments and Field Evaluations).　　　　**N.7**

Depending on the results of the assessment work further archaeological work may be required; such requirements are normally determined by the planning archaeologist or curator (but see 3.2.5), will form part of an agreed mitigation strategy and may be implemented by way of a planning condition or other agreement.
Environmental Assessment (EA) applies to projects potentially having significant environmental effects (as defined in Council Directive 85/337 EEC, and as implemented in the UK via the various Statutory Instruments etc). EA involves Appraisal and Desk-based Assessment and in many instances Field Evaluation; the resulting

Environmental Statement (ES) will contain recommendations for mitigating impact on the archaeological resource. The agreed mitigation strategies may include archaeological excavation; such work would not normally take place before a Planning Inquiry or Public Local Inquiry.

In response to a development *outside the planning process*, the principles of Desk-based Assessment and/or Field Evaluation, leading to the formulation of mitigation strategies as appropriate, should similarly apply.

3.1.2 *In a research context*, excavation area(s) will have been identified and selected by an archaeologist based on specific aspects or themes relating to defined research interests. This could include work undertaken through universities, central government agencies, local authorities, museums, independent trusts, amateur organisations and societies, private companies or private individuals.

3.1.3 *Management proposals by private landowners or others* may also result in Excavations, to obtain information in order to enhance the understanding and management of the environmental or archaeological resource.

3.1.4 **Whether the Excavation has arisen through the planning framework (including Environmental Assessment), from research interests, or management proposals, an archaeologist should only undertake an Excavation which is governed by a written *Specification* or *Project Design* (see Code of Conduct), discussed in advance with the relevant planning archaeologist or curator, as this is the tool against which performance, fitness for purpose, and hence achievement of Standard can be measured.**

3.1.5 The *Specification* or *Project Design* is therefore of critical importance.

3.2 Briefs/project outlines, specifications and project designs

N.8 3.2.1 The planning and preparation stage of any project is crucial to its success. This section addresses the initial design stages of an Excavation.

3.2.2 A *Brief* (or *Project Outline* in Scotland) is a simple outline of the circumstances to be addressed, with an indication of the scope of works that will be required (IFA By-Law; ACAO 1993). It does not provide sufficient detail to form the basis for a measurable standard; but it could form the basis for a *Specification* or a *Project Design* (see Appendix 3).

3.2.3 A *Specification* sets out a schedule of works in sufficient detail for it to be quantifiable, implemented and monitored (ACAO 1993). It should be sufficient to form the basis for a measurable standard.

3.2.4 A *Project Design* also sets out a schedule of works in sufficient detail to be quantifiable, implemented and monitored, and therefore also forms the basis for a measurable standard. However, a *Project Design* may include additional information which covers contractual details such as staffing levels or cost relevant to the commissioning but not necessarily the monitoring body. *Project Designs* are normally produced by those undertaking the work, and can either be a response to the *Brief/Project Outline* or *Specification* or be initiated as part of a research or management proposal generated independently of the planning framework. (Project Designs and their contents are further addressed in Appendix 3, and English Heritage 1991, Appendix 2.)

3.2.5 A *Brief/Project Outline* or a *Specification* may form the basis for a *Project Design*. For Excavations within the planning framework, the *Brief/Project Outline* or *Specification* will usually be prepared by the planning archaeologist or curator and issued by the commissioning body (the developer or their agent) to selected tenderers, who respond with a costed Project Design. The *Brief/Project Outline* or a *Specification* may be prepared by the applicant or their agent, but it is essential that the planning archaeologist/curator has agreed the proposals, so that they have been accepted as "fit for purpose".

3.2.6 *Briefs/Project Outlines, Specifications* and *Project Designs* must be prepared by suitably qualified and experienced persons, using specialist advice where necessary.

3.2.7 In the case of Environmental Assessment, the *Brief/Project Outline* or *Specification* will usually be prepared by the developer or their agent, discussed with the planning archaeologist/curator and issued to tenderers who again respond with a costed *Project Design*. This may also apply to management proposals.

3.2.8 Proposals for Excavations *not* prompted by a threat to the archaeological remains will normally take the form of a *Project Design* prepared by the researching archaeologist, and agreed with any sponsoring body. If there is no external sponsor there must nevertheless be a written design so that the validity of any models or questions posed can be properly assessed.

3.2.9 No Excavation should take place on the basis of a *Brief/Project Outline* alone, as it could not achieve the appropriate standard (there being nothing to measure performance against).

3.2.10 When preparing either a *Specification* or a *Project Design* an archaeologist must give full consideration to all available practicable methods of excavation (Appendix 2) and decide upon the most appropriate and best available to meet the purpose of the work, seeking specialist advice where necessary. The *Project Design* should include an agreed collection and disposal strategy for artefacts and ecofacts (see also 3.6.2 and 3.6.3).

3.2.11 In both the planning and execution of excavations where there is no immediate threat to the archaeological resource the archaeologist must ensure that the excavations cause the minimum damage or destruction necessary to meet the stated research aims of the project.

3.2.12 It follows that such fieldwork may be properly terminated (as long as the resource is left in a stable condition) before the *Project Design* is fulfilled, if remains of such significance are discovered as to call into question the decision to excavate. In such circumstances the archaeologist should inform the relevant bodies and seek to ensure that appropriate management measures are taken (see also 3.3.1).

N.9 3.2.13 The *Specification* or *Project Design* must be suited to the project under consideration; any methods advocated must reflect the nature of archaeological remains likely to be found and should not become inflexible irrespective of site; standard templates should therefore be used with care. Other considerations include "reasonableness" in relation to scale of threat, presence of buildings, land-use etc.

3.2.14 Any archaeologist preparing a *Specification* or *Project Design* must consider the need to examine appropriate sources; they must be fully apprised of all relevant legislation, and must abide by it.

3.2.15 When preparing a *Specification* or *Project Design* consideration should be given to the need to include appropriate contingency arrangements with respect to field procedures (and thus often to resourcing). In many cases it may prove impossible to meet the project objectives without a reasonable degree of flexibility to apply professional judgment in the field. Sponsors should be helped to understand that overly rigid requirements may unavoidably result in a failure to meet their own non-archaeological objectives. Contingency arrangements should not be open-ended but should be properly specified in their own right and reflect prior knowledge of the site, the physical context of the site and the primary objectives of the excavation. Contractors must be in a position to justify in detail the eventual implementation of contingency arrangements.

3.2.16 The *Specification* or *Project Design* should contain, as a minimum, the following elements:

- Non-technical summary
- Site location (including map) and descriptions
- Context of the project
- Geological and topographical background
- Archaeological and historical background
- General and specific aims of fieldwork
- Field methodology
- Post-fieldwork methodologies
- Report preparation, contents and distribution
- Copyright
- Archive deposition
- Publication and dissemination proposals
- Timetable
- Staffing
- Health and safety considerations, and reference to any other legislation
- Monitoring procedures
- Contingency arrangements (if appropriate)

3.2.17 The contents, and different weighting of detail between *Specification* or *Project Design* contents are further amplified in Appendix 3. *Briefs/Project Outlines* and *Specifications* are also discussed in detail in ACAO 1993 and Historic Scotland 1993.

3.2.18 An archaeologist responding to a tender which includes a *Brief/ Project Outline* or *Specification* may refer to these elements in the *Project Design*, taking care to include sufficient detail and not merely repeat them. Any variation to the *Project Design* or *Specification* must be agreed with the sponsor and all relevant parties.

3.3 Fieldwork

3.3.1 All fieldwork undertaken must conform to the agreed *Specification*   **N.10** and/or *Project Design*. Variations must be confirmed in writing by all relevant parties.

3.3.2 All techniques used must comply with relevant legislation and be demonstrably fit for the defined purpose(s).

3.3.3 Full and proper records (written, graphic, digital and photographic as appropriate) should be made for all work, using pro forma records and sheets appropriate to the work (see Appendix 2).

3.3.4 All staff, including sub-contractors, must be suitably qualified and experienced for their project roles, and employed in line with IFA Codes and practices. The site director and/or manager should preferably be a member of IFA.

3.3.5 All staff, including sub-contractors, must be fully briefed and aware of the work required under the specification, and must understand the projects aims and methodologies.

3.3.6 Sufficient and appropriate resources (staff, equipment, accommodation etc) must be used to enable the project to achieve its aims, the desired quality and timetable, and to comply with all statutory requirements. It is the role of the archaeologist undertaking the work to define appropriate staff levels.

3.3.7 All equipment must be suitable for the purpose and in sound condition and comply with Health and Safety Executive recommendations. It should be noted that diving equipment in particular is subject to statutory controls under the *Diving Operations at Work Regulations*, over and above suitability for purpose and sound condition.

3.3.8 Artefact and environmental data collection is a standard element of any excavation. Project collection and discard policies, strategies and techniques must be fit for the defined purpose, and understood by all staff and sub-contractors. (See also *Guidelines for Finds Work*, IFA 1992, and *Standard and Guidance for Finds and Ecofact Studies and Curation*, IFA forthcoming).

3.3.9 All retained artefacts and ecofacts must be treated and packaged in accordance with the requirements of the recipient museum/repository and national guidelines (Museums and Galleries Commission 1992, Society of Mueum Archaeologists 1992, UKIC 1983, 1984, 1988 and 1990).

3.3.10 The site archive must be prepared in accordance with the requirements of the recipient museum/repository and national guidelines (ibid).

3.3.11 Health and Safety requirements cannot be ignored no matter how imperative the need to record archaeological information; hence Health and Safety will take priority over archaeological matters. All archaeologists undertaking fieldwork must do so under a defined Health and Safety Policy. Archaeologists undertaking fieldwork must observe all safe working practices; the Health and Safety arrangements must be agreed and understood by all relevant parties before work commences. Risk Assessments must be carried out and documented for every field project. All archaeologists have a responsibility to report unsafe practice. For further guidance refer to the bibliography (Appendix 7).

3.3.12 Copies of a site summary (see English Heritage 1991) must be submitted to the appropriate Sites and Monuments Record, the National Archaeological Record and, where appropriate the central government conservation organisation within 6 months of completion of the fieldwork.

3.3.13 Where an excavation has been carried out as part of the planning process, the report must contain sufficient information to enable the planning archaeologist to determine whether or not any condition has been discharged.

3.4 Post-excavation Assessment

N.11 3.4.1 A *Post-excavation Assessment* should normally be carried out after the completion of the fieldwork and site archive to assess the potential for further analysis and publication (English Heritage 1991, 15ff) (but see 3.4.5 on Data Structure Reports for Scotland). This involves the assessment of the project against the original Project Design to determine the extent to which the original research aims have been met (see 3.2), and forward planning and the identification of any new research questions to be incorporated in an Up-dated Project Design (3.5).

3.4.2 All Post-excavation Assessment work must be carried out by suitably qualified and experienced staff, who must be apprised of the Project Design before commencing work, and who should understand the work required of them.

3.4.3 The level of assessment of records and materials should be appropriate to the aims and purpose of the assessment project.

3.4.4 A Post-excavation Assessment Report should be produced, and this Report will form part of the project archive. It should include a characterisation of the quantity and perceived quality of the data in the site archive, a statement of the archaeological potential of the data to answer the project research aims, and recommendations on the data storage and curation requirements. Details of the contents of the post-excavation Assessment Report are given in Appendix 4.

3.4.5 In Scotland the primary product of an excavation is the Data Structure Report (historic Scotland 1993) with a costed assessment for further fieldwork and/or post-excavation and publication. This report does not have a broad equivalent in England (see Appendix 1).

3.5 Up-dated Project Design

3.5.1 The research aims of the project may be revised following the **N.12**
Post-excavation Assessment. Even if the research aims remain
unchanged, the identification of which material would merit further
study will require the Project Design (see 3.2 above) to be up-dated.

3.5.2 The Up-dated Project Design should be a document which will form
part of the project archive. (See Appendix 5 for details).

3.5.3 In up-dating the Project Design, archaeologists should be aware of
future research and/or resource management needs, and requirements
for the effective short- and long-term curation of the project archive
(including retention/disposal considerations) and ensure that these
are addressed and raised with the planning archaeologist or other
relevant authorities.

3.6 Analysis

3.6.1 All analysis must conform to the Up-dated Project Design; any **N.13**
variation must be confirmed by all relevant parties.

3.6.2 All techniques used must be demonstrably fit for the defined
purpose(s), and comply with relevant legislation.

3.6.3 Those carrying out the work should be suitably qualified and
experienced, and fully aware of the work required under the Up-dated
Project Design.

3.6.4 All data generated as a result of the analysis phase should be included
in the project archive. Many of the data and their interpretation will
form part of the Publication (3.7).

3.7 Publication and dissemination

3.7.1 The publication format should conform to the synopsis in the **N.14**
Up-dated Project Design.

3.7.2 Subject to the Up-dated Project Design, the publication report should
normally contain sufficient data and references to the project archive
to permit interpretations to be challenged. Similarly, reports should
normally integrate the results of specialist researches with the site
sequence, in order to ensure both that important data are not
overlooked, and that an informative and interesting account is
produced. The assistance of independent referees may be sought to
enhance academic quality.

3.7.3 As a minimum, a site summary should be published; copies should be
submitted to the appropriate Sites and Monuments Record and

3.7.4 Consideration should be given to publicising the results of the project
through a range of outlets, from conventional archaeological publications to, for example, site viewing platforms, interpretation panels
and lectures, open-days and school visits, radio and television
programmes, videos and popular publications.

3.8 Monitoring

N.15 3.8.1 All work must be monitored by the archaeological organisation undertaking the work (*i.e.* tracking) and, if appropriate, by the planning archaeologist and commissioning body, or their nominated representatives (see for example Darvill in Hunter and Ralston 1993, 169ff). The guidance below is directed in general at monitors from outside the organisation undertaking the work. However, many of the points apply equally to internal monitors or managers.

3.8.2 A monitor should be suitably experienced and qualified, or have access to appropriate specialist advice, in order to monitor field and post-excavation work properly.

3.8.3 Monitoring must be undertaken against the written *Specification* and/or *Project Design*.

3.8.4 Monitors, where not representing the commissioning body, should bear in mind the need for flexibility, within the stated parameters, in contractual matters such as staff numbers, budgets or timetable.

3.8.5 All monitoring visits must be documented by both parties.

3.8.6 Non-compliance with the agreed *Specification* or *Project Design* must be pointed out by the monitor to the archaeologists undertaking the work. and their client if appropriate, at the earliest opportunity (see ACAO 1993, section E(vii), 17).

3.8.7 All monitoring arrangements must be mutually agreed at the outset of the project; the archaeologist undertaking fieldwork must inform the planning archaeologist or other monitor of the commencement of work with reasonable notice.

3.8.8 Whilst monitors may choose to visit at any time, normally they should inform the archaeologist undertaking the work of any intended visits in advance. Monitors must respect reasonable requests from the client commissioning the work to attend only at pre-arranged times and, if necessary, in the company of the client's representative.

3.8.9 Any costs for monitoring to be charged by the planning archaeologist or other monitor must be agreed at the outset of the project.

3.9 Archives, ownership and deposition

N.16 3.9.1 The requirements for archive preparation and deposition must be addressed at the outset of the project.

3.9.2 The proposed recipient museum or other repository must be contacted at the beginning of the project planning stage, and particular project arrangements for deposition of the site archive should be detailed in the *Specification* and/or *Project Design*.

3.9.3 Archive deposition must take account of the requirements of the recipient museum or repository, and the relevant sections of the Museums and Galleries Commissions Guidelines relating to the preparation and transfer of archives or the appropriate national guidelines. A copy of the paper archive should be lodged with the appropriate national archaeological record, in accordance with their specific requirements.

3.9.4 In Scotland, the paper archive is lodged with the National Monuments Record of Scotland although finds are deposited in a museum; a second copy of all or part of the paper archive should be made available to the museum receiving the finds.

3.9.5 The site and research archives (English Heritage 1991) generated during fieldwork and post-excavation should be deposited with the recipient museum or other repository in the required format. Artefacts and environmental remains form part of those archives. The treatment of human remains will be governed by the relevant legislation and government regulations.

3.9.6 In England, Wales, Northern Ireland the Isle of Man ownership of objects rests with the landowner, except where other law overrides this (eg Treasure Trove; *Burials Act* 1857). The archaeologist undertaking the fieldwork or the planning archaeologist must make this clear at the inception of the project (in the *Brief/Project Outline, Specification* or *Project Design*).

3.9.7 It should be noted that the different areas have, *inter alia*, differing reporting procedures for Treasure Trove, differing requirements for finds deposition, and the material cannot be exported from the Isle of Man without a licence. A licence is required for excavation work in the Isle of Man and Northern Ireland. Archaeologists unfamiliar with the procedures in any area should seek guidance from the appropriate authorities (see Appendices 7 and 8).

3.9.8 Except in Scotland, it is the responsibility of the archaeologist undertaking the fieldwork to endeavour to obtain the consent of the landowner in writing for finds donation and deposition with the recipient museum where this is appropriate.

3.9.9 Except in Scotland, in the event that the landowner is unwilling, for whatever reason, to donate the finds to the appropriate recipient museum, the archaeologist undertaking the fieldwork must endeavour to ensure all artefacts and ecofacts are recorded, safely packaged and conserved where appropriate before transfer to the owner, and that their location and ownership is stated in the site archive and public record. It should be noted that the owner's explicit (written) permission is required before entering such personal information in the public record (see *inter alia* the *Data Protection Act* 1984).

3.6.10 In Scotland all newly-discovered ancient objects, whether precious metal or not, may be claimed as on behalf of the Crown if their owner cannot be traced. The law applies no matter where, or on whose property, objects may be found and whether such objects were hidden or lost. All finds should be reported to the Procurator Fiscal and Queen's and Lord Treasurer's Remembrancer. The ownership of artefacts from excavations undertaken by central government, where the Crown does not claim them as Treasure Trove, is passed to the Secretary of State for Scotland. Ownership is then passed, on the recommendation of the Finds Disposal Panel, to the appropriate museum (Historic Scotland 1993).

3.9.11 The rules of ownership applicable to material which has come from a vessel (*i.e.* all those classified as 'wreck'), differ from those applicable to material on land and materials found on the seabed which is not wreck. Under the *Merchant Shipping Act* 1894, original owners have one year in which to claim ownership, after which the material is sold with the proceeds going to the Crown. The Act is implemented such that ownership of historic wreck may be passed to the salvor in lieu of a salvage award. The Department of Transport, which administers the Act, have said that it favours the retention of material by museums, but this does not always happen. In cases of wreck material the Marine Emergency Administration Division of the Department of Transport should be contacted. (For further information see Firth 1993, 65ff.)

3.10 Other considerations

N.17 3.10.1 It is advisable for Excavation projects to be governed by a written contract or agreement, to which the agreed *Specification* or *Project Design* may be attached. Such contracts or agreements should be dated, signed by both parties and include reference to the defined area of study outlined on a map, to the *Specification* or *Project Design*, to conditions for access, programme, method and timetable for payment and copyright arrangements (see IFA Technical Paper no. 8).

3.10.2 Unless otherwise agreed in a contract, the copyright of any written or graphic or photographic records and reports rests with the originating body (the archaeological organisation undertaking the fieldwork and analysis), who will licence their use in relation to the specific project by the client or sponsoring body. Such agreements on copyright should be agreed with the sponsoring body at the outset of the project (see Appendix 6).

3.10.3 Material copied or cited in reports should be duly acknowledged; and all copyright conditions (such as those for Ordnance Survey maps) observed.

3.10.4 All aspects of publicity must be agreed at the outset of the project between the commissioning body and the archaeological organisation or individual undertaking the project.

3.10.5 The archaeologists undertaking work must respect the sponsor's or client's requirements over confidentiality, but the archaeologist must emphasise their professional obligation to make the results of archaeological work available to the wider archaeological community within a reasonable time.

3.10.6 The archaeologist or archaeological organisation undertaking such projects must ensure that they have adequate insurance policies, Public and Employer's Liability, some relevant form of civil liability indemnity or Professional Indemnity.

APPENDIX 1: GLOSSARY OF TERMS USED

Appraisal a rapid reconnaissance of site and records to identify **N.18** (within the planning framework) whether a development proposal has a potential archaeological dimension requiring further clarification (ACAO 1993, 4); **or** a rapid reconnaissance of site and records to identify whether a particular project or study area has potential for further academically-oriented research involving non-intrusive or intrusive methods

Assessment (Desk-based) an assessment of the known or potential archaeological resource within a specified area or site (land-based, inter-tidal or marine), consisting of a collation of existing written and graphic information, in order to identify the likely character, extent and relative quality of the actual or potential resource. (See also *Standard and Guidance for Archaeological Desk-based Assessments*.)

Brief/Project Outline an outline framework of the archaeological circumstances which have to be addressed, together with an indication of the scope of works that will be required. In Scotland the Brief may be reffered to as a Project Outline (see Historic Scotland 1993).

Client the individual or organisation commissioning and funding the project

Curator a person or organisation responsible for the conservation and management of archaeological evidence by virtue of official or statutory duty, including for example County or District Archaeological Officers, Regional Archaeology Officers, national bodies such as English Heritage and Cadw.

Data Structure Report an initial organisation on paper, of the information retrieved from an excavation, comprising a narrative account of the site sequence, indices, or contexts, drawings, photographs, small finds, and environmental samples, and a list of project documentation. This report is relevant in Scotland and there is no broad equivilent elsewhere in the UK. Details are given in Historic Scotland 1993.

Environmental Assessment a systematic analysis of a project's potential effects on all aspects of the environment including cultural heritage, in order to provide information for the deciding agency to consider in the decision-making process, and further give bodies with relevant environmental responsibilities the opportunity to comment before consent is given. EA applies to projects having significant environmental effects as set out in Directive 86/337/EEC and as implemented in the UK, which came into effect in July 1988.

Evaluation
a limited programme of non-intrusive and/or intrusive fieldwork which determines of the presence or absence of archaeological features, structures, deposits, artefacts or ecofacts within a specified area or site; and, if present, defines their character and extent, and relative quality. It enables an assessment of their worth in a local, regional, national or international context as appropriate.

Planning archaeologist see curator.

Post-excavation Assessment
the process carried out after the completion of fieldwork in order to assess the potential for further analysis and publication. This involves the assessment of the findings (as represented in the site archive) against the original Project Design. It may result in the production of an Up-dated Project Design, which will incorporate any new research questions identified. Post-excavation Assessment must result in the production of a report.

Project Design
a written statement on the project's objectives, methods, timetable and resources, forming the framework for the execution of the project through to completion, set out in sufficient detail to be quantifiable, implemented and monitored. Normally prepared by an archaeologist or organisation undertaking the fieldwork, frequently in response to a Brief or Specification.

Project Outline
see brief

Specification
a written schedule of works required for a particular project (by a curator, planning archaeologist or client), set out in sufficient detail to be quantifiable, implemented and monitored. Normally prepared by or agreed with the relevant curator.

APPENDIX 2: EXCAVATION TECHNIQUES AND RECORDING TECHNIQUES

N.19   This standard covers the following methods of excavation: Hand-excavated open areas and/or trenches; Machine-stripped and hand excavated open areas and/or trenches; Auguring; and Probing (frequently used underwater). An excavation project may be supplemented by non-destructive means of investigation, such as: Geophysical survey; Remote sensing; Geochemical survey; Earthwork survey; Field scanning (*i.e.* observation and mapping of artefact and other distributions); and Standing building survey.

There are a number of techniques available for archaeological excavation. In many instances several techniques may be valid under the terms of the brief/project outline, and it will be necessary to explain the criteria for selection. The methods selected must be fit for the defined purpose and therefore related to the research objectives. Where the use of machinery is specified this must be under the direct supervision of an archaeologist.

Full and proper records (written, graphic, digital and photographic as appropriate) should be made for all work, using *pro forma* records and sheets appropriate to the work. A range of recording systems is available, and many archaeological contractors have produced manuals to govern their recording procedures and ensure internal consistency.

The recording system used should be one that is appropriate to the requirements of the project in question and should be agreed with relevant parties including the body that is to receive the archvie. It should entail: relating the site and excavation areas to the National Grid and the Ordnance Survey datum; relating all plan and section drawings to the site grid; maintaining written registers of all plans, drawings, photographs, special finds, samples, etc; and compiling records on suitable, durable materials.

APPENDIX 3: CONTENTS OF PROJECT DESIGN

The Project Design should contain, as a minimum, the following elements: **N.20**

1 Non-technical summary (intelligible to the lay reader);
2 Site location including map(s) and description (NGR, size, geology, land-use, topography, physical constrains)
3 Context of the project: planning background, planning policies, other environmental matters, Scheduled Monument and listed building constraints, Protected Wrecks, relevant legislation, details of proposed development if relevant;
4 Geological and topographical background;
5 Archaeological and historical background (including built, landscape and technical, plan or NGR, site status);
6 Aims of fieldwork (clearly stated in both general and specific aims);
7 Field methodology (techniques selected, with justification for selection; detailed exposition of techniques, artefact collection policies, discard policies, environmental collection strategy and implementation, recording techniques, and any measures for the conservation/reburial of surviving deposits);
8 Post-fieldwork methodologies (cleaning, conservation, cataloguing, packaging, dating techniques, archive preparation);
9 Report preparation, contents;
10 Copyright;
11 Archive deposition (including finds ownership, recipient museum/ repository);
12 Publication and dissemination proposals;
13 Timetable;
14 Staffing;
15 Health and Safety policies and implementation, including Risk Assessment;
16 Insurances;
17 Monitoring procedures (internal, curatorial, contractual);
18 Costs (or these may be presented in a covering letter).

A contracting archaeologist responding to a tender with a Specification may refer to these elements if defined in a Brief/Project Outline or Specification set by curator or client, rather than repeat them in a Project Design.

APPENDIX 4: CONTENTS OF POST-EXCAVATION ASSESSMENT REPORT

N.21 The level of detail required in the Post-excavation Assessment Report will depend on the quantity and complexity of data and the extent to which those factors have required additional study of the material in order to form a reliable assessment.

A Post-excavation Assessment Report will normally contain:

1 Introduction:
    Scope of the project (eg sites involved)
    Circumstances and dates of fieldwork and previous work
    Comments on the organisations of the report
2 Original research aims
3 Summary of the documented history of the site(s)
4 Interim statement on the results of fieldwork
5 Summary of the site archive and work carried out for assessment:
    Site records: quantity, work done on records during Post-excavation Assessment;
    Finds: factual summary of material and records, quantity, range, variety, preservation, work done during Post-excavation Assessment;
    Environmental material: factual summary of human and animal bone, shell and each type of sample (eg bulk organic, dendrochronological, monolith), quantity, range, variety, preservation, work done on the material during Post-excavation Assessment;
    Documentary records: list of relevant sources discovered, quantity, variety, intensity of study of sources during Post-excavation Assessment.
6 Potential of the Data:
    — A discursive appraisal of the extent to which the site archive might enable the data to meet the project's research aims. Different classes of data should be discussed in an integrated fashion, sub-divided according to the research aims of the project.
    — A statement of the data's potential to develop new research aims, to contribute to other projects and to advance methodologies.
7 A summary of the potential of the date of local, regional, national and international importance.
Additional information will normally include:
    Supporting illustration at appropriate scales (ref archive deposition guidelines);
    Sufficient supporting data, tabulated or in appendices, and/or details of the contents of the project archvie, to permit the interrogation of the stated conclusions; and
    Index, and references.

APPENDIX 5: UP-DATED PROJECT DESIGN

The Up-dated Project Design should be a written document. It should **N.22** include:

1 The methodology used to answer each research aim
   — detailed methodologies for each type of data
   — non-analytical procedures, eg proposals for disposal/retention and for archive deposition
2 Preliminary publication synopsis
   — the proposed publication outlet(s)
   — a chapter by chapter breakdown of the report, supported by estimates of word counts and figure lists
   — how it is intended to integrate specialist reports and to cross-refer between different parts of the text
3 Resource requirements
4 Cascade chart

It may be helpful to include or append a copy of all or part of the original Project Design, for ease of reference.

APPENDIX 6: COPYRIGHT

Under the *Copyright, Designs and Patents Act* 1988 the organisation or **N.23** person undertaking field and reporting work retains the copyright to the written and graphic material, unless this has been varied in the contract for the work. This position should be made clear to all relevant parties at the outset of work.

The circumstances under which the report or records can be used by other parties should be made clear at the inception of the project. For example one of these clauses could be incorporated into the Specification or Project Design:

> The ..... [name or organisation carrying out work] ..... shall retain full copyright of any commissioned reports, tender documents or other project documents, under the *Copyright, Designs and Patents Act* 1988 with all rights reserved; excepting that it hereby provides an exclusive licence to the client for the use of such documents by the client in all matters directly relating to the project as described in the Project Design/Specification.
>
> or
>
> The ..... [name of organisation] ..... will assign copyright to the client upon written request but retains the right to be identified as the author of all project documentation and reports as defined in the *Copyright, Designs and Patents Act* 1988 (Chapter IV, s. 79).

In the last instance a further letter actually granting copyright needs to be sent to the client.

The proposals for distribution of the report must be made clear to all parties at the outset of the field project.

Appendix O

STANDARD

An Archaeological Watching Brief will record the archaeological resource **O.1**
during development within a specified area using appropriate methods of
study which satisfy the stated aims of the project, and which comply with
the Codes of Practice of the Institute of Field Archaeologists.

DEFINITION OF WATCHING BRIEF

Archaeological Watching Brief is defined as a formal programme of observa- **O.2**
tion and investigation conducted during any operation carried out for
non-archaeological reasons within a specified area or site or underwater,
where there is the possibility that archaeological deposits may be disturbed
or destroyed. The programme will result in the preparation of a report and
ordered archive.

This definition and Standard do not include chance observations, which
should lead to an appropriate archaeological project being designed and
implemented, nor do they include monitoring for preservation of remains *in
situ.*

PURPOSE

An Archaeological Watching Brief will in all cases be intended: **O.3**

- to allow, within the resources available, the preservation by record of
  archaeological deposits, presence and nature of which could not be
  established (or established with sufficient accuracy) in advance of
  development or other potentially disruptive works.
- to provide an opportunity, if needed, for the watching archaeologist to
  signal to all interested parties, before the destruction of the material in
  question, that an archaeological find has been made for which the

resources allocated to the watching brief itself are not sufficient to support a treatment to a satisfactory and proper standard.

An Archaeological Watching Brief will not be intended to reduce the requirement for excavation or preservation of known or probable deposits, and it will be intended only to guide, not to replace, any requirement for contingent excavation or preservation of possible deposits.

An Archaeological Watching Brief will be intended to establish and make available information about the archaeological resource existing on a site.

OCCURRENCE

O.4 Watching Briefs may occur:

- in response to a proposed development which threatens the archaeological resource;
  as part of the planning process (within the framework of appropriate national planning policy guidance notes) and/or development plan policy;
  as part of an Environmental Assessment (see 3.1 below);
  or outside the planning process (eg ecclesiastical development, agriculture and forestry, works by statutory undertakers).
- within a programme of research not generated by a specific threat to the archaeological resource.
- in connection with the preparation of management plans by private, local or national bodies.

Watching Briefs may therefore be instigated or commissioned by a number of different individuals or organisations, including Local Planning Authorities, national advisory bodies, government agencies, private landowners, developers or their archaeological researchers etc.

GUIDANCE

1 INTRODUCTION

O.5 1.1 This guidance seeks to define best practice for the execution of Archaeological Watching Briefs and concomitant reporting in line with the By-laws of the Institute of Field Archaeologists (in particular *The Code of Conduct* and *The Code of Approved Practice for the Regulation of Contractual Arrangements in Field Archaeology*). It seeks to expand and explain general definitions in the Codes for the actual practice of fieldwork and reporting.

1.2 The Standard and guidance apply to watching briefs which are land-based, inter-tidal and underwater, whether generated by research, by management proposals, through the planning framework or by any other proposals which may affect the archaeological resource within a specified area.

1.3 In addition the guidance seeks to amplify that given in *Planning Policy*

Guidance Note 16 (PPG 16; Dept of Environment 1990) and its equivalents, and to be compatible with current guidelines issued by regulatory authorities.

1.4 The terminology used follows PPG 16, guidance issued by the Association of County Archaeological Officers (ACAO 1993) and English Heritage (1991), with amplifications where necessary. It tries to take account of different terminology, legal and administrative practice in different parts of the UK. A glossary of terms used may be found in Appendix 1.

1.5 This document provides guidance for work carried out in the British Isles. Whilst general guidance is given, this document cannot be exhaustive; archaeologists working in the different countries and regions must ensure that they are familiar with the specific laws and regulations pertinent to those areas.

2 PRINCIPLES: THE BY-LAW OF THE INSTITUTE OF FIELD ARCHAEOLOGISTS

2.1 An archaeologist undertaking Archaeological Watching Briefs must adhere to the four principles enshrined in the Institute of Field Archaeologists' Code of Conduct and the rules governing those principles: **O.6**

1 The archaeologist shall adhere to the highest standards of ethical and responsible behaviour in the conduct of archaeological affairs.
2 The archaeologist has a responsibility for the conservation of the archaeological heritage.
3 The archaeologist shall conduct his or her work in such a way that reliable information about the past may be required, and shall ensure that the results be properly recorded.
4 The archaeologist has responsibility for making available the results of archaeological work with reasonable dispatch.

2.2 Further, the *Code of Approved Practice for the Regulation of Contractual Arrangements in Field Archaeology* specifically addresses professional conduct in situations where work is sponsored or commissioned on a contractual basis, especially as part of development controlled by the planning process. It provides guidance on professional behaviour where more than one individual or body are competing for the same piece of work, and seeks to ensure that the terms and conditions for all work are clearly defined, normally by contract.

3 PROCEDURES

3.1 Project identification

3.1.1 *Within the planning framework* in England, Wales and Scotland the desirability of preservation of archaeological deposits is now a material consideration, and consequently "developers and local authorities should take into account archaeological considerations **O.7** and deal with them from the beginning of the development control process" (*Planning Policy Guidance Note 16* and Scottish Office Environment Department 1994). Local planning authorities can reasonably attach conditions to grants of consent in order to safeguard the resource. Such conditions may require specific courses of action or may use a negative condition; alternatively a developer may conclude a voluntary planning agreement (Section 106 Agreements) to enable certain works to take place. Even where careful consideration of the likely archaeological resource has occurred and appropriate strategies for its preservation devised the possibility of unexpected discoveries occurring during development remains.

3.1.2 An Archaeological Watching Brief will normally be attached as a condition of consent or form part of a scheme of investigation devised by an applicant to satisfy a negative condition in instances where other forms of action would not be appropriate for the identified or potential archaeological resource.

3.1.3 Certain developments fall within special regulations or statute different from or additional to the standard planning process (*e.g.* some projects initiated by Statutory Undertakers, Crown Commissioners, Ministry of Defence etc). Certain of these organisations subscribe to codes of practice (*e.g.* the Water Companies) or agreements (formal or informal) with the lead national archaeological bodies to take into consideration the effects of development proposals on the archaeological resource.

3.1.4 **Whether the Watching Brief has arisen through the planning framework (including Environmental Assessment), from research interests, or management proposals, an archaeologist should only undertake a Watching Brief which is governed by a written *Specification* or *Project Design* prepared in consultation with or approved by the relevant planning archaeologist or curator, as this is the tool against which performance, fitness for purpose, and hence achievement of Standard can be measured.**

3.1.5 The *Specification* or *Project Design* is therefore of critical importance.

3.2 Briefs/project outlines, specifications and project designs

O.8   3.2.1 A *Brief/Project Outline* is a simple outline framework of the situation to be addressed, with an indication of the scope of works that will be required (IFA By-Law; ACAO 1993). It does not provide sufficient detail to form the basis for a measurable standard; but it could form the basis for a *Specification* or a *Project Design*.

3.2.2 A *Specification* sets out a schedule of works in sufficient detail for it to be quantifiable, implemented and monitored (ACAO 1993). It should be sufficient to form the basis for a measurable standard (Appendix 2).

3.2.3 A *Project Design* also sets out a schedule of works in sufficient detail to be quantifiable, implemented and monitored, and therefore also forms the basis for a measurable standard. However, a *Project Design* may include additional information which covers contractual details such as staffing levels or cost relevant to the commissioning but not necessarily the monitoring body. A *Project Design* may be prepared in response to a *Brief/Project Outline* or *Specification*; or it may be a research proposal generated independently of the planning framework. (Project Designs and their contents are further addressed in Appendix 3 and English Heritage 1991, Appendix 2.)

3.2.4 A *Brief/Project Outline* or a *Specification* may form the basis for a *Project Design*. For Watching Briefs within the planning framework, the *Brief/Project Outline* or *Specification* will usually be prepared by the planning archaeologist or curator and issued by the commissioning body (the developer or their agent) to selected tenderers, who respond with a costed *Project Design*. The *Brief/Project Outline* or a *Specification* may be prepared by the applicant or their agent, but it is essential that the planning archaeologist has agreed the proposals, so that they have been accepted as 'fit for purpose'.

3.2.5 *Briefs/Project Outlines, Specifications* and *Project Designs* must be prepared by suitably qualified and experienced persons, utilising specialist advice where necessary.

3.2.6 An archaeologist shall only undertake an Archaeological Watching Brief, which is governed by a written and agreed *Specification* or *Project Design* prepared in advance of work commencing. The *Specification* or *Project Design* must identify the objectives, scope, geographical area, and means of dissemination of the results of the watching brief, and incorporate a method statement and work programme. The *Specification* or *Project Design* should conform to the *Brief/Project Outline* if one has been set, and must in any case be approved in advance by the planning archaeologist or curator.

3.2.7 No Watching Brief should take place on the basis of a *Brief/Project Outline* alone, as it could not achieve the appropriate standard (there being nothing to measure performance against).

3.2.8 In preparing a *Specification* or *Project Design* for the work, the archaeologist shall establish the intention of the work, and the extent to which archaeological considerations will be allowed to affect the development schedule. The archaeologist shall establish the scope of the watching brief, whether comprehensive (present during all groundworks), intensive (present during sensitive groundworks), intermittent (viewing the trenches after machining), or partial (as and when seems appropriate).

3.2.9 An archaeologist preparing a *Specification* or *Project Design* must be fully apprasied of all relevant legislation, and must abide by it.

3.2.10 The *Specification* should contain the following elements:-

- Introduction (occasion circumstance)
- Context of the project (scope, objectives)
- Archaeological and historical background
- General and specific aims of fieldwork
- Field methodology

- Procedure for signalling unexpectedly significant or complex discovery
- Post-fieldwork methodologies
- Report preparation and contents
- Archive deposition
- Publication

3.2.11 The *Specification* or *Project Design* must be agreed by all parties concerned before work commences.

3.2.12 The *Specification* or *Project Design* should contain, as a minimum, the following elements:

- Site Location (including map) and description
- Context of the project
- Geological and topographical background
- Archaeological and historical background
- General and specific aims of project
- Field methodology
- Post-fieldwork methodologies
- Report preparation, contents and distribution
- Copyright
- Archive deposition
- Publication and dissemination proposals
- Timetable
- Staffing
- Health & Safety Statement
- Any other specific necessary reference to legislation
- Monitoring procedures
- Contingency arrangements (if appropriate)

3.2.13 The contents, and different weighting of detail between *Specification* and *Project Design* contents are further amplified in Appendices 2 and 3. *Briefs Project Outlines* and *Specifications* are also discussed in detail in ACAO 1993.

3.2.14 An archaeologist responding to a tender which includes a *Brief/ Project Outline* or *Specification* may refer to these elements in the *Project Design* if they are set out in sufficient detail, rather than repeat them. Any variation to the *Project Design* or *Specification* must be agreed in writing with the sponsor and all relevant parties.

3.2.15 The *Project Design* must include the *Specification* and the following additional elements:-

- Insurance
- Staff (levels and competence)
- Timetable
- Health & Safety Arrangements
- Monitoring procedures
- Costings (including any contingency)

3.3 Fieldwork

3.3.1 All fieldwork undertaken must conform to the agreed *Specification* **O.9** and/or *Project Design*. Variations must be confirmed in writing by all relevant parties.

3.3.2 All techniques used must comply with relevant legislation and be demonstrably fit for the defined purpose(s).

3.3.3 Full and proper records (written, graphic, digital and photographic as appropriate) should be made for all work, using pro forma record forms and sheets, and/or text descriptions appropriate to the work.

3.3.4 All staff, including sub-contractors, must be suitably qualified and experienced for their project roles, and employed in line with IFA Codes and practices. The site director and/or manager should preferably be a member of IFA.

3.3.5 All staff, including sub-contractors, must be fully briefed and understand of the work required under the *Specification*, all Health and Safety implications and of any restrictions placed on the watching archaeologist because of the nature of the site and/or development type.

3.3.6 Sufficient and appropriate resources (staff, equipment, accommodation etc) must be used to enable the project to achieve its aims, the desired quality and timetable, and to comply with all statutory requirements. Any contingency elements must be clearly identified and justified. It is the role of the archaeologist undertaking the work to define appropriate staff levels.

3.3.7 All equipment must be suitable for the purpose and in sound condition and comply with Health and Safety Executive recommendations. It should be noted that diving equipment in particular is subject to statutory controls under the Diving Operations at Work Regulations, over and above the suitability for purpose and sound condition.

3.3.8 Artefact and environmental data collection is a standard element of any intrusive field evaluation. Project collection and discard policies, strategies and discard policies must be fit for the defined purpose, and understood by all staff and sub-contractors. (See also *Guidelines for Finds Work*, IFA 1992 and *Standard and Guidance for Finds and Ecofact Studies and Curation*, IFA forthcoming.)

3.3.9 The requirements of Health and Safety cannot be ignored no matter how imperative the need to record archaeological information; hence Health and Safety will take priority over archaeological matters. All archaeologists undertaking fieldwork must do so under a defined Health and Safety Policy. Archaeologists must observe all safe working practices, whether required by their own policies or those of the principal development contractor, and they should ensure that health and safety arrangements must be agreed by all relevant parties before commencement of work. Risk Assessments must be carried out and documented for every field project. For further guidance refer to the bibliography (Appendix 6).

3.3.10 On arrival on site, the archaeologist(s) should report to the site manager or other identified representative of the principal contractors or developer, and conform to their arrangements for notification of entering and leaving site.

3.3.11 Where the archaeologist has by instruction or agreement the power to suspend development work, he or she shall, in exercising such power, follow procedures previously agreed with the other contractors on the site. Within the constraints of the nature of the archaeological resource, the archaeologist shall not cause unreasonable disruption to the maintenance of the work schedules of other contractors.

3.3.12 An archaeologist should keep a record of the date, time and duration of all visits, the number of staff concerned and any actions taken.

3.4 Monitoring

O.10 3.4.1 All work must be monitored, by the archaeological organisation undertaking the work (*i.e.* tracking), and if appropriate by the planning archaeologist and commissioning body, or their nominated representatives see for example, Darvill in Hunter and Ralston 1993, 169ff). The guidance below is directed in general at monitors from outside the organisation undertaking the work. However, many of the points apply equally to internal monitors or managers (*e.g.* 3.4.2).

3.4.2 A monitor should be suitably experienced and qualified, or have access to appropriate specialist advice, in order to monitor field and post-field work properly.

3.4.3 Monitoring must be undertaken against the written *Specification* and/or *Project Design*.

3.4.4 Monitors, where not representing the commissioning body, must be careful not to instruct the archaeologist undertaking the work to vary the agreed *Specification* or *Project Design* without consultation with all relevant parties, particularly if this will result in a variation of contract and cost.

3.4.5 Monitors, where not representing the commissioning body, should bear in mind the need for flexibility, within the stated parameters, in contractual matters such as staff numbers, budgets or timetable.

3.4.6 All monitoring visits must be documented by both parties.

3.4.7 Non-compliance with the agreed *Specification* or *Project Design* must be pointed out by the monitor to the archaeologists undertaking the work, and their client if appropriate, at the earliest opportunity (see ACAO 1993, section E(vii), 17).

3.4.8 Monitors should be aware of their legal duties, particularly regarding Health and Safety and the reporting and advising against bad and unsafe practice.

3.4.9 All monitoring arrangements must be mutually agreed at the outset of the project; the archaeologist undertaking fieldwork must inform the planning archaeologist or other monitor of the work with reasonable notice.

3.4.10 Whilst the monitor may choose to visit at any time, they should normally inform the archaeologist undertaking the work of any intended visits in advance. Monitors must respect reasonable requests from the client commissioning the work to attend only at pre-arranged times and, if necessary in the company of the client's representative.

3.4.11 Any costs for monitoring to be charged by the planning archaeologist or other monitor must be agreed at the outset of the project.

3.5 Post-fieldwork analyses and reports

3.5.1 All retained artefacts and ecofacts must be cleaned, conserved and packaged in accordance with the requirements of the recipient museum and/or national guidelines. **O.11**

3.5.2 The project archives must be prepared in accordance with the requirements of the recipient museum and national guidelines.

3.5.3 All analytical and assessment work must be carried out by suitably qualified and experienced staff.

3.5.4 All staff, including sub-contractors, must be fully appraised of the Specification or Project Design before commencing work, and should fully understand the work required of them.

3.5.5 The level of recording and analysis of artefacts and ecofacts should be appropriate to the aims and purpose of the project, and should not exceed the requirements of the *Specification* or *Project Design* unless variation has been agreed.

3.5.6 An archaeologist shall ensure that the results of the watching brief are disseminated in a reasonable time through appropriate means. Copies of the report should be submitted to the relevant Sites and Monuments Record within six months.

3.5.7 Copies of a site summary (see English Heritage 1991) must be submitted to the appropriate Sites and Monuments Record, the National Archaeological Record and, where appropriate the central government conservation organisation within 6 months of completion of the fieldwork.

3.5.8 In Scotland the primary product of fieldwork is the Data Structure Report (Historic Scotland 1993) with a costed assessment for further fieldwork and/or post-excavation and publication. This report does not have a broad equivalent elsewhere in the UK (see Appendix 1).

3.6 Archives, ownership and deposition

3.6.1 The requirements for archive preparation and deposition must be addressed at the outset of the project. **O.12**

3.6.2 The proposed recipient museum or other repository must be contacted at the project planning stage, and particular project arrangement for the deposition of the site archive should be detailed in the *Specification* and/or *Project Design*.

3.6.3 Archive deposition must take account of the requirements of the recipient museum or repository, and the relevant sections of the Museums and Galleries Commissions Guidelines relating to the preparation and transfer of archives or the appropriate national guidelines. A copy of the paper archive should be lodged with the appropriate national archaeological record, in accordance with their specific requirements.

3.6.4   In Scotland, the paper archive is lodged with the National Monuments Record of Scotland although finds are deposited in a museum; a second copy of all or parts of the paper archive should be made available to the museum receiving the finds.

3.6.5   The site and research archives (English Heritage 1991, appendices 3 and 6) generated during fieldwork and post-fieldwork should be deposited with the recipient museum in the required format. Artefacts and environmental data form part of those archives.

3.6.6   In England, Wales, Northern Ireland the Isle of Man ownership of objects rests with the landowner, except where other law overrides this (*e.g.* Treasure Trove; *Burials Act* 1857). The archaeologist undertaking the fieldwork or the planning archaeologist must make this clear at the inception of the project (in the *Brief*, *Specification* or *Project Design*). But, in advance of fieldwork, the landowner's consent should be obtained, if possible, to donate and deposit the finds with the site and research documentary archive in the appropriate recipient museum.

3.6.7   It should be noted that the different areas have, *inter alia*, differing reporting procedures for Treasure Trove, differing requirements for finds deposition, and that material cannot be exported from the Isle of Man without a licence. A licence is required for excavation work in the Isle of Man and Northern Ireland. Archaeologists unfamiliar with the procedures in any area should seek guidance from the appropriate authorities (see Appendices 6 and 7).

3.6.8   Except in Scotland, it is the responsibility of the archaeologist undertaking the fieldwork to endeavour to obtain the consent of the landowner in writing for finds' donation and deposition with the recipient museum.

3.6.9   Except in Scotland, in the event that the landowner is unwilling, for whatever reason, to donate the finds to the appropriate recipient museum, the archaeologist undertaking the fieldwork must endeavour to ensure all artefacts and ecofacts are recorded, safely packaged and conserved where appropriate before transfer to the owner, and that their location/ownership is stated in the site archive and public record. It should be noted that the owner's explicit (written) permission is required before entering such personal information in the public record (cf. *inter alia* the *Data Protection Act* 1984).

3.6.10 In Scotland all newly-discovered ancient objects, whether precious metal or not, may be claimed as on behalf of the Crown, if their owner cannot be traced. The law applies no matter where, or on whose property, objects may be found and whether such objects may be hidden or lost. All finds should be reported to the Procurator Fiscal and Queen's and Lord Treasurer's Remembrancer. The ownership of artefacts from excavations undertaken by central government, where the Crown does not claim them as Treasure Trove, is passed to the Secretary of State for Scotland. Ownership is then passed, on the recommendation of the Finds Disposal Panel, to the appropriate museum (Historic Scotland 1993).

3.6.11 The rules of ownership applicable to material which has come from a vessel (*i.e.* all those classified as a 'wreck') differ from those applicable to material on land and material found on the seabed which is not wreck. Under the *Merchant Shipping Act* 1894 original owners have one year in which to claim ownership, after which the material is sold with the proceeds going to the Crown. The Act is implemented such that ownership of historic wreck maybe passed to the salvor in lieu of a salvage award. The Department of Transport, which administers the Act, have said that it favours the retention of material by museums, but this does not always happen. In cases of wreck material the Marine Emergency Administration Division of the Department of Transport should be contacted. (For further information see Firth 1993, 65ff.)

3.7   Other considerations

3.7.1   An archaeologist or archaeological organisation undertaking such projects must ensure that they have adequate insurance policies, Public Liability, some relevant form of civil liability indemnity or Professional Indemnity.   **O.13**

3.7.2   It is advisable that archaeological projects are by a written contract to which the agreed *Specification* is attached. Those for *Archaeological watching Briefs* will often be of the *standard form* or *fixed price* type (cf Darvill & Atkins 1991). They should be dated and signed by both parties and include reference to area of development outlined on an attached map, reference to the Specification, permission for access, indemnification arrangements, completion of report, method and timetable of payment and/or retention, and copyright arrangements.

3.7.3   Unless otherwise agreed in a contract, the copyright of any written or graphic or photographic records and reports rests with the originating body (the archaeological organisation undertaking the fieldwork and analysis), who will licence their use in relation to the specific project by the client or sponsoring body. Such agreements on copyright should be agreed with the sponsoring body at the outset of the project (see Appendix 5).

3.7.4   Material copied or cited in reports should be duly acknowledged; and all copyright conditions (such as those for Ordnance Survey maps) observed.

3.7.5   All aspects of publicity must be agreed at the outset of the project between the commissioning body and the archaeological organisation or individual undertaking the project.

3.7.6   All archaeologists undertaking work must respect the sponsor's or client's requirements over confidentiality, but the archaeologist must endeavour to emphasise their professional obligation to make the results of archaeological work available to the wider archaeological community within a reasonable time (see 3.5.11).

3.7.7   Statutory requirements regarding archaeological matters vary within the United Kingdom, commissioning bodies and others may therefore find it useful to consult the relevant documents listed in Appendix 5 and can obtain further guidance from the appropriate advisory bodies listed in Appendix 6.

APPENDIX 1: GLOSSARY OF TERMS USED

O.14   **Appraisal**   a rapid reconnaissance of site and records to identify (within the planning framework) whether a development proposal has a potential archaeological dimension requiring further clarification (ACAO 1993, 4); **or**
a rapid reconnaissance of site and records to identify whether a particular project or study area has potential for further academically-oriented research involving non-intrusive or intrusive methods

Assessment (Desk-Based)   an assessment of the known or potential archaeological resource within a specified area or site (land-based, inter-tidal or marine), consisting of a collation of existing written and graphic information, in order to identify the likely character, extent and relative quality of the actual or potential resource. (See also *Standard and Guidance for Archaeological Desk-Based Assessments*.)

Brief/Propject Outline an outline framework of the archaeological circumstances which have to be addressed, together with an indication of the scope of works that will be required. In Scotland the Brief may be reffered to as a Project Outline (see Historic Scotland 1993).

Client   the individual or organisation commissioning and funding the project

Curator   a person or organisation responsible for the conservation and management of archaeological evidence by virtue of official or statutory duty, including for example County or District Archaeological Officers, Regional Archaeology Officers, national bodies such as English Heritage and Cadw.

Data Structure Report an initial organisation on paper, of the information retrieved from an excavation, comprising a narrative account of the site sequence, indices, or contexts, drawings, photographs, small finds, and environmental samples, and a list of project documentation. This report is relevant in Scotland and there is no broad equivalent elsewhere in the UK. Details are given in Historic Scotland 1993.

Environmental Assessment	a systematic analysis of a project's potential effects on all aspects of the environment including cultural heritage, in order to provide information for the deciding agency to consider in the decision-making process, and further give bodies with relevant environmental responsibilities the opportunity to comment before consent is given. EA applies to projects having significant environmental effects as set out in Directive 86/337/EEC and as implemented in the UK, which came into effect in July 1988.
Evaluation	a limited programme of non-intrusive and/or intrusive fieldwork which determines of the presence or absence of archaeological features, structures, deposits, artefacts or ecofacts within a specified area or site; and, if present, defines their character and extent, and relative quality. It enables an assessment of their worth in a local, regional, national or international context as appropriate.
Planning archaeologist	see curator.
Project Design	a written statement on the project's objectives, methods, timetable and resources, forming the framework for the execution of the project through to completion, set out in sufficient detail to be quantifiable, implemented and monitored. Normally prepared by an archaeologist or organisation undertaking the fieldwork, frequently in response to a Brief or Specification.
Specification	a written schedule of works required for a particular project (by a curator, planning archaeologist or client), set out in sufficient detail to be quantifiable, implemented and monitored. Normally prepared by or agreed with the relevant curator.

APPENDIX 2: PREPARATION OF SPECIFICATION

The Specification should contain, as a minimum, the following elements: **0.15**

- Non-technical summary (intelligible to the lay reader)
- Site location and description (NGR, size, geology, land-use, topography, physical constrains)
- Planning Background (proposed details, planning policies, other environmental matters, Scheduled Monument constraints, Protected Wrecks etc)
- Archaeological and Historical Background (including plan or NGR, site status)
- Purpose/aims of fieldwork (clearly stated in both general and specific aims)
- Field methodology (techniques selected, with justification for selection; detailed exposition of techniques, artefact collection policies, discard

policies, environmental collection strategy and implementation, recording techniques)
- Post-fieldwork methodologies (cleaning, conservation, cataloguing, packaging, dating techniques, archive preparation)
- Report preparation, contents and distribution
- Copyright
- Archive deposition (including finds ownership, recipient museum)
- Publication and dissemination
- Timetable, if appropriate
- Staffing—in general terms only—*e.g.* the site director should be a member of the Institute of Field Archaeologists, but **not** the number of staff
- Health and Safety statement
- Monitoring procedures required by the curator, including any charges
- Procedures for reporting unexpectedly significant or complex discovery

APPENDIX 3: PROJECT DESIGN CONTENTS

O.16   The Project Design should contain, as a minimum, the following elements:

- Non-technical summary (intelligible to the lay reader)
- Site location and description (NGR, size, geology, land-use, topography, physical constraints)
- Planning Background (proposal details, planning policies, other environmental matters, Scheduled Monument constraints, Protected Wrecks), if appropriate
- Geological and topographical background
- Archaeological and Historical Background (including built landscape and technical, plan or NGR, site status)
- Purpose/aims of fieldwork (clearly stated in both general and specific aims)
- Field methodology (techniques selected, with justification of selection; detailed exposition of techniques, artefact collection policies, discard policies, environmental collection strategy and implementation, recording techniques, and any measures for the conservation/reburial of surviving deposits)
- Post-fieldwork methodologies (cleaning, conservation, cataloguing, packaging, dating techniques, archive preparation)
- Report preparation and contents
- Copyright
- Archive deposition (including finds ownership, recipient museum)
- Publication and dissemination proposals
- Timetable
- Staffing
- Health and Safety policies and implementation, including Risk Assessment Insurances
- Monitoring procedures (internal, curatorial, contractual)
- Procedures for reporting unexpectedly significant or complex discovery
- Costs (or these may be presented in a covering letter)

A contracting archaeologist responding to a tender with specification may refer to these elements if defined in a *Brief* or *Specification* set by curator or client, rather than repeat them in a *Project Design*.

APPENDIX 4: REPORT CONTENTS

The specific requirements of any report will necessarily vary according to the scope of works, the nature of the results or other factors. However, the following sections will occur in most reports:

O.17

Non-technical summary
    This should outline, in plain, non-technical language the principle reason for the work, its objectives and main results; and should include reference to authorship and commissioning body.

Introductory statements
    These could include acknowledgements, circumstances of the project such as planning background, the archaeological background, an outline nature of work, the site description (including size, geology and topography, location), when the project was undertaken and by whom.

Aims and Objectives
    These should reflect or reiterate the aims set out in the *Project Design* or *Specification*.

Methodology
    The methods used, including the detail of any variation to the agreed *Project Design* or *Specification* should be set out carefully, and explained as appropriate.

Results
    These should be set out as a series of summary objective statements, organised clearly in relation to the methods used, and describing both structural data and associated finds and/or environmental data recovered. Descriptive material should be clearly separated from interpretative statements. Technical terminology (including dating or period references) should be explained where necessary if the report is aimed at a largely non-archaeological audience. The results should be amplified where necessary by the use of drawings and photographs; and by supporting data contained in appendices (below).

Conclusions
    It may be appropriate to include a section which sums up and interprets the results and puts them into context (local, national or otherwise). Other elements could include a confidence rating on techniques used, or on limitations imposed by particular factors (*e.g.* weather or problems of access).

Archive location
    The final destination of the archive (records and finds) should be noted in the report. If the archive is likely to remain with the originating body for some time, that should also be noted in the report, along with the reason.

Appendices
    These should contain essential technical and supporting detail, including for example lists of artefacts and contexts or details of

measurements, gazetteers etc. It may also be appropriate to include the *Project Design* or *Specification* for ease of reference.

Figures & Plates

Most reports will need to include one or more illustrations for clarity; as a minimum a location plan should be included. Any plans or sections should be clearly numbered and easily referenced to the National grid and related to the specified area.

References and Bibliography

A list of all sources used should be appended to the report.

Copy of Specification

It may be helpful to include a copy of the original *Specification* in order to assess whether or not the defined aims and objectives have been met. The report can then be used for reference without recourse to other documentation.

APPENDIX 5: COPYRIGHT

O.18 Under the *Copyright, Designs and Patents Act* 1988 the organisation or person undertaking field and reporting work retains the copyright to the written and graphic material, unless this has been varied in the contract for the work. This position should be made clear to all relevant parties at the outset of work.

The circumstances under which the report or records can be used by other parties should be made clear at the inception of the project. For example one of these clauses could be incorporated into the *Specification* or *Project Design*:

The .... [name or organisation carrying out work] shall retain full copyright of any commissioned reports, tender documents or other project documents, under the *Copyright, Designs and Patents Act* 1988 with all rights reserved; excepting that it hereby provide an exclusive licence to the client for the use of such documents by the client in all matters directly relating to the project as described in the Project Specification.

or

The .... [name of organisation] will assign copyright to the client upon written request but retains the right to be identified as the author of all project documentation and reports as defined in the *Copyright, Designs and Patents Act* 1988 (Chapter IV, s. 79).

In the last instance a further letter actually granting copyright needs to be sent to the client.

The proposals for distribution of the report must be made clear to all parties at the outset of the field project.

Appendix P

CODE OF PRACTICE FOR SEABED DEVELOPERS
(JOINT NAUTICAL ARCHAEOLOGY POLICY
COMMITTEE (1995))

INTRODUCTION

Recommended procedures for consultation and co-operation

This Code set out recommended procedures for consultation and co-oper- **P.1** ation between seabed developers and archaeologists. While the general principles can be applied throughout the UK, specific arrangements for consultation may vary between England, Northern Ireland, Scotland and Wales. The recommendations represent current best practice and they will be reviewed in the light of future policy developments.

The sea and seabed have been used by many for thousands of years and today they support a multitude of commercial and leisure uses. However, the diverse uses do not always work in the interests of conservation. This Code is concerned with the underwater archaeological and historical resource. Its purpose is to provide a framework within which the concerns for the maritime archaeological heritage and the interests of other sea users can be reconciled.

The Government's policy on archaeology is stated in Planning Policy Guidance Note no. 16 "Archaeology and Planning":

> Archaeological remains should be seen as a finite and non-retrievable resources, in many cases highly fragile and vulnerable to damage and destruction. Appropriate management is therefore essential to ensure that they survive in good condition. In particular, care must be taken to ensure that archaeological remains are not needlessly or thoughtlessly destroyed. They can contain irreplaceable information about our past and the potential for an increase in future knowledge. They are part of our sense of identity and are valuable both for their own sake and for the sake of education, leisure and tourism.

The same principles apply throughout the UK.

Maritime archaeological sites are equally valuable. There has been a growing awareness in recent years of underwater archaeological sites and discoveries. These include ancient crafts, historic wrecks, drowned settlements and harbours.

The Code's objective is to encourage commercial seabed developers to seek advice on the possible maritime archaeological potential of their proposed development at the earliest opportunity. The involvement of archaeologists during the planning stages of a development will allow the archaeological implications to be considered in line with the overall assessment of the development's environmental impact. Consideration of archaeology under water should be an integral element of environmental assessment.

The Code can assist the tailoring of specific agreements to suit individual situations. Its adoption should open up a non-statutory channel of communication between seabed developers and maritime archaeologists. An early understanding of the maritime archaeological resource will be beneficial to all parties.

For the purposes of this Code, the "seabed" is defined as the area below mean low water. "Development" is defined as "activities directed to the construction, alteration or renewal of any works in or under the seabed and the excavation, removal, movement or deposit of materials, substances or articles in the sea or under the seabed."

The JNAPC Code of Practice for Seabed Developers

P.2   The following undertaking has been made by the British Marine Aggregates Producers Association:

Companies carrying out operations on the seabed who are members of the British Marine Aggregates Producers Association will co-operate with the Joint Nautical Archaeology Policy Committee in the pursuit of aims to preserve archaeological remains.

In the case of a company seeking a licence for seabed mineral extraction, it is normal for the company to carry out a seismic and a bathymetric survey of the area as a first priority and before any other activity takes place. Companies who are members of the British Martine Aggregates Producers Association will be glad to make relevant details of such surveys available to an archaeologist or a body proposed by the Joint Nautical Archaeology Policy Committee, provided that they undertake to guarantee complete commercial confidentiality of the information supplied. When possible, companies will invite an archaeologist to witness the surveys and also to witness a dredging operation.

1   Seabed developers acknowledge the potential scientific value of archaeological evidence on, or concealed within the seabed and will make every effort to report, promptly, unexpected discoveries encountered.

2   The practice of developers making provision for archaeological survey and investigation in advance of development on and is supported by Government, the CBI and local authorities. Seabed developers should therefore take account of the need for co-operation to record and assess the nation's maritime heritage.

3   At the earliest opportunity the developers should seek informed archaeological advice to establish whether potential development programmes

would be likely to affect a site of archaeological interest. Normally, the developer will consult appropriate archaeological bodies see list enclosed.

4   The above bodies will make available to the developer information contained within the appropriate National Monuments Record and the coastal section of the Sites and Monuments Record maintained by the appropriate local authority or equivalent. This will enable the developer and the licensing authority to give due consideration to Government's desire to see archaeological sites physically preserved or recorded.

5   Where such consultation or the developer's own research indicate that important archaeological remains may exist, the developer may make provision for the carrying out by appropriately qualified archaeologists of an underwater survey of the area. The survey will be designed to ascertain the archaeological potential before development commences and what action should be taken to preserve any important archaeological remains located.

6   Consideration will be given to the physical preservation of important archaeological remains in line with the Government's archaeological policies. Where development is unavoidable because of economic or social needs and physical preservation is not possible, archaeological survey and investigation may be an acceptable alternative. Such work will include the establishment of a site archive and the publication of the results of the investigation and survey according to the recommendations in "The Management of Archaeological Projects" published in 1991 by English Heritage or an equivalent standard.

7   Seabed developers and archaeologists will recognise the laws relating to sites, including the Protection of Wrecks Act 1973, and the issues of reporting and ownership of finds under the Merchant Shipping Act 1894.

8   In co-operation with the Receiver of Wreck, seabed developers will ensure that archaeologists may, for the purposes of study and analysis. retain artefacts and records for a reasonable time. Seabed developers will also recognise the desirability of depositing all artefacts and records in an appropriate museum as a complete permanent archive for future study. Copies of all site records should be sent to the relevant local authority Sites and Monuments Record or equivalent and to the appropriate National Monuments Record.

9   The archaeologists will be conscious of the potential public relations benefits to developers of publicising their work, and that in any publicity, financial or other support from the developer should be recognised in a manner agreed by the developer.

10 The developer will present to the licensing authority a copy of the advice provided by archaeological bodies consulted along with his own pro-posals for accommodating any archaeological constraints which have been identified.

Appendix Q

USEFUL NAMES AND ADDRESSES

ANCIENT MONUMENTS SOCIETY
St Ann's Vestry Hall
2 Church Entry
London EC4V 5HB
Tel: 0171-236 3934
Fax: 0171-329 3677

ARCHITECTURAL HERITAGE FUND
27 John Adam Street
London WC2N 6HX
Tel: 0171-930 0295
Fax: 0171-925 0199

AREA MUSEUMS COUNCILS:
AREA MUSEUM COUNCIL FOR THE SOUTH WEST
Hestercombe House
Cheddon Fitzpaine
Taunton TA2 8LQ
Tel: 01823 259696
Fax: 01823 413114

ASSOCIATION FOR INDUSTRIAL ARCHAEOLOGY (AIA)
c/o Amber Patrick, Hon Secretary
Ironbridge Gorge Museum
The Warfage
Ironbridge
Telford
Shropshire TF8 7AW
Tel: 01952 435 522

ASSOCIATION OF INDEPENDENT MUSEUMS (AIM)
Mr Andrew Petterson, Hon Secretary
c/o Hotties Science & Arts Centre
PO Box 6826
Chalon Way
St Helens
Merseyside WA9 1LL
Tel: 01744 22766

ASSOCIATION OF LOCAL GOVERNMENT ARCHAEOLOGICAL OFFICERS (ALGAO)
S Bryant, Secretary
County Archaeologist
County Planning and Environment Department
Hertfordshire County Council
County Hall
Hertford SG13 8DN
Tel: 01992 555 244
Fax: 01992 555 648

BRITISH ARCHAEOLOGICAL ASSOCIATION (BAA)
Dr Lindsay Grant, Hon Secretary
c/o Courtauld Institute
Somerset House
Strand
London WC2R 0RN
Tel: 0171 872 0220

CADW (WELSH HISTORIC MONUMENTS)
Brunel House
2 Fitzalan Road
Cardiff CF2 1UY
Tel: 01222 500200
Fax: 01222 500300

CAMBRIAN ARCHAEOLOGICAL ASSOCIATION
Dr J M Hughes, General Secretary
The Laurels
Westfield Road
Newport
Gwent NP9 4ND
Tel: 01633 262449

CATHEDRAL FABRIC COMMISSION FOR ENGLAND (CFCE)
Fielden House
10 Little College Street
London SW1P 3SH
Tel: 0171 222 3793

CENTRE FOR THE CONSERVATION OF HISTORIC PARKS & GARDENS
Institute of Advanced Architectural Studies
University of York
King's Manor
York YO1 2EP
Tel: 01904 433966

CIVIC TRUST
17 Carlton House Terrace
London SW1Y 5AW
Tel: 0171 930 0914
Fax: 0171 3210180

COMPASS (Planning Magazine's database)
  Suite 3
  Fullers Court
  38 Lower Quay Street
  Gloucester GL1 2LW
  Tel: 01452 310566
  Fax: 01452 310551

COUNCIL FOR BRITISH ARCHAEOLOGY
  Bowes Morrell House
  111 Walmgate
  York YO1 2UA
  Tel: 01904 671417
  Fax: 01904 671384

COUNCIL FOR SCOTTISH ARCHAEOLOGY
  c/o National Museums of Scotland
  Queen Street
  Edinburgh EH2 1JD
  Tel: 0131 225 7534, ext. 311

COUNCIL OF MUSEUMS IN WALES
  32 Park Place
  Cardiff CF1 3BA
  Tel: 01222 225432
  Fax: 01222 668516

COUNTRYSIDE COMMISSION
  John Dower House
  Crescent Place
  Cheltenham
  Gloucestershire GL50 3RA
  Tel: 01242 521381
  Fax: 01242 584270

COUNTRYSIDE COUNCIL FOR WALES
  Plas Penrhos
  Ffordd Penrhos
  Bangor
  Gwynedd LL57 2LQ
  Tel: 01248 370444
  Fax: 01248 355782

DEPARTMENT OF THE ENVIRONMENT
  Planning Policy Directorates
  2 Marsham Street
  London SW1P 3EB

	Fax: 0171 276 4995
	Telephone numbers:
General Inquiries	0171 276 3000
Development Plans and Policies	0171 276 3901
Development Control	0171 276 3810
Land Compensation and EIA	0171 276 3866
Minerals	0171 276 3986

341

Enforcement Policy and Specialist Planning Appeals
PDC2 Division
Tollgate House
Houlton Street
Bristol BS2 9DJ   *Fax:* 0117 9878639
Enforcement Policy   0117 9878605

DEPARTMENT OF THE NATIONAL HERITAGE
Heritage Division
2-4 Cockspur Street
London SW1Y 5DH
                                                  Telephone numbers:
Underwater Archaeology Inquiries   0171 211 6367
Listed Building Inquiries   0171 211 6371
PPG 15 Inquiries   0171 211 6371
Conservation Policy Inquiries   0171 211 6364
Listed Building Urgent Work/Compulsory
Purchase Orders Inquiries   0171 211 6364
Ecclesiastical Exemption Inquiries   0171 211 6364
General Inquiries   0171 211 6372
General Inquiries (switchboard)   0171 211 6000
Listing of Buildings   0171 211 6383
Scheduling of Ancient monuments   0171 211 6363
Scheduled Ancient Monument Consent
Inquiries   0171 211 6352
General   *Fax:* 0171 211 6382

EAST MIDLANDS MUSEUMS SERVICE
Courtyard Buildings
Wollaton Park
Nottingham NG8 2AE
Tel: 0115 9 854534
Fax: 0115 928 0038

ENGLISH HERITAGE
23 Savile Row
London W1X 1AB
Tel: 0171 973 3000
Fax: 0171 973 3001

ENGLISH NATURE
Northminster House
Peterborough
Cambridgeshire PE1 1UA
Tel: 01733 340345
Fax: 01733 68834

GARDEN HISTORY SOCIETY
76 Clapham Common North Side
London

EC4V 5HB
Tel: 0171 236 3934

HISTORIC FARM BUILDINGS GROUP
Roy Brigden
Museum of English Rural Life
Rural History Centre
University of Reading
Whiteknights
Reading RG6 2AG
Tel: 01734 318663

HISTORIC MONUMENTS & BUILDINGS (NORTHERN IRELAND)
Environment Service
Department of the Environment for Northern Ireland
5-33 Hill Street
Belfast BT1 2LA
Tel: 01232 235000

HISTORIC SCOTLAND
Longmore House
Salisbury Place
Edinburgh EH9 1SH
Tel: 0131 668 8600
Fax: 0131 668 8765

INSTITUTE OF ENVIRONMENT ASSESSMENT
Gregory Croft House
Fen Road
East Kirkby
Lincolnshire PE23 4DB
Tel: 01790 763613
Fax: 01790 763630

INSTITUTE OF FIELD ARCHAEOLOGISTS
University of Manchester
Oxford Road
Manchester M13 9PL
Tel: 0161 275 2304

INTERNATIONAL COUNCIL ON MONUMENTS AND SITES (ICOMOS)
75 Rue du Temple
75003 Paris
FRANCE
Tel: + (33) 1 42 77 35 76
Fax: + (33) 1 42 77 57 42

ICOMOS (UK)
10 Barley Mow Passage
Chiswick
London W4 4PH
Tel: 0181 9946477

343

INTERNATIONAL COUNCIL OF MUSEUMS (ICOM)
Ms Nell Hoare
Hon Secretary, ICOM UK
c/o The Textile Conservation Centre
Apartment 22
Hampton Court Palace
East Moseley
Surrey KT8 9AU

JOURNAL OF PLANNING AND ENVIRONMENT LAW
Sweet & Maxwell Limited
100 Avenue Road
Swiss Cottage
London NW3 3PF
Tel: 0171 393 7000
Fax: 0171 393 7010
DX: 38861 Swiss Cottage

LANDS TRIBUNAL
48 Chancery Lane
London WC2A 1JR
Tel: 0171 936 7200
Fax: 0171 404 0986
DX: 44452 The Strand

MANX NATIONAL HERITAGE
Manx Museum & National Trust
Manx Museum
Douglas
Isle of Man
Tel: 01624 675522

MANX NATIONAL TRUST
Manx Museum
Douglas
Isle of Man
Tel: 01624 675522

MEDIEVAL ARCHAEOLOGY RESEARCH GROUP (SCOTLAND)
Nigel Ruckley, Secretary
British Geological Survey
Murchison House
West Mains Road
Edinburgh EH9 3LA
Tel: 0131 667 1000

MUSEUMS ASSOCIATION, THE
42 Clerkenwell Close
London EC1R 0PA
Tel: 0171 608 2933

MUSEUM DOCUMENTATION ASSOCIATION
Lincoln House
Cherry Hinton Road
Cambridge CB1 4DH
Tel: 01223 242848
Fax: 01223 213575

MUSEUMS AND GALLERIES COMMISSION
16 Queen Anne's Gate
London SW1H 9AA
Tel: 0171 233 4200
Fax: 0171 233 3686

NATIONAL HERITAGE MEMORIAL FUND (NHMF)
10 St James' Street
London SW1A 1EF
Tel: 0171 9300963

NATIONAL TRUST (NT), THE
36 Queen Anne's Gate
London SW1H 9AS
Tel: 0171 222 9251
Fax: 0171 222 5097

NATIONAL TRUST FOR SCOTLAND
5 Charlotte Square
Edinburgh EH2 4DU
Tel: 0131 226 5922
Fax: 0131 243 9501

NORTH OF ENGLAND MUSEUMS SERVICE
House of Recovery
Bath Lane
Newcastle upon Tyne NE4 5SQ
Tel: 0191 222 1661
Fax: 0191 261 4725

NORTH WEST MUSEUMS SERVICE
Griffin Lodge
Cavendish Place
Blackburn BB2 2PN
Tel: 01254 670211
Fax: 01254 681995

NORTHERN IRELAND HERITAGE GARDENS COMMITTEE
42 Osborne Park
Belfast BT9 6JN
Tel: 01232 668817

NORTHERN IRELAND MUSEUMS COUNCIL
185 Stranmillis Road
Belfast BT9 5DU

Tel: 01232 661023
Fax: 01232 661715

PLANNING AND ENVIRONMENT BAR ASSOCIATION
The Assistant Secretary, PEBA
2 Harcourt Buildings
Temple
London EC4Y 9DB
Tel: 0171 358 8415

PLANNING INSPECTORATE
Tollgate House
Houlton Street
Bristol BS2 9DJ

	Telephone numbers:
Highway Inquiries	0117 9878909
Local Plan Inquiries	0117 9878579
Enforcement Inquiries	0117 9878561
Environmental Protection Inquiries	0117 9878919
General Inquiries	0117 9878754
Switchboard	0117 9878000
	Fax numbers:
Planning Appeals	0117 9878769
Enforcement Appeals	0117 9878782
General	0117 9878406
Chief Planning Inspector	0117 9878408

PLANNING MAGAZINE
Ambit Publications Limited
Suite 1
Fullers Court
40 Lower Quay Street
Gloucester GL1 2LW
Tel: 01452 417553/4

PREHISTORIC SOCIETY
Dr Robert Bewley, Hon Secretary
c/o University College London
Institute of Archaeology
31-34 Gordon Square
London WC1H 0PY
Tel: 0171 3877050

RESCUE, THE BRITISH ARCHAEOLOGICAL TRUST
15a Bull Plain
Hertford SG14 1DX
Tel: 01992 553377

ROYAL ARCHAEOLOGICAL INSTITUTE
Jonathan Coad, Hon Secretary
c/o Society of Antiquaries of London
Burlington House
Piccadilly
London W1V 0HS
Tel: 0171 734 0193

ROYAL COMMISSION ON THE ANCIENT AND HISTORICAL MONU-
MENTS OF SCOTLAND
John Sinclair House
16 Bernard Terrace
Edinburgh EH8 9NX
Tel: 0131 662 1456
Fax: 0131 662 1477/1499

ROYAL COMMISSION ON ANCIENT AND HISTORIAL MONUMENTS
IN WALES
Crown Buildings
Plas Crug
Aberystwyth
Dyfed SY23 2HP
Tel: 01970 621233
Fax: 01970 627701

ROYAL COMMISSION ON THE HISTORICAL MONUMENTS OF
ENGLAND
National Monuments Record Centre
Kemble Drive
Swindon SN2 2GZ
Tel: 01793 414700 (RCHME Switchboard)
01793 414600 (NMR Enquiries)
Fax: 01793 414707 (RCHME)
01793 414606 (NMR)

Regional Offices:
The Lodge
Anstey Hall
Maris Lane
Trumpington
Cambridge
Cambridgeshire CB2 2IE
Tel: 01223 841210

Quern House
Mill Court
Hinton Way
Great Shelford
Cambridge
Cambridgeshire CB2 5LD
Tel: 01223 843156

Rose Duryard
Lower Argyll Road
Exeter
Devon EX4 4PB
Tel: 01392 213338

Shelley House
Acomb Road
York
North Yorkshire YO2 4HB
Tel: 01904 784411

Darwin Building
Keele University Science Park
University of Keele
Newcastle under Lyme
Staffordshire ST5 5SP
Tel: 01782 632118

Line Building
Haymarket Lane
The University
Newcastle upon Tyne NE1 7RU
Tel: 0191 222 7962

ROYAL FINE ART COMMISSION
7 St James's Square
London SW1Y 4JU
Tel: 0171 839 6537
Fax: 0171 839 8475

SCOTTISH MUSEUM ARCHAEOLOGISTS
Mike King, Secretary
North East Fife District Council Museum Service
County Building
St Catherine's Street
Cupar KY15 4TA
Tel: 01334 653722 ext. 141

SCOTTISH MUSEUMS COUNCIL
County House
20-22 Torphichen Street
Edinburgh EH3 8JB
Tel: 0131 229 7465
Fax: 0131 229 2728

SOCIETY OF ANTIQUARIES OF LONDON
Burlington House
Piccadilly
London W1V 0HS
Tel: 0171 734 0193
Fax: 0171 287 6967

SOCIETY OF ANTIQUARIES OF SCOTLAND
c/o National Museums of Scotland
Queen Street
Edinburgh EH2 1JD
Tel: 0131 225 7534 ext. 327/328

SOCIETY FOR LANDSCAPE STUDIES (SLS)
Carenza Lewis, Hon Secretary
c/o RCHME
Kemble Drive
Swindon SN2 2GZ
Tel: 01793 414700

SOCIETY FOR MEDIEVAL ARCHAEOLOGY
Dr Paul Stamper, Hon Secretary
The Archaeology Unit of Shropshire
Winston Churchill Building
Radbrook Centre
Radbrook Road
Shrewsbury SY3 9BJ
Tel: 01743 254009

SOCIETY OF MUSEUM ARCHAEOLOGISTS
Dr Robin Holgate, Secretary
c/o Luton Museum
Wardown Park
Luton LU2 7HA
Tel: 01582 36941

SOCIETY FOR POST-MEDIEVAL ARCHAEOLOGY
Dr David Gaimster, Secretary
Department of Medieval and Later Antiquities
British Museum
Great Russell Street
London WC1B 3DG
Tel: 0171 323 8734

SOCIETY FOR THE PROMOTION OF ROMAN STUDIES
Dr H M Cockle, Hon Secretary
Roman Society
31-34 Gordon Square
London WC1H 0PP
Tel: 0171 387 8157

SOCIETY FOR THE PRESERVATION OF ANCIENT BUILDINGS
37 Spital Square
London E1 6DY
Tel: 0171 377 1644
Fax: 0171 247 5296

SOUTH EASTERN MUSEUMS SERVICE
Ferroners House
Barbican

London EC2Y 8AA
Tel: 0171 600 0219
Fax: 0171 600 2581

SUBTERRANEA BRITANNICA
Paul W Sowan, Chairman
c/o CNHSS Ltd
96a Brighton Road
Croydon CR2 6AD
Tel: 0181 6569755

UNITED KINGDOM INSTITUTE FOR CONSERVATION (UKIC)
6 Whitehorse Mews
Westminster Bridge Road
London SE1 7QD
Tel: 0171 6203371
Fax: 0171 6203761

UKIC Archaeology Section:
Helena Jaeschke, Secretary
3 Park Gardens
Lynton
Devon EX35 6DF
Tel: 01598 53245

VERNACULAR ARCHITECTURE GROUP
Mr Bob Meeson, Hon Secretary
16 Falna Crescent
Colton Green
Tamworth
Staffs B79 8JS
Tel: 01827 69434

WELSH OFFICE/SWDDFA GYMREIG
Cathays Park
Cardiff CF1 3NQ
Tel: 01222 825111
Fax: 01222 825622

WEST MIDLANDS AREA MUSEUM SERVICE
Hanbury Road
Stoke Prior
Bromsgrove
Worcestershire B60 4AD
Tel: 01527 872258
Fax: 01527 576960

YORKSHIRE & HUMBERSIDE MUSEUMS COUNCIL
Farnley Hall
Hall Lane
Leeds LS12 5HA
Tel: 01532 638909
Fax: 01532 791479

Appendix R

SELECT BIBLIOGRAPHY

In addition to publications which have been referred to directly in the main text, details are provided of various books which provide useful introductions to various aspects that may be of interest to the reader. For those who might require a general background to field archaeology, *An Introduction to Archaeology* by Lesley and Roy Adkins (1992) is a good beginning. The same authors have produced *A Thesaurus of British Archaeology* (Adkins and Adkins, 1982) which, in addition to explaining many archaeological technical terms, provides bibliographies for individual topics.

Two series of specialised publications on archaeology are particularly worthy of note: *Shire Archaeology* by Shire Publications Ltd, and the series published jointly by B T Batsford Ltd and English Heritage.

In addition to the journals published by various archaeological learned societies, a useful way of keeping up to date with recent discoveries and activities is *Current Archaeology* which is published six times a year and available from Current Archaeology, 9 Nassington Road, London NW3 2TX.

Finally, for those who have got to grips with archaeological jargon and would like an antidote there is nothing better than Paul Bahn's *A Bluffer's Guide to Archaeology* (Bahn, 1989).

Adkins, L. and Adkins, R. A., *A Thesaurus of British Archaeology* (1982, Newton Abbot, David and Charles).

Adkins, L. and Adkins, R., *An Introduction to Archaeology* (1992, London, Tiger Books International).

Arup (Ove Arup & Partners and the Department of Archaeology, University of York in association with B Thorpe), *York Archaeology and Development Study* (1991, Manchester, Ove Arup (Ove Arup & Dept Archaeol Univ York for City Council and English Heritage)).

Ashbee, P., *The Bronze Age Round Barrow in Britain* (1960, London, Phoenix House).

Bahn, P., *Bluff Your Way in Archaeology* (1989, Horsham, Ravette).

Bahn, P. (ed.), *Collins Dictionary of Archaeology* (1992, Glasgow, Harper Collins).

Baker, D., *Models Briefs and Specifications for Archaeological Assessments and Field Evaluations* (1993, Association of County Archaeological Officers).

Barclay, G. J., *Forestry and Archaeology in Scotland* (1992) 46 *Scottish Forestry* 27–47.

Barker, P., "The Origins and Development of RESCUE" in Rahtz (1974), pp. 280–85.

Barley, M. W., *The English Farmhouse and Cottage* (1961, London, Routledge and Kegan Paul).

Bateman, T., *Ten Years' Digging* (1978, Buxton, Moorland Reprints).

Bapps, S. and Bell, S., *Environmental Law* (2nd ed., 1994, London, Blackstone Press).

Bell, A. S., *The Scottish Antiquarian Tradition* (1982, Edinburgh, John Donald Publishers).

Beresford, M. and St Joseph, J. K. S., *Medieval England. An Aerial Survey* (1977, Cambridge, Cambridge University Press).

Biddle, M., "The Future of the Urban Past" in Rahtz (1974), pp. 95–112.

Biddle, M., *What future for British Archaeology?* (1994, Oxford, Oxbow Books).

Bowden, M., *Pitt Rivers: The Life and Archaeological Work of Lieutenant-General Augustus Henry Lane Fox Pitt Rivers, DCL, FRS, FSA.* (1991, Cambridge, Cambridge University Press).

Bradley, R., *The Prehistoric Settlement of Britain*, (1978, London, Routledge and Kegan Paul).

Bray, W. and Trump, D., *Dictionary of Archaeology* (1982, Harmondsworth, Penguin).

Broodbank, C. "Review: Among the New Books" (1995) 69/*Antiquity* 285–92.

Brunskell, R. W., *Illustrated Handbook of Vernacular Architecture* (1971, London, Faber and Faber).

Buchanan, R. A., *Industrial Archaeology in Britain* (1972, Harmondsworth, Penguin).

Butcher, S. and Garwood, P. *Rescue Excavation 1938 to 1972* (1994, London, English Heritage).

CADW, *What is CADW? An Introduction to the work of CADW: Welsh Historic Monuments* (1995, Cardiff, CADW).

Chart, D. A., *A Preliminary Survey of the Ancient Monuments of Northern Ireland* (1940, Belfast, HMSO).

Clarke, H., *The Archaeology of Medieval England* (1984, London, British Museum Publication).

Cleere, "British Archaeology in a Wider Context" in Hunter and Ralston (1993), pp. 115–124.

Colt Hoare, *The History of Ancient Wiltshire* (1810, London).

Countryside Commission, English Heritage, English Nature, *Conservation Issues in Strategic Plans* (1993, Countryside Commission, English Heritage, English Nature).

Crook, J. M., *The British Museum: a case study in architectural politics* (1972, Hardmonsworth, Penguin).

Crossley, D., *Post-Medieval Archaeology in Britain* (1990, Leicester, Leicester University Press).

Cunliffe, B. W., *The Report of a Joint Working Part of the Council for British Archaeology and the Department of the Environment* (1982, London, Department of the Environment).

Cunliffe, B. W., *Iron Age Communities in Britain* (1991, London, Routledge).

Cunnington, R. H., *From Antiquary to Archaeologist* (1975, Princes Risborough, Shire Publications).

Daniel, G., *The Origins and Growth of Archaeology* (1967, Harmondsworth, Penguin).

Daniel, G. E., *A Hundred and Fifty Years of Archaeology* (1975, London, Duckworth).

Darvill, T., *Ancient Monuments in the Countryside: An Archaeological Management Review* (1987, London, HBMC).

Darvill, T., *Prehistoric Britain* (1987, London, Batsford).

Darvill, T., Saunders, A., Stantin, B. "A Question of National Importance: Approaches to the evaluation of Ancient Monuments for the Monuments Protection Programme in England" (1987) 61 Antiquity 393–408.

Department of the Environment, *Principles of Publication in Rescue Archaeology* (1975, Report by a Working Part of the Ancient Monuments Board for England, Committee for Rescue Archaeology, London, DOE).

Department of the Environment, *Planning Policy Guidance Note 16: Archaeology and Planning* (PPG 16) (1990, London, HMSO).

Department of the Environment (Northern Ireland), *Finding and Minding 1986–89: A Report on the Archaeological Work of the Department of the Environment for Northern Ireland* (1990, Belfast, DOE (NI)).

Department of National Heritage, *Notes for The Guidance of The Finders of Historic Wrecks* (1992, London, Department of National Heritage).

Department of National Heritage, *Preserving The Past, Shaping the Future* (1994, London, Department of National Heritage).

Department of National Heritage, *Protecting Our Heritage* (1996, London, Department of National Heritage and Welsh Office).

DMRB, *Environmental Assessment Design Manual for Roads and Bridges* (1993, Vol. II., London, Department of Transport (with revisions 1994)).

Dyer, J. (ed.), *Discovering Prehistoric England* (1993, Princes Risborough, Shire Publications).

Encyclopedia of Planning Law and Practice, London (Sweet & Maxwell Office).

English Heritage, *Exploring Our Past: Strategies for the Archaeology of England* (1991, London, HBMC).

English Heritage, *The Management of Archaeological Projects* (2nd ed., 1991, London, HBMC).

English Heritage, *Development Plan Policies for Archaeology: Advice Note for Local Planning Authorities* (1992, London, HBMC).

English Heritage, *Managing England's Heritage: Setting Our Priorities for the 1990s* (1992, London, English Heritage).

English Heritage, *The Visitor's Guide to English Heritage 1995–96* (1995, London, English Heritage).

English Heritage, *Geographical Survey in Archaeological Field Evaluation* (1995, London, English Heritage).

Evans, D.M., Pugh-Smith, J. and Samuels, J., "World Heritage Sites: Beauty Contest or Planning Constraint" [1994] J.P.L. 503–508.

Evans, J., *A History of The Society of Antiquaries* (1956, Oxford, The Society of Antiquaries).

Forestry Commission, *Forests and Archaeology: Guidelines* (1995 Forestry Commission).

Fowler, P. J., "Motorways and Archaeology", in Rahtz (1974), pp. 113–29.

Frere, S. S., *Britannia* (1974, London, Cardinal).

Fulford, M. G. and Huddleston, K., *The Current State of Romano-British Pottery Studies: A Review for English Heritage* (1991, English Heritage Occas Pap 1., London, HBMC).

Gaffney, C. F., Gater, J. A. and Ovenden, S. M., *The Use of Geophysical Techniques in Archaeological Evaluations* (1991, IFA Techn Pap 9., Birmingham, IFA).

Green, S., *Prehistorian: A Bibliography of V. Gordon Childe* (1981, Bradford-on-Avon, Moonraker Press).

Grimes, W. F., *Excavations on Defence Sites, 1939–1945* (1960, London, HMSO).

GPES, *The Preparation of Environmental Statements for Planning Projects that Require Environmental Assessment—A Good Practice Guide* (1995, London, Department of the Environment).

Health and Safety Commission, *Designing for Health and Safety in Construction* (1995, Sudbury, Health and Safety Executive).

Health and Safety Commission, *Managing Construction for Health and Safety* (1995, Sudbury, Health and Safety Executive).

Heap, D., *An Outline of Planning Law* (1991, London, Sweet & Maxwell).

Highway, C. M. (ed.), *The Erosion of History: Archaeology and Planning in Towns* (1972, CBA).

Hewison, R., *The Heritage Industry* (1987, London, Methuen).

Heyworth, M. (ed.), *British Archaeological Yearbook 1995–96* (1995, York, CBA).

Hill, G. F., "The Law and Practice of Treasure Trove" (1930) *Antiquaries Journal* pp. 228–241.

Hill, G. F., *Treasure Trove in Law and Practice from the Earliest Time to the Present Day* (1936, Oxford, Clarendon Press).

Hingley, R. (ed.), *Medieval or Later Rural Settlement in Scotland: Management and Preservation* (1993, Edinburgh, Historic Scotland).

Historic Scotland, *Corporate Plan 1991–94* (1991, Edinburgh, Historic Scotland).

Historic Scotland, *A List of Ancient Monuments in Scotland 1993* (1993, Edinburgh, Historic Scotland).

Historic Scotland (with Scottish Office), *Protecting the Built Heritage: A Green Paper* (1996, Edinburgh, HMSO).

Hoskins, W. G., *The Making of the English Landscape* (1970, Harmondsworth, Penguin).

House of Commons, Committee of Public Accounts, Treaty with Report. *Protecting and Managing England's Heritage Property* (1992, London, HMSO).

Hudson, K., *A Social History of Archaeology* (1981, London, Macmillan).

Hunter, J. and Ralston (eds.), *Archaeological Resource Management in the UK: An Introduction* (1993, Stroud, Alan Sutton Publishing).

IFA (Institute of Field Archaeologists), *The Institute of Field Archaeologists: Memorandum and Articles of Association* (1987 Birmingham, IFA (as amended)).

IFA, *By-Laws of the Institute of Field Archaeologists: Code of Conduct* (1988, Birmingham, IFA (as amended)).

IFA, *The Institute of Field Archaeologists Annual Report No. 11* (1994, Birmingham, IFA).

Jessup, R., *Man of Many Talents: an informal biography of James Douglas 1753–1819* (1975, London, Phillimore).

Johnston, D. E. (ed.), *Discovering Roman Britain* (1993, Princes Risborough, Shire Publications).

Joint Nautical Archaeology Policy Committee, *Heritage at Sea: Proposals for the better protection of archaeological sites underwater* (1989, London, National Maritime Museum).

Jones, G. D. B., *Past Imperfect: The Story of Rescue Archaeology* (1984, London, Heinemann).

Kelley, R., *Towards producing a list of historic landscapes in Wals to inform the production of a register of landscapes, parks and gardens of special Historic Interest in Wales* (1994, Cardiff, CADW).

Kendrick, T. D., *British Antiquity* (1950, London, Methuen).

Lamber, D., Goodchild, P. and Roberts, J., *Researching a Garden's History: A Guide to Documentary and Published Sources* (1995, Reigate, Landscape Design Trust).

Leland, J., *The Itinerary of John Leland the Antiquary* (1745) (9 Vols) (Oxford, James Fletcher and Joseph Tote).

Longworth, I. and Cherry, J., *Archaeology in Britain since 1945* (1988, London, British Museum Publications).

Major, J. K., *Fieldwork in Industrial Archaeology* (1975, London, Batsford).

Manley, J., "Archaeology and Planning: A Welsh Perspective", [1987] J.P.L. pp. 466–84, 552–63.

Marsden, B., *The Early Barrow Diggers* (1974, New Jersey, Noyes Press).

McGill, G., *Building on the Past* (1995, London, E. and F. N. Spon).

Mcgaw, J. V. S. and Simpson, D. D. A. (eds.), *Introduction to British Prehistory* (1981, Leicester Univ. Press).

Mellor, M., *Medieval Ceramic Studies in England* (1994, London, English Heritage).

Mynors, C., *Listed Buildings and Conservation Areas* (2nd ed., 1995, London, Longman).

MGC (Museums and Galleries Commission), *Standards in the Museum Care of Archaeological Collections* (1992, London, Museums and Galleries Commission).

Olivier, A. C. H., *Archaeology Review 1993–94* (1994, London, English Heritage).

Page, W. (ed.), *The Victoria History of the County of Nottingham* (1906, London, Archibald Constable).

Pagoda Projects, *An Evaluation of the Impact of PPG 16 on Archaeology and Planning* (1992, London). Public report (dated January 31, 1992) Commissioned by English Heritage.

Piggott, S., *Ruins in a Landscape: Essays in Antiquarianism* (1976, Edinburgh, Edinburgh Univ. Press).

Piggott, S., *William Stukeley* (1985, New York, Thames and Hudson).

Pitt Rivers, A. H. L. F., *Excavations in Cranborne Chase* (1887–98, London, 4 vols).

Pugh-Smith, J. and Samuels, J., "PPG 16: Two Years On" [1993] J.P.L. 203

Rackham, O., *Trees and Woodland in the British Landscape* (1976, London, Dent).

Rahtz, P. A. (ed.), *Rescue Archaeology* (1974, Penguin, Harmondsworth).

Renfrew, C., *Before Civilisation* (1976, Harmondsworth, Penguin).

RCHME, *An Inventory of the Historical Monuments in Buckinghamshire* (1912, Vol. 1., London, HMSO).

RCHME, *Recording England's Past: A Review of National and Local Sites and Monuments Records in England* (1993, London).

RCHME and English Heritage, *Thesaurus of Archaeological Site Types* (1992, London, RCHME & EH).

Salway, P., *Roman Britain* (1981, Oxford, Oxford University Press)

Samuel, R., *Theatres of Memory* (1994, London, Verso).

Saunders, A. D., "A Century of Ancient Monuments Legislation 1882–1982" (1983, *Antiquaries Journal* Vol LXIII, part 1., Oxford, Oxford University Press).

Sawyer, P., *Anglo-Saxon Charters* (1968, London, Royal Historical Society).

Schofield, J. and Vince, A., *Medieval Towns* (1994, London, Leicester University Press).

Scottish Office (Environment Dept), *National Planning Policy Guideline NPPG 5: Archaeology and Planning* (1994, Edinburgh, SOEnD).

Scottish Office (Environmental Department), *Planning Advice Note PAN 42: Archaeology—the Planning Process and Scheduled Monument Procedures* (1994, Edinburgh, SOEnD).

Scottish Office (with Historic Scotland), *Protecting the Built Heritage: A Green Paper* (1996, Edinburgh, HMSO).

Scrase, T., "Archaeology and Planning—a Case for Full Integration" [1991] J.P.L. 1103.

Simmons, J. (ed.), *English County Historians* (1978, Wakefield, E.P. Publishing).

Simpson, and Brown, N. D., *The Care of Historic Buildings and Ancient Monuments by Government Departments in Scotland* (London, Department of National Heritage).

Sorrell, A., *Reconstructing the Past* (1981, London, Batsford).

Spoerry, P., *Archaeology and Legislation in Britain* (1993, Hertford, RESCUE).

Stukeley, W., *Hinerarium Curiosum* (1724, London).

Suddards, R. W. and Hargreaves, J. M., *Listed Buildings: The Law and Practice of Historic Buildings, Ancient Monuments and Conservation Areas* (3rd ed., 1996, London, Sweet & Maxwell).

Tate, W. E., *The Parish Chest* (1969, London, Cambridge University Press).

Taylor, C., *Fieldwork in Medieval Archaeology* (1974, London, Batsford).

Thompson, M. W., *General Pitt-Rivers: Evolution and Archaeology in the Nineteenth Century* (1977, Bradford-on-Avon, Moonraker Press).

Thompson, M. W., *Ruins: Their Preservation and Display* (1981, London, British Mus. Publ.).

Tym, R. and Pagoda Associates, *Review of the Implementation of PPG 16 Archaeology and Planning* (1995 Report for English Heritage).

UNESCO, *The World Heritage Convention: An Idea in Action* (1991, Paris, UNESCO).

Wallis, H., *Historians' Guide to Early British Maps* (1994, London, Royal Historical Society).

Wainwright, G. J., "The Management of Change: Archaeology and Planning" (1993) 67 *Antiquity* 416–21.

Welsh Office, *WO Circular 61/81: Historic Buildings and Conservation Areas—Policy and Procedure* (1981, Cardiff, HMSO).

Welsh Office, *Planning Policy and Guidance Note 16: Archaeology and Planning* (1991, Cardiff, HMSO).

Welsh Office, *Planning Guidance (Wales): Planning Policy* (1996, Cardiff, HMSO).

Welsh Office, *Protecting our Heritage* (1996, London, Department of National Heritage and Welsh Office).

Whimster, R. P., *The Emerging Past* (1989, London, RCHME).

Wood, J. (ed.), *Buildings Archaeology: Applications in Practice* (1994, Oxford, Oxbow, Monograph 43).

Young, C. J. (ed.), *Guidelines for the Processing and Publication of Roman Pottery From Excavations* (1980, London, Department of the Environment).

Index

(Main text references are, first, to chapter and, secondly, to paragraph. Thus, the reference 6.10 is to Chapter 6 paragraph 10. Appendix references are, first, to appendix and, secondly, to paragraph. Thus, the reference G.6 is to Appendix G, paragraph 6. Appendices can be found after the main text.)